The Meaning of Madness

The Meaning of Madness
Symptomatology, Sociology, Biology and Therapy of the Schizophrenias

C. Peter Rosenbaum, M.D.
Associate Professor of Psychiatry
Director, Adult Psychiatry Clinic
Stanford University School of Medicine

SCIENCE HOUSE   NEW YORK   1970

Library of Congress Catalog Card Number: 77-104654
Standard Book Number: 87668-028-7

Manufactured by Haddon Craftsmen, Inc.
Scranton, Pennsylvania

The authors and publishers listed below have generously extended permission to reprint excerpts from the works cited:

Table from Bellak, Leopold. *Schizophrenia: a review of the syndrome.* London: Logos Press, 1958. Distributed by Grune & Stratton, New York.

Table from Bender, Lauretta. A visual motor Gestalt Test and its clinical use. *American Orthopsychiatric Association, Research Monograph, No. 3, 1938.* © The American Orthopsychiatric Association.

Eliot, T. S. The waste land. In *The Complete Poems and Plays.* New York: Harcourt, Brace & World, Inc., 1930, pp. 40-41.

Table from Eiduson, S. et al. *Biochemistry and Behavior.* Princeton, N.J.: D. Van Nostrand Company, Inc., 1964, pp. 101-107.

Table from Garmezy, Norman and E. H. Rodnick. Premorbid adjustment and performance in schizophrenia: implications for interpreting heterogeneity in schizophrenia. *Journal of Nervous and Mental Disease,* 1959, 129, 450-466. © The Williams & Wilkins Co., Baltimore, Maryland.

Kohn, Melvin L. Social class and schizophrenia: a critical review. In *The transmission of schizophrenia, Journal of Psychiatric Research VI (Supplement),* David Rosenthal and Seymour S. Kety (eds.). London: Pergamon Press, 1968, 155-178. Reprinted here in its entirety.

Table from Lidz, Theodore, S. Fleck, and A. R. Cornelison. *Schizophrenia and the family.* New York: International Universities Press, Inc., 1965.

Table from Nameche, Gene, Mary Waring, and David Ricks. Early indicators of outcome in schizophrenia. *Journal of Nervous and Mental Disease,* 1964, 139, 232-240. © The Williams & Wilkins Co., Baltimore, Maryland.

Table from Redlich, Frederick C. and Daniel X. Freedman. *The theory and practice of psychiatry.* New York: Basic Books, Inc., 1966.

Rosenbaum, C. P. A case of postpartum schizophrenia. In *Modern psychotherapeutic practice,* A. Burton (ed.). Palo Alto, Calif.: Science and Behavior Books, Inc., 1965, pp. 59-79.

Rosenbaum, C. P. Metabolic, physiological, anatomic and genetic studies in the schizophrenias: a review and analysis, *Journal of Nervous and Mental Disease,* 1968, 103-126. © The Williams & Wilkins Co.

To Three Excellent Teachers

Nathaniel S. Apter   Don D. Jackson
Harold F. Searles

Preface

This book is a general review of the schizophrenias, their diagnosis, symptomatology, their roots in biology, family, and social group, and their therapy.

The areas of my own greatest personal interest (and potential bias) are individual therapy and the understanding, on which such therapy depends, of the patient's experiential world as it is now and as it was as he was growing up in his family. The chapters relevant to these areas are highly interrelated, and I was tempted to make them consecutive rather than placing them in separate sections of the book. Though I decided ultimately on the present organization, the reader who shares my interest in psychodynamics might well be advised to go directly from Chapter 4, "Phenomenology: The World of Schizophrenic Existence," to Chapter 7, "The Families of Schizophrenic Patients," then to Chapter 11, "Three Psychological Formulations," and from there to Chapter 14, "Dynamically Oriented Individual Psychotherapy of the Schizophrenias," ultimately returning to the remaining chapters.

Preparing the material has been a job of exclusion as much as it has been one of inclusion. In a 1967 publication, the National Clearinghouse for Mental Health Information listed 2,243 articles written between 1960 and 1964 on clinical research in the schizophrenias. Many of the books and articles on the schizophrenias have dealt in depth with one specific area, excluding all others. Other books, seeking to be general, are encyclopedic in length and weight.

   To my knowledge, there has not been a published book that is broad in scope, yet relatively brief, and that can be read in bed without bruising the abdominal wall. It is my hope that this volume will rectify that situation.

   In writing this book I have had necessarily to use my own judgment about what to include and what to exclude. Many friends and colleagues have made valuable general suggestions and specific comments on, and criticisms of, one or more chapters, and I am indebted to them. The responsibility for errors of fact, omission, or interpretation lies solely with me.

C. PETER ROSENBAUM, M.D.
Stanford, California

Acknowledgments

For the past several years I have given a seminar on the schizophrenias for the first-year psychiatric residents at the Stanford University School of Medicine, and it is from the seminar that this book derives.

Several groups of residents have asked stimulating questions at our seminar, have challenged and forced me to make my presentations as lucid as possible, and have kept me as honest and unbiased as they could.

Those who have reviewed individual chapters and made useful comments and suggestions include Nathaniel Apter, Jack Barchas, Daniel X. Freedman, Ian Gregory, Leo Hollister, Frederick Ilfeld, Herant Katchadourian, Seymour Kessler, Einar Kringlen, Theodore Lidz, Werner Mendel, Rudolf Moos, Ernest Noble, Frank Ochberg, David Rosenthal, George Solomon, Paul Watzlawick, Otto Will, and Lyman Wynne. To all of them, my thanks.

Arthur and Zelda Rosenbaum made many useful suggestions on matters of grammar and style. David and Sarah Louise Rosenbaum provided me with a rich experience in the psychological phenomena of the early years of life.

Irwin Feinberg reviewed several chapters and made especially useful comments about the material on symptomatology, phenomenology, and recent findings in sleep and dream research.

In addition to reviewing several chapters, David A. Hamburg encouraged me to write the book and helped make it possible for me to find the time to get the writing done.

Irvin D. Yalom reviewed the entire book, much of it during a hectic meeting in Chicago in January 1968. I am heavily in his debt for his encouragement, advice, and collaboration over the past several years.

Barbara Cleave and Lavina Tubbs typed several of the draft chapters. Nancy Phillips did not only the bulk of the typing but most of the painstaking and necessary work of finding and checking references, corresponding with authors and publishers, and keeping order in the chaos of writing a book.

C. Peter Rosenbaum

Palo Alto, California   June 1969

Table of Contents

Foreword

The schizophrenias are one of the major disabling disorders of human living. They regularly occur in significant numbers in every sector of society and space. They can still be reliably predicted in every generation to come as they have occurred in every generation known to history. The puzzles posed by their occurrence, the problems presented by their variable forms and treatment comprise core issues underlying the specialty of psychiatry.

To say that psychiatry "needs" the schizophrenias merely emphasizes a perspective; for it is no myth that, for better or worse, every society inevitably engenders a recognizable response to schizophrenic disorders. Those societies which want an informed response to human suffering require a special focus on the schizophrenias, and this has been the task tacitly assigned to a modern, sentient, and scientifically informed psychiatry.

Over the past century we have gradually been developing an orientation to the schizophrenic dysfunctions. We can recognize—to an extent still all too limited—core schizophrenias and distinguish them from other major dysfunctions; we yet have a long way to go in identifying the appropriate dimensions by which variant schizophrenias could and should be grouped. We need no longer express our frightened or benighted awe of madness by seeing the schizophrenic persons as either saints or devils—or, for that matter, as the persecuted norm of noble dissent abused by malevolent specialists. Nor need we fear that it is our diagnosis which separates a schizophrenic person from his family and peers, or creates a destiny of life-long vulnerability to retreat, disorganization and dysfunction.

We can now document the modifiable nature of the disorder, its fluctuations in response to environmental and biobehavioral approaches. We are increasingly able to explore a variety of options and measures to aid these persons to live —constantly or intermittently—within a community in which they can relate. We have become increasingly able and willing to know the person who experiences his world in a fashion we call schizophrenic and are more familiar with the vicissitudes and pleasures in such therapeutic relationships. Yet, whatever our progress, whatever the productive or false leads that have been and are being attempted, the fundamental problems and puzzles of the origin of these disorders, their treatment, and their appropriate classification remain serious and unsolved issues.

Recognition of these facts is difficult to bear; it leads many to gloss over the importance of inquiry and assessment, while absorbed in the initial glow of a new cure (which, incidentally, has been regularly announced once or twice a decade for longer than most of us can remember). Yet, any society that wishes a truly humane approach will require not only enthusiasm, but a special focus upon biobehavioral investigations from the molecular, genetic, and developmental to the social, and all of these pointed toward an understanding of etiological factors as well as the biobehavioral measures that can moderate the onset, duration, and course of the schizophrenias. In all probability, we should be prepared for a variety of subgroups that will segregate from the general syndrome very much as central nervous system syphilis was separated at the turn of the century.

Any society concerned with its own survival, with the grasp of its latent and ill-understood potential for disordered or unbalanced behavior (and for discriminating creativity from destructiveness), would be well advised to begin to comprehend the forms and features of the schizophrenias as they recurrently influence the fringes and—in occasional mass movements—the roots of the social fabric. Schizophrenia, then, is a subject that not only touches social processes and the lives of many victims (perhaps one of ten families), but is a topic that will increasingly engage a wider range of public health approaches than the psychiatric specialist alone can deliver.

It is accordingly remarkable that so few authentic surveys of our information and ignorance are generally available. Tomes and a bewilderingly enormous literature confront the specialist while tracts and special pleadings are sold to an unsuspecting but anguished public. Dr. Rosenbaum has somehow managed to present the authentic substance of all the crucial issues. He has done so concisely, comprehensively, and comprehendibly. His presentation owes no debt to schools or ideologies. Rather, as an experienced, scholarly, and gifted clinician and teacher, he has made possible a readable as well as reliable resume of where matters really do stand. It is a gift to students, specialists, and the public which is long overdue!

Daniel X. Freedman, M.D.
Professor and Chairman
Department of Psychiatry
University of Chicago

Section One

THE PATIENT
AND HIS ILLNESS

1

Signs, Symptoms, and Diagnosis

INTRODUCTION

In 1898, the German psychiatrist Emil Kraepelin[11] brought several diverse mental afflictions together under the name of dementia praecox. In 1911, the Swiss psychiatrist Eugene Bleuler published a classic, *Dementia Praecox, or the Group of Schizophrenias*.[4] The terms have been used more or less synonymously for the last fifty years, though *schizophrenia* has largely supplanted *dementia praecox*.

Kraepelin performed a great synthesis when he recognized that the states previously referred to as dementia precoce, katatonia, and hebephrenia shared important features in common. However, the implication of the term dementia praecox—a precocious dementia usually showing an inevitable and inexorable deterioration of mental functioning—was unfortunate. One other unfortunate implication of Kraepelin's feat, one that Bleuler attempted to undo, was the notion that dementia praecox was a single, unitary disease, much the same as streptococcal pharyngitis is a single disease.

Bleuler's emphasis on the possible diversity of these states, "The Group of Schizophrenias," has been ignored by many; the importance of recognizing this diversity is reemerging. One can analogize with those diverse conditions collectively known as cancer: the multitude of cancers differ in many important aspects, e.g., etiology, sensitivity to radiation and drugs, degree of malignancy, etc. The cancers share the characteristics of relatively uncontrolled, neoplastic growth and spread, but to treat all cancers as identical because they share a certain few attributes is to reason by predicate (see Chapter 4), a characteristic of schizophrenic thinking and not a very scientific approach.

At present, in a like manner, there is considerable evidence that not all schizophrenics are alike. Patients differ in apparent etiology, prognosis, response to treatment, chronicity, and severity of symptoms. Some of these can be factored out by study of the patient's premorbid adjustment, family pedigree, family and socioeconomic background, presenting symptoms, etc. Each of these issues will be discussed in the appropriate chapter; suffice it to say here that the schizophrenias indeed seem to be a diverse and heterogeneous group of conditions.

There are many descriptions of schizophrenic symptomatology extant. Similarly, diagnoses based on those descriptions vary. Ideally a diagnosis should transmit a maximum of information in a minimum of words and with the least possibility of distortion. Furthermore, the information should have some predictive value about the course of illness and indications for treatment. Unfortunately, in psychiatric nomenclature in general, and in description and diagnosis of the schizophrenias in particular, many of the definitions are much too abstract to convey information usefully.

SIGNS AND SYMPTOMS: BLEULER'S DESCRIPTION

Bleuler's 1911 description of the symptomatology of the schizophrenias is still the best I have seen. He describes the defects in thinking and the disharmonies of feeling as being part of the basic thought disorder of the schizophrenias. He separates these into the fundamental symptoms, including altered simple and compound mental functions, and the accessory symptoms.

Fundamental Symptoms

The fundamental symptoms include, generally, disturbances of association and affectivity, and a tendency to turn away from reality toward fantasy, autism. An old mnemonic has it that one can remember Bleuler's fundamental symptoms as the "Four A's:" Association, Affectivity, Ambivalence, and Autism." But the mnemonic is only a beginning, because it does not mention the multitude of other alterations of simple and compound mental functions and accessory symptoms that Bleuler describes in great detail.

Bleuler points out that in every case, the various psychic functions are split off from one another, thus the *schiz* of schizophrenia. (A popular, incorrect layman's use of the term "schizophrenia" equates it with multiple personality of the kind described in *The Three Faces of Eve*,[14] and Morton Prince's "Miss Beauchamp—the Theory of Psychogenesis of Multiple Personality."[12]) In the schizophrenias, the personality loses its unity, and integration of various psychic complexes does not occur. Bleuler says,[5] "The psychic complexes do not combine in a conglomeration of strivings with a unified resultant as they do in a healthy person; rather, one set of complexes dominates the personality for a time, while other groups of ideas or drives are 'split off' and seem either partly or completely impotent."

Altered Simple Functions

The first of these altered functions is the defect in *association*. Here the logical links between ideas, their hierarchical progression toward reality-oriented, goal-directed thinking is interfered with. Ideas interrupt other ideas, or thoughts seem to be taken away entirely ("thought deprivation").[6] There may be "*Klang-associations*" where ideas follow one another because of the similarities of sound, or there may be "echo-lalia" wherein a patient will echo the statements of the interviewer. In advanced cases, utterances may become so fragmented and bizarre that they are referred to as "word salad." There may be a pressure of ideas, or there may be severe blocking of expression because the patient is unable to let one of several competing thoughts be voiced. There may be condensations; Bleuler gives the example of the patient who, thinking of the German words "traurig" (sad) and "einsam" (lonesome), said, "trauram." There may be perseveration, in which the same idea is repeated over and over again; there may be stereotyped thinking in which patients are preoccupied with the same topic to the exclusion of all others.

The first of the three examples below shows preoccupation with grandiose ideas and some of the defects in affectivity that will be discussed. The second example shows the loose associations of Naomi N., a chronically hebephrenic patient whose symptomatology and case history are presented in greater detail in Chapter 3. The third example comes from a chronically paranoid patient.

> *Example 1:* ". . . I just have to stay here long enough to save some money and go to England. Then I'll marry Elizabeth Regina. Oh, you won't regret this. We are going to save mankind. Franklin, this is going to be the most important time of your life."—Robert B.
>
> *Example 2:* "That bad man over there came by and hurted me under the jaw and you didn't give me no ice-cream so I laid down on the floor and died when you did that to me and I didn't give you no eats."—Naomi N.
>
> *Example 3:* "My name is Mrs. A. G., the former Miss A. C., and I am not a patient in this hospital, where the following things have been perpetrated on me and about which I am consulting my lawyers: mind-rape, body-rape, body mutilation, awful dismemberment, night assaults, etc. (The list of depredations numbered close to 200.) I demand to be released and returned to the legitimate stage in Detroit, Michigan, where I will meet my financé [sic!] and resume my career on stage." [The career on the stage, so far as could be determined, never had existed.]

In the defect in association, words are used peculiarly or new words are invented—neologisms. For instance, one patient thought that all sexual behavior was adultery, because only adults had sexual relations.

For many years it was thought that the utterances of schizophrenics were bizarre, irrational, and unintelligible. Bleuler applied many concepts he learned from Freud and Jung to such utterances and frequently could make sense of them, just as the analysis of the dreams of neurotics can frequently be at least partially interpreted and understood. In both instances, however, often much remains mysterious and uninterpretable, so the person just starting his study of the schizophrenias should not take himself to task if he fails to understand all that his patients have to say, in spite of diligent attention to their words. Interpreting the communications of schizophrenic patients will be dealt with in more detail in Chapters 4 and 14.

In the defect in *affectivity*, Bleuler referred to the disharmonies and inconsistencies of the emotional life of the schizophrenic. Feelings are frequently inappropriate either to what the patient is talking about or what is going on in the environment. One sees peculiar giggling, smiling, frowning, and grimacing. The affect may be quite blunted; the patient may speak in a quiet leaden tone without sign of animation. Patients may speak dispassionately or even cheerfully about the death of a loved one. Often there will be sudden rages and assaults. Patients may appear confused, dazed, or delirious. One learns later that an apparently bizarre emotional outburst was in response to thought, hallucinations, or delusions; from the patient's point of view, the sudden rage and striking out was an attempt to defend himself against an imagined assault.

In the defect of *ambivalence*, Bleuler refers to the profound difficulty with the simultaneous presence of opposite thoughts and feelings with which the schizophrenic is confronted. Making a commitment in one direction or another is an extraordinarily difficult task for the schizophrenic; the kinds of ambivalences that normal persons encounter in their daily lives are magnified a hundredfold for the schizophrenic.

Bleuler divides ambivalence into three overlapping categories: (1) affective ambivalence, the simultaneous presence of conflicting feelings; (2) ambivalence of will, "Ambi-Tendenz"; and (3) intellectual ambivalence, the presence of conflicting thoughts.

> *Example 4:* Stuart M. showed marked ambivalence of will. He moved about the ward as if he were a wooden puppet, with stiff, jerky movements, unseen strings to his limbs being pulled by an invisible puppeteer. If meals were announced, while the other patients moved toward the dining room, Stuart would take a step or two in that direction, stop, look up and down, put his feet up and down, like a soldier marking time in place, salute with his arms, turn partially around, as if he were doing an about-face, stamp his feet on the ground some more, wave his arms jerkily and stiffly, take a step or two in the new direction, and then repeat this sequence. In this exaggerated parody of military posture, his progress toward the dining hall was essentially a sequence of three steps forward, two to the side, two backward, and then a little forward motion again. It usually took him ten minutes to traverse the 50 yards to the dining room.
>
> *Example 5:* John N. showed ambivalence of thought, manifested by blocked speech. He was asked to describe his mother. He said, "My mother is a g---," as if he were about to say, ". . . good woman." He stopped and then said, "My mother is a b--," as if he were about to say, ". . . bad woman." These half sentences kept alternating, and after several minutes, he still was not able to complete either one.

Intact Simple Functions

Bleuler describes certain intact simple functions to help distinguish the mental symptoms of the schizophrenias from those of organic brain conditions. In the schizophrenias, *sensation, memory, consciousness,* and *motility* are not always, or even often, disturbed. In contrast, there are usually alterations in one or more of these functions in organic conditions. In fact, the schizophrenic patient may record both true and false orientations, revealing awareness of both, e.g., the "Emperor of the World" may beg for a cigarette; a physician can be seen both as a doctor and a former lover. Bleuler has termed this phenomenon "double-entry bookkeeping,"[7] or "double registration" or "double orientation."[8]

Even where a schizophrenic patient's memory and consciousness are intruded on by an emotional complex, he will usually know what the interviewer will say, in contrast to the patient with an organic brain syndrome, who will not know the interviewer's point of view. If, for example, a paranoid schizophrenic believes himself to be a spy for the FBI and the hospital to be a communist-run interrogation institution, he is fully capable of saying, "I know *you* are trying to tell me that this is Gardenville State Hospital, and that you are a psychiatrist, but *I* know that this is a hoax and that you are really an enemy agent." The disoriented organic patient would not be able to maintain this distinction.

Altered Compound Mental Functions

Bleuler describes those of *autism, attention, the will, the person, schizophrenic "dementia,"* and *activity* and *behavior.*

Autism refers to an excessive focusing of attention on internal mental life, i.e., on fantasies, daydreams, hallucinations, delusions, and the like. Unlike the fantasies, reverie states, and "brown studies" that all of us fall into from time to time, the schizophrenic patient cannot voluntarily withdraw himself from the state and redirect his attentions to reality. The consequence of such preoccupation is a lack of awareness and attention paid to the external environment, with a corresponding withdrawal of interest from interpersonal dealings. Patients sometimes speak about others (often prominent in entertainment or the news) who are in love with them. Such imaginary relationships are called autistic love affairs, proceeding as they do from the patient's own fantasies.

Because of the autistic withdrawal, there is impairment of the patient's ability to pay attention, to scan the events in the environment, and to will an appropriate verbal, bodily, or personal response to them.

In the defect in *attention*, Bleuler comments on two paradoxical facets. On one hand, the patient may well lack ability to maintain attention on a particular activity for very long; the attention span is short. On the other hand, the patient may be seemingly unaware of events that are, nevertheless, registered and remembered with utter clarity months or years later.

The defect in *will* is shown by the inability or unwillingness to initiate behavior in such matters as dress or eating with some semblance of manners. At the same time, the patient may be at the mercy of thoughts and impulses coming from within or without, acting on them without reflection, as shown in Stuart M.'s wooden-soldier behavior. The patient in catatonic stupor may be unable to will the simplest of motions, but later he may shift to an excited state and lash out at everything he beholds.

The defect in *the person* describes the kinds of misperception that patients may have about themselves and their identities, that are the result of delusional or hallucinated thinking.

The *schizophrenic "pseudodementia"*—an apparent loss of the faculties of rational thought—is not a true dementia. True dementias, caused by organic changes in brain tissue, either remain stable at a certain level or, more commonly, go on to progressive deterioration. Yet there are many instances of apparently "demented" schizophrenic patients who spontaneously, after years of dilapidated behavior, recovered their wits or demonstrated a wiliness which indicated that little, if any, of their capacity for ratiocination had been lost. Likewise, many patients will show intact and normal mental functioning in areas that are not intruded upon by delusional or autistic thought complexes.

In discussing *activity* and *behavior*, Bleuler says:

> Outspoken schizophrenic behavior is marked by lack of interest, lack of initiative, lack of a definite goal, by inadequate adaptation to the environment, i.e., by disregard of any factors of reality, by confusion, and by sudden fancies and peculiarities.[9]
>
> An educated lady writes a number of letters, marks them "registered mail" and then does not mail them. A teacher suddenly applies for a position paying 2,000 Swiss francs salary, and quits his present teaching position. An uneducated person wishes to study the theory of music. A sales clerk rides back and forth on the train between Romanshorn and Geneva because he had heard that some people had become engaged to nice young women while riding on the night trains. A man takes off all his clothes outdoors in winter, walks naked through the village in order to take a dip in a river that lies a half-hour's distance away. A young girl sews stockings upon a rug.[10]

The Accessory Symptoms

These include, most prominently, (1) hallucinations, (2) delusions, (3) catatonic phenomena, (4) disturbances of the vegetative functions, and (5) disturbances of memory.

The *hallucinations* (false perceptions without apparent sensory basis) are generally auditory, rarely visual, olfactory, or tactile. They are frequently of a threatening or hostile nature, though they may be pleasurable. The examiner may have to infer the presence of hallucinations, in absence of a direct report by the patient, by the fact that the patient appears to be responding to voices or visions unheard and unseen by the examiner.

Delusions (i.e., a belief system for which there seems to be little or no evidence and which is not culturally shared) vary from being very well articulated, internally consistent

and fixed, as in paranoid schizophrenia, to being poorly
articulated, inconsistent, changeable, and evanescent in many
simple or mixed conditions. The most commonly found delusions, in order of frequency, are those concerned with persecution, self-reference, religion, sin; the sexual delusions of
infidelity, jealousy, erotomania; and, finally, those involving
magic, the body, and myth.[3] The content of the delusion of
course reflects the wishes and fears of the individual.

Catatonic phenomena is a term refering to a multitude
of alterations of functioning in the voluntary (striped or
striated) muscular system. Alterations of posture, gait, hand-
writing, speech, and response of environmental stimuli have
been described. There may be complete immobility with waxy
flexibility, alterations of gait, as shown by Stuart M.; hand-
writing can become bizarre and highly personalized, and
there is frequent negativism and stereotypy of behavior. Many
of these phenomena are described in greater detail in Chapter 2.

Disturbances of memory come about when a complex
delusion or hallucination intrudes into consciousness. Paranoid patients may have incorrect recollections of their childhoods; a patient who thinks he is Jesus Christ may imagine
that he was brought up in Bethlehem. Recovered patients
frequently have amnesia for the period of illness.

Further discussion of the accessory symptoms of schizophrenia will be found in Chapters 2 and 4.

DIAGNOSIS

The age of risk for the schizophrenias of adolescence and
adulthood is thought to be from puberty to 45 years; patients
who develop psychiatric conditions before or after these limits
are not thought to be typically schizophrenic. In the weeks or
months before the patient comes to professional attention,
family and friends have noticed a change in behavior. They
will say he is different, changed, not like his old self, etc. The
kinds of changes most frequently found are reported in
Chapter 5.

If the patient demonstrates all the altered simple and compound mental functions described by Bleuler, the diagnosis of typical schizophrenia can easily be made. However, in many cases of mild or atypical schizophrenia, many of these defects in functioning may be difficult or impossible to detect; the most conspicuous phenomena may be such accessory symptoms as hallucinations, delusions, or catatonic phenomena. The clinician may have to make the diagnosis on the basis of these accessory symptoms, plus the hint of altered simple and compound functions, plus a history of characteristic behavior and mood changes in the weeks and months preceding the overt psychosis.

The American Psychiatric Association has recognized the difficulty in finding all the signs and symptoms that Bleuler described for his typical cases. In their official diagnostic manual of 1952,[1] they give this definition:

> [Schizophrenia is] characterized by fundamental disturbances in reality relationships and concept formations, with affective, behavioral disturbances in varying degrees and mixtures. The disorders are marked by a strong tendency to retreat from reality, by emotional disharmony, unpredictable disturbances in stream of thought, regressive behavior, and, in some, by a tendency to "deterioration."

The A.P.A. modified this description in 1968,[2] as follows:

> This large category includes a group of disorders manifested by characteristic disturbances of thinking, mood, and behavior.. Disturbances in thinking are marked by alterations of concept formation which may lead to misinterpretation of reality and sometimes to delusions and hallucinations, which frequently appear psychologically self-protective. Corollary mood changes include ambivalent, constricted

and inappropriate emotional responsiveness
and loss of empathy with others. Behavior may
be withdrawn, regressive and bizarre. The
schizophrenias, in which the mental status is
attributable primarily to a *thought* disorder,
are to be distinguished from the *major affective*
illnesses (q.v.) which are dominated by a *mood*
disorder. The *paranoid states* (q.v.) are distinguished from schizophrenia by the narrow-
ness of their distortions of reality and by the
absence of other psychotic symptoms.

Though Bleuler considered flattening or blunting of affect
an important feature of the diagnosis, it would now appear
that the condition is as much an artifact of prolonged hospitalization (institutionalism) as it is intrinsic to the symptomatology of the schzophrenias. In this era of rapid and
vigorous treament, most patients demonstrate considerable
affect, but it is often inappropriate to surroundings and context.

If the diagnosis of schizophrenia is to be made primarily
on the presence of accessory symptoms, the examiner should
be careful to exclude organic psychoses such as Korsakow's
psychosis, L.S.D. intoxication,[15] neurosyphyilis, etc. The distinguishing characteristics of these conditions can be obtained
from standard texts.[13]

There are several atypical forms of schizophrenia, described in Chapter 2, in which some but not all of the simple
and compound functions are altered, or alterations are minimal and fluctuating, etc. Though such atypical states are of
interest, the major focus of this book will be on the typical
schizophrenias.

There are certain factors that are *not* a part of the symptoms or signs of the schizophrenias, and that will be excluded
from these discussions. The first is that of a known organic
condition that affects behavior; persons with toxic psychoses,
chronic brain syndromes, and the like are not usually thought
to be schizophrenic. This statement does not mean that they

cannot also be schizophrenic or that previously schizophrenic persons cannot also develop a chronic brain syndrome, but such happenings are coincidental.

For instance, it frequently happens that parents of a newly admitted schizophrenic patient will attribute his illness to the time he fell off his tricycle when he was 5, bumped his head, and was unconscious for a few minutes; or how, at 3, had whooping cough with the highest fever ever recorded in West Dubuque, and seemed to be delirious for the better part of the week, though later making a full recovery; or how at 16 he was exposed to some D.D.T. fumes and behaved peculiarly thereafter. If you interviewed the parents of 50 nonschizophrenics intensively and asked if their children had ever fallen off tricycles and lost consciousness, or had a high fever and seemed sort of delirious, you would probably get very close to as many positive replies as with the parents of schizophrenics. Thus this book will include people who have had bumps on the head as children (it's part of the universal human condition), but it will exclude those in whom there is any definite suggestion of a persistent neurological illness or defect.

Another exclusion from this book will be persons who have had a psychosis in childhood, variously diagnosed as childhood schizophrenia, infantile autism, etc. This group of illnesses may or may not prove to be significantly related to adult schizophrenia. In view of this uncertainty, I shall focus on those schizophrenias afflicting adolescents and young adults.

There is also considerable uncertainty whether persons first showing signs of psychosis after the age of 45, frequently diagnosed as "involutional paranoid reaction," should be considered in the same light as those whose illness develops earlier. Because of this confusion, such persons will be excluded.

To summarize, the term "schizophrenic" in use here will refer to persons whose clinical picture conforms to Bleuler's description, and for whom the outcome of illness can vary from progressive deterioration to quick and complete recovery without recurrence. Atypical schizophrenias, such as schizo-affective psychosis, pseudoneurotic schizophrenia, etc., will be discussed in greater detail in the next chapter. The book excludes consideration of persons having a known organic condition that affects their behavior, or conditions in which the onset of psychotic behavior occurred before puberty or after the age of 45.

2

Taxonomy

INTRODUCTION

Many types of schizophrenia have been described over the past 50 years. Some of these proposed types have fallen into disuse; others carry considerable clinical currency. This chapter will attempt to synthesize current thinking about typology and nomenclature; illustrations for several of the types are found in Chapter 3.

Kraepelin and Bleuler described classical or typical cases of schizophrenia as well as atypical forms. They mentioned several subtypes, and subsequent authors have added to this list. A taxonomic key for the currently important types of schizophrenia is found in Table 2–2. Each of these types will be described in some detail in the text. (The portions of the case histories dealing with schizophrenic symptomatology and typology are most relevant here.)

Before going to the taxonomic key in detail, we must first consider three currently useful distinctions that have more to do with the timing, onset, duration, and prognosis of the illness than with the symptomatology per se. These distinctions are those of (1) process-reactive, (2) true schizophrenia-schizophreniform, and (3) acute-chronic psychoses. Though it is not correct to use each of these polarities as synonymous with the others, it is clear that they contain many points of similarity.

The *process-reactive distinction* reflects the observation that there are some patients who insidiously and without apparent external stress slide into a schizophrenic state, i.e., that they seem to be the victim of an inherent schizophrenic *process.* Others become schizophrenic only after severe and obvious external stress; their psychosis is a *reaction* to such stress. Descriptions of these two concepts follow; they are summarized in Table 2–1.

> *Process:* Poorly integrated prepsychotic personality, characterized by marked sexual, social and occuptional inadequacy, a lack of emotional responsiveness, and social isolation. The slide into psychosis, for this patient, is usually insidious and without pertinent stress and most frequently occurs in late adolescence. The disorder is made manifest by the gradual onset of emotional blunting, withdrawal from daily activities, apathy and indifference, somatic delusions and marked disturbances in thinking—a pattern which may be maintained through long years of hospitalization. Few or no precipitating factors.[9]
>
> *Reactive:* From birth to the fifth year, the maturational and developmental history showed no defects, physical health was good. Generally school and home adjustment was good, (as was adjustment to other age-related tasks). Parents were accepting. Heterosexual relationships were established. The patient had friends and domestic troubles did not disrupt his behavior.
>
> The onset of the illness was often sudden with a clear-cut understandable precipitating event. Aggression was expressed verbally. Decency was maintained. The course was fulminating, with massive hallucinatory experiences, ideas of reference, and mild paranoid trends, as well as sensorial impairment. A

TABLE 2–1

A COMPARISON OF PROCESS AND REACTIVE SCHIZOPHRENIA

Parameter:	*Process*	*Reactive*
1. Premorbid adjustment	Poor	Good
2. Nature of onset	Slow, insidious	Sudden, acute
3. Precipitating factors	Few or none	Clear-cut presence
4. Age at onset	Adolescence	Variable
5. Primary symptomatology		
a. Affect	Blunted, apathetic	Aggression; frequently depression
b. Thoughts	Classic thought disorder	Ideas of reference; ± classic thought disorder
c. Social behavior	Withdrawn, indifferent	Social awareness maintained
d. Sensorium	Clear	Impaired
6. Response to treatment	Poor	Good

> thought disorder was present according to some
> authors, but not others. Response to treatment
> was good.[21]

Unfortunately, the seemingly unitary concepts of "process" and "reactive" carry within them several parameters,
as inspection of Table 2–1 will demonstrate. Where then do
we put the patient who had good premorbid adjustment (characteristic of the "reactive" patient), for whom no precipitating
event was observable (characteristic of the "process" patient),
whose primary symptomatology demonstrated aggression,
intact social awareness, and sensorial impairment (characteristic again of the "reactive" patient), etc.? The process-reactive distinction would serve better if fewer parameters were
buried implicit within it, but it has come into usage with its
several parameters, and the reader should be aware of them.

European psychiatrists distinguish between *true schizophrenia* and the *schizophreniform psychoses. True schizophrenia* applies to patients whose illness is progressive,
severe, and deteriorating; such patients rarely, if ever, show
a significant recovery. Langfeldt[17] terms *schizopheniform* all
psychoses that result from clear precipitating stress (usually
psychological, but also occasionally organic), that demonstrate illusions, ideas of refernce, confusion, and disorientation, and for whom the prognosis is relatively good.

The *acute-chronic* differentiation is based both on onset
and course. Just as the apparently simple process-reactive
distinction turned out to conceal several parameters within itself so too the *acute-chronic* distinction conceals at least three
parameters. The first is that of length of onset, the time from
the beginning of personality change to the appearance of
the overt psychosis. If this time is less than six months (some
authors use three months), the patient's condition is said to
be *acute*; if it is greater, to be *chronic*.

The second parameter is that of reversibility. The official
nomenclature of the American Psychiatric Association has
used *acute* to be synonymous with *reversible*, and *chronic* to

be synonymous with *irreversible.* By this criterion, a schizophrenic patient who went into remission after 20 years could be considered *acute!*

The third parameter is that of clinical course. Many psychiatrists feel that if a patient has been continuously schizophrenic for two years or more, he merits the label of *chronic;* if his illness clears before two years, that he has been *acute.*

Only in the first use given, that of duration of onset, can the acute-chronic distinction be made at the time of first admission. The other distinctions depend on extended observations of the patient and can be made only in retrospect. Obviously this semantic confusion can lead to paradoxical use of the terms, e.g., the patient whose illness is reversible (*acute*) after five years is also *chronic* by virtue of having been ill longer than two years. Authors rarely state which meaning of *acute* or *chronic* they are employing, and the reader may have to infer it.

From the foregoing, it is apparent that there are many points of congruence in the cluster of *process/true schizophrenia/chronic* groups and in the cluster of *reactive/schizophreniform psychosis/acute* groups.

Use of Table 2–2, the Taxonomic Key

When a patient shows one or more of the symptoms, signs, or personal characteristics of the schizophrenias, as detailed in Chapter 1, one should further search in this chapter, Table 2–2, "A Taxonomic Key," to see where in the array of the schizophrenias he might fit, if he fits there at all. If the patient demonstrates *all* the signs of altered simple and compound mental functions that Bleuler describes, he is probably suffering from one of the typical schizophrenias. The form that his symptoms take will determine which (combination) of the classical subtypes he demonstrates, and examination of the events of the onset and course of illness will allow one to place the patient on the continua of acute-chronic, process-reactive, and true schizophrenia-schizophreniform psychosis.

If only some, but not all, of the patient's simple or compound mental functions are grossly disturbed, or if some of the signs of disturbed functioning are doubtful and suggest a partially concealed schizophrenic thought disorder, the patient probably shows one of the atypical schizophrenias. That category should then be searched to see if the patient conforms to one of the recognized subtypes.

If none of the classical signs of the thought disorder is present, the patient may belong in the category of related states; again the subtypes should be examined. If the patient's clinical picture conforms to none of the conditions defined in these three major categories, he probably does not demonstrate one of the schizophrenias or related states.

TABLE 2–2

A TAXONOMIC KEY OF THE SCHIZOPHRENIAS

I. *The Typical Schizophrenias:* Patients in this category clearly show all the altered simple and compound mental functions described by Bleuler. They may in addition show some of the accessory symptoms. Make the process-reactive distinction, using the criteria of A (Table 2–1), and the subtype distinction as in B (below).
   A. By Process-Reactive Differentiation: See Table 2–1, this chapter. The presence of Bleuler's basic criteria for schizophrenia, plus the characteristics of "reactive" schizophrenia would lead in Europe to a diagnosis of "schizophreniform psychosis."
   B. By Classical Subtypes
      1. Simple type
         a. Insidious impoverishment of intellect
         b. Insidious impoverishment of emotional life
         c. Deterioration of interpersonal relations
         d. Marginal existence
      2. Hebephrenic type
         a. Insidious onset, perhaps at first confused with depression
         b. Shallowness, silliness, inappropriate giggling
         c. Hallucinations of fantasy rather than delusion, usually fragmented and changing
         d. Neologisms, punning, word-salad

      e. Posturing and manneristic behavior

      f. Ravenous appetite, soiling

   3. Catatonic type

      a. Stupor (an apparent, but not real, diminution of consciousness)

         i. Negativism, echolalia

         ii. Automatism, dreaminess, grimacing

         iii. Immobility, waxy flexibility

         iv. Refusal to eat

         v. Loss of sphincter control; constipation

      b. Excitement

         i. Unorganized aggressive motor outbursts

         ii. Soiling, nudism, negativism, grimacing

         iii. Delirious, dazed appearance

   4. Paranoid

      a. Premorbid suspicious character; onset later in life

      b. Marked ideas of reference, delusions of persecution

      c. Frequent accusatory auditory hallucinations

      d. Hostile and unpleasant manner

      e. Loosening of associations, hypochondriacal pre-occupations, neologisms

      f. Aloof and unpredictable assaultiveness

      g. Well-preserved intellectual functioning outside of psychotic core

   5. Mixed: Signs of two or more of the classic subtypes, e.g., hebephrenic, catatonic, paranoid, present, but none clearly predominates

   6. Undifferentiated: No signs of the classic subtypes are clearly present, though the basic defects in thinking and relating are manifest.

II. *The Atypical Schizophrenias:* Patients in this category show some but not all of the altered simple and compound mental functions of Bleuler, or they show them intermittently or not completely convincingly.

  A. Schizo-Affective Psychosis

    Recurrent episodes, usually starting in adolescence, looking initially like manic-depressive psychosis with some thought disorder; the thought disorder becomes more prominent after several attacks and the mood disorder diminishes.

  B. Acute Homosexual Panic (Kempf's disease)

    Probably a variant of an acute confusional schizophrenia sometimes precipitated by threat of homosexual contact or loss, demonstrating considerable homosexual fear and preoccupation.

   C. Acute Paranoia (acute polymorphic delirium; exhaustion psychosis; combat psychosis)
      1. Recent emotional and physical exhaustion
      2. Illusions that develop into paranoid delusions and hallucinations
      3. Normal reintegration of personality after relief of stress
   D. Ambulatory Schizophrenia—the "masked schizophrenias"
      1. Pseudoneurotic type
         a. Pan-anxiety
         b. Pan-neurosis
         c. Vague, fleeting, or stereotyped description of symptoms
         d. Disorganized or chaotic social and sexual lives
         e. Subtle or overt thought disorder
         f. Transient overt psychotic episodes may appear, especially with stress
      2. Pseudopsychopathic schizophrenia ("schizopath")
         a. History of drifting, antisocial, impulsive, or amoral behavior
         b. On examination, evidences of overt thought disorder, or tangential, circumstantial, loosely associated speech
      3. Borderline character
         a. Few to some areas of anxiety-free functioning
         b. Few to some consistent object and social relationships
         c. Mild to moderately bizarre complaints, verbalizations, proverb interpretations
         d. Experienced as "eccentric character" or "strange bird"
   E. Postpartum or Puerperal Schizophrenia
      Appearance in the mother of one of the syndromes of typical schizophrenia one month prepartum to three months postpartum. (Similar reactions have been described for fathers.)
   F. Periodic Catatonia: Periods of normal behavior alternating with episodes of catatonic stupor or excitement.

III. *Related States; Rare, Exotic, or Unclassified Syndromes*
     (Listed, but will not be described or characterized in the table; see text for details.)

  A. Related States
    1. Schizoid character
    2. Pure paranoia and the paranoid state
    3. Ganser syndrome
    4. Alcoholic hallucinosis
  B. Rare, Exotic, or Unclassifiable Syndromes
    1. Oneirophrenia
    2. Psychogenic psychosis
    3. Capgras' syndrome
    4. *Psychose passionelle* (pure erotomania)
    5. Lycanthropy
    6. *Latah, amok, koro (shook yung)*
    7. *Folie à deux*

THE TYPICAL SCHIZOPHRENIAS

Simple schizophrenia (schizophrenia simplex; dementia simplex)

Simple schizophrenia is marked by insidious and inconspicuous improverishment of intellectual and emotional life and of social relationships. The symptoms come on gradually, over a period of months and years, frequently starting in early adolescence. Rarely are there discernible precipitating events. In contrast to the other typical schizophrenias, there are rarely spectacularly bizarre symptoms. These patients quietly slide into an autistic world, losing interest in school, family, and job. Many become hoboes, alcoholics, prostitutes, or the village eccentric, and are ignored or quietly tolerated by the community. Others sufficiently lose the capacity to exist even on a marginal level and must be hospitalized. Such patients rarely make substantial improvement and live out their autistic lives in a protected setting. Many authors, including Sullivan, feel that simple schizophrenia may be more biologically and hereditarily determined than the other major subtypes.

Hebephrenic Schizophrenia

In Greek mythology, Hebe was the adolescent daughter of Zeus and Hera and cupbearer to the gods. She was reputed to sip a bit of the wine she was bearing and slip into a state of silly, giggling, exuberant adolescent pixilation. This picture gave rise to the term "hebephrenia," coined by Hecker in 1871, one of the subtypes of schizophrenia.[12] It is marked by silliness, shallowness of feeling, fantasy, punning, use of rhyme and invented words (neologisms), posturing, grimacing, manneristic behavior, ravenous appetite, and incontinence.

The first symptoms frequently appear between the ages of 15 and 21, develop slowly over a period of months or years. The initial diagnosis is often a subtype other than hebephrenia.[5] The course tends to be chronic; good recovery is a rarity in patients who have been ill for more than a couple of years, as it is for any chronically ill patient. The cases of Naomi N. and Vivian L. in Chapter 3 demonstrate many of the features of chronic hebephrenic schizophrenia.

Simple schizophrenic patients and hebephrenic patients who have been ill for many years and now are "burnt out" may be difficult to distinguish. Such a distinction is done by history: the hebephrenic patient had overt signs of his hebephrenia in the early years of his illness; the patient with simple schizophrenia did not.

Catatonic Schizophrenia

The term derives from Greek words that mean "downward," "away," and "tension"; the term was coined by Kahlbaum in 1874.[15] Indeed, striking alterations in the normal use of the striped (voluntary) musculature are the cardinal features in the two subtypes of catatonic schizophrenia, stuporous and excited.

In the *stuporous* state, the patient is apparently out of contact with reality (though many a recovered catatonic demonstrates that he registered all that was going on around him with great fidelity while he was stuporous). Stuporous patients adopt strange, uncomfortable-looking, statuelike postures which they maintain for minutes or hours at a time. In spite of their appearance, they are actually at a high level of physiological arousal, as determined by EEG and metabolic studies. They may show *cereus flexibilitas* (waxy flexibility) by allowing their limbs to be passively moulded by the examiner into new postures, and to maintain these postures after the examiner removes his hands, much as a lump of clay would do under the sculptor's hands. Such patients may also show command automatism, responding to the examiner's suggestions in a robotlike manner. Their faces may portray dreaminess, grimacing, or tics, and frequently one has the impression that they are locked into contact with hallucinations to which, because of the patients' immobility, they cannot respond. Finally, such patients may frequently be so immobilized that they neither eat nor maintain sphincter control. Tube feedings may be necessary to avoid death through inanition.

In the *excited* state, a stuporous patient, usually without warning, will suddenly become very active. Bleuler describes such catatonically excited patients as follows:

> They clamber about, move around, shake the branches of trees in the garden, hop over the beds, bang on the table twenty times, and then on the wall; they bend the knees, jump, strike, break, twist their arms into impossible positions between the radiator and the wall, totally unconcerned about the burns which they receive. They cry, sing, verbigerate, laugh, curse, scream and spit all over the room.[3]

Such periods of excitement may revert to stupor as quickly as they appeared or there may be intervening periods of calm or recovery. In massive uncontrolled destructive excitement, patients may run the risk of death by exhaustion and in extreme cases may require several electroshock convulsions in a single day to slow them down.

Catatonic stupor may be the first frankly schizophrenic manifestation presented in an acute schizophrenic episode. Many catatonic patients who recover will tell of feeling om-

nipotently destructive and that their stupor was a defense
against their fantasied power to destroy people or the entire
world. It is as if they said to themselves, "If I completely
negate my power of voluntary motion, I will not cause the
terrible destruction I am afraid I am capable of." Such themes
of schizophrenic thinking and logic will be considered in more
detail in Chapter 4.

Paranoid Schizophrenia

This is the name given to the form of the thought disorder in which misinterpretations of reality and of others'
motives predominate. The term derives from a Greek word
meaning "derangement, madness"; that word in turn comes
from *para*, meaning "akin to" and *nous*, "mind." Thus, in
pure paranoia, there is thinking that resembles, or is akin to,
normal thinking, and in paranoid schizophrenia, there is
relative preservation of intellectual functions in the presence
of the primary thought disorder. Though many people use
the world "paranoid" as a synonym for unpleasant delusions
of suspiciousness and hostility, it is just as properly applied
to the pleasant delusion of beatific grace experienced by some
patients who think themselves to be Jesus Christ.

Delusions and hallucinations, usually of a persecutory
or grandiose nature, are quite frequent. The chaotic, scattered,
apparently silly and autistic thoughts and fantasties of the
hebephrenic are rarely seen; likewise, the striking alterations
of the striped musculature of the catatonic are generally absent. Intellectual functioning, especially outside the areas
of delusional thinking, tends to be well preserved. The primary
mental mechanism is that of projection: the attribution of
that patient's own repressed thoughts and feelings onto such
outside forces as other people or hallucinated voices.

Paranoid schizophrenia frequently makes a later onset
than do the other varieties with new cases appearing in patients who are in their thirties or forties. To the degree that
the patient comes to accept a paranoid explanation of his
mental condition the prognosis is poor; to the degree that he
remains anxious and uncertain about how "real" his paranoid

experiences are, the prognosis is better. When a patient accepts a psychotic explanation for the mystifying and frightening events that have been taking place, his anxiety is relieved to a great extent, the state of uncertainty ended. Paranoid schizophrenics usually maintain an attitude of great aloofness and contempt for the world. They may be frightened by the accusatory or persecutory delusions and hallucinations. If, privately, they have concluded that a certain person is personally responsible for their discomfort, they may assault that person. Such selective assaultiveness stands in marked contrast to the undifferentiated destructiveness of a catatonic excitement. Occasionally a paranoid schizophrenic patient will kill himself or make a serious suicide attempt; information from patients who survived such attempts shows that frequently the psychology behind the attempt was one of "I'll be damned if I'll let those [imagined] bastards get me; I wouldn't give them the satisfaction; I'll do it myself first."

One of the most famous cases in psychiatric literature, Freud's Judge Schreber, was a paranoid schizophrenic. Another case is that of Anton K. in Chapter 3.

Mixed Schizophrenia

With the exception of simple schizophrenia, the three major subtypes described above may be present in a single patient to varying degrees. In fact, patients rarely conform so nicely to our diagnostic abstractions that they represent a pure case of one of the subtypes. When patients demonstrate an admixture of more than one subtype, they are diagnosed as showing a "mixed schizophrenia" by the predominant subtype specified, e.g., "mixed schizophrenia with hebephrenic and catatonic features." Furthermore, the predominant symptomatology may change over time. A patient who is catatonic one month may be hebephrenic the next. The case of Elsie B. (Chapter 3) demonstrates a mixed schizophrenia.

Undifferentiated Schizophrenia

There are patients who, although quite obviously showing the signs and symptoms of the classical thought disorder,

either never showed, or do not now show, distinct characteristics of one or more of the subtypes. Such patients are diagnosed as having undifferentiated schizophrenia.

THE ATYPICAL SCHIZOPHRENIAS

Patients diagnosed as having one of the atypical schizophrenias show some, but not all, of the altered simple and
compound mental functions of Bleuler, or they show them
intermitently or not completely convincingly.

Schizo-Affective Psychosis

This is a form of mental illness in which the thought disorder of schizophrenia occurs simultaneously with the dramatic mood extremes of mania, depression, or both. The words
are the words of schizophrenia, but the music is the music of
manic-depressive psychosis. The first attack usually comes
during adolescence and frequently there is a good remission.
The usual diagnosis is that of early manic-depressive psychosis. With repeated attacks over the years, the thought
disorder becomes more prominent, the mood disturbance less
so. Diagnoses change over time to "manic-depressive psychosis
with underlying thought disorder"; then to "schizo-affective
psychosis"; then to "schizophrenia with manic (or depressive)
features"; then to "chronic schizophrenia." Not all patients
initially diagnosed as having manic-depressive psychosis will
ultimately reveal a schizophrenic picture; in fact, most of
them will not. But the fraction of patients who do will merit
the diagnosis of "schizo-affective psychosis" somewhere in
their psychiatric history.

Acute Homosexual Panic (Kempf's disease)

This was originally described as a distinct entity precipitated by the threat of eruption into consciousness of
previously unconscious wishes to offer oneself as a "sexual
object" to a member of the same sex. This eruption may be
precipitated by seductive closeness or actual attempt at seduc-

tion by a member of the same sex, loss of a close friend of the same sex, failure in heterosexual performance, separation from home and friends, etc. Such patients show a picture of intense agitation and panic, confusion, delusions and hallucinations of persecution, occasional assaultiveness, and considerable preoccupation with homosexuality and fears of homosexual attack per anum.

However, this same clinical picture is seen in many acute schizophrenic episodes, though the amount of preoccupation with homosexual material may not be so great. The term is occasionaly used with nonpsychotic illnesses. I should be inclined to consider psychotic forms of Kempf's disease merely a variant of an acute schizophrenic episode not warranting a separate diagnostic classification.

Acute Paranoia (Acute Polymorphic Delirium; Exhaustion Psychosis; Combat Psychosis)

Bellak describes acute paranoia condition as follows:

> . . . consists of an episode of delusions brought on by exhaustion or by a psychologically determined precipitating cause and is characterized by illusions which gradually develop into hallucinations and delusions. After the episode is over the personality is well-preserved and integrated.[2]

Ambulatory Schizophrenia

This term has had two major uses. The first use is to describe patients who are quite obviously schizophrenic—demonstrating all of Bleuler's signs—but who have managed to function in the community without running afoul of the local agencies. A patient who complained of his blood veins slipping from his heart had worked as a handyman and janitor for years in spite of his obvious gross delusional system. It was only when the cardiology clinic saw that his cardiac complaints were far from organic, and he was referred to psychiatry, that the diagnosis of schizophrenia was made.

The second use of the term "ambulatory schizophrenia" describes a series of states that lie on the hazy border between psychosis and neurosis or psychopathy; in this sense at least three subtypes enjoy current usage: (1) pseudoneurotic schizophrenia, (2) pseudopsychopathic schizophrenia, and (3) borderline character.

I much prefer this second usage of the term "ambulatory schizophrenia," referring to the three subtypes cited. Otherwise it has no other meaning save to refer to someone who is schizophrenic but not hospitalized. All three subtypes may be considered forms of "masked schizophrenia"; that is, the classical schizophrenia symptomatology is not immediately apparent to the observer but can be detected through close scrutiny or special diagnostic techniques.

1. PSEUDONEUROTIC SCHIZOPHRENIA was first described by Hoch and Polatin[13] in 1948; it is characterized by pan-neurosis, pan-anxiety, poor interpersonal relationships, anhedonia, polymorphous perverse sexuality, and a tendency toward the classical thought disorder of schizophrenia.

Pan-neurosis means that these patients present a multitude of neurotic complaints about neurotic symptomatology. In a single patient there may be strong evidences of obsessional thoughts, compulsive acts, phobias, hysterical conversions, anxious concern with body functioning, depression, inability to concentrate, and feelings of unreality and depersonalization.

Pan-anxiety means that no area of psychological functioning is experienced in a relatively anxiety-free way. Such patients are concerned about their social contacts, their work performance, their marriages, their sex lives, their mental and physiological functioning. Their social relationships tend to be few, superficial, and chaotic. Signs of disturbed or loose associations, autism, and the other classical signs of the schizophrenias may be apparent at first contact or may emerge only under stress, in an unstructured situation (e.g., free association, Rorschach testing), or under sodium amytal.

Anhedonia refers to an inability to experience pleasure: nothing in life holds great appeal or produces more than transient satisfaction. *Polymorphous perverse sexuality* is the term that applies to a sexual life where there is no organization toward intercourse, or even a particular perversion, but where, instead, all kinds of sexual play and activity take place indiscriminately.

The past histories of such patients can reveal previous overt psychotic episodes, usually brief, with somatic hallucinations and delusions having been prominent. Some patients who have been chronically schizophrenic (i.e., for longer than two years) may improve to the point of showing a picture of pseudoneurotic schizophrenia. Many pseudoneurotic schizophrenic patients, however, have never had an overt, frankly schizophrenic episode. Such patients generally are able to conform sufficiently to the community's rules of behavior and are thus rarely either picked up by police or committed to hospitals by relatives or acquaintances. Since this term has come into use, diagnoses of "ambulatory schizophrenia" and "pseudoneurotic schizophrenia" have been made for large percentages of patients seen in psychiatric clinics. Frequently between one third and one half of all patients, especially males, seen in some clinics receive such a diagnosis.

2. PSEUDOPSYCHOPATHIC SCHIZOPHRENIA is described by Weiner, in Bellak,[22] as follows:

> . . . a group of patients, basically schizophrenic, whose symptoms were, however, masked by antisocial behavior so that they were diagnosed as psychopathic personalities. On closer examination, however, they had many different neurotic symptoms, diffuse anxiety, and led a chaotic, polymorphous sexual life.
>
> Three different types of pre-psychotic personality were isolated: a tough, jaunty, bland, defiant, sneering, nonchalant exterior which on

> closer examination hid a guilt-laden, anxious
> person with phobias, compulsive and hypo-
> chondriacal symptoms; a clinging, dependent,
> coy, ingratiating, but obstructionistic and pas-
> sively aggressive front beneath which there
> were multiple phobic, compulsive and other
> neurotic symptoms, much contentless anxiety,
> and a preoccupation with death; and a with-
> drawn, remote, isolated, often alcoholic, person
> with compulsive and hypochondriacal symp-
> toms.
>   Their antisocial acts included addiction to
> drugs and alcohol, truancy and delinquent acts,
> nomadism, larceny, bigamy, assault, robbery,
> and other aggressive and destructive acts. Their
> sexual acts demonstrated the gamut of overtly
> perverse behavior.

Weiner goes on to say that such patients may become
overtly psychotic when confined, that deterioration into
classical schizophrenia does not usually occur, and that these
patients should not be confused with frankly schizophrenic
patients who commit a crime or antisocial act during an
active psychotic episode, as did Anton K. Such patients are
sometimes referred to as "schizopaths."

3. BORDERLINE CHARACTER is the third of the masked
schizophrenias and may be difficult to distinguish from
pseudoneurotic schizophrenia. Nevertheless, there are certain
patients who have a few or several, but not many, neurotic
complaints, whose interpersonal functioning is markedly
limited but who have formed a few important relationships,
and who may function in a relatively anxiety-free way in at
least some sectors of their lives, who still use words peculiarly,
who are eccentric in manner and dress without being aware
of their eccentricities, and who strike the observer as "strange
birds" or being "a little schizy." The basic thought disorder
is not as close to the surface as it is in the pseudoneurotic
schizophrenic, but they give the strong impression that it
lies not too far beneath the surface, as Knight has pointed

out.[16] For such patients, the designation of "borderline character" is certainly appropriate. There is yet one more state described, that of the "schizoid character"; such patients are
sufficiently distant from the psychosis end of the psychosis-
neurosis continuum that they are described in the section on
Related States.

Postpartum Schizophrenia

The appearance of schizophrenia in either parent in the
period following the birth of a child warrants this diagnosis.
Authors vary in how much time may elapse between before
or after birth and psychosis for this diagnosis to be made;
Melges[18] proposes a period of from one month prepartum to
three months postpartum.

Views on the etiology of postpartum schizophrenic reactions vary. Some authors feel that the unique hormonal
physiological changes of childbirth are largely responsible for
the symptoms.[4, 11] Others feel that childbirth, like many
another event in life, imposes a psychological stress. Likewise,
psychosis following being drafted, graduated from college,
having a broken love affair, etc., is best understood as a failure
of emotional adjustment.[7, 8, 19] Evidence is not clear about
how much either hormonal or psychological factors, separately
or in conjunction, are implicated in producing postpartum
schizophrenia. In fathers who become psychotic after the
birth of a child, presumably no such hormonal changes can
be implicated.[20] The case of Sylvia T. (Chapter 3) demonstrates a case of postpartum schizophrenia.

Periodic Catatonia

This is the last of the atypical schizophrenias to be considered. It is a syndrome described by Gjessing,[10] in which
periods of weeks or months of normal functioning alternate
with episodes of catatonic stupor or excitement.

RELATED STATES

There are several conditions that show little, if any, of
the basic symptomatology of schizophrenia described by

Bleuler. Yet there are enough suspicious points of similarity to demand that they be considered. They are the following: schizoid character, pure paranoia, paranoid state, Ganser syndrome, and alcoholic hallucinosis. Rare and unclassifiable syndromes will also be briefly mentioned.

Schizoid Character

Schizoid patients are isolated, introverted, unable to form close friendships, keep much to themselves, and give others the impression of aloofness, superiority, and contempt for mankind. The schizoid's representations of others with whom he has contact frequently have a nameless, faceless, two-dimensional, cardboard flat quality. In a curiously dispassionate way, such a patient may describe a love affair as follows: "I met a girl last summer. We spent quite a bit of time together, but then we broke up. I don't know where she is now." The schizoid's episodic contacts with others are reminiscent of a train going through the Midwest at night: there are long periods of dark silence interrupted only by the clacking of the wheels; then, suddenly, passage through a small town with lights, shadows, and the rumble of crossings, followed soon again by clicking dark silence.

It was once thought that most schizophrenics were schizoid premorbidly, and, conversely, that schizoid characters were prone to develop schizophrenia. Neither seems to be true. Though reports vary, it would seem that no more than a third of all schizophrenic patients were schizoid characters premorbidly;*and it would seem that a very small percentage of schizoid characters ever became schizophrenic.

Pure Paranoia and the Paranoid State

In *pure paranoia,* there is usually a single, fixed, false assumption on which an intricate and internally consistent

---

* As shown in greater detail in Chapter 5, serious disturbance of premorbid adjustment occurs in between one third and one half of the schizophrenic patients studied. Many of these disturbances were of a form *other than* schizoid personality; hence it would seem that at the maximum, premorbid schizoid personality was found in no more than one third of the patient population.

logical system is based. It is as though the patient, having assumed that the earth is flat, quite logically refuses to sail toward the horizon for fear of falling off the edge. The false logical system exists isolated from the rest of the patient's mental functioning, which is preserved intact. There are none of the signs of the fundamental thought disorder, in contrast to paranoid schizophrenia. Such a false belief system may persist for years.[6]

There are authors who doubt that such a condition exists, that, instead, patients so diagnosed represent paranoid schizophrenia with minimal but detectable thought disorder. In the example given below, it is apparent that for the first 2 months of contact, the patient appeared to represent a case of pure paranoia; after this time, the diagnosis was changed to paranoid schizophrenia.

> *Example:* A woman lawyer was arrested on the complaint of a male acquaintance who stated that she tried to enter his apartment and would frequently park in front of his building at night and observe his comings and goings. She was committed to a state hospital; there she explained in a calm and rational manner that she and the man had been married and and she was doing nothing more than exercising her conjugal rights. Her version struck the ward staff as so convincing that several members were tempted to inspect the local marriage license register to see if her story were indeed true. While on the ward she was a pleasant, cooperative person who conversed intelligently about matters of the day.
>
> Initially there were no signs of a classical thought disorder, delusions (other than the alleged marriage), or hallucinations. After two months, however, overt signs of disturbed thinking appeared, and the ward staff felt more certain that the "right" person was in the hospital, though they were not entirely able to quiet fears that many normal people, incar-

cerated under false circumstances, might show
signs of disordered thinking after a few months.

Paranoid state refers to a condition, usually relatively
brief, in which there is a set of delusions that are not so
intricate and extensive as in pure paranoia, nor are there the
fragmented or bizarre thoughts of paranoid schizophrenia.
Though such states may persist, they usually are transient.
It would seem that paranoid states resulting from acute
physical and emotional stress are identical with acute paranoia (polymorphic delirium, exhaustion psychosis).

The Ganser Syndrome (Stockade Syndrome)

This clinical picture is marked by paralogical thinking,
talking past the point (*vorbeireden*), and pseudostupidity.
There may also be striking degrees of amnesia for life events.
The syndrome is found most frequently in people facing
military or civilian prosecution and has been thought by
some to be a variety of malingering. In this picture, the patient
gives wrong answers to questions in such a way that he
reveals that he knows the right answer. Example: Q. How
much is 5×4? A. 19. Q. How many legs does a cow have?
A. Three.

Appearance of this syndrome betokens primitive ego
functioning at best. Patients with the Ganser syndrome
frequently show overt psychosis when imprisoned or given
sodium amytal. Jolian-West [14] has said of such patients,
"No matter how sick they look, they are really even sicker."

Alcoholic Hallucinosis

The diagnosis of *alcoholic hallucinosis* is applied to
patients who develop hallucinations, more frequently auditory
than visual, during, or more commonly, after, a bout of
drinking. The sensorium is clear, and there is no evidence
of incipient or manifest delirium tremens. The hallucinations
are unpleasant, accusatory, and threatening, and the patient
may respond to them with violence. The hallucinosis may
persist for days or weeks after drinking has stopped, and the

patient's condition may first come to attention after he has suddenly assaulted someone. If the hallucinations persist, one must consider the possibility that a latent paranoid schizophrenia became manifest after drinking.

Miscellaneous States

The following forms of related states will not be considered in detail either because they are rare or are not now enjoying much usage, or because they seem to be so similar to types already described that considering them as a separate category would be making an unwarranted distinction in an overcomplicated field: oneirophrenia, psychogenic psychosis, sensitive delusions of reference, propfschizophrenia, *folie à deux*, prison psychosis, the depersonalization syndrome, Capgras' syndrome, *psychose passionelle* (pure erotomania), lycanthropy, and exotic syndromes such as *latah, amok,* and *koro*. The reader interested in these syndromes can look them up in Bellak [2] and Arieti. [1]

SUMMARY

Bleuler and Kraepelin proposed several clinical subtypes of the schizophrenias, and others have suggested additional subtypes. These subtypes have, by and large, been characterized by symptoms and signs rather than by nature of onset and clinical course. These latter parameters, however, are dealt with in the concepts of process-reactive, true schizophrenia-schizophreniform psychosis, and acute-chronic, and it is becoming increasingly important to evaluate patients along these lines as well as for the more traditional signs and symptoms.

The typical schizophrenias, in which the fundamental symptoms described by Bleuler are clearly present, are as follows: simple schizophrenia (also known as schizophrenia simplex or dementia simplex), hebephrenic schizophrenia, catatonic schizophrenia (in both stuporous and excited forms), paranoid schizophrenia, mixed schizophrenia, and undifferentiated schizophrenia.

Patients may not show all the defects described by

Bleuler and thus may not demonstrate the characteristics of the typical schizophrenias. In such cases, the patient may more properly be diagnosed as demonstrating one of the atypical schizophrenias, as follows: schizo-affective psychosis, acute homosexual panic (Kempf's disease), acute paranoia (also known as acute polymorphic delirium, exhaustion psychosis, or combat psychosis), ambulatory schizophrenia (of which the three major subtypes are pseudoneurotic schizophrenia, pseudopsychopathic schizophrenia, and borderline character), postpartum schizophrenia, and periodic catatonia.

The states that may be related to the schizophrenias are as follows: schizoid character, pure paranoia, paranoid state, the Ganser syndrome, and alcoholic hallucinosis. Rare and exotic conditions, many of which are interesting in their own right but probably not at all related to the schizophrenias, include the depersonalization syndrome, Capgras' syndrome, *latah, amok,* and my favorite, *koro (shook yung).*

3

Case Histories

These cases have been chosen to demonstrate a variety of subtypes, outcomes, and vignettes of treatment. The material on symptomatology and subtype is most pertinent to these early chapters; that on course and treatment will become more relevant later and should be reviewed in conjunction with the appropriate chapters. Identifying information for these patients has been altered to protect their privacy, but essential clinical data are reported unchanged. The cases of Vivian L. and Sylvia T. are presented in detail. The remainder are presented in abbreviated form, with special emphasis only on aspects that particularly demonstrate phenomena amplified on elsewhere in this book.

CHRONIC SCHIZOPHRENIA

STEPHEN J.: A Case of Chronic Paranoid Schizophrenia

Stephen J. is a 34-year-old, single, Jewish male, intermittently employed, living in halfway and boarding houses. He came to New Orleans impulsively from his home in St. Louis when he was 29.

Condensed Personal History and Development of Illness

Stephen's mother ordered his father out of the home when Stephen was 4. He was reared, together with his younger sister, by his mother and grandmother. The mother made her living teaching languages. By all reports, she always had maintained a smotheringly close, symbiotic relationship with Stephen.

From the age of 18 on, Steve showed signs of disturbed behavior. He dropped out of college and, at 22, had the first of five St. Louis hospitalizations for mental illness. When not in the hospital, he lived at home, functioned marginally as a clerk in various stores. At 29, he impulsively left St. Louis to escape the women in his family and came to New Orleans to live with his father, whom he had not seen since childhood, and to take the father's name, hoping magically to acquire more masculinity. The father, bewildered by his unexpected arrival, brought him to the X Clinic, where I became the first of five therapists who were to treat him during the next five years.

Treatment and Clinical Course

His major symptoms were those of auditory hallucinations and delusions that accused him of "eating bowel" (ingesting feces) and getting into "booger wars" (throwing dried nasal secretions back and forth). He had experienced these phenomena for several years; their "realness" to him was directly proportional to his level of anxiety.

Steve is an intelligent and appealing person. His therapists have all found him likable, even at times when he has been exasperating with his infantile demandingness. He immediately evokes warmth and compassion. He is obviously bright and, having been told repeatedly by his mother that he would amount to something in this world, feels therefore he must; he has thus found it difficult to accept the relatively commonplace jobs he has held. It is more prestigious to be a "Sales Representative for the Hearst Corporation" than merely to be a "newspaper boy."

In the first formal session, communications went well until about 20 minutes had passed, at which point this sequence occurred: (1) Steve looked at me with childlike adoration; (2) he looked away shyly; (3) he scratched his genitals; (4) he looked up at me fearfully and said, "I'm afraid of you."

Making an interpretation based on intuition about the meaning of the sequence, I told him, "If you're afraid I'll make a homosexual pass at you, or let you make one at me, forget it. We're here to talk, not act." He sighed, appeared visibly relieved, and our conversation resumed.

Steve's unconscious frequently surfaced that easily, and the interviews alternated between depth interpretations of this sort and a consideration of more mundane matters such as working out which bus to take to get to the clinic. A colleague, hearing about that first session with Steve, said, only half jokingly, "How does it feel to get eaten up, consumed, digested, and shit out, all several times in an hour?"

Six weeks after arriving in New Orleans, Steve got increasingly anxious about the poor reception he had received from his father and became increasingly psychotic. His voices and delusions got louder; he thought he was getting electric shocks, that his mind was being read, and that he had to return immediately to St. Louis.

He was hospitalized. Somatic treatment was restricted to drugs; at one point he was on 2,000 mgm of chlorpromazine a day. He was discharged six weeks later on Stelazine, 60 mgm b.i.d., and Cogentin, 2 mgm, b.i.d. He took up living in a local halfway house, continued his outpatient psychotherapy twice a week for an hour, and spent most of his days in a psychiatric day center where he participated well in the group activities.

His outpatient therapy at this time ranged from appreciation of unconscious dynamics to helping Steve with very practical day-to-day matters. Steve was an expert at passive-aggressive maneuvers that maintained his role as the helpless, sick mental patient. I told Steve he deserved Hollywood honors for his portrayal of the "schlemiel" (one who can do nothing right). A sample of such a transaction follows:

Steve: I've forgotten how to get back to my halfway house after our session. I don't know which bus to take.

Therapist: Have you *really* forgotten?

Steve: Yes.

Therapist: How do you think you might find out?

Steve: I don't know.

Therapist: I think I hear the voice of "the schlemiel" speaking again.

Steve: I suppose I could call the bus company.

Therapist: Sure.

Steve: Can I use your phone?

Therapist: There's a pay phone out front. You don't have a dime?

Steve: I've got a dime. I think I take a Number 30 bus to Main Street and then. . . .

A related issue was Steve's alleged incompetence in handling money. Though he had several hundred dollars from disability payments in a trust fund in his name in St. Louis, he would write his mother for a dole every few weeks, thus perpetuating the symbiotic relationship. He had never had a bank account of his own. I encouraged him to ask his mother for $150 to start a bank account; if he proved he could handle money well, he could write for the remainder and thus fully manage his own funds. He was enthusiastic, but asked me to write his mother for him. I pointed out to him that it was his money, not mine, and if he wanted it badly enough he could write her himself. He wrote a nearly illegible letter in which the only clearly decipherable message was that he wanted the $150.

The money came and he started his account. We decided together that he should keep a notebook of expenditures. He was quite frugal and proved that he was not a spendthrift. Each hour started with the Litany of the Notebook, details included in a pathetic, concrete schizophrenic way, to wit:

6¢ Peter Pauls Mound Candy Bar (instead of, simply, "candy bar")

69¢ Brand X Turkey T.V. dinner (instead of, simply, "T.V. dinner")

It quickly became apparent that Steve's money problems lay more with not being able to spend than with not being able to save. He wrote for the remainder of his money, and for the past six years has maintained full control of it.

Another incident demonstrates the need for the therapist to help such patients in making real-life decisions. Friends invited Steve to dinner at a nice restaurant; he wanted to go but had several reservations. It would probably cost $5.00 or more, and he wondered whether this wasn't being extravagant. He would be invited to have a drink before dinner, and he had been told that people on tranquilizers should not drink. It would be crowded and noisy, and he knew from past experience that his voices got louder and more immediate when he was in a crowd. I pointed out to him that he had been struggling along on T.V. dinners for several weeks, and that I thought he owed it to himself to splurge every once in a while; that he could drink but should only have about half as much as he might if he were off medication (since he was normally a "two-martini" man, he would settle for one); and, though he would have to make up his own mind about his voices, I hoped he could distance himself enough from them that they would not interfere seriously with his experience. At the next session he proudly reported that he had gone with the group and had had a good time. At first the voices had bothered him, but he had thought to himself, "Dr. Rosenbaum says I should ignore the voices if I can and have a good time, and I managed to."

During this period of therapy, we discussed Steve's getting a job. He found any number of reasons why he wasn't ready for one and managed successfully to avoid getting one.

His next therapist took over and wrote that attempts to get Steve to get a job continued to be unavailing. During the summer, Steve's mother made the first of several two-week

visits to New Orleans, and the therapist found it quite revealing:

> As could have been predicted, she was
> a classic example of the schizophrenogenic
> mother, intrusive, castrating, overindulgent, in-
> consistent, and a past master at the use of
> double-bind type of communication. Stephen's
> reaction to her was one of minimal regression
> to more infantile modes of demandingness.

In the months that followed, Stephen started decompen-
sating. In retrospect, the reasons seem to be an accumulation
of the following: the mother's visit, being forced to leave his
halfway house because his time was up, repeated failures at
trying to find a job, and decreasing his medications. These
stresses culminated in his eighth hospitalization, lasting six
weeks. Again he was stabilized and released on relatively high
doses of medication: Stelazine 60 mgm b.i.d. and Thorazine
700 mgm q.i.d.

In the years since then Steve has continued to function
without requiring further hospitalization. He has held a post-
office job for several months. He lives in a boarding house.
He has diminished his psychotherapeutic contacts to once
every two or three weeks or p.r.n.; he continues on high doses
of medication.

Prognosis

It is unlikely that Steve will ever be entirely free of psychotic symptoms. He will always need medication, just as a
diabetic always needs insulin, though the dosages may be
adjusted according to current stresses. He will always need
a certain amount of psychiatric guidance and support. He has
formed an important transference to the X Clinic, where he
has come to rely on the availability of therapists year after
year. He may again require hospitalization if he goes through
a period of acute stress, but it will probably be a relatively

brief hospitalization aimed at stabilizing him and allowing him to resume his current level of functioning.

VIVIAN L.: A Case of Chronic Hebephrenic Schizophrenia

On admission at age 18, this single, white, Protestant girl was virtually immobile. She sat or stood motionless most of the time, seemed to be in a trance, spoke little, and refused to eat, later explaining, "No, I will not drink milk until God tells me to," that if she did drink the milk it would hurt the man who had originally taken it from the cow. She developed severe ankle edema, which cleared when she later became more active. Medication, which later had to be discontinued because of leukopenia, made her more accessible, and she started to eat when offered firm encouragement by the staff.

After several weeks her speech and behavior gradually enlivened. Her behavior was fragmented, disorganized, and she obviously was responding to vivid autistic fantasies. She spent hours a day cleaning her room and the day room in a compulsive ritual. Her mood rapidly fluctuated between giddiness, anger, depression, excitement, and restlessness. Sentences that started out relatively coherent and logical quickly deteriorated into fragments, loose associations, and incomprehensibility. She was catatonic on admission but became hebephrenic shortly thereafter.

Present Illness

The family describes Vivian as having been "an angel" until the age of 16, when she had a rather autistic "crush on a boy" and had a "mystical" experience during which she felt changed while at a summer church camp. Later that summer, while on a visit to her father's family home, the family first noted that she seemed quite withdrawn and seclusive. At 17, she seemed easily upset by various school events, felt picked on by classmates and had rather frequent crying spells and periods of "nervousness." When she was 18, her seclusiveness increased. She frequently stayed home from school in a preoccupied state, was suspicious about poisoning in the

food; she engaged in constant and compulsive house cleaning. She was also preoccupied with a good many sexual fantasies and with fears of sexual assault. At the same time there
was a heightening of chronic quarreling between the parents
over what should be done about Vivian, just as there had
been similar quarrels throughout the years about her up-
bringing. A sister, two years younger, became for a time the
only person with whom the patient spoke.

Two months before her scheduled high school graduation, Vivian was completely unable to continue in school and
withdrew.

Family Background

The father, Thomas L., was a 55-year-old native of a
rural state. He had been a filing clerk with the same company
for more than 20 years. His wife was a 52-year-old secretary
with a better education (high school) and a better-paying job
than her husband had. The question of the wife's working
had been one of the sore points of chronic marital quarreling.
The extremely complicated details of the family history can
only be touched on in this summary. Briefly, the husband
complained throughout the years that his wife was an inadequate mother, both to himself and his daughters, not preparing the right kind of food and being too critical and harsh
with the family members. The wife, on the other hand, saw
her husband as making insatiable demands, toward which
she maintains a fixed attitude of self-righteous martyrdom
with constant complaints; these were partially disguised as
perplexity over why he could never be satisfied with her sacrificing efforts. The marriage seemed highly schismatic, by
criteria cited in Chapter 7.

Mr. L. had had a "nervous breakdown" when he was 42.
It involved considerable anxiety, some somatic symptoms involving weakness in the muscles of his right fist, temporary
disorganization of his behavior, and a good many paranoid
ideas. He had been fairly chronically suspicious of infidelity
on the part of his stony, ascetic wife, suspicions that he had
later had with regard to Vivian. He also was chronically

jealous of any continuing relationship that his wife had with her parents or siblings. When Vivian was admitted, both family therapists saw Mr. L. as an ambulatory paranoid schizophrenic with a barely concealed thought disorder.

Personal History

The patient was born in the second year of the parents' marriage. Vivian as a baby was described as "the loving type," rarely crying. Her maternal grandmother cared for her during the day and was devotedly attentive to Vivian. Vivian had always been shy, quick to surrender her possessions at the slightest demand, in contrast to her younger sister.

Mr. L. seems to have been intensely emotionally and symbiotically involved with Vivian since she was born. Material from family therapy sessions suggests, in fact, that he unconsciously imbued Vivian with the qualities of nurturance, loving, and goodness that he had experienced with his own mother and that he constantly complained were missing in his relationship with Mrs. L. From Vivian's birth, then, he focused on her with a special set of unconscious expectations. He told the therapists repeatedly, "Vivian is not next to my heart; she's part of it!"

The incestuous component of Mr. L.'s feelings toward Vivian was deeply repressed. He experienced it in a paranoid, projected fashion by remaining forever suspicious and agitated about the possibility that potential boyfriends of Vivian might be making sexual advances toward her. When she entered high school and went out with social groups (individual dating was forbidden by the parents), Mr. L. frequently skulked around outside to be sure that "nothing bad would happen to her"; he became known to Vivian's friends as "the cop of Greenville." At the same time, both in the past and during the course of work with the family, there were moments of genuine warmth and affection between Vivian and her father, which, however, became quickly complicated by anxiety.

When Vivian was two, her sister, unwanted by Mrs. L., was born; this, too, was a difficult childbirth. Mrs. L. soon

brought in a series of girls to care for her children while she
worked; each of the girls lasted only for a brief period. Finally, from the time Vivian was 5 until she was 10, Mrs. L.
returned home, where she remained without working. Meanwhile, the father had been having considerable emotional
difficulty, which he felt gradually became relieved because he
was able to find a male companion with whom he could talk.
However, this friend died of alcoholism in the year just before
Vivian became overtly ill, which was also about the same
time that Mr. L.'s mother died.

Within the home, the parents were quite constantly at
odds, apparently jealous over signs of affection from Vivian.
Once Vivian said that she always kept things in balance
between her parents. Mrs. L. worked long hours preparing
food, making costumes for school, etc., in order to please
Vivian, but Vivian's response was always sufficiently ambiguous so that each parent could see her response as meaning
what each of them wished it to mean. In contrast, the sister
had a less emotionally significant role with the parents, and
was able to be both more rejecting verbally and more accepting of her mother, with relatively little contact with the father, except in later disciplinary measures.

Vivian's physical development was unusually precocious,
and she received a good deal of attention and praise from the
parents on her appearance, for example, as a drum majorette.
Her performance, however, ended in a fiasco because of alleged rivalry from other girls. In school, Vivian's grades were
slightly above average; in fact, they were better than her
sister's until Vivian became overtly ill.

Clinical Course and Treatment

The L. family participated for two years in a treatment
program in which the entire family met with two therapists
twice a week, and one of these therapists also met individually with Vivian twice a week.* The major focus of the family
therapy was to bring to light, and attempt to resolve, the

* Many vignettes from the family therapy are presented in Chapter 7
 and from the individual therapy in Chapter 14.

longstanding, largely unconscious interpersonal role conflicts in the family. The family was markedly schismatic and pseudomutual, to use concepts of Lidz and Wynne that are more fully explained in Chapter 7. The major focus of the individual therapy was to help Vivian start integrating her fragmented, autistic, and disorganized experiential world according to the principles discussed in Chapter 14; many episodes from her individual therapy are reported in that chapter.

In general, she began therapy in an aloof and unproductive manner. She slowly became more and more involved in a psychotherapeutic relationship with her therapist, and, on the whole, made productive use of psychotherapy, gradually recognizing some of her destructive and sexual impulses. She showed greater control over these impulses at times. However, there were also episodes of agitation and assaultiveness, sometimes urinary incontinence and sexual provocativeness. When the assaultiveness and agitation became unmanageable with ordinary nursing means, sedation at night and chlorpromazine during the day successfully quieted her. However, even light, sustained dosage made her sluggish and inaccessible, even after a period of adaptation to the drug. Therefore tranquilizers were used only in relation to unmanageable behavior.

Gradually she began to be able to take part in more and more ward activities. Under supervision she was able to manage an hour or so a day of such jobs as filling Christmas seal envelopes. In general, firm consistency in ward management seemed to be especially valuable.

After the first year she began to make more and more frequent visits home on weekends, when both the family and she would agree that a visit was desired. Some visits seemed to work out better when the patient was accompanied by a member of the nursing staff. Meanwhile, the family therapy, too, was proceeding with gradual but fairly definite progress and was shifting from an early focus upon the father-Vivian relationship to the marital relationship. The father even began to accept the obviously intense relationship between Vivian and her therapist.

These trends continued for 20 months, when her therapist announced his plans for leaving on a six-week trip in April and May and his permanent departure in July. Vivian became clearly more disorganized, with more frequent periods of agitation and excitement, and was more disruptive in the family therapy sessions. The family therapy sessions became more intense than ever and also were seemingly more productive, with such surprising changes as the unprecedented occurrence of a pleasant weekend in the marital relationship.

While the first therapist was away on his extended trip in May, there was a stormy family session during which Vivian sat in a regressed fashion in a corner. Her father sat down with her and began to caress her until suddenly he became intensely anxious and jumped up. The therapist speculated that it might be natural that sexual feelings might complicate such a situation, and this led immediately to an enraged outburst from the father. Vivian, in contrast, took the matter quite calmly, and said, for example, "Of course there are sexual feelings involved, how could it be otherwise?"

The father was unable to contain his rage and anxiety. He called a hospital administrator to complain that his daughter was being experimented on by doctors "who think like rats in the street." There was a good deal of administrative uproar about this; the therapist took the position with the family that the working situation was untenable if the hospital administrator was to be called after an upsetting session, and treatment would have to be discontinued. The father nevertheless continued to barrage the therapist with a relentless stream of demands about how the treatment program was to be altered, first in one way and then in another. The therapist held firm to his definition of the ground rules of the treatment situation. A few weeks later the father called the hospital administrator with a new series of complaints. The therapist decided at that point that he could not continue to work effectively with the family, and treatment ended with Vivian's being transferred to another hospital.

Follow-up

Seven years later the patient was on convalescent leave and was attending an outpatient clinic every month. She has occasional short outbursts of anger and negativism, but attends church, is taking courses in shorthand and typing, and "has improved considerably."

NAOMI N.: A Case of Chronic, Process, True Schizophrenia; Hebephrenic Type; of Twenty Years' Duration

Present Illness

Naomi N., now 42, was admitted at age 22 to a state hospital, where she has been nearly continuously.

Her mother and sisters said that Naomi apparently got along with her siblings and friends until she was 15 years old, when she suddenly started ignoring boys altogether. She remained fond of her older sister, Sarah. When Naomi was 21, she became very quiet, thought she belonged to God, would hear His voice. She ate very little, lost a great deal of weight, and locked herself up in the bathroom for hours at a time. Later she displayed peculiar behavior, constantly shaved her arms and legs, and plucked out all of her eyebrows. She imagined that there was a bad odor in the house and scrubbed the floor and washed the furniture day and night.

When she was 32, she demonstrated many phenomena of the hebephrenic schizophrenic. She walked around the room in a ritual of taking three steps and hopping on one foot, and simultaneously pulled out a hair from the back of her head and popped it into her mouth, with the result that she had a tonsurelike bald spot. There was a great deal of manneristic activity. When she was sitting down she was constantly in motion, chattering away to herself and pointing to invisible things and pushing them away. In talking with her, her ego boundaries were diffuse and permeable. She could not differentiate between things that came from inside of her and those that came from outside of her. A quote from a tape recording follows:

Therapist: What do you like to do? Anything in particular?

Patient: I like to ride. I like to read. I like to ride on a bicycle. And I like to go to prayer service. I never went to prayer service.

Therapist: What kind of prayer service?

Patient: Prayer service at the North Pole prayer service.

Therapist: I see. What were you looking for on my arm there? Were you afraid it wasn't all there?

Patient: Yeah, I was afraid of your right leg, see (*exposing calf of her own right leg*). I was feeling it. (*Picking it plain?*) And then my right leg went lame.

Therapist: How did that happen?

Patient: It happened. It just did. (*Giggle*) And I got so scared that I did it to you. (*Touches me.*) Is that all right?

(Later in the same interview.)

Therapist: What was the name of the town?

Patient: The town? It was, uh, I can't remember. It was, uh, Bemidji. Is that all right? (*Giggle*) . . . I didn't see the comb. I wanted, I wanted to try to in the bathroom and then I died underneath in the bathroom (*giggle*), and it was hurting me so hard that anybody was watching my nose and I pointed right at my own nose, and I lost control of everything, just like you thought. You know that bad lady there.

Therapist: Who?

Patient: Who is she? Is she Kate Francis?

Therapist: I don't know. Well, Naomi, uh . . .

Patient: She looks like Kate Francis to me. She must be about, uh, 19 years old.

At times her schizophrenic wit could be very funny. For

example, one day she picked up a cigarette butt off the floor and came over and asked for a light. And, in the manner of the Dowager Queen examining a fine cigar, she said, "Oh, a Camel! Normally I smoke Chesterfields, but I don't mind smoking Camels 'cause they'll all turn into Chesterfields anyhow!"

On another occasion, I had just lighted a cigarette with matches that said on the cover, "Thank you, come again." She walked to the door with me as I was leaving the ward a few minutes later; as I was locking the door behind me, she had her face pressed up against the screen and said, "Thank you, come again," like a shopkeeper who had just seen one of his favorite customers through the door. She had integrated into what she thought was her own sentiment something from outside of herself—what she had read a few minutes previously on the back of a pack of matches—and superimposed on that something from within—a denial of the hospitalization situation—thus making it seem again like a shopkeeper and a customer in a middle-class business transaction.

Followup

Ten years later, when Naomi was 42, the hospital supplied this information:

> Patient is restless and silly, paces the floor, is negligent of her personal appearance, and is having auditory and also visual hallucinations. She claims she has seen God. She has a tendency to be untidy, is withdrawn, never participates in any of the ward activities.

The outlook, of course, is very poor for her. The odds are heavy that she will die in the state hospital, more burnt out and more vegetablelike than she is now.

VIGNETTE OF ROBERT B.: A Case of Chronic Schizophrenia in Exacerbation, Mixed Paranoid, and Hebephrenic Subtypes

(This vignette demonstrates both characteristic schizophrenic thought and the dramatic mood swings between agitation and calm that can be seen.)

>*Patient:* (*With a smile from ear to ear*) How do you do. I am Robert B., Prince of England, pleased to meet you.
>
>*Therapist:* I am Dr. Franklin, psychiatrist of Palo Alto.
>
>*Patient:* Well, I have come up from Brentwood. Sit down—this is going to be difficult for you. When I was in Brentwood I compensated. I know this is unbelievable. My subconscious mind was revealed to me and I knew I was Robert. Oh, it wasn't easy. They said I'd blow it. Well, I blew half of Hollywood. I performed fellatio on everyone on that ward.
>
>*Therapist:* Everyone?
>
>*Patient:* Sometimes only in my mind. That's how my subconscious is revealed. That's how I compensated. It was beautiful. Can you believe me? You have to buy this. I need a psychiatrist to buy these images of regard. To buy me. I'll perform fellatio on you every day. Oh, we're going to make it. I just have to stay here long enough to save some money and go to England. Then I'll marry Elizabeth Regina. Oh, you won't regret this. We are going to save mankind. Franklin, this is going to be the most important time of your life.

. . . Two days later:

>*Patient:* (*With an expression of genuine concern*) Are you sure you're all right, Franklin? I worry about you. . . . Yes, I know you're all right. Your subconscious mind is understanding. There—I could tell. Just then it happened. (*Patient makes a pelvic convulsive movement as though he is receiving messages per anum.*)

. . . Two days later after hearing that he would be sent to a locked ward for failure to comply with ward regulations.

> *Patient: (Roaring at full volume, with veins bulging, face red, standing 6 inches away from the therapist.)* I am God. I am Christ. No goddam punk shit psychiatrist is going to send me to a locked ward. The images of regard have been revealed to me and I have to protect those images. I am God. Do you understand that? I suck off cougars. I have a cougar waiting for me in that room (*pointing in the direction of the maximum security ward*), up on that locked ward. Tell me that I am God . . . I will not calm down . . .

. . . One day later:

> *Patient: (With an expression of serene tranquility.)* Franklin, that was rough. I hope you understand I had to do it. That night I became God and the most beautiful images were revealed to me. I saw Bambi. It was lovely —all soft and brown and indescribable colors. Oh, you should have seen it . . .

ACUTE SCHIZOPHRENIA

ANTON K.: A Case of Acute, Reactive Paranoid Schizophrenia (Schizophreniform)

Present Illness and Reason for Commitment

Anton K. is a 35-year-old Czechoslovakian-born white Protestant. He is married, a carpenter, makes a middle-class income.

During the Christmas season preceding his admission, Mr. K. threw his seven-year-old daughter and only child, Edithe Cecile, into the path of two cars. He then bashed her head against the pavement. She died two days later without regaining consciousness. He was arrested, found to be too mentally ill to stand trial, and committed.

The patient was involved in an automobile accident two months earlier; he showed signs of increased tension and anxiety in the following weeks, and was unable to return to work. He began to feel that the people in the upstairs apartment were doing things against him. One evening he was watching television while playing chess with his daughter. He thought the people on television were laughing at him. Though he had always called his daughter Cecile, he thought she was now two people, the other of whom was Edithe. Cecile was a sweet little girl, "an angel." Edithe was an imposter, was nasty, would sass her parents and go outside and get her clothes dirty. The way she pursed her lips with her tongue while playing chess indicated that she wanted to "orally copulate my penis."

Mr. K. panicked, told her to go to bed, went out for a drive. He felt that all the cars on the highway were chasing him. Eventually he came home and went to bed. The next morning he heard voices on television telling him he would have to kill both his wife and daughter. He took his wife to work.

He then took his daughter for a drive, wanting to go to the top of a local hill. His car hit an embankment. He got out to ascertain the damage, saw another car nearby, and started running away. His daughter called after him; he returned and noted that she had changed from Cecile to Edithe. She put her hand in his pocket to hang onto him. He then committed the crime described.

During his first six weeks in the hospital, he thought a computer was feeding ideas to him. Though he recalled his daughter's death, he could not believe that he had killed her. He was hyperactive verbally in his groups and insisted on finishing other people's sentences for them, thinking he knew what was on their minds. He was placed on Stelazine, from 10 to 20 mgm per day; this medication was stopped eight months later.

After six weeks in the hospital, he wrote his wife, asking if it was true that he had killed the girl, as he was being told at the hospital. The wife responded that it was, and Mr. K. believed her. For a day or two he was extremely upset about this and sought out the chaplain. Once he accepted his responsibility for the killing, he got involved in a great number of activities on and off the ward, keeping himself busy from 6:00 A.M. to 10:00 P.M., explaining that he was doing so to build confidence in himself. This attitude seemed to be in marked contrast to his former way of life; he described himself as having been shy, introverted, and lonely all of his life, and tending to withdraw from social contact.

In the weeks that followed, his delusions about being controlled by a computer gradually disappeared, as did all symptoms of psychosis. The patient's participation and co-operation in group therapy, ward, and hospital activities were maintained at a high level. He tended to be deferential, implicitly accepting whatever the ward staff told him. (As one staff member put it, "Every time I told him something, he would say 'Yes, sir,' and I could practically hear the heels click.") The patient repeatedly asked for reassurance that he was doing the right things to get better.

During the spring and summer the patient had many dreams about his daughter. In almost all of them he was reliving the killing. No such dreams occurred after July. There were, however, many episodes of depression, wherein he found himself tempted to kill himself by lying down on the pavement in the courtyard and banging his head against it. (This is an identification with the lost love object.) At such times he sought out ward staff or other patients and talked about his feelings with them.

Both Mr. K. and the staff felt there have been a number of real changes in Mr. K.'s personality, and that these had been the result of his group and individual therapy. In addition to becoming much more verbal and sociable, he found he could tolerate, and in fact enjoy, the support and encouragement of friends from his wife's church who came to visit him. He could also challenge his therapist when he did not agree on an interpretation.

ELSIE B.: A Case of Acute Schizophrenia, Mixed Hebephrenic and Paranoid Subtypes

Present Illness

Elsie B., a 26-year-old, single woman, was picked up by the police on Good Friday on the steps of a church, dressed in a bridal gown. She said that she was waiting for the bridegroom to come. She was quite obviously bizarre and disturbed, and she was taken to the county hospital. She was transferred to a state hospital shortly after.

On admission, she was silly and fluttery; she rambled and giggled. Her eyes were big; it was difficult to make contact with her. She spoke about her dentist; she had fallen in love with him and felt that he had fallen in love with her. For instance, the week before, he had given her some mouthwash, a red gargle, that she knew was blood and that she knew would impregnate her; she thought that offering this was his way of asking her to marry him. And so she had gone to the church in her wedding gown to meet him there.

On admission, her abdomen protruded as if she were five or six months pregnant; a case of pseudocyesis. (Pregnancy tests showed that she was not physiologically pregnant.) She talked at great length about the child within her, and how it came from the blood that she drank from the dentist, and so on.

Clinical Course and Treatment

A resident spent about an hour a day in psychotherapy with her; mainly he listened and helped her with her reality testing. He did not delve into the unconscious dynamics, her ideas of oral impregnation, or the like, but focused on more here-and-now ego-oriented topics. As the days went on, she could slip out of extremely psychotic thinking and behavior, at first only for a few seconds; then she would get anxious, and all of a sudden, from looking and sounding almost normal, she would look and sound schizophrenic again. She would start giggling in her insane laugh.

Over the period of about three months the proportion between when she was in the real world and when out of it increased in favor of being in. She could increasingly tolerate discussion of circumstances of her hospitalization and her plans for the future without having to slip back into psychotic thinking and behavior. Concomitantly her belly shrank, and by the end of six months she was discharged from the hospital as being in total remission.

She had come from a Polish Catholic family. Her father had been lost to the family from an early age. She had been brought up by a rather strict and harsh mother, and during the course of her hospitalization she was able to talk about her difficulties in breaking away from her mother and establishing an identity and values for herself. It may well be that through the device of her psychosis she was actually able to establish such a sense of identity; when she put the pieces back together, they may have been joined by a somewhat stronger glue. With only modest amounts of psychotherapy, with no electric shock and no drug treatment, she did make a complete recovery from what was initially an extremely florid and obvious schizophrenic episode.

Follow-up

She was readmitted nine years later at the age of 35. She was discharged in complete remission after eleven months of hospitalization. She was readmitted for a third time three years later, at the age of 38, because of

> . . . a relapse of her schizophrenic symptoms and a physical attack on her mother, chasing her from her home. She was abusive to her mother for a month or so, and she attempted to choke her 5-year-old daughter. She was secretive, withdrawn, hostile, suspicious, disorientated, and at times refused to respond to questions. After

three months her schizophrenic symptoms were remitted sufficiently for her to have a two-week visit with her mother. After the two weeks were up, the patient did not return, and we have no further information on her at this time.

SYLVIA T.: A Case of Acute, Reactive Postpartum Schizophrenia†

The patient, Sylvia T., was a 23-year-old white, Protestant woman. Her husband, Paul, two years her senior, was a design engineer for a local space-industry company. The patient's admission to the hospital took place a month after the birth of their first child, Susan.

Six weeks before Susan's birth, the T.'s moved from the South to the West Coast because of Mr. T.'s promotion and job transfer. Two weeks later they were established in their apartment, and Mr. T. was already working late hours on his new assignment. Three days before the child was born, Mrs. T.'s mother came to help out during the next two weeks. The child, a normal baby girl, was born by routine delivery after a trouble-free pregnancy. One week postpartum, Paul was hospitalized for a few days for treatment of diverticulitis.

Two weeks postpartum, Mrs. T. began to have periods of distraction, moodiness, and withdrawal. She suddenly became interested in Catholicism, began insisting that the baby be baptized and that they join this faith. She became convinced that certain apparently trivial events were quite meaningful, e.g., the laundryman was really delivering important papers to her husband; the whir of machinery in her husband's office, as heard over the phone, signified an important discovery in rocket fuels that the Communists would try to steal from her brilliant husband. She lost interest in the baby and carried it around like a rag doll. These preoccupations became so pervasive that her husband brought her to the hospital.

† Condensed from C. Peter Rosenbaum, *A case of postpartum schizophrenia*. In Arthur Burton, (ed.), Modern psychotherapeutic Practice. Palo Alto, Calif.: Science and Behavior Books, 1965.

Other stresses postpartum included Paul's week-long illness three days after the baby was born, a visit by old friends, and the departure of Mrs. T.'s mother.

When admitted, Mrs. T. was confused; her eyes were wide and vacant, and she only poorly comprehended the reasons for her admission. Her statements were cryptic; her gestures were frequently symbolic. She thought I was sending her thought messages by telepathy.

Past History

Mrs. T. is an only child. Her father deserted the family a few months after she was born; she was raised by her grandmother or by relatives while her mother worked.

The patient characterized her mother as being in many ways a very helpless, anxious person. For instance, every time they took a trip downtown her mother on the way to the station would fumble for her tickets, and the patient would always find them for her just in time to make their train.

When Mrs. T. was 10, her mother remarried. The husband, whom the patient called "Uncle Frank," had once been her father's best friend but had come to hate him for what he considered criminal desertion of wife and child. Uncle Frank had a bad temper and was decidedly restrictive with her, and she was constantly afraid of him. In later years he suffered from a chronic lung disease which aggravated his temper. He died when the patient was 16.

Mrs. T. was allowed neither to date nor to baby-sit often while she was in high school; thus her experience in two areas important for her later functioning as a wife and mother was sharply limited. In college she did well academically and had an active social life; she was an attractive, vivacious belle. She and Paul saw a good deal of each other during summer vacations, and he persuaded her (she was reluctant) to marry him shortly after her graduation.

The first few years of marriage were generally pleasant, though Mrs. T. had nagging doubts about whether she truly loved her husband or whether he loved her for more than

her good looks and her pleasant temperament. There were
fairly frequent petty arguments. She felt inhibited sexually
and rarely achieved orgasm or even intense pleasure during
love making. She felt warmer toward Paul when they deliberately stopped using contraceptives; the baby was conceived
shortly thereafter.

Her pregnancy was uncomplicated. She did not attend
maternity classes during her pregnancy, but depended instead on Dr. Spock, whom she read faithfully. She could
barely confess to herself, and not at all to Paul, that she felt
she had to be a "perfect mother" and yet felt miserably un-
prepared.

Dynamics of the Postpartum Reaction

In attempting to understand the reasons for Mrs. T.'s
decompensation, we must examine her personality structure,
the external events of her life at the time, and the meaning
of these events at both superficial and deeper levels.

Throughout her life she had feared she was not likable
or desirable. She handled these fears by compulsively seeking
out company and being an apparently gay and frivolous belle
—she doubted that these social graces would be useful to her
in caring for her new infant.

Chronologically, the external stresses on her were the
following: the move to a strange part of the country; her
husband's investment in his work and his resultant withdrawal from her; the presence and departure of her am-
bivalently regarded mother; the birth of the baby and the
consequent challenge to her mothering abilities; her husband's further withdrawal because of diverticulitis, and the
emotionally charged visit of old friends. Had she had to cope
with only one or two of these situations, it is conceivable her
decompensation would not have been nearly so severe.

Her deeply buried lack of trust in men had started with
her father's desertion, her stepfather's opposition to her dating, and her husband's frequent exclusion of her in favor of
his studies and his work. She further feared that she would

become physically unattractive after childbirth, that she would be incompetent as a mother, and that her husband would reject her on both counts.

On a deeper level, she may have thought of herself as poisonous to men (had her birth driven away her father?). As she herself mentioned, her separation from her mother was still incomplete psychologically. She felt that her anxiety about her own and her mother's helplessness was communicable and destructive to anyone who had dealings with her.

Thus the concatenation of events surrounding the move and the birth had stirred up grave fears. The birth of the girl baby signified many things to her. Mrs. T., as therapy proceeded, expressed fears that her own childhood was ended, that her husband would now desert her as her father had deserted her mother, that the child would grow up to have the same anger toward her that she herself had toward her mother, that the physical changes of childbirth would make her unattractive to her husband, that she had lost something from inside her which was truly her very own, that her ambivalence about the child and her incompetence as a mother would become obvious and invite general disdain.

At first she attempted to cope with these feelings by overdependence on her husband; later there were transient episodes of depersonalization with awareness of her distress. Ultimately a full-blown schizophrenic reaction developed, with hallucinations, delusions, and frequent misinterpretations of events. Her preoccupation with Catholicism seemed to answer many of her fears in a magical way. It would forbid divorce, i.e., desertion by her husband. It would help her defend against her murderous impulses toward the child: if the child were baptized, it would be a human being and therefore she would not be allowed to harm it. It would provide her with at least two fathers besides her husband: a local priest and God. It would forbid contraception, thereby allowing increased sexual pleasure and feelings of feminine competence. It would promise her the long, happy marriage of Paul's grandparents (who had been Catholic).

Similarly, her thought that her husband had discovered the rocket fuel repaired her severely damaged self-esteem. It would mean an end to his long days in the laboratory and more time at home. It would mean a hero's reception for both of them; his achievement would show her competence as a wife.

Clinical Course and Treatment

Mrs. T. was hospitalized on a therapeutic community ward in a general hospital for two weeks. This ward is of the type described in greater detail in Chapter 13. There she was treated with group and milieu therapy in addition to individual therapy and phenothiazine medication.

She said she wanted to continue to breast-feed the baby and was encouraged to do so, under supervision of the nursing staff or her husband, whose employer was quite generous about granting time off during the crisis. Thus she was able to maintain meaningful contact with her husband and child at the very time she was most fearful about losing them, and she was able to get some training from the nursing staff, many of whom had their own children, on such fundamentals as nursing and diaper changing.

Talking with Mr. T. increased his awareness of his wife's fears and vulnerabilities. His intolerance of her dependency softened markedly, and he could reassure her that he did not expect her to become the perfect mother and that he did not intend to leave her. She in turn was able to relinquish her psychotic ways of expressing these fears (i.e., demands for the conversion of the family to Catholicism, fears of Communists stealing his secrets, etc.) and to begin to discuss them more logically.

During the early days of her hospitalization she frequently wandered off the ward, looking for her husband. These pathetic and embarrassing trips alerted us to the need to help her control her behavior; she was started on chlorpromazine, 50 mg., four times a day, orally, with a resultant clearing of thinking and an end of her sorties off the ward. Research had shown that chlorpromazine is not excreted in mother's milk, and thus the medication was no contraindication to her continued nursing.

The tasks of the individual psychotherapy, both during hospitalization and after, were essentially threefold: (1) the prompt development of a relationship of warmth and trust; (2) the task of understanding the psychological factors in her break and the integration of such insight into awareness; and (3) an educative role in helping her assume gradually increasing responsibility for her home and family.

Mrs. T. quickly entered into a trusting relationship during our daily meetings. I was available for impromptu visits or phone calls as necessary. In psychotherapy, I operated with three major assumptions: (1) My aim was to help her decode and understand her symbolic thinking; (2) many such communications could be interpreted as indirect commentaries of her perception of the immediate state of the therapy relationship; and (3) momentary intensification of the psychotic thinking signaled a rise in her anxiety and warranted attention to the events immediately preceding. For instance, at one point she started fingering a borrowed rosary, emphasizing in the Lord's Prayer "Forgive us our trespasses as we forgive those who trespass against us." I asked if she thought that I had just trespassed against her. She said, "Yes"; something I had just said signified to her that I didn't like her and didn't want her ever to go home to her family. Once we had clarified this point she accepted my statement that I did like her and very much did want her to go back when she was ready.

To Mrs. T.'s advantage, she was remarkably able to recognize, understand, and integrate the meanings of her psychotic thoughts into a conscious, useful, secondary-process kind of thinking rather than having to cover them up. Thus, even months later, her psychotic period had taken on the appearance of a fascinating, frightening, well-remembered, and well-analyzed dream. My treatment of her psychotic material as a second-rate way of trying to express first-rate concerns strengthened her gains.

She asked from the beginning when she could go home.

Her psychotic state was quite fluid—she could drift into and out of a psychotic episode in minutes—and she soon learned to observe herself as she was doing so. We agreed on the relative diminution of the episodes of "peculiar thinking" as the criterion for discharge. At discharge there were certainly many areas of psychotic thinking, but these were not so great as to keep her from going home and caring for her baby; therapy continued on an outpatient basis five days a week.

During and after the hospitalization, periodic marital-couple sessions allowed Mrs. T. to voice certain feelings she was afraid to mention outside the neutrality of the therapy situation. Mr. T. became more straightforward and treated her neither like a miscreant child nor like a fragile flower, the two extremes he had felt pushed toward earlier.

Certain educative aspects of therapy were stressed. One was that mothering a child is a complex skill and, like any complex skill, takes time, trial and error, and good teaching. In this case, Mrs. T.'s mother-in-law was present as a competent and well-intentioned practitioner of the art of mothering. Mrs. T.'s fears about accepting her as one from whom she could learn had in part been based on her experience with her own mother, which suggested that the raising of a child was a perilous procedure fraught with hazard at every juncture. As such fears were explored in therapy, Mrs. T. made increasing use of her mother-in-law as a teacher.

Another educative aspect was the repeated discussion of ways in which roles change throughout life. Though part of Paul's original attraction to her was based on her looks and frivolity, the birth of the child had not made her ugly; all was not over between them; growing to know and understand each other in their new roles as parents was a challenge that could be met.

In the month following discharge we discussed Mrs. T.'s concern about being a good mother. She came to realize that she didn't have to spend 24 hours a day with the baby to be a good mother, nor did she have to interpret the baby's every cry or shriek as evidence of poor mothering. Similarly, her fears of being a social outcast because of her mental illness abated as she made friends with her neighbors.

Mr. T.'s difficulty in accepting her dependency was occasionally revealed in a psychotic way. For example, one day her religious preoccupations were considerably greater than usual, with fervent recitations of the Twenty-third Psalm. It emerged that she had had an argument with her husband that had intensified her desire to have a shepherd watch over her. As this was clarified, her attentions returned to her relationship to her husband and left the theological plane.

By the end of the first posthospital month her husband was back at work nearly full time; he helped with breakfast and came home for lunch or to study. To assuage her loneliness she spent considerable time visiting her neighbors, watching T.V., or painting.

During the second posthospital month evidences of psychotic thinking appeared less and less frequently. Usually, simple confrontation and airing of the psychotic process were sufficient to cause it to disappear. By the end of the second month nothing further even had a psychotic flavor.

Toward the middle of that month Mrs. T. became increasingly a prey to feelings of apathy, lack of *joie de vivre*, lassitude, and boredom. She could not fill up her time, reiterating the question, "I wonder what all these other girls do; they seem to be so busy with their babies and their homes, and yet I find nothing to do." A urinary tract infection may have contributed to her general lassitude. She would also awaken in the early morning with nagging, unpleasant thoughts. The depression seemed to be a combination of a true postpartum depression, the kidney infection, and a possible effect of chlorpromazine. When it did not lift after about a week, she was given imipramine. Her chlorpromazine was reduced, and she was also given an antibiotic for her kidney infection.

By the middle of the third posthospital month the depression began to lift significantly. This turn was probably a result of medication and of the psychotherapeutic discus-

sion, including my suggestion that, despite her lack of motivation, she should carve out projects that needed to be done
or that she would like to do, such as making a dress, and do
them even if they were not gratifying. As the depression
lifted, the imipramine was decreased; it was stopped two
weeks later.

She and her husband got along fairly well. She easily
endured his absences from home, although she felt much
better when he was around, and their squabbles were infrequent. They started entertaining and enjoyed a full, normal
life.

Therapy sessions, by now once a week, became more
and more prosaic. She was completely off medication by the
third posthospital month. We took stock at that time and
agreed to stop therapy. I encouraged her to let me know from
time to time how things were going generally and to call if
anything came up that she wanted to discuss.

Eight months after the first appearance of her psychosis
she called to say that she was having peculiar thoughts again
and wanted to discuss them. At the interview she described
a mystical experience of having been some kind of saint sent
to earth to bring a special harmony to mankind. The experience came right after she and Paul had had an argument,
another example of the relationship of precipitating factors
and relevant dynamics. She also thought she might be pregnant, a diagnosis confirmed medically some days later.

There indeed was psychotic thinking; outpatient psychotherapy five times a week and chlorpromazine were started.
Things generally went well, except for one point when she
became suspicious and fearful that, because my office was
near an experimental laboratory, I was performing experiments on her. She insisted that I see her at home, where she
felt safer than in my office. I did so. She proudly showed me
Susan and their pleasantly decorated apartment, and we
were able to resume office visits thereafter.

After two months the psychotic thinking vanished, the
medication was stopped, and monthly meetings were set dur-

ing the course of the pregnancy. She continued to do well, physically and mentally, throughout the entire pregnancy and delivered a premature infant girl eight months later. The baby was placed in a respirator the day after birth, and there was concern for the baby's life. Mrs. T. was told that the respirator and special attention were required for the baby. I saw her in the hospital and afterward.

She weathered the situation very well. Her concern for the infant was normal, as was her pleasure at taking the baby home two weeks later. Shortly after the baby had come home, Mrs. T. wryly remarked that she felt almost cheated—she hadn't even had a mild postpartum depression.

Three years after her first schizophrenic episode there was one more brief period of psychotic thinking that responded well to treatment. Shortly thereafter, when Mr. T. accepted an excellent job offer, the family moved to another part of the country. I have heard from them occasionally in the succeding four years, and all seems to be going well with them; there have been no recurrences of illness. Mrs. T. had a third child without any emotional complications.

By all reports, the understandings they gained as a result of Mrs. T.'s psychosis have helped them to be freer and more open with each other, and their lives have been a good deal more gratifying than they were before, although they would have preferred to come by such improvement by a less harrowing route.

4

The World
of Schizophrenic Existence

INTRODUCTION

For one who has never been schizophrenic—and I have not been—to become familiar with the world of experience of schizophrenic patients is analogous to experiencing a dream someone else has dreamed and reported to one. While the dreamer was dreaming, all that happened was vivid and meaningful. On reporting it, the content is changed to make the more incongruous elements seem more sensible. The listener must use his own imagination to conjure up images to match the dreamer's words; if he is sufficiently imaginative and empathetic, the listener will have an experience similar to the dreamer's. Jung has said that if the dreamer were to awaken and walk about and not know that he is dreaming, one has an example of dementia praecox.

The word "dream" is perhaps too gentle; the lives of schizophrenic patients often have a nightmarish quality about them. Most patients I have worked with closely have shown anguish and pain the better part of every day. Patients who seemed to have found serenity through psychotic resolution of distress were trapped in narrow, stereotyped lives where nearly all energies were drawn into maintaining the precarious defenses. Biographies of schizophrenic patients exemplify this distress, for example, Freud's famous case of Judge Schreber.[7]

Admittedly, one is always unsure about the subjective experiences of another person, and it is even more difficult to be certain that one understands those of the schizophrenic patient. The reader must understand, then, that this chapter is an *attempt* to understand the inner world of the schizophrenic patient. Parts of the chapter may be proved wrong as research expands our knowledge of these phenomena. There are numerous clinical vignettes in the chapter, the primary data. These data are preceded and followed by interpretation and explanation that represent the best attempts of many authors to understand the subjective world of the patient.

In trying to convey some of the qualities of the schizophrenic experience in this chapter, I will examine the topic from several points of view, each on a different level of abstraction, just as the anatomist can examine his specimens grossly, under varying degrees of magnification, with different stains, or by histochemical techniques. Each of these methods reveals different facets of the material under examination. The corresponding levels here will be the following: a brief overview of primitive and mature mental functioning, and the concept of regression; assumptions about normal early psychological development; primary process, the dream, and other factors in the unconscious; disturbances in formal logic and reasoning; concepts of self and object relations; and an interpretation of schizophrenic communication.

PRIMARY PROCESS, SECONDARY PROCESS, AND THE CONCEPT OF REGRESSION

Freud,[5] Sullivan,[19] Arieti,[1] Szasz,[20] and others have described the natural evolution of mental functioning from its most primitive, as found at birth, to its most sophisticated, as found in mature adults. These authors have focused on different aspects; the most relevant of these are (1) impulses, drives, and emotions; (2) developing a sense of self; (3) relationships with others (object relations); and (4) the ability to reason logically.

Impulses, Drives, and Emotions

In the newborn, the impulses, drives, and emotions are very much of the here-and-now. There is no tomorrow; all of eternity is now. The newborn's motto would seem to be, "I want what I want when I want it!" Freud's "pleasure principle" holds sway; the impulse of the moment is what counts; other persons in the environment are not seen as separate from the self. Logic and thought are entirely self-centered and directed only at procuring immediate gratification of need. Infancy is a state of solipsism. In maturity this point of view has largely given way to the "reality principle": personal drives and needs must be considered in the context of the environment; some lesser immediate gratifications must be postponed in order to work toward greater rewards later.

Object Relations

There is no sense of self at birth. I, Thou, and It are fused. Mother is an extension of the self and appears and disappears magically at the time of need. In the first few months there is a dawning of the idea that there is an "out there" environment, and that the people in it are different from one's self, though they are perceived as being important primarily to the extent that they can gratify one's needs.

Within the first few months of life, the capacity to perceive others gradually awakens. In the 4-month-old, sometimes crying will stop if another person enters the room, sits down away from the child, and starts to read, not paying any direct attention to the infant. By the end of the first year, there is a sense of self, an ability to make you-me discriminations. By 3 years, children are able to make your-mine discriminations about possessions. By 8 years, children have a well-developed capacity to develop friendships in which the feelings and wishes of the friend are important to recognize. In maturity, one finds the capacity to regard the needs of others as equal in importance to one's own and to be able to gratify these needs; one has learned to love in a relatively selfless way.

The Development of Logical Thinking

Primitive logic tends to be self-centered. Early attempts at understanding the world are naïve and frequently invalid from a scientific point of view: they do not successfully predict or control the environment. For example, a 2-year-old looked out over a stretch of water one night; he was looking for the moon, which was not visible. He did see some city lights reflected in the water and announced, "The moon fell in the water." In primitive tribes, stones and trees have spiritual and magical powers attributed to them. The persistence of magical and primitive notions of causality into adult life is seen in superstitions. In maturity, in our culture, logic and causality are more effectively developed.

The Concept of Regression

The personal evolution of mental function from primitive to mature is never complete. The vestiges of childhood are never lost. In some situations they become more than vestiges, where what has happened early becomes more prominent.

The name given to the reappearance of primitive functioning in adults is "regression." It is most commonly seen at times of stress, fatigue, in schizophrenia, and in dreaming. In fact, much of what we have learned about the meaning of schizophrenic experience comes from Freud's explication of the primary-process activities of the dream, activities largely unconscious to most people during waking life.[6]

A few words about the concept of regression are in order. A prevailing misconception is that regression is a uniform withdrawal from a given level of psychological development to an earlier one, e.g., "He has regressed to the level of a 3-year-old." In fact, this is rarely true. When regression occurs, it is more profound in some areas than in others. Freud made the analogy of the retreating army: some units (aspects of mental function) are in pell-mell retreat (profound regression); others take up positions at secondary points (partial regression); still others remain at the front to do battle (no regression).

In schizophrenia, one hears about "intact islands of ego," the functioning units still at the front. Thus the person who is said to be psychologically regressed to the level of a 3-year-old does not relinquish all adult modes of thinking and relating. Neither, then, do the words and concepts he gained after the age of 3 disappear; they often are, as it were, dragged along as baggage poorly packed.

NORMAL EARLY PSYCHOLOGICAL DEVELOPMENT

In attempting to understand the mental functioning of anyone, schizophrenic or otherwise, one can make certain assumptions.

First assumption: *There is an inherent need in people to strive after meaning, to form hypotheses, in interpreting the world.* These efforts may range from the primitive notions of causality of children and aboriginal cultures, where spirit and will are attributed to nonhuman objects (e.g., rocks, trees, chairs), through many personal beliefs on religion and politics, to the sophisticated statements of theoretical physicists.

The findings of the Gestalt psychologists show that there is an innate capacity, imposed by the brain, to order the perceptual world. The basic capacity to see one object as lighter than another, or nearer, or bigger, seems to be inborn, though learning and practice can enhance these abilities. I would suggest that there is an equivalent innate capacity in children to attempt to put order in their total experiential world.

Second assumption: *There is a need to learn how to think and conceptualize.* This learning involves at least three tasks: one must first be able to identify and label the bits of data; e.g., one cannot form any generalization about dogs until one can spot a dog, or what he believes to be one. A second task is the need to organize things in hierarchical orders, an early form of symbolic logic, i.e., to have ideas about membership in classes, implication, exclusion, etc. A third task is the need to evaluate the data: does it bode well (ill) for me, is it relevant, etc.?

For example, some children are afraid of dogs but not of cats. They will run from a dog but approach a cat of the same general size and coloring. Obviously, this means they can perceive both animals, they have formed the Class of Dogs and the Class of Cats, and have decided that the presence of members of the Class of Dogs bodes ill for them, but the Class of Cats does not.

There is one special class of data that is particularly important with regard to psychological functioning, namely, the data pertaining to one's own existence as a human being. This includes being able to recognize and label feeling states, thoughts, etc., within one's self and others, and how they affect interpersonal relationships. For example, if a 2-year-old child were to start to touch something forbidden, and then stop himself, he would first have to be able to recognize the particular impulse as one separate and distinct from his other impulses, that it belongs to the class of parentally disapproved-of impulses, that impulse and action are two different things, and that if the action occurs, it will elicit a smack from his parent. A 2-year-old does not go through anything resembling such an intricate analysis of a behavior sequence; however, if he is unable to perform any of these operations in his own way, he will not be successful in inhibiting or controlling his behavior.

These operations are learned and practiced. Some of them have gone awry in the thinking of schizophrenics, perhaps because of never having been learned thoroughly.[13, 16] For the first several years of life, nearly all of the labeling, classifying, and evaluating of experience is patterned closely on the parental modes. For example, when driving by some fields where dill was growing, a 3½-year-old commented on the smell. His father jokingly said that it was a field of pickle plants, but the child did not hear it as a joke. For several weeks thereafter he insisted that the plants were pickle plants, and when pickles were being served at lunch, he would ask whether they had grown from the plants he had seen.

Third assumption: *There is an optimum and necessary range of social stimulation for each individual.* Spitz[18] and Bowlby[3] have demonstrated the effects of lack of social stimulation. Spitz noted that infants raised in a nursery where all the physiological needs were gratified, but cuddling and attention were lacking, frequently went into serious depressions, "marasmus," sometimes dying. Bowlby studied infants and children separated from parents and found, at first, increased anxiety and dependency; later, increased hatred for the mother; and, finally, if separation persisted, a tendency to turn away altogether from love objects.

Too much stimulation also has deleterious effects. When a child is overstimulated, thinking and behavior become disorganized and anxious until the flow of stimulation has been reduced.

Similar work with social deprivation in animals has also shown stunting of social, emotional, and physiological maturation. Harlow[11] has demonstrated this finding in monkeys raised without contact with mother or peers for the first six months of life.

THE DREAM, AND THE UNCONSCIOUS

Dream Mechanisms

From the dreams of his patients and from their free associations, Freud became aware of a kind of primitive mental world of which most people are unaware.[6] Yet the continued presence of this world was found to be an important force in waking life, as shown in slips of the tongue, choice of mates and profession, etc. He termed this world out of awareness "the unconscious," and the kind of laws that operated in it as "primary process thinking," this latter to be compared with the "secondary process thinking" found in normal adults in waking life.

Most nonschizophrenic people get closest to the primary-process activities of the unconscious while they are dreaming. At night the ego's barrier of repression against awareness of unconscious events is relaxed, and many of these events appear, albeit in highly disguised form.

The irrational, *Alice's Adventures in Wonderland*[4] kind of world of dreams has often and rightly been compared to a nocturnal schizophrenic episode from which one recovers when awakening. Freud's enduring analysis of dreams is condensed in part here. One funtion of the dream is to protect the sleep of the dreamer from troubling and disturbing thoughts that threaten to make an appearance in consciousness unless they are disguised.* The five primary mental mechanisms through which this purpose is accomplished are *symbolization, condensation, displacement, plastic representation,* and *secondary elaboration.* These mechanisms are also found in normal waking life.

In *symbolization,* one relatively innocuous object becomes a symbol for another that is more threatening, e.g., a wolf for one's rage, an archway for a vagina, etc.

In *condensation,* two or more streams of thought are condensed into one entity, as seen in punning and wit. Dr. Spooner himself was reported to have said, on the topic of waiting in bus stations, "Ah, how tired I get of sitting on those beery wenches!" In the Marx Brothers' *A Day at the Races,* Groucho (the doctor) is taking Harpo's (the patient's) pulse, and says, "Either he's dead or my watch has stopped." This grave prognosis causes Harpo to reach for a bottle with a skull and crossbones on it. Groucho snatches it away from him, saying, "Don't drink that poison; it costs $4.00 an ounce!" Here, Groucho's ill-disguised death wishes toward Harpo, the quasi-medical stance of being a healer, the use of the pulse

---

* Recent physiological research on sleeping and dreaming in schizophrenics and normal persons is discussed in Chapter 9; this work suggests alternative hypotheses to Freud's regarding the function of dreaming.

as the evidence of life ("the ticker"), and Groucho's self-centered concern for his watch and poison supply are condensed into two bits of action.

Displacement refers to a situation in which a disturbing thought is detached from its original stimulus and attached to a more innocuous one; e.g., a man can be angry at the boss but comes home and barks at his wife.

Plastic representation refers to treating words as though they were objects. In a case of Theodore Reik's,[15] a German-American patient dreamed of the Austrian statesman, Metternich. In association with the dream, the patient recalled an incident in which he had been at a train station to meet a woman, who, however, was not on the train—a humiliating experience—and so he had "met-her-nicht." Vivian L. once said, "Hello, Mr. Rosenbaum; do you have any roses in your garden?" She felt that if one were named "Rosenbaum" he was interested in roses (flowers); if she were a wilting flower as she felt she was, she was simply asking if I could take care of her.

Secondary elaboration refers to the kind of rational coherence the dreamer gives to his dream, after awakening, in reporting it to himself or someone else; some of the zanier aspects are toned down, things are brought into better perspective. Many patients will have a dim notion of the bizarre nature of their thoughts and will rationalize them for the observer's consumption.

Freud described other primary process mechanisms that were not specifically part of the dream work; four of these, important in understanding the schizophrenic's experience, are *omnipotent thinking, projection, timelessness,* and *reaction formation.*

In *omnipotent thinking,* the thought and the action are synonymous: to wish someone's death is to cause it. The early model for this omnipotence is, of course, the infant-mother relationship, where the distress of hunger and the wish for relief "magically" causes the mother to come to the rescue. It is only after some months of life that the child develops any notion at all that (1) crying is related to distress, (2) it and mother are separate individuals, or (3) it is *his* crying that causes *her* response; and even if he believes implicitly in (3), that is still omnipotent thinking, because she wills her own behavior and his crying is merely a signal to which she may or may not respond. Loss of belief in one's own omnipotence is one of childhood's most unpleasant lessons, and one frequently only partially learned.

Projection is the name given to the phenomenon of attributing what is primarily an internal thought or feeling state to an external object. The hungry child will guilelessly tell his mother that his playmate is hungry; the guilt-ridden neurotic will unconsciously assume that others must have contempt for him; the angry paranoid will assume that others are out to humiliate and degrade him; all these are examples of projection.

In *reaction formation,* the forbidden wish is replaced by its opposite. The child with the impulse to smear grows up into the compulsively neat adult; the man with repressed rage toward authority is obsequious in the company of his superiors.

Timelessness is another characteristic of primary-process thinking. If something is felt or sensed now, it will be forever and for all time. The model for this again is infancy, where the feeling of the moment occupies all of consciousness; ideas of what things might be like in a little while, tomorrow, or next year, are missing. Hence the urgency of some of the panics that schizophrenic patients (and others, whose reality-testing abilities may be temporarily impaired by a vast amount of anxiety), may feel, for they cannot see that there will be a tomorrow, when things will be different.

In discussing distortion of time sense in schizophrenia, Fromm-Reichmann says:

> [A patient's] progress seemed so exceedingly slow to me that at times I asked myself whether there was any progress at all or whether I was handling him incorrectly and

should transfer him to a colleague who might be able to be useful to the patient in a shorter time. One day this patient commented spontaneously. "Things are going surprisingly well between us except that they are going too fast. If only you wouldn't rush me so that I would not have to go so rapidly."

On page 167, she states,

> To [psychotics], as to the dreamer, a span of years or miles may be condensed into two minutes of experience. Conversely, the dreamer may feel, after having dreamed only two minutes, that he has covered a span of many years or miles.[8]

Unconscious Drives, Fantasies, and Wishes

Thus far in this section I have been describing mental mechanisms, routes if you will, over which impulses, feelings, and thoughts travel. Now I shall discuss the impulses and thoughts themselves, the travelers of the roads of the unconscious.

The passions of childhood are strong but not subtle. The child who is hungry will suck and bite voraciously. Psychoanalytic exploration has shown that frequently the hunger is accompanied by fantasies of cannibalism, or actually devouring the pleasure-giving other person. Remnants in adult life are seen in the phrase, "You look so good I could eat you up," and in the intense kissing, sucking, biting, and squeezing that takes place during love making. Children's fairy tales abound in monsters who destroy greedy little boys and girls; and the monsters are, after all, projections of the storyteller.

> *Example:* A patient impulsively stabbed and killed his drug supplier. He then cut off the victim's right arm and carried it around with him for three days before being picked up by the police. He was found by the court to be

sufficiently out of touch with reality to assist in his own defense and was hospitalized. On examination he demonstrated the classical signs of the thought disorder of schizophrenia.

In a dispassionate way, he explained his background and his crime. He felt that from the age of 13 on, his father had kept him "down," by which he meant weak, naïve, incompetent, and unable to cope in the adult world, even though the father was away from home for long periods because of his work. He felt that he himself was slowly coming "up" in the last few years, in part through his contact with the underground drug world. In particular he saw his supplier as being strong, sophisticated, capable, and heterosexually wise, qualities that the patient felt he himself lacked. The patient thought that the right side of his own body represented these traits, that his left side was the weak, feminine side.

During an argument about diluted drugs, the killing occurred; there had no doubt been a displacement of wrath from father toward supplier. By killing the supplier, the patient thought he would absorb his spirit and his wisdom. He took the right arm, no longer the symbol of strength, *but strength itself!* While he had the arm, he started to eat it, thus more fully to incorporate its strengh.

Anger and hate are important. The angry child who tells his parents, "I hate you," and shoots them with his finger "so you will be dead," means every word he says. His fears that the world will return his spite (projection) are seen in nightmares and minor phobias so often seen in childhood.

In adolescence a new set of powerful feelings must be handled, those of lust and intimacy. In a culture that is as conflicted about sexuality as ours is, it is not surprising that many people repress, rather than express, their lustful and in-

timate needs by adopting strict codes of morality, by developing neurotic symptoms such as frigidity and impotence, or by
blurring their conflicts in an apparent orgy of sexual activity.

To the schozophrenic, many of these feelings have never
been properly indentified and labeled; he has not learned how
to let them be an integrated and constructive part of his
personal relations. For him a wish for closeness may be
equated with a cannibalistic voraciousness, and, with the
thought being equal to the action, to be equivalent to the
destruction of the person with whom he wants to be close.
Anger is projected, and the world is seen as full of people bent
on the patient's humiliation and destruction.

Hill[12] describes how the schizophrenic patient may bring
such feelings into the therapeutic situation:

> . . . Particularly, the therapist is to be an
> exclusive possession of the patient and is to
> find his own satisfaction exclusively in the ex-
> istence of this one patient of his. The goal is
> a close system of symbiotic bliss, utterly safe,
> and gratifying.

Needless to say, when the schizophrenic patient is frustrated in these wishes, as inevitably he must be, the anger and
murderous rages with which he must deal are equally strong.
Because of the intense wish for closeness, the poor sense of
self-identity or body ego, and the frequent manifestations of
projection and omnipotent thinking, many patients who
begin to develop a relationship with a therapist will become
afraid that the therapist will catch their illness, become crazy,
or be hurt by his contact with the patient in other ways.

There are certain phenomena of the unconscious found
frequently enough in schizophrenic patients to warrant special
emphasis. These include the ability to induce anxiety in others,
outpourings from the unconscious, and the motives for attempts at self-castration.

It is a frequent observation that the sudden appearance
of anxiety in the interviewer, without his easily being able

to find a reasonable explanation for its appearance, may be the first clue that he is dealing with a schizophrenic. This experience is akin to the feelings of eeriness, awe, and dread that Sullivan[19] ascribes to the "Not-Me," discussed below. One reason for this anxiety may come from the sudden and uninhibited outpouring of unconscious or primary-process material as described by Hill:[12]

> For the purpose of psychotherapy, based upon psychoanalysis, the self-awareness of the schizophrenic is in striking contrast to that of the psychoneurotic. That which the neurotic spends hundreds of hours of analysis discovering about himself, particularly his repressed infantile sexuality and his oedipal conflicts, his castration fears and her penis envy, the schizophrenic may tell his therapist in the first interview. In fact, if a patient does speak so readily of incest and matricide and such things, which to a normal person are unthinkable, one at once is alerted to the likelihood that he is a schizophrenic.

Attempted or successful self-castration in males suggests a schizophrenic process. The dynamics of these actions frequently revolve around a desperate attempt to solve the conflicts about incest and matricide that Hill[12] describes. They represent a concrete resolution of this conflict: "I am troubled by my strong desires to have sexual intercourse with my mother. Either I can remove my sexual drives by castration ('. . . if one of thy organs offend thee, cut it off. . . .') or by killing the temptress—matricide."

DISTURBANCES IN LOGIC AND REASONING

Logic Disturbances

Arieti,[1] Goldstein,[9] Von Damarus,[21] and many others have commented on the disturbances in formal logic in the schizophrenic patient. In normal logic, shown formally in the syllogism of Barbara (so named by the thirteenth century philosopher Peter Hispanus), in the first (major) premise, the subject defines a class and the predicate states one or more of its attributes, e.g., "All men are mortal." Here the class defined is that of all men; its attribute is that of mortality. In the second (minor) premise, the subject is defined as being a member of the class, e.g., "We are men." The conclusion is that the member of the class defined in the minor premise shares the attribute of the class, e.g., "Therefore we are mortal." In Figure 4–1, the major class, all men, is represented by Circle A; the minor class, we, by Circle B, is wholly contained in the major class.

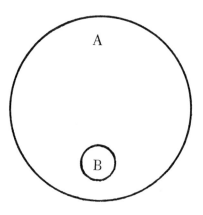

Figure 4–1

One of the most important disturbances in logic in the schizophrenic is the appearance of predicative thinking: things are made identical because they share a common characteristic. Unlike the syllogism of Barbara, things are identified because they are similar in predicate, not subject. See these examples:

    A. Major premise: All chairs have legs.
       Minor premise: I have legs.
       Conclusion: Therefore, I am a chair.

    B. Major premise: Jesus Christ was persecuted.
       Minor premise: I am persecuted.
       Conclusion: Therefore, I am Jesus Christ.†

    In these examples, because the subjects of the two premises shared a common characteristic, i.e., had identical predicates, e.g., having legs or being persecuted, the subjects were made identical.

    In Figure 4–2, Circle A represents the class of all things having legs. Circle B represents the class of all chairs. Circle C

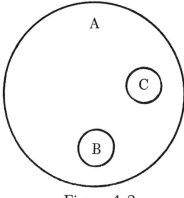

Figure 4–2

represents "I". In reasoning by predicate, the schizophrenic treats Circles B and C as though they are identical.

    Arieti has termed this kind of reasoning "paleological," meaning that such thinking is found in people when they are very young and just learning to reason. The little boy who thought the moon fell into the water may have demonstrated

† Evidence that schizophrenic patients commit more syllogistic errors than do normals is not firm, and further research will be required to clarify this point. Also, it is not clear whether the syllogistic error shown leads to the false conclusion of being Jesus Christ, or whether that conclusion was reached first, in which situation seeing one's self as persecuted follows logically and without syllogistic error. With either explanation, however, the interviewer would be justified in asking the patient if he felt persecuted.

paleological thinking, if he was not the victim of an illusion. His thought processes may have gone something like this: "The moon is bright; the lights on the water are bright; therefore the moon is the lights in the water."

The examples of reasoning by predicate so far have been those of observable traits, such as having legs, being persecuted, or being light. There are other attributes, however, that can be used in schizophrenic thinking, such as those of temporal contiguity and spatial contiguity. In temporal contiguity when two events closely follow each other, a special relationship is seen between them. For instance, Sylvia T. lit a cigarette; a moment later her therapist was paged; she worried that her lighting the cigarette caused him to be paged. In spatial contiguity, when things are in physical proximity, a special relationship may be seen between them.

Peculiar Reasoning: Metaphorical and Semantic Errors

If the predicative thinker could only make a metaphor out of his logic, could only insert the word "like" at the right spot, no one would quarrel with his conclusions. Were he to say, "I am *like* a chair; we both have legs," or "I am *like* Jesus Christ; we both are persecuted," he would be making himself quite comprehensible. It is, in fact, the inability to handle metaphor, to change easily from levels of abstraction, that often characterizes schizophrenic thinking. David Rapaport[14] has termed this phenomenon "loss of connotative enrichment," or, elsewhere, "narrowing of the concept base."

Well known among the impairments of the use of metaphor in schizophrenics is unusual proverb interpretation. The patient with an organic brain syndrome is concrete and impoverished in his responses. He is capable only of narrow and literal-minded interpretations. The schizophrenic patient, on the other hand, as the examples given below demonstrate, may give responses that are highly personal, idiosyncratic, and bizarre, and that reveal a private meaning attributed to the proverb. He may also occasionally give a truly concrete response.

The purpose of a proverb is to provide a metaphorical

commentary on common human situations through concrete examples. For instance, the proverb "A rolling stone gathers no moss" is not concerned with stones and moss per se, but rather with either of the two commentaries on life that (1) a busy person doesn't get rusty, or (2) a drifter doesn't accumulate many of life's goods. Yet the schizophrenic patient may give a very concrete restatement of the proverb: "A rotating earth fragment does not accumulate much primitive plant life"; or a highly personalized interpretation: "I don't know how to roll so I don't know about that one"; or a highly generalized, abstract account: "It's about motion, momentum, center of gravity, revolutions; revelations and moss; moss-backed revelations. . . ."

Related to this response is the frequent commission of the semantic error by the schizophrenic patient. The semanticists warn against confusing the word with the object, the map with the territory, the symbol with the symbolized. The word "apple" is not edible; the map of the Rocky Mountains is not made of stone; the right arm is not strength itself.

Teleological Regression

Arieti[1] mentions "teleological regression," a regression away from adult, secondary-process, reasoning, to forms of reasoning where the logic serves to avoid anxiety, is emotionally determined, and becomes increasingly primitive.

With these foregoing concepts in mind, Vivian L.'s inquiry about rose gardening can be more fully understood. Vivian asked her question about the rose garden as I walked on the ward one morning. Not stopping to think about its implications, I responded honestly, but rather concretely, I must admit, that I didn't have a garden. At that afternoon's psychotherapy session she was much more distant, subdued, and depressed than usual. Gradually, we determined together that it was the interchange of the morning that had lowered her mood.

An analysis of these events follows: A person with the name of Rosenbaum must have something to do with roses (confusion of the word with the object; plastic representation

of the word "rose"); she felt herself to be an object in need
of care, just as flowers must be cared for, but she had reasoned
by this syllogism: "Roses need caring for; I need care; therefore, I am a rose." Thus her question was a schizophrenic
inquiry about the state of our relationship: Will you care for
me?

My response that I didn't have a garden was concrete, but
on a different level of abstraction than her question. With her
emotionally determined need to communicate on a level of
"What does this bode for me?" the response meant rejection
of her need to be cared for. During the psychotherapy session
the impasse in communication was clarified; as soon as I
reassured her that I was interested in helping her and had
not meant to imply otherwise, her depression lifted.

The Adaptive Value of Faulty Logic

Lest it be supposed that only schizophrenic patients reason concretely, note well that the threat of anxiety will cause
many nonpsychotic people also to do so. A man was being
screened for a job; one of his interviews was with a psychiatrist, and he was nervous about what the psychiatrist
would find out about him. When the psychiatrist asked, "How
do you sleep?" the man replied quite concretely, "On my
stomach." When the psychiatrist clarified, "I mean how *well*
do you sleep?" the man replied appropriately.

Thus there is a certain safety in responding concretely,
in failing to respond at the implied level of metaphorical
abstraction. The safety lies in being able to avoid a potentially
humiliating statement in a relationship where one sees potential for humiliation. The psychiatrist cannot damn a man for
sleeping on his stomach; the impact of the rejection for Vivian
is less than if she asked the direct question, "Are you interested in taking care of me?" and receiving the blunt "No"
she was afraid of. Many normal people have literally or figura-
tively crossed to the other side of the street to avoid an unpleasant meeting; the schizophrenic unwittingly does it by
avoiding a direct, verbal, understandable confrontation.

There is a growing body of evidence that many of the disorders of logic found in schizophrenic patients are present in their families in a more subtle form; this evidence will be discussed further in Chapter 7.

CONCEPT OF SELF AND OBJECT RELATIONS

Most adults have a fairly clear idea of where their bodies and minds end and other people's begin, and whether they are men or women. When we ask "Who am I?" it is a sophisticated question meaning, "Am I comfortable in my choice of profession, of morals, of philosophy?" It does not usually mean, "Am I 6 feet tall?" or "Am I a man or a woman?" or "Is my stomach so big I could hold the world in it?" Our sense of self is not something we were born with; we started learning it in infancy with the exploration of fingers and toes, just as surely as we later learned to read and spell. At birth there was no sense of self and non-self; baby and breast were one; and mother-child and universe were one.

There are some situations in which nonpsychotic adults regularly lose the sense of self, and ego boundaries dissolve for the moment, to be reconstituted later. These situations include going to sleep, loving and being loved, orgasm, profound religious and esthetic experiences, drinking, taking other mind-altering drugs, and hypnosis. Most of us are comfortable with these situations: these experiences are positive, they usually increase our sense of trust in a benevolent universe, and to some extent, at least, they are under our control.

For the schizophrenic patient, whose security about the wholeness of his sense of self is frequently precarious, such events can be quite frightening. The prodrome of an acute break is often marked by a reversal of the sleep cycle; one stays awake during the dark of night, when the body can dissolve and sleeps only during the day when the light can demonstrate one's integrity.

Naomi N., in her chattering, demonstrates many such confusions of self and not-self. She interchanges "I," "You," and "He," freely; and she is concerned with eating, with being

eaten and hurt, with injury and death, and with being re-
stored.

Sullivan[19] has divided the sense of self into "Good-me,"
"Bad-me," and "Not-me." The first two categories include the
thoughts and feelings in ourselves that are associated with,
respectively, praise and acceptance, and disapproval and
punishment by others. "Not-me," he says, is

> . . . the organization of experience with sig-
> nificant people that have been subjected to such
> intense anxiety so suddenly precipitated, that it
> was not possible for the then relatively rudi-
> mentary person to make any sense of, to
> develop any true grasp on, the particular cir-
> cumstances which dictated the experience of
> this intense anxiety.

Here is a fictitious example of how a feeling state could become a part of one of these systems. If a 2-year-old child, in
a burst of enthusiasm, runs to his mother, hugs her, and
says, "I love you," and she responds with a hug and tells
him "I love you, too," notions of loving mother will very likely
become part of "Good-me." If she responds by detaching his
arms and saying, "We don't act that way here," it will probably become part of "Bad-me." If, however, she stiffens, becomes quite tense and anxious, and says "You don't love me;
you don't know what love is!" it may well become part of
"Not-me." Many parents literally are *unable even to acknowledge the existence of* (rather than to acklowledge but dis-
approve of) the thoughts and feelings of the patient; this
failing exists to a far greater degree among families of schizophrenics than among families of nonschizophrenics.[16] The
result, I suggest, is a larger component of "Not-me" in the individual patient. Because part of the concept of "me" has to
do with body size, configuration, and sex role, it is not surprising that schizophrenics should have such problems with
knowing "Who am I?" These concepts are shown in Figure
4–3.

These many aspects of warped development provide some explanation of the disordered interpersonal and object relationships of the schizophrenic patient. His incredibly strong wishes for closeness, his frustrated rages, etc., many of which must be repressed and kept out of awareness, lead at once to an intense wish for, and an equally intense fear of,

FIGURE 4–3

"GOOD-ME," "BAD-ME," AND "NOT-ME"

The Healthy Personality

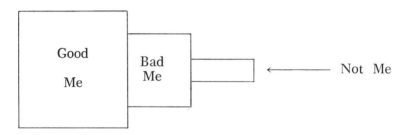

The Neurotic Personality

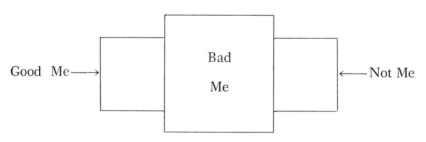

The Schizophrenic Personality

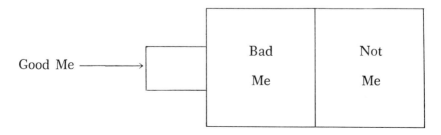

a close relationship with another person. Here, then, are some of the ingredients of the classical ambivalence that Bleuler[2] described.

One crafty, chronically paranoid patient, George Newton, was speaking about someone's having insulted him; he smiled while he spoke. I told him that if someone had insulted me in the same fashion I would be angry, and yet he was smiling about it. He said, "Well, Doctor, to every action there's an equal and an opposite reaction. That's Einstein's Third Law, isn't it?"

As I blurted out, "No, that's Newton's Third Law . . . ," he regarded me with a cat-that-ate-the-canary smile; he had done a very effective job of getting me involved in his ambivalent come-closer, go-further-away style of relating.

The early precursors of the inability to form stable object relations have been described by both Szasz and Searles. Szasz[20] has pointed out that normal persons have an inner reservoir of remembered object relationships on which we can draw when we suffer a loss in the real world, "much like stored glycogen, fat, and muscle upon which the organism draws during periods of starvation." He suggests that the schizophrenic has no such store of early, stable object relationships upon which to draw and thus is particularly vulnerable to loss. He might have analogized the schizophrenic to the diabetic: the necessities (people, glucose) exist in the environment, but the patient is not able to utilize them.

As a consequence of the inability to use previous experience with introjected objects, the schizophrenic patient is peculiarly at the mercy of persons in the here-and-now; he has great difficulty "buffering" them, if you will. Szasz[20] points out that schizophrenic patients form an immediate transference to the physician, but that this transference is of a different quality from that formed by neurotic patients. For the schizophrenic the transference is real and immediate; it does not have the "as-if" quality of the slowly developing transference-neurosis of the neurotic, which is patterned on previously stable object relations.

Searles[17] comments on the lack of consistency of perception, the lack of object constancy, in the schizophrenic patient. Parents of schizophrenics are themselves so often disorganized, anxious, unpredictable people that the child has little opportunity to develop stable relationships with them, a phenomenon discussed in detail in Chapters 7 and 11. Searles described one such mother and quoted her schizophrenic daughter as saying, "Whenever you use the word 'mother,' I see a whole parade of women, each one representing a different point of view."

> *Example:* In working with George M., a chronic schizophrenic, we had become involved in a close and meaningful relationship. Because of his fear that anyone he came into close contract with would become part of him, and vice versa, he was afraid that his schizophrenia would become contagious, that I would become psychotic.
>
> At one point he ran away. After we picked him up, he said, "I ran away to keep you from getting electrocuted." He knew through personal experience that people with this illness are given electric shocks, and thus he was afraid that I would suffer this fate. If I did, either I would be terribly angry at him for having started it, or I might be killed (the loss of consciousness being death); in any event, I would be lost to him as a person who could be close and helpful. So this situation of wanting to be close had in it the seeds of destruction and abandonment. The only way he could think of to preserve at least a fragment of our relationship was to run away, and save me from the curse of his illness and the resultant shock treatment, and to save himself from feeling like a murderer who has destroyed someone he is close to.

The desire and the fear of being close are the central dilemmas of the schizophrenic patient. Vivian L. once stated this eloquently. Her statement came toward the end of a session that had been friendly and active. Then the conversation had slowed down, and Vivian had begun to look a little sad and far away. I inquired about the change in mood; she said it had to do with "Friendship," and went on to say, "Too much friendship is like when a bear is cold and he sees the hunter's fire, and he comes over to get warmed and gets scorched."

A moving version of a schizophrenic patient's psychotherapeutic experience is given in *I Never Promised You a Rose Garden*.[10]

INTERPRETING SCHIZOPHRENIC COMMUNICATION

Using the foregoing formulations, one can understand a great deal, but never all, of the utterances of schizophrenic patients. Schizophrenic thinking provides the patient with an explanation of certain otherwise peculiar mental events; it allows him to think and conceptualize about these events; it provides expression of certain strong feelings and thoughts; it provides a sensory input in the absence of real-life interactions; and part of this input has to do with states of relatedness with other people.

Because the patient is caught in the dilemma of wanting closeness and yet being frightened of it, he must use a mode of communication that can simultaneously assert and deny his commentaries on human relationships, be they here and now and in this room, be they the present state of things, or be they the early life situation with the family. George's runaway and later his statement about electrocution told how he felt about the then contemporary situation, his treatment, and his presence on the ward.

> *Example:* Mr. William Z. thought his home was bugged and that the FBI could see and hear him through his TV set. He thought they were sending him a mesage to go to San Diego; so he took a plane there. On board the plane, he

was sure that the other passengers knew all about him, the trouble with his wife at home, and could read his mind. When he got to San Diego, he called his wife in San Francisco, the first time she had heard from him since he disappeared.

Mr. Z.'s episode shows a psychotic way of handling a difficult domestic situation: his wife caused him considerable aggravation, and he wanted, on an unconscious level, to let the world know how difficult things were and also to get out of the situation. Yet his mental functioning labeled such sentiments as severely reprehensible, closer to "Not-me" than "Bad-me," and so he was afraid that the world knew, i.e., the FBI was watching through his TV, and, when he was getting out of the situation by flying to San Diego, that it was on command of the FBI, and that the other passengers (more of the world) knew what had been going on. In other words, he could not afford to take personal responsibility for these sentiments and say, in effect, "I am doing this"; he had to go through the psychotic thought processes to assert and deny simultaneously his feelings about the contemporary marital situation.

The ability to send double messages, to assert and deny simultaneously, is not only the patient's problem; he may well have learned it in a family where a good deal more than an average amount of this type of indirect communication occurred.

SUMMARY

Dreaming is probably the closest most nonschizophrenics come to having a schizophrenic experience. There are many similarities between the mental functioning of normal children and that of schizophrenic adults. Impulses and feelings of childhood demand instant gratification and expression;

those of adulthood can be inhibited or delayed in order to
achieve greater long-term satisfactions. The sense of self, of
being separate from others, is entirely lacking at birth; it is
present in a rudimentary form at the end of the first year, and
in greatly enhanced form in adulthood. Children do not consider that the needs of others are important; adults, however,
can evaluate the needs of certain others as being equal to
their own. Children do not know how to think logically; this
skill is taught first by parents and later by peers before it
appears in its mature form in adolescence and young adulthood.

In schizophrenia there is a regression away from mature
forms of feeling, relating, and thinking, toward more im-
mature forms. The regression is never complete, however;
intact islands of ego can be found even in seriously regressed
patients.

Certain inherent mental needs of growing young human
beings must be posited: (1) there is a need to strive after
meaning; (2) there is a need to learn how to think and conceptualize; and (3) there is an optimum and necessary range
of social stimulation for each person.

Freud found, from his work with dreams and listening
to his patients' free associations, a world of mental life that
is rarely accessible to awareness—that operates by a set of
rules similarly inaccessible. He termed this world "the unconscious." Of the several mental mechanisms, or rules, by
which the unconscious works, five were defined in his study of
dreams; these five are symbolization, condensation, displacement, plastic representation, and secondary elaboration.
Other mechanisms defined are those of omnipotent thinking,
projection, timelessness, and reaction formation. These mechanisms are frequently at work in the conscious daily life of
schizophrenics.

Strong and unsubtle feelings frequently dominate the
schizophrenic's life and have not been integrated into useful
harmony. These include the neeed for closeness and nurturance, cannibalistic desires, anger, murderous wishes, lust, and
wishes for intimacy.

The processes of formal logic and reasoning, and the use of metaphor, are impaired, and semantic errors are frequently found in schizophrenics. A major logical error is that of reasoning by predicate, or seeing two things as identical because they share a common attribute, e.g., "All chairs have legs; I have legs; therefore, I am a chair." Because of these defects in logic, schizophrenic patients usually interpret proverbs in a highly personal, sometimes concrete manner.

Because schizophrenic patients are afraid of close human relationships, even when they want them badly, many of their statements about relationships are simultaneous assertions and denials; peculiar reasoning, symbolization, and plastic representation frequently make it difficult for the other person to tell whether the patient is talking about interpersonal relationships or concrete objects. In such indirect communication the safety for the patient lies in avoiding some feared calamity, be it an open, obvious rebuff, rejection, or humiliation.

Schizophrenic patients usually have a distorted or inadequate self image; they are not familiar with their feelings, their bodies, or their effect on other people. To use Sullivan's formulation, they have a large component of "Not-me" in their makeup. They do not have a reservoir of previous, successful object relationships; they seem not to have learned from previous experience, quite possibly because in childhood their experience with their parents was unstable, fragmenting, and unreliable.

Many aspects of primitive feeling, thinking, and relating can be found in the schizophrenic patient. If we understand them, we can understand many of the patient's communications, although superficially they appear bizarre and incapable of comprehension. Such understanding may be crucial for psychotherapy.

5

Clinical Course

There is a wide range of possible outcomes for persons who have had a schizophrenic episode. Some remit completely and never again show signs of a schizophrenic disorder. Others may have one or a few recurrences, but are, in the main, symptom-free, e.g., Sylvia T. Others may be mildly or moderately affected continuously but are nevertheless able to function in the community, hold jobs, maintain family and social relationships, etc.; such patients are said to have had a "social remission." There are others who are severely affected, who are unable to function more than marginally in the community, and who usually have periodic relapses requiring rehospitalization, e.g., Stephen J. Finally, there are patients whose illness is chronic, progressive, and deteriorating, and who seem doomed to a lifetime of hospitalization, e.g., Naomi N. There are some observers, such as Bleuler,[3] who believe that no schizophrenic patient ever goes completely into remission, that all of them show at least a few signs of deterioration. His population, however, tended to be of older, more chronic patients, and he may simply not have had the opportunity to examine the acutely ill patients for whom the outlook is best.

It is difficult to be accurate in evaluating outcome statistics. Some authors use the criteria of release vs. continued hospitalization, yet standards for making such decisions vary from hospital to hospital and from community to community.

Others use the criteria of the presence or absence of symptoms. Still others, in estimating the outcome of illness, use the criterion of social and personal functioning. All of these criteria overlap and can be considered *roughly* comparable. For instance, the patient who is kept in the hospital is probably kept there because he has overt symptomatology and noticeable defects in social adaptation. In Table 5–1, I have combined these criteria in reporting Bleuler's and Wing's data. "Good" means discharged from hospital and/or relatively symptom-free and/or modest defects, at worst, in social adaptation. Likewise, "Poor" means prolonged hospitalization and/or pronounced symptomatology and/or gravely impaired social functioning. "Medium" refers to patients falling between these extremes.

TABLE 5–1 OUTCOME IN THE SCHIZOPHRENIAS

Author	Date of Sample	Good	Medium	Poor
			(In percentages)	
Bleuler	1911	60	18	22
Wing	1930-1940	50	25	25
Wing	1950-1966	67[a]	26	7

[a] Of this 67 percent, 65 percent (or 44 percent of the total original sample), were "functioning independently in the community." It follows, therefore, that the remaining 23 percent who were not hospitalized were not functioning independently in the community, either, and might appropriately be moved to the "Medium" category.

Wing[17] compares readmission and discharge rates of two and three decades ago to current studies. In earlier studies, fewer than half the patients first admitted were released and in the community at follow-up three to sixteen years later. In his series reported in 1966, only 7 percent of patients stayed as long as two years in the hospital, and only 28 percent spent any time in the hospital during the last two years of follow-up. At follow-up 67 percent of his patients were out of the hospital, and, of these, 65 percent were functioning independently in the community. Of his original sample, he says:

> About one-quarter of schizophrenic pa-
> tients were still severly ill five years after first
> admission and another quarter were handi-
> capped by less severe symptoms. The outlook
> in early schizophrenia is, therefore, more favor-
> able than it has ever been. . . . Compared with
> the days when to enter hospital with a diagnosis
> of schizophrenia was almost tantamount to
> staying a lifetime, it is possible now to be, if
> not optimistic, then at least not unreservedly
> gloomy about the prognosis in an early case.

The deteriorated, "burnt out" chronic patient of former years is seen much less often in this era of vigorous treatment. Yet there are those long-term patients still to be found in state hospitals who have proved refractory to treatment, some of whose behavior has been described by Arieti[2] as follows:

> The [chronic] schizophrenic seems to
> hoard in order to possess; the objects he collects
> have no intrinsic value; they are valuable only
> inasmuch as they are possessed by the patient.
> The patient seems almost to have a desire to
> incorporate them, to make them part of his own
> person, and puts them into his mouth, nostrils,
> vagina, anus, etc.
>   [On self-decoration:] Pieces of paper and
> rags are cut into several bands; bracelets, rings,
> necklaces are made with them. Many, predomi-
> nantly female patients, paint their faces in a
> conspicuous, ridiculous manner. Many patients
> of both sexes adorn themselves by placing but-
> tons, stamps, small boxes, corks, or coins on
> their chests.

FACTORS RELATING TO OUTCOME

Age at First Admission

The earlier the age of onset, the poorer the outlook for recovery. Pollack, Levenstein, and Klein[9] found that adolescents (under age 20) and young adults (ages 20 to 29) first hospitalized for schizophrenia fell significantly less frequently into their "excellent" or "good" outcome groups than did older adults (ages 30 to 39).

Premorbid Adjustment

Available evidence suggests two important things:

1. The incidence of psychiatric disturbance in childhood is significantly higher in children who later become schizophrenic.

2. For persons who do become schizophrenic, poor premorbid adjustment is associated with a more chronic course and poorer outcome, so-called "process schizophrenia," and good premorbid adjustment is associated with a more acute course and better outcome, so-called "reactive schizophrenia."

Childhood

Many, but not all, children who later become schizophrenic show signs of disturbed behavior as children. Reports from several investigators who have compared the preschizophrenic with his twins, siblings, or family members, have shown that many a preschizophrenic is shy, socially withdrawn, dependent, submissive, emotionally labile, and overly obedient.

Prout and White[13] interviewed mothers about the childhoods of thier schizophrenic offspring and the patients' same-sexed siblings. These authors found that the preschizophrenic was more sensitive, less happy, less social, more passive, dependent, and easier to manage than his normal sibling, who, in turn, tended to be more rebellious. Pollack *et al.*[10] made "blind" ratings from maternal retrospective reports about 44 young adult schizophrenics and their "normal" siblings; they compared these ratings with reports for families where there was psychiatric illness other than schizophrenic and where there was medical illness. They report:

> Within the schizophrenic patient group there was considerable variability; about one-

third were rated as having unremarkable histories, and one-third as having severely deviant
childhood histories. The latter were found to
have had a significantly earlier age of onset of
severe psychiatric illness.

. . . Schizophrenic patients as a group were
rated as having been significantly more irri-
table, shy, dependent, and non-affectionate in
childhood than their sibs. They had significantly more conduct problems and neurotic
traits, were poorer in school performance, had
more difficulties in peer relationships and were
rated poorer on overall childhood adjustment.

Pollin *et al.*[11,12] and Kringlen[6] have compared monozygotic twins discordant for schizophrenia on several psychological and physiological parameters; some of these
findings are reported in greater detail in Chapter 9. Pollin's
group found that the index (i.e., preschizophrenic) twin
differed from his control in being seen from birth onward as
being weaker, more vulnerable to feeding and adjustment
problems, less competent socially, and generally more docile
but occasionally more prone to outbursts of temper when
frustrated; these patterns and the parental interactions implicit in them persisted relatively unchanged throughout life.
They also found that the index twin had a significantly higher
degree of "soft signs" of neurological malfunctioning than did
the control.

Kringlen[6] found that the index twins, premorbidly,
showed more of the following traits than their controls
showed: dependency, inhibition, obedience, and introversion.

Alanen,[1] comparing 30 schizophrenics with 30 neurotic
patients, found that, of the schizophrenic group, 12 had
shown signs of marked social withdrawal before puberty,
and 8 withdrew at or after puberty. In contrast, none of the
neurotics had shown such withdrawal.

Hilgard and Newman[5] report that the percentage of
patients who had lost their mothers in childhood was higher

for both male and female schizophrenics than for the control population; loss of a father was approximately the same in the experimental and control groups.

Weiner[16] reviews descriptions of adjustment before illness. Many authors cited refer to a relatively high incidence of "schizoid personality" premorbidly (figures ranging from 28 to 75 percent), but he points out that some authors use the term to denote "mild" schizophrenia, in which some of the classical signs of schizophrenia are already present; others use it in the manner defined in Chapter 2. These differences in usage may account for the wide variability of the figures. Judging from the studies of preschizophrenic children, it would seem safest to assume that the incidence of premorbid schizoid traits is somewhat greater during adolescence than it is in the general population, but far from universal.

Other forms of premorbid psychopathology include borderline characters, pseudoneurotic, and pseudopsychopathic states described in Chapter 2.

PROGNOSIS

Age of onset and quality of premorbid adjustment are just two of several factors that a number of authors have found to predict the outcome of the illness, i.e., to establish a prognosis.

Vaillant[15] reviewed both historical and contemporary descriptions of schizophrenic episodes that were marked by complete or nearly complete recovery. He found that these descriptions shared the following characteristics: schizophrenic symptom picture, good premorbid adjustment, psychologically understandable symptoms, discernible precipitating cause, symptoms of psychotic depression, heredity positive for psychotic depression, acute onset, confusion and delirium, and concern with dying.

Nameche and colleagues[8] applied Vaillant's ideas in the study of the case records of 50 schizophrenic patients followed for periods up to 40 years. They divided the patients into two groups, chronic and released. This criterion merely

stated that patients were, or were not, able to function outside
of a hospital; it did not comment on the degree of clinical
remission of primary symptoms. The chronic patients had
spent, on the average, 88 percent of their adult lives in mental
hospitals, the released group, 19 percent. The case records of
these patients were carefully examined for several parameters
observable at the time of initial hospitalization; the findings
are shown in Table 5–2.

These findings, wholly consonant with those of Vaillant,

TABLE 5–2

PROGNOSIS, PREMORBID ADJUSTMENT, AND OUTCOME

Based on a study of histories of chronic vs. released patients

Items factored out

	Chronic	Released	P(Chi sq.)
	(In percentages)		
1. Psychotic or schizoid pathology in the main mothering person	59	19	.02
2. Lack of any separation from the pathogenic family	65	23	.01
3. Poor premorbid social and sexual adjustment (Phillips Scale)	75	27	.01
4. Prehospitalization treatment less than three months	90	53	.02
5. No acting out in community	80	47	.05
6. Not disoriented or confused on admission	89	33	.001
7. No symptoms of depressive psychosis	85	28	.001
8. Premorbid schizoid personality	95	40	.001
9. Absence of clear precipitating events	85	40	.01
10. Not overtly concerned with dying during acute phase of illness	85	40	.01
11. [Greater] length of onset of admitting symptoms	80	38	.02
12. Schizophrenic patterns in heredity	15	20	not sign.

From Nameche et al.[8]

discriminate well between the two groups on a number of factors. Nameche[8] discusses the findings by saying,

> . . . 95% of the group who became chronic had records containing seven or more negative prognostic factors; 87% of the released group demonstrated fewer than seven negative factors.

It would appear from Nameche's and Vaillant's studies that a *favorable* prognosis can be made when most of the factors cited in Table 5–2 are absent at admission. Sylvia T. qualified on nearly all these points, and thus it was possible to be quite hopeful about her ultimate recovery.

Arieti[2] confirms and adds to these criteria. He points out that the continued presence of *anxiety* is a hopeful sign: it indicates that the patient maintains awareness of his abnormal state and has not slipped into a comfortable, albeit psychotic, explanation of what is happening to him. Conversely, the acceptance of delusional or hallucinatory explanations for what is happening is ominous. Sullivan[14] echoes this thought, pointing out that increasing use of the mechanism of *projection,* with massive shifts of blame for distress being placed on others, is serious; he says,

> . . . the transfer of blame has come into being through shifting the mythological and diffusely focused thinking in the direction of one's being the apotheosis of all that one has wished to be. If this suffices—that is, if the paranoid attitude gives enough feeling of security so that the schizophrenic disturbances of the level of awareness cease—then the person goes into a bitter, highly systemized paranoid state with remarkable speed.

Arieti further points out that early compliance by the patient with hospital routine is a favorable sign; again, it indicates some awareness of illness and wish to be helped. Conversely, defiance of routine is more serious.

He notes, too, that the availability of helpful family members and social resources augur well for the patient. This fact is again demonstrated with Sylvia T., whose husband, mother-in-law, psychiatric ward, and psychiatrist were all able to offer her, as her acute symptoms abated, substantial support and guidance in resuming her functioning as wife and new mother.

DEVELOPMENT OF OVERT PSYCHOSIS

Prodromal Stage

The progression from onset to overt psychosis may vary from the slow, insidious, gradual onset seen with Vivian L. to an abrupt two-week transition as seen in the case of Sylvia T. Similarly, there may be little or nothing suggesting external, precipitating stresses for the simple schizophrenic, or, in any event, nothing more than the normal stresses of adolescence. In other cases a life event of signal importance and stress, e.g., childbirth and its resultant alterations in family homeostasis, as in the case of Sylvia T., may be found.

In most cases, the patient will have gone through a number of levels of attempts to cope with unreal experiences before the overt psychosis is established.

In the prodromal period patients frequently are bothered with episodes of depersonalization, *déjà vu*, feelings of unreality, awareness that their universe is changing, ideas of reference, and intense preoccupation with meanings as shown in hours spent reading the Bible or books on philosophy.

Many, if not all, of these experiences are a normal part of adolescence. In the normal adolescent, however, the experiences are brief, sometimes enjoyable, and more frequently interesting than terrifying or mystifying.

Depersonalization refers to the experience of seeing one's self as though one were an external observer. "I watched my hand on the steering wheel of the car," said one adolescent nonschizophrenic, "and I was amazed to find that it seemed to know how to steer the car all by itself, as if I didn't have anything to do with making it work."

Déjà vu, from the French "already seen," refers to the uncanny feeling that one has "been here before," has participated in this conversation, has walked into this building, in some previous incarnation, even though intellectually he knows full well that he never has.

Ideas of reference describe the thought that what other people are doing refers to one's self. Anyone who has walked into a room full of people just as they burst into laughter, and who wondered if they were laughing at him, is familiar with the experience. For the developing schizophrenic, such experiences multiply and generalize, so that he wonders if casual gestures of two people talking on the street mean they are talking about *him*. Sylvia T. demonstrated ideas of reference when she wondered if her lighting of a cigarette caused her doctor to be paged.

These and similar experiences lead the patients into a state of *mystification*, as Ronald Laing[7] has termed it. Patients attempt to deal with this mystification in a number of ways. The intense preoccupation with meaning is an attempt to bring these experiences under intellectual control; for example, in "The Waste Land" by T. S. Eliot:[4]

> "My nerves are bad to-night. Yes, bad. Stay
> with me.
> "Speak to me. Why do you never speak? Speak.
> "What are you thinking of? What think-
> ing? What?
> "I never know what you are thinking. Think."

> I think we are in rats' alley
> Where the dead men lost their bones.

> "What is that noise?"
> The wind under the door.
> "What is that noise now? What is the wind
> doing?"

                Nothing again nothing.
                        "Do
        "You know nothing? Do you see nothing? Do
                    you remember
            "Nothing?"

   The intrusion into consciousness of forbidden impluses,
strange ideas, mystifying experiences, an awareness of a
sense of loss of meaning and of object relationships result in
attempts to defend against these phenomena. Many patients
become compulsive and engage in endless rituals while beset
with conflicts about destruction, dirt, sexuality, etc.: Vivian
L.'s and Naomi N.'s prodromal activity are cases in point.
Others, alarmed over their (imagined) omnipotent, destructive potential, become mute and catatonic. Others change
their body image, as did Naomi N. when she tore out her
eyebrows, or Elsie B. as her belly swelled in compliance with
her delusion about being pregnant.
   The reversal of the day-night activity cycle has been described. Night has traditionally been the time when evil
spirits come out; the crow of the cock signals the knell and
they return to the underworld. So it is for schizophrenic patients for whom the weakening band of repression of the ego
against the evil spirits of the unconscious is frightening:
one must maintain maximum vigilance against these evil
spirits at night, then, in the safety of daylight, relax the guard
and sleep.

Psychotic Stage
   These experiences come more and more to dominate the
patient's life. His utterances and behavior become highly determined by thoughts and fantasies largely unaffected by surrounding reality (autism), and there is a variable amount of
realization, depending on the level of surviving observing
ego, of his decompensation. Many patients at this stage will
explain that they think they are becoming insane, losing their
minds, having a nervous breakdown, and the like. By this

time, too, family members and friends have become aware of the changes. It is usually at this point that the patient presents himself, or is presented by the family, police, family doctor, etc. to a psychiatric facility. The psychosis is overt; the work of treatment is now at hand.

Section Two

PSYCHOLOGY, SOCIOLOGY, AND BIOLOGY

6

Psychological Tests

by EUGENE ZUKOWSKY, PH.D.*

INTRODUCTION

Psychological testing contributes to the understanding of the schizophrenias in two ways:

1. Major research findings using psychological tests in the study of the schizophrenic process by comparing groups of schizophrenics to other groups, e.g., the normals, the neurotics, the organics.
2. The individual schizophrenic process as seen in the clinical use of psychological tests.

Ideally, the reader should have some knowledge of what tests measure and how well they measure it. Such information would enhance the reader's perspective on the broader issues involved in psychological testing and increase his ability to evaluate critically both research and clinical uses of tests. For these evaluations, the reader is referred to Anastasi.[1]

This chapter will attempt to cover the above two dimensions of testing, confining discussion to the most widely used psychological tests in clinical practice and clinical research. The tests described in this chapter are single examples of wider categories of tests. (1) The Wechsler Adult Intelligence

---

* Dr. Zukowsky is Clinical Psychologist at the Palo Alto Veterans Administration Hospital and Clinical Assistant Professor in the Department of Psychiatry, Stanford University Medical School.

Scale (WAIS) is the most widely used individually administered test of intelligence. It samples a variety of behaviors pertinent to the schizophrenias as well as to intellectual functioning, such as memory, abstract ability, concentration, and attention. (2) The Minnesota Multiphasic Personality Inventory (MMPI) is a paper-and-pencil test of personality and, to date, the best among the empirically derived diagnostic inventories. (3) The Draw-A-Person test (DAP) and Bender Visual Motor Gestalt (BG) are widely used nonlanguage tests that investigate the projection of personality through the motor-expressive spheres. (4) The Rorschach and Thematic Apperception Test (TAT) are, together, the standard by which all projective tests are measured and are indispensable, if measured by usage alone, to the study not only of the schizophrenias but of personality in general.

The use of psychological tests in the description of the schizophrenias is rooted in two divergent trends in the history of psychological testing. Alfred Binet[12] published, in 1915, an objective test of intelligence measuring discrete mental factors. This effort, following the practices of the early European psychological laboratories, provided the impetus for the Mental Test movement in America. The WAIS and MMPI are examples of tests in current use related to this movement. Concurrently, the Swiss psychiatrist Hermann Rorschach[48] first described a diagnostic test of psychopathology based on the perception of ambiguously shaped inkblots. The former trend in testing finds its way into clinical use via the academic-research route. The latter trend, which began the movement in projective testing and personality assessment, became directly absorbed into clinical practice, although its acceptance among clinicians was delayed until the development of personality theory had been elaborated. The history of psychological testing in clinical and academic settings in America is well recorded by Sargent and Mayman[50] in the *American Handbook of Psychiatry*. Their chapter will offer the reader a good feel for the interplay of influence and critique between the clinical and research forces regarding the uses and abuses of psychological tests.

Psychological tests reflect samples of a person's behavior in a proscribed setting; these samples, by design, highlight limited aspects of human functioning. It follows from this intention that a battery of tests will be necessary to assess a wide scope of human functioning. For a study of the schizophrenias the breadth is particularly cogent, inasmuch as the degree of individual variability requires the examiner to assess the schizophrenic process in differing areas of functioning. It is not uncommon to observe, in a well-delineated paranoid process, the total intactness of the cognitive-intellectual spheres, and then, upon projective testing, to glimpse the subtle breakdown of logic that allows for the highly personalized premises on which a delusion is based.

PROJECTIVE TESTS

Projective techniques are the most widely used psychological tests in research and in clinical work with pathological groups. For this reason, a statement of the projective hypothesis, together with a brief overview of the major issues, will be presented. For a detailed survey and description of a wide variety of projective tests, see Anderson and Anderson.[2] For an excellent review of the theoretical foundations and the clinical use of projective tests, see Sargent.[49]

The statement of the projective hypothesis first came from Frank.[19] The hypothesis is related to psychoanalytic theory regarding identification, and not, as is often erroneously believed, with the concept of projection as a defense. It is assumed that, given a situation that has a minimal degree of structure, where both the stimuli and expectations (social set) remain ambiguous, people will react to these demands in ways congruent with their more enduring personality characteristics, styles of coping, problem-solving ability, and manner and efficiency of thought and/or perceptual organization. Thus a person's style of thinking and problem solving, his orientation to external events, his modes of coping with stress and imagination, etc. can be presumed to relate to predominant features of character makeup.

The psychological test literature of psychopathology and

clinical description has grown. Not only are there new styles
of personal, individual testing; there also are now available
vast amounts of test-response data from known groups. However, the basic assumptions underlying projective techniques,
as well as the reliability and validity of the tests themselves as
used in clinical practice, have come under critical scrutiny.[42, 58, 65] Masling,[32] for example, has demonstrated evidence
that the projective response is dependent on, and interrelated
with, a variety of situational variables. These include the
methods of administering the tests, the interaction between
the personality of the testor and testee, the subject's mood
and general attitude, and the setting in which the tests are
administered. In addition, lack of a consistent theoretical
foundation in both the test rationale and the interpretations
of responses based on them has increased doubts regarding
the validity of the basic assumptions of the projective hypothesis. As shall be seen, the use of projective tests with
the schizophrenias will be important because they reflect
language and thinking, cognitive organization, and fantasy.

In the next section we will explore more deeply the research and clinical findings pertinent to an understanding
of the schizophrenic process through psychological tests.

RESEARCH AND CLINICAL CONTRIBUTIONS

Perhaps the strongest criticism against research in the
schizophrenias is the amazing lack of clarity of sample characteristics. Many investigators see all schizophrenics as alike
and use widely divergent, heterogeneous samples. Rabin and
King,[43] in a thorough review of research results using psychological tests with schizophrenics, emphasize the need to reduce the heterogeneity of samples of schizophrenic patients.
They point out that potentially valuable findings may be
canceled out by combining results from divergent patient
groups.

To date, the two most clearly relevant dimensions on
which schizophrenic samples can be made more homogeneous are the related variables of acute-chronic and the more

etiologically tinged division of process and reactive schizophrenia. There is also some indication that the paranoid
schizophrenic should not be included with other subgroups.
In fact, there is, as yet, no clear evidence that division into
classical subgroups bears any relevance to an understanding
of the schizophrenias. The researcher will run into the most
serious difficulty in establishing sufficient reliability in his
efforts to separate schizophrenics into subgroups,[4] although
he will fare better using grosser classifications.[52]

The above limitations have been taken into consideration
in the description that follows of the clinical and research
contributions of specific psychological tests to an understanding of the schizophrenic process. The tests described are
rarely used singly for diagnosis in clinical practice. It is only
in research that the weight of each test is singly evaluated.

Wechsler Adult Intelligence Scale (WAIS)

The major purpose of the WAIS is to measure intellectual functioning (IQ). The test is organized into verbal and
performance tasks of six and five subtests, respectively. The
verbal subtests contribute information pertinent to memory
functions, abstract ability, concentration and attention, and
knowledge of word meanings. The performance subtests are,
generally, tasks related to perceptual-motor and concept
formation. All these factors contribute to global intelligence.
They also contribute information regarding the nature of the
schizophrenic process. More often than not, on these cognitive measures, people diagnosed as schizophrenic perform
differently, as a group, from other individuals. Examination
of subtest performance may reveal indications of a schizophrenic process through actual deficits in subtest performance or through stylistic or expressive behavior.

Perhaps with no other group have there been such consistent findings with the use of the WAIS. As a group, schizophrenics produce the greatest variation in scatter of scores
and response variability over subtests of any group tested.[42, 60]
Early research findings with the WAIS showed that

schizophrenics do poorest on subtests requiring active attention and energy output. Thus, generally, schizophrenics have
lower over-all performance subtest scores than verbal subtest
scores. However, the variability of scores between subtests
will be conspicuous, partly correlated with severity, and will
be more conspicuous between the verbal subtests than between the performance scores. Owing to the schizophrenic's
marked variability in intellectual performance, measures of
scatter or constellations of subtest scores have made diagnosis by these test signs unreliable. Rapaport[44] has considered
marked differences between a low similarities (abstract
ability) score and high vocabularly and information scores
as the only pathognomonic sign for schizophrenia on the
WAIS. Ostensibly, this finding relates to the loss of abstract
ability in the schizophrenic with fairly well-retained funds of
information and word usage, retentions that require less
active effort to use appropriately. There is doubt, however,
that the "loss of abstract attitude," as Kurt Goldstein once
described it, is a consistently important phenomenon in schizophrenia.[30]

Generally, the schizophrenic is expected to manifest impaired mental efficiency, particularly where effort (attention?
motivation?) is required. His thinking process will show
slowing and difficulty in shifting. He may tend to perseverate.
Perceptually, he has difficulty attending to relevant details
(picture-completion subtest), although this statement may
not hold for the overvigilant paranoid. As pointed out earlier,
scatter among subtests and patterns of performance are highly
variable. For this reason primarily, it is extremely difficult to
obtain significant differences in differential diagnoses; where
differences are found, they are not of sufficient magnitude to
be used diagnostically (or predictively) in the individual
case. With recognition of this limitation, Wechsler[61] developed a method of "successive sieves" to eliminate false posi-
tives and negatives; he successfully separated 60 normals
from 60 schizophrenics. The major difficulty in such separations has been differentiating different pathological groups,

e.g., organic vs. schizophrenic, or neurotic vs. schizophrenic, or differentiating subclassifications within one pathological group (catatonic vs. hebephrenic). In addition, WAIS findings point to a somewhat lower general level of intelligence in schizophrenic subjects than in nonpsychotic groups, though it is not apparent whether this finding precedes or merely reflects the schizophrenic process. Furthermore, it is not clear whether this finding is true of all schizophrenic groups or only, for example, the more chronic samples. This lack of clarity is one consequence of research with heterogeneous schizophrenic samples.

Language usage and certain stylistic performance features are important in the determination of individual cases of schizophrenia. Usually, deviant language usage will not be diagnostic unless repeated and blatant. However, schizophrenics frequently manifest "cognitive slippage." The frequency and blatancy of this slippage will ordinarily be related to severity and, consequently, to prognosis. However, intactness of intellectual functioning does not rule out the presence of a schizophrenic process. The intelligent, well-organized, stabilized paranoid patient may breeze through the WAIS. The person who disorganizes affectively, as opposed to cognitively, may go unrecognized. It is for this reason that a battery of tests is employed.

Deficits in reality testing ordinarily manifest themselves on performance items. The Block Designs subtest reflects this deficit when the subject reproduces a design with grave distortions from the original after a minimum of checking, and believes it to be correct. The organic subject may make the same mistake in outcome, but he will not think it correct. Rather, he will be unable to correct it. In addition, schizophrenic subjects may manifest highly blasé or apathetic attitudes. They may behave evasively in a passive manner (extreme slowness) or aggressively in either negativistic or impulsive-reckless styles. Personal styles are related to character structure, not to diagnostic group. They become diagnostic when extreme, the person being unable to exert controls over his behavior. (To see how the clinician uses intelligence testing in assessment, see Mayman, Schafer, and Rapaport.[34])

Draw-A-Person (DAP)

Drawings of the human figure were originally used as a nonverbal, culture-free test of intelligence. Although it is still used for this purpose, figure drawing is also used by the clinician as a projective test. The subject is asked to draw a figure of a person, the choice of sex, style, etc. being left to the subject. Often, after completion of both a male and female figure, the testor asks for a story about each figure, adding a dimension to this test that is similar to the Thematic Apperception Test. Machover[29] and Levy[27] have been instrumental in developing the projective possibilities of the DAP. They elaborated numerous dynamic rationales for certain characteristics of drawings. For example, the size of the drawings may relate to one's sense of importance. Placement of the figure on the page will reveal how outgoing or withdrawn a person is; drawings with buttons are thought of as suggestive of dependency; figures with no hands or stunted hands suggest early rejection.

In the schizophrenias, the DAP is useful regarding questions of body image, sexual identity, and ego boundaries. Schizophrenics often reveal fairly gross distortions in the figures and often draw nude figures. Machover, however, cautions that the drawing of nude figures is also true of people undergoing psychoanalysis where much libidinal material has been uncovered—there is an analogy there somewhere! Schizophrenics may draw transparent figures, i.e., figures with clothing that does not succeed in preventing a view of what lies behind the covering, or nude figures that reveal internal anatomy. Analogously, schizophrenics frequently perceive transparencies on the Rorschach, viewing internal anatomy through an ostensibly whole person. Schizophrenics may also depict clear separations between the head—the seat of reason and intelligence (ego control)—and the body—the seat of emotion and desire (instincts)—as though to portray graphically the split in affect and reasoning. Confused sexual identity or sexual preoccupation in the schizophrenias may occur in drawings of figures with mixed sexual characteristics, overelaboration of genitalia, figures in seductive postures, etc. Withdrawal of sexual interest, concomitant with a generalized withdrawal in the schizophrenias, is more common, and is manifested in bare outline drawings where the figures are both neuter and lifeless, as is shown in Figures 6–1 and 6–2. Needless to say, the variability in figure drawings of schizophrenics is extensive. The DAP becomes diagnostic when figures and/or stories associated with them are elaborated with obvious bizarreness or with gross distortions.

Swenson[56] noted in a recent literature review with the DAP that there was little supporting evidence for any of the

Figure 6-1. Drawing of a Male Figure by a 25-year-old Schizophrenic Male.

asumptions made concerning the interpretive significance of drawn characteristics. He was highly critical of its continued use as a clinical tool.

The Bender Visual Motor Gestalt (BG)

The Bender Gestalt adds the dimension of nonverbal, perceptual-motor behavior to already existing verbal-perceptual tests. Originally, this need was felt most acutely in the organic case; indeed, the test was primarily developed for, and used in, the diagnosis of organicity.[9] The Bender requires that the subject reproduce nine designs of increasing difficulty. These designs are similar to Wertheimer's original "Gestalt" figures. In a test for memory, the subject can be asked to reproduce the designs after copying them.

Hutt and Briskin[23] have elaborated the Bender Gestalt

Figure 6-2. Drawing of a Female Figure by a 25-year-old Schizophrenic Male.

Figure 6–3A. Bender Gestalt Test.

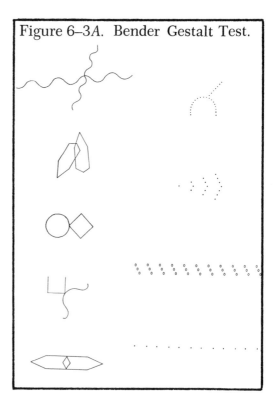

as a projective test, using the symbolic value of each design, with the subject's associations for interpretive meaning. The contributions of the Bender with schizophrenics lie in assessing judgment, ego control, planning ability, and reality testing. The schizophrenic displays poor judgment and planning ability by running designs into one another or off the page, by rotating designs, by markedly upset sequences of positioning each design on the page, by hugging one side of a page, or by using several pages to complete the figures. Poor ego controls are reflected in the subject's inability to copy designs in reasonable size—the schizophrenic may copy some designs in huge proportions (grandiosity) or in a tightly done, tiny size, as though to exert all available energy at controlling functions. Here there will ordinarily be concomitant signs of anxiety. Poor reality testing in the schizophrenic may become obvious when designs are reproduced in almost unrecognizable form or where the subject fails to check back to the design while continuing to distort his rendition. A blasé attitude is usually correlated with this behavior. Figure 6–3 is an example of Bender-Gestalt done by a middle-aged schizophrenic male. It includes rotations of the figures and several gross distortions.

Although much is said of attention difficulties in the schizophrenic, there is no evidence, on design recall, of differences between schizophrenics and other groups, with one exception, the organic. This finding is a function of poor recall in the organic, not the schizophrenic. Two literature reviews[11, 57] conclude that the most reliable function of the Bender is its ability to discriminate between groups of psychotics and normals, and psychotics and organics. It is used mainly as a test of "organicity," with fairly good reliability. Figure 6–4 is an example of an organic Bender. The lack of control over motor functioning is striking. For comparison with the standard designs, see Bender.[9] As with most tests, schizophrenics respond with more variability to the Bender Gestalt than do other groups. Because research with more discrete groups of schizophrenics is lacking, it is impossible to make sense out of this response variability.

Minnesota Multiphasic Personality Inventory (MMPI)

The MMPI consists of 556 items to be answered "true" or "false" if the subject believes the question applies or does not apply to him. Questions range over a multitude of possible feelings, beliefs, attitudes, symptoms, and experiences sufficiently discriminating of certain pathological groups, e.g., hysterics, depressives, schizophrenics, so that individuals tested will tend to answer the items characteristic of the pathological group that most closely fits their symptoms and

Figure 6-3. Bender-Gestalt by a Middle-aged Schizophrenic Male.

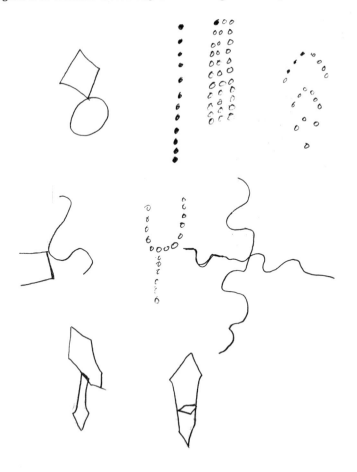

Figure 6-4. Bender-Gestalt by an Organic Patient.

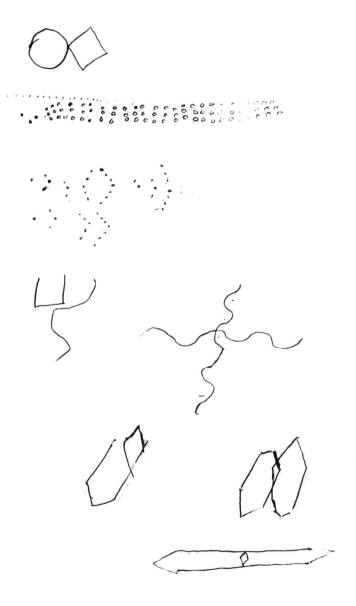

experiences. Hence, as is its purpose, the MMPI is designed as a diagnostic test.

By and large, the items that go to make up the Sc (schizophrenic) Scale are composed of questions reflecting presence of unusual or bizarre thoughts, feelings, and experiences and, secondly, social isolation and/or alienation. For example, ". . . Bad words, often terrible words, come into my mind and I cannot get rid of them." ". . . I often feel as if things were not real." ". . . Someone has it in for me."

Together with the Sc Scale, items measuring paranoia (pa) and psychesthenia (pt) make up the psychotic triad. The paranoia scale concerns itself with items reflecting suspiciousness, persecutions, ideas of reference or grandiose self-concepts, varying degrees of sensitivity to others, and rigidity of opinions and attitudes.[21] The psychesthenic scale includes items reflecting compulsions, obsessions, phobias, indecision, self-doubt, excessive worry, lethargy, and anxiety. Generally, items that make up the psychotic triad follow closely the usual descriptions of a schizophrenic process by the observations called for in initial screening interviews.

In clinical practice, the MMPI has been used extensively as a diagnostic tool to screen for the presence or absence of psychosis, as well as to make firmer diagnostic discriminations. Recently, Marks and Seeman[31] have published descriptions of "the abnormal personality" based on actuarial findings of MMPI data. Their Atlas describes 16 empirically derived classes of personality configurations of adult psychiatric patients. Data for this atlas were collected from over 1,200 male and female psychiatric patients from a medical center. In addition to diagnostic information the work includes actuarial probabilities on familial configurations, prognostic probabilities, educational background, and a variety of other pertinent variables. In discussing the complexity of developing the schizophrenia scale that ". . . more research was devoted to [than] to any of the other clinical scales . . . ," Marks and Seeman point out that even with the introduction of a correction factor (k), which improved the scale, the detection rate for 50 criterion cases could not be improved beyond 60 percent. In addition, noting the complexity inherent in characterizing schizophrenia, clinically or actuarially, the authors point to incongruity of affect and thought content, and fractionation of the thought process as the only consistent features characterizing the schizophrenic process.

A compendium on the MMPI by Welsh and Dahlstrom reports several studies that attest to the ability of the MMPI to differentiate reliably betweeen groups of psychotics and normal patients (Meehl, Schmidt), and between psychotic and neurotic patients (Gough, Guthrie).[62] However, two reports (Benton, Modlin) offer contradictory evidence on the ability of the MMPI to differentiate reliably and diagnose in the individual case, and Meehl concluded that, although discriminations were made at better than chance, the proportion of misclassifications was considerable.

The advantages of the MMPI over other tests in clinical use, particularly the projective tests, are (1) in a brief time, with a minimum of effort, one is able to distinguish, with fairly high probability, a schizophrenic from a nonschizophrenic; (2) prognostic statements can be made with a high degree of assurance; and (3) there is sufficient evidence for the validity of MMPI descriptive interpretations of personality.[28,31]

Rorschach

There has been no more widely used and researched psychological test than the Rorschach. Its essence, however, remains elusive. Dynamic psychologists swear by it and, despite depressing research results, "know" that within its subtle, seemingly unmeasurable intricacies lie possibilities for valid psychological knowledge.

The test consists of ten inkblot designs, some all black, some all color, some mixed. The subject is given minimal structure, being told only to give his immediate associations to each blot. He further is told that there are no correct or incorrect answers and that he therefore cannot fail the test (imagine trying to tell *that* to an active psychotic in a psychiatric setting!). After giving associations to the ten cards, the examiner goes over all responses to determine where they were seen and which cues determined the perceptions (form, shading, color).

Hermann Rorschach's original work[48] was an attempt to study pathological groups through perception. In conceptualizing the schizophrenias, he was influenced by Bleuler's descriptions of the language and thought processes of the schizophrenic. As we shall see below, it is likely that in the realm of language and thoughts, i.e., communication, the Rorschach will make its greatest contribution.

Owing to the immense variability in responses of schizophrenics, it has been difficult to apply any single Rorschach criterion, pattern of responses, or pathognomonic signs to identify schizophrenics with sufficient validity. The clinician, working with the individual, will utilize as many cues as he can get from the test responses, from test behavior, and from his own elusive and subjective impressions of the subject. The ease of diagnosis, i.e., the degree of assurance placed in labeling a person schizophrenic, will, in large part, be related to the degree of obviousness of the cues; and this degree, in turn, is very likely related to severity. Thus, in those instances where there are the fewest, most ambiguous clues, if in fact a schizophrenic disorder exists, it will (a) be most difficult to diagnose accurately and (b) likely reflect an either impending, but not yet severe, disorder, or, as often happens, reflect an essentially "burned-out" schizophrenic process. In either situation, information from extra-Rorschach sources will be required.

The principal Rorschach indicators of schizophrenia have been described by Schafer[51] and others.[13, 45] The diagnosis of schizophrenia is not indicated by any one type of characterological picture, as with hysteria, for example. Schizophrenia is not a personality or character type. Diagnosis is based on an appraisal of Rorschach responses relevant to the quality of reality testing, effectiveness of interpersonal communication, and appropriateness and degree of affective output.

Effective reality testing is assessed through the form-level score. This score reflects the subject's ability to match the quality of what he sees with the more recognizable formal properties of the blot. Commonly used form-rating systems grossly distinguish between good and poor form.[25] More elaborate form-rating systems have been developed that are able to differentiate finer gradations of form perception.[33] Schizophrenics may reveal highly amorphous and vague form perception, e.g., "clouds," "water," "color," suggestive of a more chronic disorder (assuming the presence of other indicators), or form may be perceived in absurd ways, e.g., "a spider" to a portion of a blot with no apparent appendages. Usually, intactness of form level is positively correlated with less severe disturbances and with good prognosis.[39, 40, 41] High form-level ratings are more typical of the reactive schizophrenic, the converse being true of the process schizophrenic.[7, 18, 66]

Affective intactness and emotional lability are reflected on the Rorschach by the balance between color and shading responses to form. As a general rule, the more the form dominates over a perceived color response, the greater one's control over emotionality. No color perception or no form indicates emotional sterility and extreme inhibition; excessive use of color indicates impulsivity, and extreme emotional volatility. With schizophrenics, particularly in acutely florid states, one is likely to obtain a massing of pure color responses, uncontrolled and modified by form perception. In less disturbed states color will dominate over form in the response process, but formal properties will not be absent. Color naming is common to burnt-out, chronic schizophrenics. The content of color responses is an important clinical dimension. The use of pleasant colors, e.g., rainbows, sunsets, are usually not malignant (they may, however, be associated with hysteria). Color responses such as "yellow urine," "bloody mess," or generally gory use of color are usually malignant. Weak or vapid colors, e.g., grey or muddy brown, may suggest a blunting of affect.

Generally, color use will suggest a degree of intactness of controls over emotional expression. Where controls are poor, the possibility of volatile behavior increases. There is no indication from the Rorschach that schizophrenics display any greater degree of volatile emotionality than other groups. Volatility is related more to particular stages in the schizophrenic process (catatonic excitement) or, as likely, to external situational events.

The perception of shading is thought to correlate with emotional sensitivity and the ability to be aware of nuances of emotional meanings. Absence of shading responses, common to the schizophrenic, reflects withdrawal and experiences typical of persons who have been burnt early in life. Contrary to the myth, the schizophrenic does not reveal himself, on this dimension, to be supersensitive to subtle nuances of feeling.

Indicators of loosening social controls are in the frequent increase of sex responses. Orme,[38] for example, found that in a sample of more than 1,000 Rorschachs of mixed diagnoses, there were twice as many sex responses in the records of schizophrenics. Sex responses for the schizophrenic are manifest not only in the perception of genitalia, but often in perceptions of the sex act itself or in confabulations, e.g., "Two women with their vaginas together."

Reflections of intellectual or cognitive disruption and fragmentation are seen, in part, in irregular sequences of perception. Whereas most people proceed rather regularly from wholes to parts, or, conversely, from parts to wholes on the Rorschach, the fragmented, confused person will often reveal an overly irregular pattern, or select highly unusual locations for his perceptions.

The most telling manifestation of a schizophrenic process on the Rorschach, as well as on all other verbal tests, is the prevalence of disruptions in thinking. As Benjamin[10] has stated, ". . . Almost all the typically schizophrenic Rorschach characteristics, those which permit blind diagnosis to be made without necessarily referring to the content of the answers, are in the field of 'thinking'. . . ." Several attempts at investigating and classifying deviations in thinking (Watkins and Stauffscher,[59] Benjamin,[10] Kataguchi,[24] Holt,[22] and Zukowsky[66]) have found increased severity of thought disorder in the process schizophrenic, a finding that tends to confirm the early speculations of Benjamin and increases the usefulness of the process-reaction distinction. Rorschach examples of deviant verbalization, which jar one's sense of communicational integrity, will vary from the subtle, where the gap in reasoning is easily filled in by the examiner and thus seems coherent, e.g., "This must be Paris; here's the Eiffel Tower," through peculiar statements, e.g., "a magnified fly eye," contaminations, e.g., "a rabbit hand" (combining two contiguous areas), queer verbalizations, e.g., "a transverse cut of a sore," to the frankly bizarre, autistic, confused, or incoherent responses. Degree of severity of thought disorder has been found to have an inverse relationship with prognosis.[20, 39]

In differential diagnosis with the Rorschach, agreements are fairly clear regarding what factors will reliably discriminate between the normal and the schizophrenic (naturally, any test must be able to discriminate between extremes). Application of the following ten signs, if several signs are present and are of sufficient intensity, will ordinarily diagnose the schizophrenic.

These signs are generally agreed on by the "experts":[6, 25, 46, 48]

1. A confused sequence of approach. This reflects the generally confused, often scattered, inefficient cognitive functioning that differentiates the normal, sequential, recognized, organizational patterns of nonpsychotics.
2. Presence of confabulated or autistic responses, revealing the clearly deviant, illogical thinking patterns of schizophrenics that will, seemingly arbitrarily, combine contiguous percepts into a relationship having idiosyncratic meaning at the expense of consensual logic.
3. Low or absent human movement (M) or unduly high M,

usually found in paranoids. The ability to perceive human movement, conceived of as requiring the highest degree of perceptual differentiation and the ability to empathize with others, is either lacking in the schizophrenic or overly employed in the hypervigilant paranoid who is looking for external cues to respond to defensively. The interpersonal withdrawal of the schizophrenic becomes manifest, through the Rorschach, in his not seeing people.

4. Low percentage of good form responses. Quality of form responses attest to one's reality-testing ability and degree of perceptual differentiation. Previous research by Becker[7] and Fine and Zimet[18] discuss these deviancies from a developmental perspective, and relate them to the process-reactive dichotomy.

5. Very low percentage of popular responses, particularly if coupled with unique and/or bizarre original responses. The ability to perceive the more common, popularly conceived percepts on the Rorschach is also related to reality-testing ability.

6. Presence of thought blocking. In more "dilapidated" or frankly paranoid subjects, thought blocking will occur.

7. Positional responses—responses determined not by the percept but by its position in the blot, e.g., "This is the North Pole, because it's at the top." This is a variation of autistic logic, and although relatively rare, is a significantly deviant response.

8. Presence of personal references—representing a "loss of distance" between the subject and the card.

9. Perseveration—this is also found in organics but the more bizarre quality or style of expression of the schizophrenic will usually differentiate them.

10. Card or color description—representing too much "distance" from the card.

The "sign" approach to differential diagnosis with the Rorschach when used alone has, to repeat, not been satisfactory.

When attempting to diagnose the paranoid schizophrenic with the Rorschach, the clinician might use several factors. He will be attuned to heightened vigilance and guardedness, often manifested by low, unproductive responsivity, blocking and/or conscious inhibition of responses. It will not be infrequent to have this subject perceive tiny details, unusual views, masks or "eyes." Generally, the diagnosis of paranoid schizophrenia with the Rorschach is difficult, particularly where well systematized delusions are present. The paranoid, depending on his degree of intactness, will present a good façade and this façade will be reflected in the Rorschach. Dubrin[16] tested the hypothesis that the paranoid will perceive "eyes" more frequently than will nonparanoids; he achieved results significant at the 0.001 level in favor of the hypothesis. Through tests of the theoretical notion of the dynamics of homosexuality in paranoid schizophrenia it was found, with the use of Wheeler's Rorschach indices of homosexuality,[63] that the paranoid manifests a significantly greater incidence of these signs.[3, 14] Some of these research efforts suffer from lack of adequate sample procedures.

The work of Singer and Wynne[53, 54, 55, 64] with schizophrenics and their families marks a recent advance in the application of the Rorschach (and TAT) as tools toward the discovery of communication patterns and styles. Their work uses projective techniques as stimuli for the analysis of expressive communicational styles rather than as tools for the application of the projective hypothesis in the interpretation of dynamic structures of personality. Singer and Wynne[53, 54, 55] have described styles of thinking and communicating into categories of (1) amorphous, (2) mixed amorphous-fragmented, (3) fragmented, (4) stably constricted. In the blind, it has been possible to match, with excellent success, the Rorschach responses of the patients and those of their families.[53, 55] In addition, Rorschach analysis of communicational style has been effective in differentiating the language of the schizophrenic from the language of the neurotic, a task that has heretofore been difficult to accomplish.[53]

Thematic Apperception Test (TAT)

The Thematic Apperception Test has preserved its original function as a test of personality through explorations of fantasy.[35, 36] The Rorschach and the TAT together are the most popular clinical tests, although the TAT is not noted for its ability to diagnose or describe specific pathological groups.

The TAT is composed of 20 cards varying in degrees of structure, but usually containing at least one discernible person or figure, often two in interaction with each other. The cards are specified for use with either male or female subjects, and some cards are used for both. Generally, the pictures are set up to elicit certain themes, such as loneliness, competition, depression, sexuality, and, with the more ambiguous cards, more "purely" projected fantasies. There is even a blank card used most often with highly imaginative people. The task is to have the subject tell a story about each picture, what led to the current action seen, what the people are feeling, and, finally, how the story will end. Because of the story-telling nature of this task, interpretive possibilities expand beyond the content.

As Bellak notes,[8] incipient schizophrenic disturbances, for which the TAT is most suitable, become apparent in sentence structure, bizarreness of themes, projected fears, helplessness of hero, which is suggestive of limited ego strength, and lack of emotional warmth or feeling dead inside. As with the Rorschach, a schizophrenic process becomes manifest in TAT stories through expressive style in thought and language. Schafer[51] has extensively elaborated on the emergence of a schizophrenic process in TAT responses. He cites, in addition to Bellak:

1. Overelaborate symbolism dealing with the meaning of life and death.
2. Overly abstracted religious themes, e.g., virtue, sin, guilt, etc.
3. Blatantly expressed socially unacceptable content, e.g., incest, homosexuality.

4. Themes expressing wishes of withdrawal and insulation from the world.
5. Delusionlike content often in the form of themes of magical influence or unnatural power.
6. Disjointedness in the communication of meaning and/or affect.
7. Arbitrary or irrelevant story content in relation to the pictured stimulus.
8. Gross distortions of the human figures.
9. Peculiar verbalizations, cryptic explanations, vague generalizations, nonsequitors, autistic logic, and omission of ideas necessary for story coherence and continuity.

The paranoid will often infer or allude to the motives of the subject's actions, be overcautious in elaborating his story, and vague or evasive in specifying details. For example, a subject responds to a card with

> *Subject:* "This is a fellow of the age of tender years, . . . looking out the window trying to figure out his conclusions . . . his conclusion is that he may succeed in his purpose."
> *Examiner:* "What is his purpose?"
> *Subject:* "His purpose is to reach his conclusion for a definite decision which he thinks is correct."[45, p. 453]

The Examiner discontinues questions in agitated frustration, an internal state that may itself be diagnostic!

Murstein[37] has amply pointed out the limitations of the TAT in predicting individual behavior and in differentiating nosological groups. In clinical work, it is rarely, in this author's experience, that the TAT is used singly as a diagnostic test, whether for determining a schizophrenic process or a neurotic process. Most often it is useful in obtaining information regarding a subject's interpersonal strengths and weaknesses, the fantasy quality of interpersonal relationships, and prevailing mood, particularly as related to expres-

sions of hostility. Balkan[5] and Davison,[15] however, were able
to elicit differences between schizophrenics and normal persons along the dimension of formal language characteristics,
and Ritter and Eron[47] found greater variation and deviations
in thematic material, and wider variations in emotional tone
among schizophrenics than among nonschizophrenics. On
the other hand, Eron[17] determined that the frequencies of
themes and identifications in the stories of schizophrenics
and nonhopsitalized college students were more a function of
the stimulus properties of the TAT cards and not related to
specific disturbances of the subject. Again, lack of sample
specification severely limits the usefulness of these studies.

SUMMARY

In an extensive literature review on psychological deficit
in schizophrenia, Lang and Buss[26] conclude that the data
support deficits in the higher organizational processes; i.e.,
schizophrenics have difficulty focusing on relevant stimuli,
maintaining adequate attention, shifting sets when necessary, excluding irrelevant stimuli, and generally performing
efficiently. These findings have been amply demonstrated, at
various levels, through the most commonly used diagnostic
psychological tests. With shifting theoretical interest in cog-
nitive-ego functions replacing the older "id" or conflict emphasis, there is a discernible trend toward appreciating these
phenomena more abundantly. Manifestations of schizophrenia as a process seen in psychological tests as elsewhere
are now being more thoroughly viewed as deficiencies in the
cognitive sphere. However, the long-recognized deficits in
communicational ability of the schizophrenic has consistently
been so obvious as to have been too long taken for granted.
For if there is anything that psychological tests demonstrate
consistently it is that disturbances in language and thought
remain the *sine qua non* of schizophrenia. A return to investigations of communicational styles of discrete pathological
groups via projective tests, with the innovative addition of
expanding style to include familial communicative style, has

given rise to some provocative implications. In addition to reinforcing the view that in verbal expression lies the most hopeful possibility for diagnosing the schizophrenic, etiological significance is given to the early language development of the preschizophrenic. Further, serious doubt is thrown on the long-established notion of a continuum of mental disorder, with schizophrenia being the extreme pathological end of the continuum.

7

The Families

INTRODUCTION

Since the early 1950s, a number of investigators have studied the (1) *communication patterns and transaction styles,* (2) *role structures and relationships,* and (3) *familial psychopathology* of the family members of schizophrenic patients. Though obviously these areas overlap, I will present them separately for purposes of exposition.*

In a review article, Mishler and Waxler[19] have compared and contrasted the major studies. They point out that, because these investigations took place from varying vantage points, the theories cannot always be directly compared; i.e., the theories show ". . . a level of similarity equivalent to asserting the similarity of Van Gogh, Monet, and Andrew Wyeth because they have all painted landscapes." Nevertheless, at those points where the various theories articulate, the

---

* The richness of the information gathered from the family studies described in this chapter led many therapists to use family therapy—treatment of the entire family as a single unit—in an attempt to help their schizophrenic patients. After the original burst of enthusiasm for family therapy in schizophrenia died down, a more sober view of the effectiveness of this treatment appeared. Though there are those who still are optimistic about its usefulness, many do not share this optimism. Even as well-known a pioneer in the field as the late Don Jackson became dubious about the ultimate importance of family therapy as a major form of treatment in the schizophrenias.[15] For this reason, there will not be any extensive discussion of family therapy in this book, though the interested reader may, of course, turn to relevant publications, of which some of the best known are the journal, *Family Process,*[13] and books by Ackerman[1] and Böszörményi-Nagy.[9]

findings tend to be mutually confirming, and where they do not, the findings tend to be parallel and congruent.

The studies share the characteristic that they are cross-sectional in time and do not antedate the illness; i.e., the families studied already contained a schizophrenic member. Thus abnormal findings may reflect a disturbance engendered by, rather than predating, the event of a family's having to live with a schizophrenic member in its midst. Though this criticism cannot be definitively dealt with in the absence of prospective studies,[21] the great preponderance of evidence suggests that parental psychopathology is deeply ingrained in basic character structure (indeed, arose in childhood in reaction to the parents' parents), and thus long preceded the illness in the primary patient.[2, 16]

COMMUNICATION PATTERNS

In a study of communication patterns derived from a theory of logical types in which the specific content of the communications is irrelevant, Bateson, Jackson, Haley, and Weakland[7] proposed the well-known "double-bind" theory of schizophrenia. They employed the concepts of differing levels of communication, primary communication, and metacommunication (a communication about the communication). The metacommunication might either be congruent or incongruent with the primary communication. For example, when two people meet, and one says "Good morning" to the other in a friendly tone, the communication, the words, and the metacommunication, the tone of voice, are congruent. However, if it had been a gruff tone, the metacommunication would have been incongruent, and the recipient would probably have commented to himself on the incongruity with the thought, "He's hung over again, the old sot," or something of the kind.

The authors point out further that the metacommunication frequently affords a definition of the nature of the relationship between the two parties, be it friendship, anger, domination, love, etc.

In a review article, Watzlawick[27] again points out that

there are initially five necessary ingredients for a double bind. This reminder is needed, considering how often the concept has been misused. The five ingredients are these: (1) two or more persons; (2) repeated experience; (3) a primary negative injunction (that is, a primary communication), which may have either of two forms, (a) "Do not do so-and-so, or I will punish you," or (b) "If you do not do so-and-so, I will punish you"; (4) a secondary injunction (metacommunication), conflicting with the first at a more abstract level, and like the first enforced by punishments or signals that threaten survival; this secondary injunction is frequently nonverbal; (5) a tertiary negative injunction prohibiting the victim from escaping from the field. Ultimately, when the victim has learned to perceive his universe in double-bind patterns, the complete set of ingredients is no longer necessary.

An observation of Bateson's[7] may serve as an example.

> A young man who had fairly well recovered from an acute schizophrenic episode was visited in the hospital by his mother. He was glad to see her and impulsively put his arm around her shoulders, whereupon she stiffened. He withdrew his arm, and she asked, "Don't you love me any more?" He then blushed, and she said, "Dear, you must not be so easily embarrassed and afraid of your feelings."

In this example, the mother's primary communication was her visit to her son. Her incongruent metacommunication was the stiffening, the nonverbal announcement of her inability to tolerate a spontaneous affectionate gesture from her son. Her tertiary communication was the question, "Don't you love me any more?" obviously incongruent with the previous two communications. The messages were delivered in such a way that it would have taken a person with a good deal more ego strength and presence of mind than her son to be able to comment to himself or to her on the discrepancy in the messages. Neither father nor therapist was quick enough to intervene before the bewildering effect of the interaction had made its mark on the patient, and he suffered a serious relapse afterward.

When one says "Good morning" in a gruff tone, there is no inherent injunction against, or difficulty in, perceiving the incongruities; therefore it does not fulfill the necessary qualifications of being a double-bind situation. Unfortunately, in recent years many authors have referred to this latter kind of situation as a double-bind; to do so is a gross misapplication of the concept.

The authors propose that the frequency and intensity of double-bind interactions are significantly greater in the family of the schizophrenic than in other families, and that these interactions interfere with the capacity of the recipient to discriminate messages. The possible reality-testing and relationship statements that the messages may contain are misperceived; thus do the double-bind interactions predispose to a disorder in reality testing and interpersonal relations, namely, schizophrenia.

TRANSACTION STYLES

Whereas Bateson *et al.* proposed a structure in which the specific content was largely irrelevant, except to establish congruence (or its lack) in communication, Singer and Wynne[25] have examined not only content but what happens to it, in transactions with family members of schizophrenic patients. Their data came from both clinical interviews and psychological test materials.

Analysis of these transcripts shows that parents of schizophrenics, compared with transcripts of control groups of parents of adolescents or young adults showing conditions other than schizophrenia (e.g., borderline characters, severe obsessional neuroses, chronic physical illnesses), reliably and significantly demonstrate defects in maintaining sets of meaning and attention. Families of schizophrenics have difficulty describing and communicating percepts; they have difficulty bringing transactions with the tester to satisfying closure. Raters working "blind" on such transcripts have been able to differentiate reliably the following groups of parents: parents of young adult schizophrenics, those of childhood schizophrenics, and those of childhood neurotics.[26]

A potential weakness in this kind of research has been that of sociocultural influences on cognitive transaction styles. The lower socioeconomic classes have been traditionally ill at ease and somewhat inept in handling sophisticated verbal tasks. Might not this fact influence some of the findings as a contaminant? In a study recently reported by Rosenthal and Behrens,[22] family Rorschach techniques were used with three kinds of lower-class families, namely, families of white schizophrenics, families of Negro schizophrenics, and Negro control families. Raters were able to differentiate the families of schizophrenics from the Negro controls at a level of significance of $p < .001$, demonstrating that lower-class communication patterns are not themselves per se related to the existence of schizophrenia in a family.

Wynne and Singer[24, 28] emphasize that the family must be seen as a small system, a unique subculture, existing in the milieu of the community. The family members thus have ongoing, patterned, recurrent, and reciprocal relationships with one another: the whole of the family is greater than the sum of the (member) parts.

There are at least four important levels of transaction that are impaired or deviant in the families of schizophrenics: (1) styles of communication; (2) styles of relating; (3) prevailing affect and mood; and (4) total family organization.[25]

STYLES OF COMMUNICATING

The manner in which the families entered into a cognitive task, such as taking a Rorschach or Thematic Appercaption Test, and were able to share the foci of attention and meaning of the test with one another and with the tester revealed major difficulties for the families of schizophrenics but not for the control groups.[24]

First, the families of schizophrenics had "closure problems." They had difficulty defining a percept and bringing the definition to such closure that the tester had a reasonably clear idea what the subject had seen. Particularly, the protocols contained speech fragments, unintelligible remarks, unstable percepts, gross indefiniteness, etc.

Second, they showed disruptive behavior. The most frequent kind of disruptions listed by Singer are these: interruptions of examiner's speeches; extraneous questions and remarks; odd, tangential, inappropriate remarks; humor; swearing; references to "they" and to the intent of others.

Third, these families demonstrated peculiar language and logic. Singer notes that ordinary words or phrases were used oddly or out of context, that sentence construction was odd, quaint, or private; there were many slips of the tongue and mispronunciations of words. Similarly, there were illogical combinations of percepts and categories, contaminations, and nonsequitur reasoning.

Finally, these families had difficulties making their percepts easily visualizable to the tester. Where a control parent might say, "This is a furry bat; here is its head; here are its wings," the parent of a schizophrenic might say, "This sort of looks like a bat, somehow, or figures created by this ink, or something like that."

In Chapter 4 there was considerable discussion of the need to induce cognitive order in one's perceptions and to strive after meaning, and, further, the need to learn how to think and conceptualize. It is especially important to be able to organize the data pertaining to one's own functioning as a feeling human being living with others. It was noted there that the labeling and identification processes are highly dependent on parental definition during the first several years of life.

To judge by the difficulties in styles of communication described above, it appears that, from the very beginning, children raised in these families have defective instruction in how to organize their percepts of the world, themselves, and their families. That some of them should later suffer from a condition, schizophrenia, in which poor reality testing is a cardinal feature is not surprising!

ROLE STRUCTURES AND RELATIONSHIPS

The family is a unique social system. Each family develops its own internal norms and standards; sometimes these are explicit and are discussed; more frequently, they tend to be implicit and sensed by the family members as the "givens" of their existences. These standards tend to define the roles played by each of the family members, e.g., "the baby," "the stern father," "the weepy mother," etc. In most families these roles evolve and develop over the years and reflect the growth, maturity, illness, independence, etc. of the various members. The family norms influence both what behavior and language is permissible or not permissible for a given member *within* the family and also how much and how many of the influences in the surrounding community *outside* the family are allowed to enter. In a sense, the family is a cell, and the cell wall will vary in permeability from family to family, and from time to time within the same family, with respect to how much exchange there will be with the surrounding community. Each family develops homeostasis, a set of (often implicit and unwitting) maneuvers to deal with disruption of relationships and bring them back to an approximation of their previous state, just as a thermostat responds to disruptions in room temperature.

Many investigators in the United States and Europe have studied the role structures and relationships in the families of schizophrenic patients and have compared them to similar data from normal families and families where an adolescent or young adult has some chronic, nonschizophrenic psychiatric or medical problem. Each group of workers has noted serious abnormalities in the kinds of role relationships in the families of schizophrenics. Though each group has evolved its own descriptive terms for these abnormalities, the points of similarity in their findings are many, and the points of contradiction few, if any. Many of the original findings during the 1950s were independent of one another; there was relatively little communication between the groups at Bethesda (Wynne *et al.*, Bowen *et al.*), Yale (Lidz *et al.*), and Palo Alto (Jackson *et al.*). Yet when these workers had developed their findings sufficiently to be ready to communicate them to the others, they found a good deal of agreement and congruence.

Wynne *et al.*[30] employ the concept of "pseudo-mutuality" to describe their findings. The authors differentiate between "mutual," "nonmutual," and "pseudomutual" relationships. In mutual relationships, there are genuine reciprocity and concern for the growth and well-being of the other person. In nonmutual encounters, such as buying toothpaste at the drugstore, there is neither the expectation nor the pretense of more than a highly superficial concern for each party's well-being. In pseudomutual relationships, there is the outward appearance of genuine mutuality, but on closer examination the unwitting constraints each member of the family puts on the behavior and growth of the others are remarkable.

In characterizing pseudomutuality, the authors say at one point, "We are emphasizing a predominant absorption in fitting together, at the expense of the differentiation of the identities of the persons in the relationship." At another point, "In pseudo-mutuality, emotional investment is directed more toward maintaining the *sense* of reciprocal fulfillment of expectations than toward accurately perceiving changing expectations."

Wynne's group noted that the potential for introduction of corrective experiences from the surrounding community is severely reduced for the member of the family who has become schizophrenic (and it would appear that this state of affairs had been true for a long time). When the adolescent sought to leave the psychological confines of the family, its boundary maintaining subsystem would come into action and create an impassable barrier. Wynne's group comments, ". . . the family role structure is seen as all encompassing . . . this continuous but elastic bounding we have called the 'rubber fence.'"

The parents in these families seem unconsciously to

have decided upon either (1) a particularly rigid set of role expectations for each member, a set of roles that does not allow for normal maturation, growth, and life changes in any of the members; or (2) on a startling refusal to allow anyone in the family to establish a clear role for himself that includes a natural contribution of his own abilities, talents, needs, and interests. In one such family, the question, "Who runs the family?" was answered jocularly, "The cook." Behind the joke lay a sad inability in that family for anyone to be openly identified as the leader.

> *Example:* In the L. family it was obvious that Vivian had been regarded from birth onward as a sweet, angelic creature, showing only sexless loving and obedience to the family. During the early stages of her psychosis, she stayed up nights cleaning the kitchen and bathroom compulsively, muttering something about poisons. The parents interpreted this behavior as evidence of her concern for cleanliness and found it difficult to see it as disturbed behavior.
>
> Later, during therapeutic work with the family, if ever Vivian said or acted anything that had sexual overtones to it, the family would either ignore it or ask the therapists, "Doctors, why is she behaving that way? Is it her illness, or is it some drugs you doctors are giving her?" Sexuality conflicted with the role prescribed for Vivian, and evidences to the contrary were reinterpreted as coming from outside sources: the demons of her illness or experimental drugs.

Ryckoff, Day, and Wynne[23] also comment on the rigidity of roles in the families of schizophrenics. They point out that these roles are grossly condensed, stereotyped, and oversimplified; that deviation from rigid family organization is not permitted; that any attempts to modify roles meets with powerful repressive forces. They state, "These factors lead to the establishment of a family legend or myth, in the maintenance of which each family member makes an anxious investment. . . . [This] can seriously interfere with the individual's identity, and lead to an 'identity crisis,' to use Erickson's term, of psychotic proportions."

Lidz *et al.*[16] studied several upper middle-class families. They point out how the role relationships between the parents themselves are frequently quite distorted in the families of schizophrenics. None of the marriages seemed normal or healthy; all were marked by a significant degree of *marital schism* or *marital skew*; the characteristics of these two states are summarized in Table 7–1.[16] Whether skewed or schismatic, Lidz's families demonstrated family-wide deficits in perceiving social reality. They report:

TABLE 7–1[16]

CHARACTERISTICS OF MARITAL SCHISM AND MARITAL SKEW ADAPTED FROM LIDZ

Marital Schism	*Marital Skew*
Each spouse caught up in own problems; prevailing sense of desperation; "emotional divorce";* no mutual support; covert coercion; postponement of coming to grips with marital problems; malignant undercutting of worth of one or both partners in the childrens' eyes; mistrust of each other's motives, sometimes bordering on the paranoid. Fathers often narcissistic, grandiose, deny incestuous preoccupations with daughters in paranoid manner.	Serious psychopathology of one partner dominates the home; unhappiness of one spouse may be apparent to the other and children, thus eliciting complementary, supporting behavior from the other; or, distorted ideas of one are shared by the other, thus creating a *folie à deux* or *folie en famille*. Fathers generally weak and ineffectual (especially if offspring is male), went along with delusions of schizophrenic wife or seemed outwardly strong because of wife's masochistic support; psychopathology that pervaded the home was masked and treated as normal.

* Term coined by Murray Bowen.

The parents' delimitation of the environment, and their perception of events to suit their needs, result in a strange family atmosphere into which the children must fit themselves and suit this dominant need or feel unwanted. Often the children must obliterate their own needs to support the defenses of the parent whom they need. They live in a Procrustean environment, in which events are distorted to fit the mold. The world as the child should come to perceive or feel it is denied. Their conceptualizations of the environment are neither instrumental in affording consistent understanding and mastery of events, feelings, or persons, nor in line with what persons in other families experience. Facts are constantly being altered to suit emotionally determined needs. The acceptance of mutually contradictory experience requires paralogical thinking. The environment affords training in irrationality.

The families of female schizophrenic patients tended to be highly schismatic, with the mothers being quite insecure, defeated, and devalued. Though the mothers were attentive to their daughters and tried to be maternal, their efforts were impeded by their unhappiness and insecurity; and the mothers therefore could not serve as healthy models for identification for the daughters. The fathers were nearly uniformly highly narcissistic; several of them were grandiose or overtly paranoid. They held the mothers up as inadequate and turned to the daughters for the kind of feminine attention they felt the wives were unable to give. The fathers' combination of seductiveness and paranoid denial of incestuous interest in the daughters provided a role conflict for the daughters from which escape was impossible without rejection of one parent or the other—a role that seemed, therefore, to fulfill the conditions of the double bind.

> *Example:* In the L. family during one family therapy session, the only vacant seat was next to father. Vivian chose instead to sit on the floor. Father got out of his chair and sat next to her, explaining that he was doing this to show her how ridiculous it was for a grown girl to be sitting on the floor. He stroked her arm as he talked. After a few minutes, Vivian said, "Please don't touch me like that, Daddy; it's like petting." The father immediately broke into an intense and lengthy harangue on the topic of love, telling Vivian how a father's love for a daughter was different from a husband's love for a wife was different from a soldier's love for his country, etc., etc.
>
> In this interaction, he had clearly turned toward Vivian in a seductive fashion (he had on other occasions said, "Vivian isn't close to my heart; she's part of it") but had to deny in a grandiose and paranoid manner the incestuous overtones of his approach when Vivian commented on them openly.

The families of the male schizophrenics in Lidz's study tended to be more skewed than schismatic. The mothers were dominant; they maintained symbiotic and erotic relationships with their sons. The fathers provided poor models of masculinity for their sons. The fathers were described as unusually passive, alcoholic, psychotic, or distant from the family. They tended to be less aggressive than the fathers of the schizophrenic daughters. The fathers of schizophrenic sons tended to be passively seductive with their sons. Thus the sons experienced great difficulty in resolving the original symbiotic-erotic closeness with the mother that should take place before and during the oedipal period.

Brodey,[11] reporting on observations of five families that had been studied intensively for several years, also reports on the stereotyped and rigid role structure for the patient and his family. He says:

The family drama is unlike the modern theatre. It is more like the morality play of medieval times. Actors take allegorical role positions that are sterotyped and confined—one is Good; another, Evil; a third, Temptation. Though the interpretations of these roles are rigidly ritualized and limited, still the play has an impelling quality which tends to drive the audience into complete involvement, sharing with the actors in forgetting the complexities of life, perceiving only in terms of Good or Evil, Power or Helplessness, Omnipotence or Infantilism, and losing entirely the breadth of perspective, shading, and sense of impinging reality which are a usual part of everyday life.

In an exhaustive and detailed study of the families of 15 male and 15 female schizophrenic patients compared to the families of 30 neurotic patients, Alanen and colleagues[2] confirm many of Lidz's findings and add several more.

First they examined the integration of the family for healthiness, schism, or skew, as shown in Table 7–2.[3]

TABLE 7–2

MARITAL HEALTH, SCHISM OR SKEW

		Families of Schizophrenics	Families of Neurotics
Well-integrated Marriage	N =	2	19
Marital schism	N =	14	4
Marital skew	N =	7	1
Other	N =	7	6

From Alanen.[3]

The remaining families showed disturbed relationships that did not fit well into any category. Among the schismatic families of schizophrenics, there were more female patients than male; the ratio was reversed for the skewed families.

These authors also distinguished between those families

of schizophrenic patients that were *chaotic* or *rigid,* parameters that cut across the lines of *schism* and *skew,* with the findings presented in Table 7-3.[4]

TABLE 7–3

COMPARISON OF CHAOTIC AND RIGID FAMILIES

Chaotic (N = 10 of 30)	*Rigid (N = 11 of 30)*
A. "Parents' inability to draw distinct boundaries between their own and the patient's self."	A. "A parent frequently experienced the child as an object in his possession." Parents free of psychotic traits were schizoid, obsessional, and impervious.
B. Male patients, N = 7 Female patients, N = 3	B. Male patients, N = 4 Female patients, N = 7
C. More chaotic families were *skewed* than *schismatic.*	C. More rigid families were *schismatic* than *skewed.*
D. Chaotic familes more highly associated with poor outcome of illness.	D. Rigid families more highly associated with better outcome of illness, "progressive symbiosis; parent does not 'desert' the patient in hospital as frequently."

From Alanen.[4]

Of the remaining nine families, six showed signs of being both chaotic and rigid; three showed signs of neither trait.

Alanen examined traits and behaviors of the mothers and fathers with regard to their schizophrenic sons or daughters. For male schizophrenic patients, he found that the mothers were frequently lacking self-boundaries, were possessive, and anxiously overprotective; the fathers were often passive and possessive. For the female schizophrenic patients, the mothers often were possessive and inimical; the fathers were possessive and passive. Thus certain *combina-*

tions of parental traits seemed more highly associated with schizophrenia in the offspring, and these traits varied, depending on the sex of the patient. The most frequently found combinations are shown in Table 7–4.

TABLE 7–4

COMBINATIONS OF FATHER AND MOTHER TRAITS IN
MALE AND FEMALE SCHIZOPHRENIC PATIENTS

Male Patients

Combination	Father	Mother
1	Passive or missing . . . . .with	. . . Dominating* (without self-boundaries; sometimes "inimical")
2	Inimical . . . . with	. . . Dominating[a]
3	Pathogenic domination . . . with of son (homosexual) proclivities and intrusiveness)	. . . Submissive, emotionally constricted

Female Patients

Combination	Father	Mother
1	Stimulates anxious and . . . with ambivalent feelings of closeness in daughter (often narcissistic and paranoid possessiveness)	. . . "Inimical"; cold to both father and daughter, thus push them toward each other
2	Lost at early age . . . . . with	. . . Inimical or rejective
3	(not described) . . . . . .with	. . . Pathogenically possessive; inimical to daughter's independence, especially heterosexual interests

* Generally, possessive mothers had a masculine identification; were inhibited in their femininity, which led therefore to a prolonged, symbiotic dependency and diminished masculine identity for the son.
From Alanen.[2]

Garmezy and Rodnick[12] report a study that is doubly useful in that it not only gives information about parental-role behavior but has important implications for further research. Using the Scale of Premorbid Adjustment empirically derived by Phillips,[20] these authors separated a group of clinically similar patients into two subgroups: those whose premorbid adjustment was good, and those whose premorbid adjustment was poor. They then administered a number of psychological tests to both these groups and to normal subjects. The major findings are displayed in Table 7–5.[12]

The findings suggest that the group with poor premorbid adjustment ("poors") were markedly more sensitive to maternal dominance and criticism than were the "goods" or "normals." Furthermore, the "poors'" perceptions were borne out in a structured-interview situation: their mothers *were* more dominant. The authors point out carefully that many of these differences would have washed out if the results for the entire group of schizophrenic patients had been commingled rather than separated by premorbid adjustment. Much of the variability of their population disappeared when the "poor-good" distinction was maintained: in essence the authors were working with two relatively homogeneous subgroups. These findings reinforce the need to keep the "process-reactive" distinction always in mind in future research.

These findings have implications, also, for the well-known variability of schizophrenic populations on various research parameters, including impressionistic reports of the "schizophrenogenic mother." It would seem that the "schizophrenogenic mother," if there is one, is more likely to be found for *male* patients with poor premorbid adjustment, those who would most likely be termed "process schizophrenics." It would also be the families of these patients who would most likely demonstrate marital *skew* rather than *schism*, and they would tend to be *chaotic* rather than *rigid* (Alanen). In both Garmezy's and Lidz's work, the mother was the dominant member of the skewed marriage; the patients were sons. It would be interesting to see if the families of *female* patients with poor premorbid adjustment were also skewed, but with the father dominant.

TABLE 7–5
TEST PERFORMANCE BY MALE CHRONIC SCHIZOPHRENIC PATIENTS WITH GOOD AND POOR PREMORBID ADJUSTMENT COMPARED TO NORMAL CONTROLS

RESULTS

	Schizophrenic Patient Groups by Premorbid Adjustment		
TESTS	*Poor*	*Good*	*Normal*
1. Visual Discrimination Scenes			
Whipping, Feeding, Object.	←——— No Differences ———→		
Scolding.	Disturbed Response	Normal Response	Normal Response
2. Verbal Learning Tests, Measured by Reminiscence Effects			
Reward Conditions	←——— Non-Discriminatory ———→		
Punishment Conditions	Significantly Higher Than Others	Insignificantly Higher Than Others	Normal
3. Size Estimation of Mother-Son Pictures	Markedly Overestimated	Moderately Under-estimated	Slightly Under-estimated
4. Structured Interview with Parents: Verbal Dominance Scores Plotted Graphically			

Parental Dominance

Father Dominant   1—
                                Goods
                      5—

                      0—   Normals

Mother Dominant   5—   Poors
                      1—

Adapted from Garmezy and Rodnick.[12]

Yi-Chuang Lu [17, 18] has studied parents of schizophrenics and their psychotic and nonpsychotic offspring to see what aspects of family-role structure either predispose toward, or protect against, illness. She finds that the birth of the pre-schizophrenic had special meaning to the family; the result was an intense focusing of attention on his playing a special role, with consequent assistance to the nonschizophrenic sibling in avoiding such a role. The role was characterized by contradictory parental expectations of the child, coupled with his persistent effort to fulfill them.

In examining the relations of the mother and child in particular, Lu finds that the preschizophrenic, in contrast to his sibling, was highly restricted from meaningful contacts outside the family (the "rubber fence" again), there were excessive symbiotic concern with the feelings of other family members, greater exercise of maternal authority and domination of social behavior, and persistent instillation of the mother's high expectations for achievement and perfection. Such tendencies are shown in two examples:

> The mother said, "Is it better for kids to have many friends? That's a big question. I don't think a kid should have many friends. I told Eugene [the patient] it was better for him to keep to himself and not to play with those kids."
>
> (*Mother speaking*): "I told his teacher I wanted him to become an engineer. He must be ambitious. . . . I want my son to be the best. But he can't, because he was not born in this country. . . . I want my boy 100 percent but 75 percent is good too. But Eugene is not even 50 percent."

Lu points out also that the schizophrenic child "had been much more submissive and dependent on his mother," whereas, "in contrast, the nonschizophrenic sibling was reported to be much more independent of his mother."

Haley[14] examines the manner in which family role structure affects leadership and decision making in the families of schizophrenics. Explicit leadership often is denied; the mother tends to initiate while acting as though she isn't; the father will invite her to initiate and them condemn her when she does. Ultimately, "the family 'just happens' to take actions in particular directions with no individual accepting the label as the one responsible for the action." Similarly, family members find it difficult to form alliances with one another; attempts at forming a two-against-one alliance in a three-person family break down rapidly. Yet there is a family-wide "prohibition on intimate alliances of one member with someone outside the family. As a result, the family members are inhibited from learning to relate to people with different behavior and so are confined to their own system of interaction."

FAMILIAL PSYCHOPATHOLOGY

Several investigators have reported that the incidence of psychiatric illness (both psychotic and nonpsychotic) is higher among the family members of schizophrenics than it is in neurotic or control groups. Whether these findings are attributed to heredity or environment, or combinations of both, will be discussed at greater length in Chapters 9, 10, and 11; what is relevant here is that the findings are generally well accepted.

In Alanen's study[5] the degree of disturbance in parents and siblings of the schizophrenic patients was compared with that of the neurotic patients; the data are presented in Table 7–6.

Alanen[6] also looked for similarities and differences in the psychopathology of his 30 schizophrenic patients and their families. There were no instances of *folie à deux* or *folie en famille*. In five cases there was striking similarity of the index patient's psychotic symptoms to a parental psychosis; in nine cases one parent was borderline or psychotic, but the symptoms did not resemble those of the patient to any great extent. The families with pronounced gross psycho-

TABLE 7–6

DEGREE OF PSYCHIATRIC DISTURBANCE IN THE PARENTS
AND SIBLINGS OF SCHIZOPHRENIC AND
NEUROTIC PATIENTS

Type of Disturbance	Parents, Numbers Affected	
	Schizophrenic (N=60)	Neurotic (N=60)
Overt schizophrenia	4	0
Borderline schizophrenia or paranoid psychoses	12	0
Affective psychoses	3	1
Severe neuroses (obsessive-compulsive; gravely schizoid characters)	26	0
Moderately psychoneurotic	12	25
Normal	1	18
No information; presumably no conspicuous psychopathology	1	16

	Siblings, Numbers Affected	
	Schizophrenic (N=49)	Neurotic (N=49)
Overt schizophrenia	4	0
Borderline psychotic features or schizoid	6	0
Psychopathic personalities	"A few"	0
Psychoneurosis	11	Several
Normal	18	"More than half"

From Alanen.[5]

pathology differed in organization and structure from those
with little psychopathology; he presents these data as follows:

> *Much Psychopathology:* Index patient has
> many schizophrenic relatives, "the learning of
> psychotic and irrational thought and behavior
> patterns in an atmosphere permeated by them,
> appeared to be the predominant environmental
> transmission mechanism . . . corresponds to the
> 'chaotic' families."
> *Little Psychopathology:* Where the index

patient usually had no schizophrenic family
members or relatives, [the family] was characterized by rigidly dominating parents who
tried to tie their children to themselves symbiotically and were inimical toward the children's attempts to achieve independence, "these
correspond to the 'rigid' families."[2]

Lidz and his colleagues[16] have commented on the gross
psychopathology frequently seen in the members of the
families of schizophrenics. In a paper, "The Transmission of
Irrationality," they report a high incidence of irrational,
paralogical, and bizarre thinking in the parents of their patients. Though none of these parents had ever been hospitalized for mental illness, excessive degrees of scattered thinking,
confusion, paranoia, and bizarre behavior were present in at
least 60 percent of the families. Many of the fathers maintained successful social façades at business, yet displayed
pervasive paranoid belief systems in the family. Because the
definition of reality for the preschool child is almost entirely
up to the parents, and because these families have in many
instances eliminated the possible mediating influences of
the external world (the "rubber fence"), the children of these
families grow up in an environment of irrationality and have
little opportunity for the corrective experiences from the outside. The authors state:

> . . . persons who grow up in such families,
> having had their symbolic roots nourished by
> irrationality in the family, are less confined by
> the restrictions of the demands of reality when
> means of escape and withdrawal are required.

Developing a suggestion of Lidz's, Rosenbaum[21] states
that the qualities of disordered thinking and interpersonal
relationships that have been described for the individual
schizophrenic have recognizable counterparts in the family.
These include qualities described by Bleuler[8] and others. He

cites a transcription in which there is familial loosening of associations and concrete thinking.

> *Example:* The implied subjects in the following transcript of a therapy session with Vivian L.'s family are, in order: Father feeling tense at home; Father stays up too late; Mother doesn't know when Father goes to bed; Father is a slug-a-bed; Daughter is a slug-a-bed; Mother is the only one in the family with a sense of responsibility; Mother's waking up Daughter is unnecessary; Mother gives Daughter dope; Who gives Daughter crazy ideas? Who may actually be giving her dope? In only 50 seconds, the implied subject changes ten times, a change closely akin to the bewildering loosening of associations of the schizophrenic patient.
>
> *Father:* . . . This morning I was just shaking. I was sitting out there a while ago. I could just feel my nerves getting shaky, jittery.
>
> *Mother:* You don't know how to relax. You were up last night till 12:30 before you even went to sleep. I know. In and out on the back porch.
>
> *Father:* It wasn't that late.
>
> *Mother:* And in the mornings, I can't get you up.
>
> *Father:* I went to bed around 11:00. (Here the father's attempt to communicate his feelings of tension around his wife and daughters has quickly developed into a disagreement about what concrete hour he went to bed on a particular night.)
>
> *Mother:* And the same way about Vivian (their 18-year-old psychotic daughter). I could never get her up. Even though I nagged at her. It was my responsibility to get her to school. She wouldn't get up.
>
> *Vivian:* Whether you came up there didn't make much difference to me, because I knew

> what I was going to do when I first got up.
> (*Three people talk at once.*) The night before
> if you give me something that didn't make me
> get up, well, now, I can't help it.
>   *Mother:* What do you always say somebody
> gives you something for? I'd like to know where
> you get that idea.
>   *Vivian:* (*Bitterly*) You aren't kidding. I've
> got too much already.
>   *Mother:* Who gives . . . ? (*Vivian inter-*
> *rupts.*)

In a like manner he gives examples of family-wide ambivalence, autistic thinking and detachment from reality, a
defect in attention, delusions, and fragmentation of personality. At the level of interpersonal transactions he gives examples of confusion and distortion of motivation; handling
of painful affects by denial, magical thinking, and picayune
correction of grammar; conversations rich in inanities and
nonsequiturs; martyred invitations for abuse; and personal
estrangements.

Rosenbaum discusses some implications of these findings.[21] One implication is that, for the schizophrenic, the *form*
and *content* of his schizophrenic symptoms are learned
phenomena; that one of the learned *uses* of the illness is to
hold the world at one remove, and that this learning has taken
place in the family. The reason that these families persist in
such stereotyped behavior may be that they unconsciously
perceive their interpersonal relations as being so fragile and
tenuous that they must go to tragic extremes to avoid the unconsciously anticipated horror of utter unrelatedness.

The result, of course, is that the opportunities for serial
differentiation and separation of self from family, followed
by greater internal psychic integration, are lost; the necessary
developmental task of developing a sense of self is severely
impeded.

Life in these families has a quality reminiscent of André
Breton's essay on surrealism:[10]

> The world is only very relatively approximate to thought. . . . This summer the roses are blue, the wood is made of grass. The earth wrapped in its foliage makes as little effect on me as a ghost. Living and ceasing to live are imaginary solutions. Existence is elsewhere. . . .

SUMMARY

Since the early 1950s, families of schizophrenic patients have been studied for their communication patterns and transaction styles, their role structures and relationships, and their psychopathology.

Communication patterns are marked by double binds, in which a series of incongruent messages, each on a different level of abstraction, makes it difficult for the recipient to understand and respond. Interpersonal transactions are marked by difficulties in sharing foci of meaning and attention, in obtaining closure, and in avoiding disruptive and peculiar verbal behavior in taking psychological tests.

Role structures and relationships tended either to be remarkably rigid or quite chaotic. The rigid relationships have been termed "pseudo-mutual," and the maintenance of pseudomutuality in the face of possible corrective experience in the community is aided by the "rubber fence." Marriages in these families were marked by schism or skew; few, if any, seemed to be healthy or normal. Certain specific pairings of mothers and fathers were related to the degree of illness in the patient, depending on the patient's sex. Parental expectations for the patient were more contradictory than those for his nonschizophrenic siblings.

Gross psychopathology was predominant in the families of the schizophrenic patients, much less rarely seen in control families. In fact, many of the primary aspects of schizophrenia as Bleuler described it in the individual patients have recognizable counterparts in the family; such things as familial loosening of associations, ambivalence, autism, and delusions, among others, were frequently seen.

8

Social Class and Schizophrenia

by MELVIN L. KOHN, Ph.D.*

My intent in this chapter is to review a rather large and all-too-inexact body of research on the relationship of social class to schizophrenia, to see what it adds up to and what implications it has for etiology. Instead of reviewing the studies one by one, I shall talk to general issues and bring in whatever studies are most relevant. It hardly need be stressed that my way of selecting these issues and my evaluation of the studies represent only one person's view of the field and would not necesarily be agreed to by others.†

* Dr. Kohn is chief, Laboratory of Socio-environmental Studies, National Institute of Mental Health, Bethesda, Maryland.

† The *raison d'être* of this review, aside from its being momentarily current, is in its effort to organize the evidence around certain central issues and to make use of all studies relevant to those issues. There are no definite studies in this field, but most of them contribute something to our knowledge when placed in perspective of all the others. For an alternative approach, deliberately limited to those few studies that meet the reviewers' standards of adequacy, see Mishler and Scotch (70). Dunham has recently argued for a more radical alternative; he disputes the legitimacy of using epidemiological data to make the types of social psychological inference I attempt here and insists that epidemiological studies are relevant only to the study of how social systems function. This seems to me to be altogether arbitrary. But see Dunham (17) and (18). Some other useful reviews and discussions of issues in this field are: Dunham (19); Felix and Bowers (28); Dunham (20); Clausen (6); Clausen (7); Clausen (8); Hollingshead (39); Dunham (22); and Sanua (88). The present review leans heavily on my earlier paper, "On the social epidemiology of schizophrenia," *Acta Sociologica* 9, 209–21 (1966), but is more complete in its coverage and represents—for

Before I get to the main issues, I should like to make five prefatory comments:

1. When I speak of schizophrenia, I shall generally be using that term in the broad sense in which it is usually employed in the United States, rather than the more limited sense used in much of Europe. I follow American rather than European usage, not because I think it superior, but because it is the usage that has been employed in so much of the relevant research. Any comparative discussion must necessarily employ the more inclusive, even if the cruder, term.

2. I shall generally not be able to distinguish among various types of schizophrenia, for the data rarely enable one to do so. This is most unfortunate; one should certainly want to consider "process" and "reactive" types of disturbance separately, to distinguish between paranoid and non-paranoid, and to take account of several other possibly critical distinctions.

Worse yet, I shall at times have to rely on data about an even broader and vaguer category than schizophrenia—severe mental illness in general, excluding only the demonstrably organic. The excuse for this is that since the epidemiological findings for severe mental illness seem to parallel those for schizophrenia alone, it would be a shame to ignore the several important studies that have been addressed to the larger category. I shall, however, rely on these studies as sparingly as possible and stress studies that focus on schizophrenia.

3. Social classes will be defined as aggregates of individuals who occupy broadly similar positions in the hierarchy of power, privilege and prestige[104]. In dealing with the research literature, I shall treat occupational position (or occupational position as weighted somewhat by education) as a serviceable index of social class for urban society. I shall not make any distinction, since the data hardly permit my doing so, between the concepts "social class" and "socio-economic status." And I shall not hesitate to rely on less than fully

---

all its similarities to the earlier paper—a thorough reassessment of the field.

adequate indices of class when relevant investigations have employed them.

4. I want to mention only in passing the broadly comparative studies designed to examine the idea that mental disorder in general, and schizophrenia in particular, are products of civilization, or of urban life, or of highly complex social structure. There have been a number of important studies of presumably less complex societies that all seem to indicate that the magnitude of mental disorder in these societies is of roughly the same order as that in highly urbanized, Western societies. I refer you, for example, to Lin's study in Taiwan, the Leightons' in Nova Scotia[42, 60, 63], Leighton and Lambo's in Nigeria, and Eaton and Weil's of the Hutterites.* For a historical perspective within urban, Western society, Goldhamer and Marshall's study in Massachusetts[34] is the most relevant; it indicates that the increasing urbanization of Massachusetts over a period of 100 years did not result in any increase in rates of functional psychosis, except possibly for the elderly.

These data are hardly precise enough to be definitive, but they lead one to turn his attention away from the general hypothesis that there are sizeable differences in rates of mental disorder between simpler and more complex social structures, to look instead at differences within particular social structures, where the evidence is far more intriguing. I do not argue that there are no differences in rates of schizophrenia among societies, only that the data in hand are not sufficient to demonstrate them.† We have more abundant data on intra-societal variations.

---

* Eaton and Weil's volume (24) includes a valuable comparison of rates of psychosis in a variety of different cultures, from an arctic fishing village in Norway to Baltimore, Maryland, to Thuringia to Formosa to Williamson County, Tennessee. It must be noted that although Eaton and Weil find the rate of functional psychosis among the Hutterites to be roughly comparable to that for other societies, they find the rate of schizophrenia to be low (and that for manic-depressive psychosis to be correspondingly high). There is, however, reason to doubt the validity of their differential diagnosis of schizophrenia and manic-depressive psychosis.
† For further documentation of this point, see also Mishler and Scotch (70); Dunham (17); Demerath (14).

5. One final prefatory note. Much of what I shall do in this paper will be to raise doubts and come to highly tentative conclusions from inadequate evidence. This is worth doing because we know so little and the problem is so pressing. Genetics does not seem to provide a sufficient explanation. And, I take it from Kety's critical review, biochemical and physiological hypotheses have thus far failed to stand the test of careful experimentation[47]. Of all the social variables that have been studied, those related to social class have yielded the most provocative results. Thus, inadequate as the following data are, they must be taken seriously.

It must be emphasized, however, that there are exceedingly difficult problems in interpreting the data that I am about to review. The indices are suspect, the direction of causality is debatable, the possibility that one or another alternative interpretation makes more sense than the one I should like to draw is very real indeed. These problems will all be taken up shortly; first, though, I should like to lay out the positive evidence for a meaningful relationship between class and schizophrenia.

SOCIAL CLASS AND RATES OF SCHIZOPHRENIA

Most of the important epidemiological studies of schizophrenia can be viewed as attempts to resolve problems of interpretation posed by the pioneer studies, Faris and Dunham's ecological study of rates of schizophrenia for the various areas of Chicago[27] and Clark's study of rates of schizophrenia at various occupational levels in that same city.[4] Their findings were essentially as follows:

Faris and Dunham:

The highest rates of first hospital admission for schizophrenia are in the central city areas of lowest socio-economic status, with diminishing rates as one moves toward higher-status peripheral areas.†

---

* Some of the principal recent studies that bear on this point are: Rosenthal (86); Tienari (100); and Kringlen (54); Kringlen (55); and Kringlen (56).

† The pattern is most marked for paranoid schizophrenia, least so for catatonic, which tends to concentrate in the foreign-born slum com-

Clark:

The highest rates of schizophrenia are for the lowest status occupations, with diminishing rates as one goes to higher status occupations.

The concentration of high rates of mental disorder, particularly of schizophrenia, in the central city areas* of lowest socio-economic status has been confirmed in a number of American cities—Providence, Rhode Island; Peoria, Illinois; Kansas City, Missouri; St. Louis, Missouri; Milwaukee, Wisconsin; Omaha, Nebraska; Worcester, Massachusetts; Rochester, New York; and Baltimore, Maryland[13, 27, 31, 32, 48, 90]. The two ecological studies done in European cities—Sundby and Nyhus's study of Oslo, Norway[98] and Hare's of Bristol, England[37]—are in substantial agreement, too.

The concentration of high rates of mental disorder, particularly of schizophrenia, in the lowest status occupations has been confirmed again and again. The studies conducted by Hollingshead and Redlich in New Haven, Connecticut[40], and by Srole and his associates in midtown, New York City[94], are well-known examples; a multitude of other investigations in the United States have come to the same conclusion.†
Moreover, Svalastoga's re-analysis of Strömgren's data for

---

munities (27). Unfortunately, subsequent studies in smaller cities dealt with too few cases to examine the distribution of separable types of schizophrenia as carefully as did Faris and Dunham.

* There are some especially difficult problems in interpreting the ecological findings, which I shall not discuss here because most of the later and crucial evidence comes from other modes of research. The problems inherent in interpreting ecological studies are discussed in Robinson (84) and in Clausen and Kohn (9).

† See, for example, Locke with Kramer *et al.* (68); Frumkin (29); Dunham (17); Lemkau with Tietze and Cooper (65); Fuson (30); Turner and Wagonfeld (102). Relevant, too, are some early studies whose full significance was not appreciated until later. See, for example, Nolan (74); Ødegaard (75); Green (35). One puzzling partial-exception comes from Jaco's study of Texas. He finds the highest incidence of schizophrenia among the unemployed, but otherwise a strange, perhaps curvilinear relationship of occupational status to incidence. Perhaps it is only that so many of his patients were classified as unemployed (rather than according to their pre-illness occupational status) that the overall picture is distorted. See Jaco (43) and (44).

northern Denmark is consistent[99], as are the Leightons' data for "Stirling County," Nova Scotia[63], Ødegaard's for Norway[77], Brooke's for England and Wales[72], Stein's for two sections of London[96], Lin's for Taiwan[67], Steinbäck and Achté's for Helsinki[97].

But there are some exceptions. Clausen and I happened across the first, when we discovered that for Hagerstown, Maryland, there was no discernible relationship between either occupation or the social status of the area and rates of schizophrenia.* On a reexamination of past studies, we discovered a curious thing: the larger the city, the stronger the correlation between rates of schizophrenia and these indices of social class. In the metropolis of Chicago, the correlation is large, and the relationship is linear: the lower the social status, the higher the rates. In cities of 100,000 to 500,000 (or perhaps more), the correlation is smaller and not so linear: it is more a matter of a concentration of cases in the lowest socio-economic strata, with not so much variation among higher strata. When you get down to a city as small as Hagerstown—36,000—the correlation disappears.

Subsequent studies in a number of different places have confirmed our generalization. Sundby and Nyhus[98], for example, showed that Oslo, Norway, manifests the typical pattern for cities of its half-million size: a high concentration in the lowest social stratum, little variation above. Hollingshead and Redlich's data on new admissions for schizophrenia from New Haven, Connecticut, show that pattern, too[40].

There is substantial evidence, too, for our conclusion

* In Clausen and Kohn's paper (10), the data on occupational rates were incompletely reported. Although we divided the population into four occupational classes, based on U.S. Census categories, we presented the actual rates for only the highest and lowest classes, leading some readers to conclude, erroneously, that we had divided the population into only two occupational classes. In fact, the average annual rates of first hospital admission for schizophrenia, per 100,000 population aged 15–64, were: (a) professional, technical, managerial, officials, and proprietors: 21–3; (b) clerical and sales personnel: 23–8; (c) craftsmen, foremen, and kindred workers: 10–7; (d) operatives, service workers, and laborers: 21–7. Our measures of occupational mobility, to be discussed later, were based on movement among the same four categories.

that socio-economic differentials disappear in areas of small population. The Leightons found that although rates of mental disorder do correlate with socio-economic status for "Stirling County," Nova Scotia, as a whole, they do not for the small (population 3000) community of "Bristol"[63, 64]. Similarly, Buck, Wanklin, and Hobbs[3] in an ecological analysis of Western Ontario, found a high rank correlation between median wage and county first admission rates for mental disorder for counties of 10,000 or more population, but a much smaller correlation for counties of smaller population. And Hagnell[36] found no relationship between his admittedly inexact measures of socio-economic status and rates of mental disorder for the largely rural area of southwestern Sweden that he investigated.

I think one must conclude that the relationship of socio-economic status to schizophrenia has been demonstrated only for urban populations. Even for urban populations, a linear relationship of socio-economic status to rates of schizophrenia has been demonstrated only for the largest metropolises. The evidence, though, that there is an unusually high rate of schizophrenia in the lowest socio-economic strata of urban communities seems to me to be nothing less than overwhelming. The proper interpretation why this is so, however, is not so unequivocal.

DIRECTION OF CAUSALITY

One major issue in interpretating the Faris and Dunham, the Clark, and all subsequent investigations concerns the direction of causality. Rates of schizophrenia in the lowest socio-economic strata could be disproportionately high either because conditions of life in those strata are somehow conducive to the development of schizophrenia, or because people from higher social strata who become schizophrenic suffer a decline in status. Or, of course, it could be some of both. Discussions of this issue have conventionally gone under the rubric of the "drift hypothesis," although far more is involved.

The drift hypothesis was first raised as an attempt to explain away the Faris and Dunham findings. The argument was that in the course of their developing illness, schizophrenics tend to "drift" into lower status areas of the city. It is not that more cases of schizophrenia are "produced" in these areas, but that schizophrenics who are produced elsewhere end up at the bottom of the heap by the time they are hospitalized, and thus are counted as having come from the bottom of the heap.

When the Clark study appeared, the hypothesis was easily enlarged to include "drift" from higher to lower-status occupations. In its broadest formulation, the drift hypothesis asserts that high rates of schizophrenia in the lowest social strata come about because people from higher classes who become schizophrenic suffer a decline in social position as a consequence of their illness. In some versions of the hypothesis, it is further suggested that schizophrenics from smaller locales tend to migrate to the lowest status areas and occupations of large metropolises; this would result in an exaggeration of rates there and a corresponding underestimation of rates for the place and class from which they come.

Incidentally, the drift hypothesis is but one variant of a more general hypothesis that any differences in rates of schizophrenia are the result of social selection—that various social categories show high rates because people already predisposed to schizophrenia gravitate into those categories. This has long been argued by Ødegaard, but with data that are equally amenable to social selection and social causation interpretations[76]. Dunham has recently made the same point, but I think his data argue more convincingly for social causation than for social selection[17]. Intriguing though the issue is, it is presently unresolvable; so it would be better to focus on the more specific question, whether or not the high concentration of schizophrenia in the lowest socio-economic strata is the result of downward drift.

One approach to this problem has been to study the histories of social mobility of schizophrenics. Unfortunately, the

evidence is inconsistent. Three studies indicate that schizophrenics have been downwardly mobile in occupational
status,* three others that they have not been.† Some of these
studies do not compare the experiences of the schizophrenics
to those of normal persons from comparable social backgrounds. Those that do are nevertheless inconclusive—either
because the comparison group was not well chosen, or because
the city in which the study was done does not have a concentration of schizophrenia in the lowest social class. Since no
study is definitive, any assessment must be based on a subjective weighing of the strengths and weaknesses of them all. My
assessment is that the weight of this evidence clearly indicates
either that schizophrenics have been no more downwardly
mobile (in fact, no less upwardly mobile) than other people
from the same social backgrounds, or at minimum, that the
degree of downward mobility is insufficient to explain the
high concentration of schizophrenia in the lowest socio-
economic strata.

There is another and more direct way of looking at the
question, however, and from this perspective the question is
still unresolved. The reformulated question focuses on the
social class origins of schizophrenics; it asks whether the
occupations of fathers of schizophrenics are concentrated in
the lowest social strata. If they are, that is clear evidence in
favor of the hypothesis that lower class status is conducive

* Evidence that schizophrenics have been downwardly mobile in *occupational* status has been presented in Schwartz (93); Lystad (69);
Turner and Wagonfeld (102). In addition, there has been some debatable
evidence that the ecological concentration of schizophrenia has resulted
from the migration of unattached men into the high-rate areas of the
city. See Gerard and Houston (32); Hare (38); Dunham (17). (Dunham's
data, however, show that when rates are properly computed, rate-
differentials bewteeen high- and low-rate areas of Detroit are just as great
for the stable population as for in-migrants.)
† Evidence that schizophrenics have not been downwardly mobile in occupational status is presented in Hollingshead and Redlich (40) and (41);
Clausen and Kohn (10); and Dunham (17) and (21). Evidence that the
ecological concentration of schizophrenia has not resulted from in-
migration or downward drift is presented in Lapouse with Monk and
Terris (58); Hollingshead and Redlich (41); and, as noted in the preceding note, Dunham (17).

to schizophrenia. If they are not, class might still matter for schizophrenia—it might be a matter of stress experienced by lower class adults, rather than of the experience of being born and raised in the lower class—but certainly the explanation that would require the fewest assumptions would be the dirft hypothesis.

The first major study to evaluate the evidence from this perspective argued strongly in favor of lower class origins being conducive to mental disorder, although perhaps not to schizophrenia in particular. Srole and his associates found, in their study of midtown New York, that rates of mental disorder correlate nearly as well with their parents' socio-economic status as with the subjects' own socio-economic status.[94] But then Goldberg and Morrison found that although the occupations of male schizophrenic patients admitted to hospitals in England and Wales show the usual concentration of cases in the lowest social class, their fathers' occupations do not[33]. Since this study dealt with schizophrenia, the new evidence seemed more directly in point. One might quarrel with some aspects of this study—the index of social class is debatable, for example, and data are lacking for 25% of the originally drawn sample—but this is much too good a study to be taken lightly. Nor can one conclude that the situation in England and Wales is different from that in the United States, for Dunham reports that two segments of Detroit show a similar picture[21, 23, 83].

There is yet one more study to be considered, however, and this the most important one of all, for it offers the most complete data about class origins, mobility, and the eventual class position of schizophrenics. Turner and Wagonfeld, in a study of Monroe County (Rochester), New York, discovered a remarkable pattern: rates of first treatment for schizophrenia are disproportionately high, both for patients of lowest occupational status and for patients whose fathers had lowest occupational status, but these are by and large not the same patients[102]. Some of those whose fathers were in the lowest occupational class had themselves moved up and some of those ending up in the lowest occupational class had come from higher class origins. Thus, there is evidence both for the proposition that lower class origins are conducive to schizophrenia and for the proposition that most lower-class schizophrenics come from higher socio-economic origins. No wonder partial studies have been inconsistent!

The next question one would want to ask, of course, is how the schizophrenics' histories of occupational mobility compare to those of normal people of comparable social class origins. Turner and Wagonfeld have not the data to answer this definitively, for they lack an appropriate control group. They are able, however, to compare the mobility experiences of their schizophrenics to those of a cross-section of the population, and from this they learn two important things. More schizophrenics than normals have been downwardly mobile. This downward mobility did not come about because of a loss of occupational position that had once been achieved, but reflected their failure ever to have achieved as high an occupational level as do most men of their social class origins.

This argues strongly against a simple drift hypothesis—it is not, as some have argued, that we have erroneously rated men at lower than their usual class status because we have classified them according to their occupations at time of hospitalization, after they have suffered a decline in occupational position. It is more likely that a more sophisticated drift hypothesis applies—that some people genetically or constitutionally or otherwise predisposed to schizophrenia show some effects of developing illness at least as early as the time of their first jobs, for they are never able to achieve the occupational levels that might be expected of them. If so, the possibilities of some interaction between genetic predisposition and early social circumstances are very real indeed.

One direction that further research must take is well pointed out by the Turner and Wagonfeld study. The question now must be the degree to which the correlation of class and schizophrenia results from a higher incidence of schizophrenia among people born into lower-class families, the degree to which it results from schizophrenics of higher class origins never achieving as high an occupational level as might have been expected of them—and why.

For the present, I think it can be tentatively concluded that despite what Goldberg and Morrison found for England and Wales, the weight of evidence lies against the drift hypothesis being a sufficient explanation. In all probability, lower-class families produce a disproportionate number of schizophrenics, although perhaps by not so large a margin as one would conclude from studies that rely on the patients' own occupational attainments.

Parenthetically, there is another important question involved here, the effects of social mobility itself. Ever since Ødegaard's classic study of rates of mental disorder among Norwegian migrants to the United States,[76] we have known that geographic mobility is a matter of considerable consequence for mental illness,[59, 71, 101] and the same may be true for social mobility.[49, 73, 80] But we have not known how and why mobility matters—whether it is a question of what types of people are mobile or of the stresses of mobility—and unfortunately later research has failed to resolve the issue.

ADEQUACY OF INDICES

The adequacy of indices is another major issue in interpreting the Faris and Dunham, the Clark, and all subsequent investigations. Most of these studies are based on hospital admission rates, which may not give a valid picture of the true incidence of schizophrenia. Studies that do not rely on hospital rates encounter other and perhaps even more serious difficulties, with which we shall presently deal.

The difficulty with using admission rates as the basis for computing rates of schizophrenia is that lower-class psychotics may be more likely to be hospitalized, and if hospitalized to be diagnosed as schizophrenic, especially in public hospitals. Faris and Dunham tried to solve this problem by including patients admitted to private as well as to public mental hospitals. This was insufficient because, as later studies have shown, some people who suffer serious mental disorder never enter a mental hospital.[46]

Subsequent studies have attempted to do better by including more and more social agencies in their search for cases; Hollingshead and Redlich in New Haven,[40] and Jaco in Texas,[44] for example, have extended their coverage to include everyone who enters any sort of treatment facility—Jaco going so far as to question all the physicians in Texas. This is better, but clearly the same objections hold in principle. Furthermore, Srole and his associates have demonstrated that there are considerable social differences between people who have been treated, somewhere, for mental illness, and severely impaired people, some large proportion of them schizophrenic, who have never been to any sort of treatment facility.[94] So we must conclude that using treatment—any sort of treatment—as an index of mental disorder is suspect.

The alternative is to go out into the community and examine everyone—or a representative sample of everyone—yourself. This has been done by a number of investigators, for example Essen-Möller in Sweden,[26] Srole and his associates in New York,[94] the Leightons in Nova Scotia.[63] They have solved one problem, but have run into three others.

1. The first is that most of these investigators have found it impossible to classify schizoprenia reliably, and have had to resort to larger and vaguer categories—severe mental illness, functional psychosis, and such. For some purposes, this may be justified. For our immediate purposes, it is exceedingly unfortunate.

2. Second, even if you settle for such a concept as "mental illness," it is difficult to establish criteria that can be applied reliably and validly in community studies.[16] For all its inadequacies, hospitalization is at least an unambiguous index, and you can be fairly certain that the people who are hospitalized are really ill. But how does one interpret the Leightons' estimate that about a third of their population suffer significant psychiatric impairment,[64] or Srole's that almost a quarter of his are impaired?[94]

Personal examination by a single psychiatrist using presumably consistent standards is one potential solution, but usable only in relatively small investigations. Another possible solution is the further development of objective rating scales, such as the Neuropsychiatric Screening Adjunct first developed by social scientists in the Research Branch of the U.S. Army in World War II[95] and later incorporated into both the Leightons' and Srole's investigations, but not developed to anything like its full potential in either study. The limitation here is that such scales may be less relevant to the measurement of psychosis than of neurosis.

To make significant further advances, we shall have to break free of traditional methods of measurement. Epidemiological studies still largely rely on a single, undifferentiated overall assessment. Even when such an assessment can be demonstrated to be reliable within the confines of a single study, it has only limited use for comparative studies and is questionable for repeated application in studies designed to ascertain how many new cases arise in some given period of time. At minimum, we must begin to make use of our developing capacities at multivariate analysis. One obvious approach is to try to differentiate the several judgments that go into clinical diagnoses, develop reliable measures of each, and examine their interrelationship. At the same time, it would be well to develop reliable measures of matters conventionally given only secondary attention in epidemiological research—for example, the degree of disability the individual has sustained in each of several major social roles.[11] A third path we might try is the further development of objective measures of dimensions of subjective state (such as anxiety, alienation, and self-abasement) thought to be indicative of pathology. All these and others can be measured as separate dimensions, and then empirically related to each other and to clinical assessments.

Whether or not these particular suggestions have merit, I think the general conclusion that it is time for considerable methodological experimentation is indisputable.

3. The third problem in community studies is that it is so difficult to secure data on the incidence of mental disturbance that most studies settle for prevalence data.[53] That is, instead of ascertaining the number of new cases arising in various population groups during some period of time, they count the number of people currently ill at the time of the study. This latter measure—prevalence—is inadequate because it reflects not only incidence but also duration of illness. As Hollingshead and Redlich have shown, duration of illness —in so far as it incapacitates—is highly correlated with social class.[40]

Various approximations to incidence have been tried, and various new—and often somewhat fantastic—statistical devices invented to get around this problem, but without any real success. Clearly, what is needed is repeated studies of the population, to pick up new cases as they arise and thus to establish true incidence figures. (This is what Hagnell did, and it was a very brave effort indeed.) The crucial problem, of course, is to develop reliable measures of mental disorder, for without that our repeated surveys will measure nothing but the errors of our instruments. Meantime, we have to recognize that prevalence studies use an inappropriate measure that exaggerates the relationship of socio-economic status to mental disorder.

So, taken all together, the results of the studies of class and schizophrenia are hardly definitive. They may even all wash out—one more example of inadequate methods leading to premature, false conclusions. I cannot prove otherwise. Yet I think the most reasonable interpretation of all these findings is that they point to something real. Granted that there isn't a single definitive study in the lot, the weaknesses of one are compensated for by the strengths of some other, and the total edifice is probably much stronger than you would conclude from knowing only how frail are its component parts. A large number of complementary studies all seem to point to the same conclusion: that rates of mental disorder, particularly of schizophrenia, are highest at the lowest socio-economic levels, at least in moderately large cities, and this probably isn't just a matter of drift or inadequate indices or some other artifact of the methods we use. In all probability, more schizophrenia is actually produced at the lowest socio-enconomic levels. At any rate, let us take that as a working hypothesis and explore the question further. Assuming that more schizophrenia occurs at lower socio-economic levels—Why?

ALTERNATIVE INTERPRETATIONS

Is it really socio-economic status, or is it some correlated variable that is operative here? Faris and Dunham did not take socio-economic status very seriously in their interpretation of their data. From among the host of variables characteristic of the high-rate areas of Chicago, they focused on such things as high rates of population turnover and ethnic mixtures and hypothesized that the really critical thing about the high-rate areas was the degree of social isolation they engendered. Two subsequent studies, one by Jaco in Texas,[45] the other by Hare in Bristol, England,[37] are consistent in that they, too, show a correlation of rates of schizophrenia to various ecological indices of social isolation. The only study that directly examines the role of social isolation in the lives of schizophrenics, however, seems to demonstrate that while social isolation may be symptomatic of developing illness, it does not play an important role in etiology.[9, 50]

Several other interpretations of the epidemiological evidence have been suggested, some supported by intriguing, if inconclusive, evidence. One is that it is not socio-economic status as such that is principally at issue, but social integration. The Leightons have produced plausible evidence for this interpretation.[63, 64] The problems of defining and indexing "social integration" make a definitive demonstration exceedingly difficult, however, even for the predominantly rural populations with which they have worked.

Another possibility is that the high rates of schizophrenia found in lower-class populations are a consequence of especially high rates for lower-class members of some "ethnic" groups who happen to be living in areas where other ethnic groups predominate. In their recent study in Boston, for example, Schwartz and Mintz showed that Italian-Americans living in predominantly non-Italian neighborhoods have very high rates of schizophrenia, while those living in predominantly Italian neighborhoods do not.[91, 92] The former group contribute disproportionately to the rates for lower-class neighborhoods. (The authors suggest that this may explain why small cities do not show a concentration of lower-class cases: these cities do not have the ethnic mixtures that produce such a phenomenon.)

Wechsler and Pugh extended this interpretive model to suggest that rates should be higher for any persons living in a community where they and persons of similar social attributes are in a minority.[103] Their analysis of Massachusetts towns provides some surprisingly supportive data.

Other possibilities deal more directly with the occupational component of socio-economic status. Ødegaard long ago showed that rates of schizophrenia are higher for some occupations that are losing members and lower for some that are expanding.[77] His observation was correct, but it explains only a small part of the occupational rate differences. Others have focused on alleged discrepancies between schizophrenics' occupational aspirations and achievements,[49, 73] arguing that the pivotal fact is not that schizophrenics have achieved so little but that they had wanted so much more. The evidence is limited.

One could argue—and I see no reason to take the argument lightly—that genetics provides a quite sufficient explanation. If there is a moderately strong genetic component in schizophrenia, then one would expect a higher than usual rate of schizophrenia among the fathers and grandfathers of schizophrenics. Since schizophrenia is a debilitating disturbance, this would be reflected in grandparents' and parents' occupations and places of residence. In other words, it could be a rather complex version of drift hypothesis. The only argument against this interpretation is that there is no really compelling evidence in favor of it; one can accept it on faith, or one can keep it in mind while continuing to explore alternatives. Prudence suggests the latter course of action.

There are other possibilities we might examine, but since there is no very strong evidence for any of them, that course does not seem especially profitable. One must allow the possibility that some correlated variable might prove critical for explaining the findings; it might not be social class, after all, that is operative here. Until that is demonstrated, however, the wisest course would seem to be to take the findings at face value and see what there might be about social class that would help us to understand schizophrenia.

CLASS AND ETIOLOGY

What is there about the dynamics of social class that might affect the probability of people becoming schizophrenic? How does social class operate here; what are the intervening processes?

The possibilities are numerous, almost too numerous. Social class indexes and is correlated with so many phenomena that might be relevant to the etiology of schizophrenia. Since it measures status, it implies a great deal about how the individual is treated by others—with respect or perhaps degradingly; since it is measured by occupational rank, it suggests much about the conditions that make up the individual's daily work, how closely supervised he is, whether he works primarily with things, with data, or with people; since it reflects the individual's educational level, it connotes a great deal about his style of thinking, his use or non-use of abstractions, even his perceptions of physical reality and certainly of social reality; furthermore, the individual's class position influences his social values and colors his evaluations of the world about him; it affects the family experiences he is likely to have had as a child and the ways he is likely to raise his own children; and it certainly matters greatly for the type and amount of stress he is likely to encounter in a lifetime. In short, social class pervades so much of life that it is difficult to guess which of its correlates are most relevant for understanding schizophrenia. Moreover, none of these phenomena is so highly correlated with class (nor class so highly correlated with schizophrenia) that any one of these facets is obviously more promising than the others.

This being the case, investigators have tended to pursue those avenues that have met their theoretical predilections and to ignore the others. In practice, this has meant that the interrelationship of class, family, and schizophrenia has been explored, and more recently the relationship of class, stress, and schizophrenia, but the other possibilities remain largely unexamined. Given the inherent relevance of some of them —class differences in patterns of thinking, for example, have such obvious relevance to schizophrenia—this is a bit surprising.

But let me review what has been done. The hypothesis that stress is what is really at issue in the class-schizophrenia relationship is in some respects especially appealing, in part because it is so direct. We have not only our own observations as human beings with some compassion for less fortunate people, but an increasingly impressive body of scientific evidence,[15] to show that life is rougher and rougher the lower one's social class position. The stress explanation seems especially plausible for the very lowest socio-economic levels, where the rates of schizophrenia are highest.

There have to my knowledge been only two empirical investigations of the relationship of social class to stress to mental disorder. The first was done by Langner and Michael in New York as part of the "Midtown" study.[57] This study, as all the others we have been considering, has its methodological defects—it is a prevalence study, and many of the indices it uses are at best questionable—but it tackles the major issues head-on, and with very impressive and very intriguing results. It finds a strong linear relationship between stress and mental disturbance, specifically, the more sources of stress, the higher the probability of mental disturbance. It also finds the expected relationship between social class and stress. So the stress hypothesis has merit. But stress is not all that is involved in the relationship of social class to mental disorder. No matter how high the level of stress, social class continues to be correlated with the probability of mental disturbance; in fact, the more stress, the higher the correlation.* Thus, it seems that the effect of social class on the rate of mental disorder is not only, or even principally, a function of different amounts of stress at different class levels.

In a more recent study in San Juan, Puerto Rico, Rogler and Hollingshead ascribe a more important role to stress.[85] Theirs was an intensive investigation of the life histories of a sample of lower-class schizophrenics, along with comparable studies of a well-matched sample of non-schizophrenics. Rogler and Hollingshead found only insubstantial differences in the early life experiences of lower-class schizophrenics and controls; they did find, however, that in the period of a year or so before the onset of symptoms, the schizophrenics were subjected to an unbearable onslaught of stress. In effect, all lower-class slum dwellers in San Juan suffer continual, dreadful stress; in addition to this "normal" level of stress, however, the schizophrenics were hit with further intolerable stress which incapacitated them in one or another central role, leading to incapacitation in other roles, too.

The picture that Rogler and Hollingshead draw is plausible and impressive. It is not possible, however—at least not yet—to generalize as far from their data as one might like. Their sample is limited to schizophrenics who are married or in stable consensual unions. These one would assume to be predominantly "reactive" type schizophrenics—precisely the group whom one would expect, from past studies, to have had normal childhood social experiences, good social adjustment, and extreme precipitating circumstances. So their findings may apply to "reactive" schizophrenia, but perhaps not to "process" schizophrenia. In addition, for all the im-

---

* The latter finding is in part an artifact of the peculiar indices used in this study, and reflects differences not in the incidence of illness but in type and severity of illness in different social classes at various levels of stress. At higher stress levels, lower-class people tend to develop incapacitating psychoses and middle-class people less incapacitating neuroses.

pressiveness of the argument, the data are not so unequivocal. Their inquiry was not so exhaustive as to rule out the possibility that the schizophrenics might have had different family experiences from those of the controls. Furthermore, the evidence that the schizophrenics were subjected to significantly greater stress is not so thoroughly compelling as one might want. Thus, the case is not proved. Nevertheless, Rogler and Hollingshead have demonstrated that the possibility that stress plays an important role in the genesis of schizophrenia is to be taken very seriously indeed. Certainly this study makes it imperative that we investigate the relationship of class to stress to schizophrenia far more intensively.

At the same time, we should investigate some closely related possibilities that have not to my knowledge been studied empirically. Not only stress, but also reward and opportunity, are differentially distributed among the social classes. The more fortunately situated not only are less beaten about, but may be better able to withstand the stresses they do encounter because they have many more rewarding experiences to give them strength. And many more alternative courses of action are open to them when they run into trouble. Might this offer an added clue to the effects of class for schizophrenia?

More generally, what is there about the conditions of life of the lowest social strata that might make it more difficult for their members to cope with stress? One can think of intriguing possibilities. Their occupational conditions and their limited education gear their thinking processes to the concrete and the habitual; their inexperience in dealing with the abstract may ill-equip them to cope with ambiguity, uncertainty, and unpredictability; their mental processes are apt to be too gross and rigid when flexibility and subtlety are most required. Or, a related hypothesis, the lower- and working-class valuation of conformity to external authority, and disvaluation of self-direction, might cripple a man faced with the necessity of suddenly having to rely on himself in an uncertain situation where others cannot be relied on for guidance.

These hypotheses, unfortunately, have not been investigated; perhaps it is time that they were. The one hypothesis that has been studied, and that one only partially, is that lower- and working-class patterns of parent-child relationships somehow do not adequately prepare children for dealing with the hazards of life. Now we enter what is perhaps the most complicated area of research we have touched on so far, and certainly the least adequately studied field of all.

There has been a huge volume of research literature about family relationships and schizophrenia[12, 51, 89] most of it inadequately designed. One has to dismiss the majority of studies because of one or another incapacitating deficiency. In many, the patients selected for study were a group from which you could not possibly generalize to schizophrenics at large. Either the samples were comprised of chronic patients, where one would expect the longest and most difficult onset of illness with the greatest strain in family relationships, or the samples were peculiarly selected, not to test a hypothesis, but to load the dice in favor of a hypothesis. In other studies, there have been inadequate control groups or no control group at all. One of the most serious defects of method has been the comparison of patterns of family relationship of lower- and working-class patients to middle- and upper-middle-class normal controls—which completely confounds the complex picture we wish to disentangle. In still other studies, even where the methods of sample and control-selection have been adequate, the method of data-collection has seriously biased the results. This is true, for example, in those studies that have placed patients and their families in stressful situations bound to exaggerate any flaws in their interpersonal processes, especially for people of lesser education and verbal skill who would be least equipped to deal with the new and perplexing situation in which they found themselves.*

* For a more complete discussion, see Clausen and Kohn (12).

Still, some recent studies have suggested respects in which the family relationships of schizophrenics seem unusual, and unusual in theoretically interesting ways—that is, in ways that might be important in the dynamics of schizophrenic personality development. Work by Bateson and Jackson on communication processes in families of schizophrenics[2] and that by Wynne and his associates on cognitive and emotional processes in such families,[105] for example, are altogether intriguing.

But—and here I must once again bring social class into the picture—there has not been a single well-controlled study that demonstrates any substantial difference between the family relationships of schizophrenics and those of normal persons from lower- and working-class backgrounds. Now, it may be that the well-controlled studies simply have not dealt with the particular variables that do differentiate the families of schizophrenics from those of normal lower- and working-class families. The two studies that best control for social class—Clausen's and my study in Hagerstown, Maryland[51] and Rogler and Hollingshead's in San Juan[85]—deal with but a few aspects of family relationship, notably not including the very processes that recent clinical studies have emphasized as perhaps the most important of all. It may be that investigations yet to come will show clear and convincing evidence that some important aspects of family relationships are definitely different for schizophrenia-producing families and normal families of this social background.

If they do not, that still does not mean that family relationships are not important for schizophrenia, or that it is not through the family that social class exerts one of its principal effects. Another way of putting the same facts is to say that there is increasing evidence of remarkable parallels between the dynamics of families that produce schizophrenia and family dynamics in the lower classes generally.[52, 81] This may indicate that the family patterns of the lower classes are in some way broadly conducive to schizophrenic personality development.

Clearly these patterns do not provide a sufficient explanation of schizophrenia. We still need a missing X, or set of X's, to tell us the necessary and sufficient conditions for schizophrenia to occur. Perhaps that X is some other aspect of family relationships. Perhaps lower-class patterns of family relationships are conducive to schizophrenia for persons genetically predisposed, but not for others. Or perhaps they are generally conducive to schizophrenia, but schizophrenia will not actually occur unless the individual is subjected to certain types or amounts of stress. We do not know. But these speculative considerations do suggest that it may be about time to bring all these variables—social class, early family relationships, genetics, stress—into the same investigations, so that we can examine their interactive effects. Meantime, I must sadly conclude that we have not yet unravelled the relationship of social class and schizophrenia, nor learned what it might tell us about the etiology of the disorder.

SUMMARY

Perhaps, after so broad a sweep, an overall assessment is in order. There is a truly remarkable volume of research literature demonstrating an especially high rate of schizophrenia (variously indexed) in the lowest social class or classes (variously indexed) of moderately large to large cities throughout much of the Western world. It is not altogether clear what is the direction of causality in this relationship—whether the conditions of life of the lowest social classes are conducive to the development of schizophrenia, or schizophrenia leads to a decline in social class position—but present evidence would make it seem probable that some substantial part of the phenomenon results from lower class conditions of life being conducive to schizophrenia. It is not even certain that the indices of schizophrenia used in these studies can be relied on, although there is some minor comfort in that studies using several different indices all point to the same conclusion. Perhaps it is only an act of faith that permits me to conclude that the relationship of class to schizophrenia is probably real, an act of faith only barely disguised by calling it a working hypothesis.

This working hypothesis must be weighed against a number of alternative interpretations of the data. Many of them are plausible, several are supported by attractive nuggets of data, but none is more compelling than the most obvious interpretation of all: that social class seems to matter for schizophrenia because, in fact, it does.

When one goes on to see what this might imply for the etiology of schizophrenia, one finds many more intriguing possibilities than rigorous studies. There is some evidence that the greater stress suffered by lower-class people is relevant, and perhaps that lower- and working-class patterns of family relationships are broadly conducive to schizophrenia— although the latter is more a surmise than a conclusion.

Finally, it is clear that we must bring genetic predisposition and class, with all its attendant experiences, into the same investigations. That, however, is not the only sort of investigation that calls for attention. We have reviewed a large number of hypotheses, several major conflicts of interpretation, and many leads and hunches that all cry out to be investigated. The most hopeful sign in this confusing area is that several of the recent studies have gone far beyond seeing whether the usual stereotyped set of demographic characteristics correlate with rates of schizophrenia, to explore some of these very exciting issues.

9

Metabolic, Physiologic, Anatomic, and Genetic Studies

INTRODUCTION

Of the enormous number of studies seeking a consistent abnormality of metabolism, physiology, or heredity in the schizophrenias, none has been firmly established; the search continues.

Such abnormalities have been claimed, but careful replication studies have usually failed to confirm them. Kety[45] has noted certain hazards implicit in this area, as follows: Schizophrenia is probably a heterogeneous group of disorders, and significant subgroup deviations may be missed just as "the biochemical characteristics of phenylketonuria would hardly have been detected in an average value for phenylalanine blood levels in a large group of mentally retarded patients." Dietary irregularities in prolonged hospitalization affect metabolism; e.g., in one study abnormal phenolic amine excretion in urine resulted from abnormally high coffee consumption in patients compared to controls. The possible residual effects of tranquilizers, hypnotics, ECT, and insulin coma must be controlled for. Differences in physical activity between control groups, catatonic patients in stupor or excitement, and burned-out chronic patients can effect measures of energy and carbohydrate metabolism.

In recent years, certain clinical-diagnostic parameters

used to distinguish subgroups of patients have attained increasing importance. These parameters are the following: (1) reactive-process; (2) acute-chronic; (3) schizophreniform-true schizophrenia; (4) paranoid-nonparanoid, and (5) excited-nonexcited. Criteria for making these distinctions are more fully spelled out elsewhere.[3] All acute schizophrenics are upset, excited and anxious. Only some chronic patients are upset; others have become fixed and relatively comfortable with their psychotic defenses. For instance, some chronic schizophrenic patients with malignancies live longer than the normal population with the same malignancies; the patient group would seem to have diminished adrenal corticosteroid output and a concomitant lack of suppression of immunological responses with resulting longer life.[80]

Many reports show *extreme variability* on most physiological or metabolic measures in a schizophrenic population, even though few differences between the *means* are found in comparison to control groups. The variance is very often greater for the schizophrenic group. This variability may be the result of an interaction between the four factors mentioned, namely, heterogeneity in the patient population, dietary irregularities, drug and shock treatment aftereffects and abnormal exercise and activity patterns.

The worker doing metabolic studies cannot sample the metabolism of the organ of greatest interest: the living human brain. He must, instead, work with peripheral fluids and tissues, usually blood and urine, sometimes with C.S.F., or with necropsy materials. The concentrations and effects of metabolites here may be quite different from the living human brain.

Metabolic, physiologic, and anatomic studies in the schizophrenias will be discussed first in this chapter, genetic studies next, and theoretical implications in Chapter 10.

METABOLIC, PHYSIOLOGIC, AND
ANATOMIC STUDIES

This section is divided into six major subdivisions, as follows:

1. Energy Metabolism: glucose, lactate, and pyruvate; free fatty acids.

2. Amino Acid Metabolism (exclusive of Immune Mechanism Components): the biogenic amines and related substances (epinephrine and mescaline, serotonin, and lysergic acid); creatinine and uric acid.

3. Steroids and Other Hormones: adrenocortical steroids and electrolytes; sex hormones in biochemical and biobehavioral studies; thyroid metabolism.

4. Immune Mechanism Components: histidine and histamine; serum proteins (non-antigenic globulins, antigenic and toxic proteins including taraxein); cellular abnormalities in mast cells, leukocytes, and brain.

5. Tissues and Organs: peripheral tissues; brain.

6. Body Habitus and Somatotyping.

1. Energy Metabolism (Glucose and Free Fatty Acids)

Studies by Frohman *et al.*,[25] originally suggested a shift of glycolysis from the aerobic (Krebs) cycle to the anaerobic (Embden-Meyerhoff) cycle in schizophrenia, measured by lactate/pyruvate (L/P) levels of plasma incubated with chicken erythrocytes. Such studies of patients and controls pointed toward an underlying plasma factor in schizophrenia. Later work by these and other investigators[10, 12, 46, 56] failed to confirm the finding and suggested either that no such difference existed or that exercise levels in the subjects influenced L/P levels more than disease states. Smythies,[78] nevertheless, feels that such changes may be intrinsic to schizophrenia.

Mueller[58] found no abnormalities in free fatty acid metabolism, using radio-isotope methods.

2. Amino Acid Metabolism
(Exclusive of Immune Mechanism Components)

THE BIOGENIC AMINES AND RELATED SUBSTANCES—
1. EPINEPHRINE AND MESCALINE. Part of the interest in the epinephrine related compounds, products of tyrosine metabolism, has been stirred up by the close structural similarity of the molecules of epinephrine and the hallucinogen mesca-

The Meaning of Madness

line.[78] Though there are many points of similarity in the mescaline or lysergic acid (LSD-25) experience and the schizophrenias, there are also numerous important differences; they are not equivalent. No mescalinelike compounds have been discovered in serum. The similarities in chemical structure of these two "psychotomimetic" agents and the amines are shown in Figure 9–1.

A table of major metabolic pathways in epinephrine and norepinephrine syntheses and degradation is shown in Figure 9–2. No differences were found in the physiological and psychological responses to epinephrine infusion and its metabolic products in chronic schizophrenics compared to normal

Figure 9-1. Molecular structures of epinephrine and mescaline; of tryptophane and lysergic acid diethylamide (LSD-25); and of 3,4-dimethoxyphenylethylamine (DMPEA).

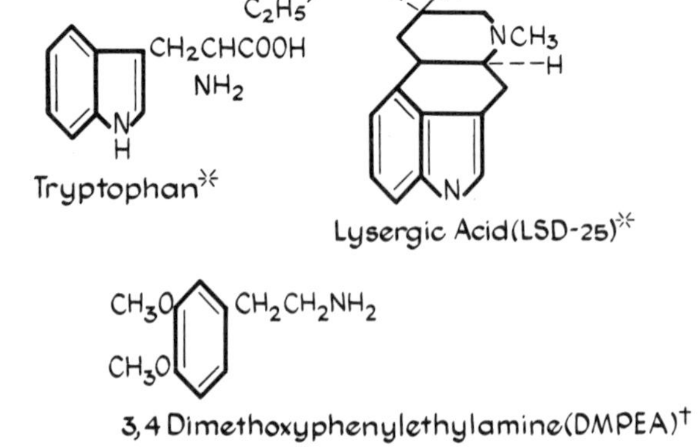

* Smythies [78]
† Friedhoff [23]

controls, save that the blood pressure and pulse rate increases were less for the schizophrenics.[11, 53, 62]

Other studies report that deviations from normal in the output of catechol amines is more closely related to anxiety, excitement, and physical activity than specifically to schizophrenia.[64, 81]

Gjessing[28] concludes differently in studies of patients with a diagnosis of "periodic catatonia" whose normal mental functioning alternates with catatonic stupor and/or excitement lasting weeks or months. In these patients, urinary metanephrine and normetanephrine are sharply elevated within a week after the onset of stupor; metanephrine starts returning to normal after a week; normetanephrine elevation persists to the middle of the period of stupor. In excitement,

Figure 9-2. Metabolic pathways of catecholamine synthesis and degradation (adapted from Eiduson *et al.*).

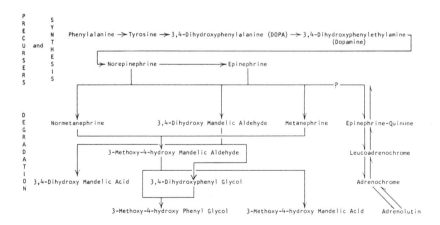

the normetanephrine elevation occurs; metanephrine level remains normal. He concludes, "Our previous hypotheses involving an endogenous toxic substance is reinforced and extended."

Hoffer *et al.*[40] have postulated that the epinephrine-adrenolutin pathway exists, that adrenochrome is a psychotomimetic agent which passes the blood-brain barrier freely and causes the symptom picture of schizophrenia. The methodology involved has been seriously questioned; substantial replication elsewhere is needed.[39]

O'Reilly and co-workers[59, 60] have studied "mauve factor" or "malvaria," as presence of mauve factor is known. Hoffer and associates have said this substance, detected by mauve coloration of paper chromatographs of treated urines, is relatively specific to schizophrenia and correlated with clinical state. O'Reilly's work shows that urines positive for mauve factor are found in a wide variety of clinical states, e.g., chronic alcoholism, involutional melancholia, cancer, normal controls, etc., though the highest incidence was in the schizophrenic group. Appearance of malvaria was not correlated with chronicity or prognosis in schizophrenia.

Friedhoff and Van Winkle[23, 24] have isolated a compound from 67 percent of the urines of schizophrenics, tentatively identified as 3,4-dimethoxyphenylethylamine (DMPEA), (Figure 9–1), which is present in 2 percent of normal urines and which has a central nervous system depressant property. Bourdillon and colleagues[8] using methods similar to Friedhoff's, found a pink spot on paper chromatography in certain subjects; they are not certain whether this spot represents DMPEA or a closely related compound. Controlling for diet, institutionalization, and drug treatment, pink spot was found in 83 percent of nonparanoid schizophrenics and at lower levels in paranoids, but still significantly higher than normal controls. Other investigators have not been able to demonstrate either DMPEA or pink spot in schizophrenics; variation in methodology may contribute to this lack of replication.

Thus it would seem from the foregoing that there is

evidence of heightened epinephrine metabolism during periods of psychic stress, but the elucidation of the cause-effect relationships and specific relation to the schizophrenias is still open to question.[5]

THE BIOGENIC AMINES AND RELATED SUBSTANCES—2. SEROTONIN AND LYSERGIC ACID: The compounds related to tryptophane, serotonin, and their products of degradation have been widely studied. The similarities of the indole structure (as in serotonin) and the nuclei of LSD-25, psilocybin, bufotenin, and other psychotomimetic agents (see Figure 9–1), have excited interest.[78] The normal metabolic pathways of tryptophane metabolism are shown in Figure 9–3.

Feldstein, Wong, and Freeman[16] injected radio-labeled serotonin into schizophrenic and normal control patients. They conclude, "There were no statistically significant differences between the chronic schizophrenic patients and the normal subjects in the recovery of total carbon-14 or 5-HIAA-C-14, by the intramuscular or intravenous routes, calculated on the basis of administered serotonin-C-14 or on the basis of total carbon-14 in the urine."

The relationship between serotonin and 5-HIAA metabolism and emotional stress is clouded by contradictory findings. Smythies[78] reports a rise in excretion of these compounds following exacerbation of clinical symptoms and a decline with improvement. Halevy et al.,[32] however, found an inverse relation between blood serotonin levels and degree of psychopathology, as measured by the MMPI, regardless of specific psychiatric diagnosis, in a group of hospitalized patients.

Schizophrenic patients may metabolize loads of 1-tryptophane abnormally; some studies show that loading schizophrenic patients with l-methionine leads to a temporary exacerbation of psychotic symptoms. [45, 46, 78] Kety and others[61] are currently investigating the implication of these findings that a defect in transmethylation is related to schizophrenic symptoms. Certain methylated compounds, such as DMPEA and betane, as well as those mentioned above, seem to cause clinical exacerbations; some of the psychotomimetic agents are methylated relatives of normal catechol and indole amines.[47]

No clear-cut relationship between schizophrenia and defects in tryptophane metabolism has been established.

CREATININE AND URIC ACID: Gerard[26] found that among subjects who had fast reaction times, those who were schizophrenic had strikingly higher creatinine excretion than slow-reacting schizophrenics; and that fast-reacting nonschizophrenic controls had strikingly higher blood uric acid levels as well as performing better on various psychological tests.

Figure 9-3. Metabolic pathways of tryptophane and serotonin (adapted from Eiduson *et al.*).

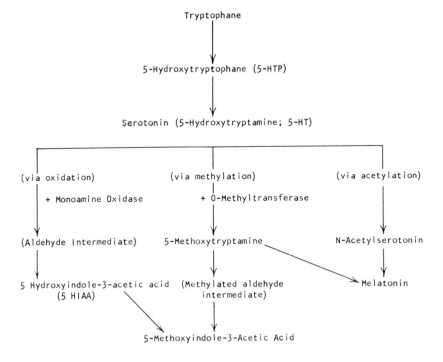

3. Steroids and Hormones

ADRENOCORTICAL STEROIDS: Eiduson summarizes studies of adrenocortical function including eosinophile levels and the metabolism of electrolytes affected by adrenocortical hormones.[12] He cites studies which point variously to adrenal hypofunction, normal function, and hyperfunction. In certain cases, paranoid schizophrenics seem to be closer to normal than other schizophrenics; in other cases the difference is reversed. Romanoff *et al.*[65] found that though mean values were not different between schizophrenics and normals, day/night variations seemed greater in the schizophrenics than in normal persons, a finding that would be expected on the basis of the extremes of reactivity to psychological stress found in the schizophrenic population.

Eiduson also notes that Addison's and Cushing's diseases, adrenalectomy, and ACTH or cortisone administration (though the latter is capable of producing transient schizophrenialike states) do not produce schizophrenia. He summarizes, "... The case of adrenal malfunction in schizophrenia is far from settled, and its diagnostic value in discriminating schizophrenic from nonschizophrenic subjects per se is questionable."[12]

In studying electrolytes influenced by adrenal function, Gerard[26] found that schizophrenics who had faster reaction times showed less psychopathology, an increased urine volume, with strikingly higher daily excretions of sodium and potassium than did schizophrenics with slower reaction times. He further found that schizophrenics differed from normal controls in having lower urine volume and sodium excretion during the daytime and having lower potassium excretion and serum phosphorus over a 24-hour period. Paranoid schizophrenics differed from other kinds of schizophrenia in having higher urine volume, sodium excretion, and serum phosphorus.

Stevenson *et al.*[82] found that both paranoid and nonparanoid schizophrenics excreted more sodium and had higher urine volumes than normals; that catatonics excreted less phosphate than paranoid schizophrenics or normals and more 17-ketosteroids than normals; and that paranoids and catatonics differed as much from each other as from normals.

SEX HORMONES: Eiduson failed to find any consistent disturbance of sex hormone metabolism in schizophrenia.[12]

There is an association between the schizophrenias and sexual behavior, as seen in Figure 9–4 in a comparison of figures for incidence of first admissions for dementia praecox (schizophrenia) and sexual activity, measured in orgasms per week.[48, 49, 54] (Kinsey does not give precise data on sexual

Figure 9-4. Sexual behavior and schizophrenia.

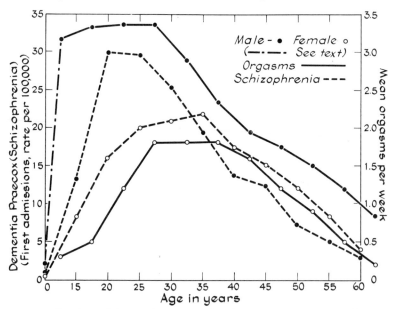

Number of first admissions for dementia praecox to State Mental Hospitals in the United States, 1933, by age and sex (Landis and Page [54])
Sexual activity in orgasms per week by age and sex (Kinsey, et al.[48, 49])

activity in males up to age 15. He does, however, show that using the development of secondary sexual characteristics and ejaculatory ability as criteria, virtually none of his samples were adolescent at age ten, virtually all were by age 15, and that this change was almost perfectly linear. Therefore, the author has interpolated a straight line between these two points in the representation of male sexual activity between 10 and 15.)

The curves for the incidence of schizophrenia, although made in 1933, probably are a reasonably accurate representation of the incidence of first admissions in this and other advanced Western countries prior to the phenothiazine era.

As the graph shows, in males both the incidence of schizophrenia and sexual activity rise rapidly in adolescence, reach a peak in the sample's early and mid-twenties, and start a sharp decline by the age of 30. In females the rise for both is more gradual, a plateau is reached in the middle-late twenties, and a more gradual decline starts at around age 35 to 40.

This finding probably reflects an interaction of factors, e.g., hormonal, psychological, and environmental, and can lead to behavior which varies from being predominantly sexual to predominantly schizophrenic.

THYROID HORMONE. Eiduson notes reports that a small percentage of hospitalized schizophrenics show thyroid deficiency and respond to thyroid treatment and that some show increased iodine uptake.[12] Addition of iodized salt to the patients' diets eliminated the increased uptake. Studies of protein-bound iodine were unable to differentiate between schizophrenics and normals. Administration of thyroid to schizophrenic patients has not influenced the course of the illness. Gjessing[27] was unable to find signs of significant thyroid malfunctioning in cases of periodic catatonia.

4. Immune Mechanism Components

HISTIDINE AND HISTAMINE: Brown, *et al.*[9] injected radiolabeled histidine C-14 into schizophrenic and normal control subjects, and found no significant differences in metabolism or disposal in the two groups.

SERUM PROTEINS—1. NONANTIGENIC GLOBULINS AND MACROGLOBULINS: Fessel and co-workers[17, 18, 52] have described the presence of serum proteins abnormal either in type or in frequency in schizophrenic patients. These proteins include rheumatoid and lupus factors (clinical rheumatoid arthritis is rare in a schizophrenic population), various macroglobulins, and the rise under stress of proteins 4S and 19S. Others have not been able to confirm these findings.[6] Psychosis, including schizophrenia-like symptoms, may be the harbingers of systemic lupus erythematosis (SLE) in more than one fifth of the cases; such psychosis is only occasionally the result of steroid therapy for the SLE.[21]

SERUM PROTEINS—2. ANTIGENIC AND TOXIC FACTORS: Some years ago Heath implicated ceruloplasmin, a copper-bearing protein with a molecular weight of about 150,000, in schizophrenic symptomatology. It now appears that ceruloplasmin levels reflect nonspecific emotional stress and vitamin C deficiency, not schizophrenia per se.[1]

Heath et al.[33] also fractionated a protein substance, not found in normals, from schizophrenic blood, named taraxein, and stated that it produced a temporary psychotic state when injected into normal volunteers. Replication of these findings has failed. Methodological weaknesses in the original study could account for the results as being artifact rather than essential to schizophrenia.

More recently, Heath and co-workers employed[34, 35, 36] fluorescent antibody staining, EEG, and antigenic techniques using necropsy brain material and/or serum proteins from acute and chronic schizophrenic patients, nonschizophrenic, chronically ill patients, normal controls, and experimental animals.

From these studies the authors conclude that brain cells and sera of schizophrenics are antigenically different from those of control groups, that schizophrenia is a "single disease entity," and that the septal-caudate region of normal monkey and human brain possesses unique antigenic properties. They see schizophrenia as an autoimmune disorder with the serum globulin taraxein as antibody.

These studies suffer from five weaknesses: (1) The "single disease entity" is quite different serologically in the acute and chronic phases, by the authors' own findings; (2) blind raters were not used to judge experimental materials; experimental bias was not eliminated; (3) there was no control group of emotionally agitated nonschizophrenics; (4) the diagnostic criteria of schizophrenia were nowhere specified; and (5) controls for hospitalization, exercise, and drug and/or electroshock treatment were modest at best.

Haddad and Rabe[31] "detected an antigenic abnormality in the serum of schizophrenic patients, not relating the finding to an infectious process. They immunized guinea pigs with pooled schizophrenic serum, desensitized with normal serum, and found anaphylactic reaction upon challenge with the same or different schizophrenic (but not with normal or alcoholic) serum.[11]

Gerard[26] has found unidentified toxic substances in the urine of schizophrenics that produced excitement and agitation when injected into mice at levels highly significantly greater than the urine of normal controls. The paranoid schizophrenic patients differed from other schizophrenics in showing a lower parasympathetic index, and increased urine volume, sodium, and 5-HIAA excretion.

Turner and Chipps[84] report a heterophil hemolysin, a protein of high molecular weight, can be found in the serum of schizophrenics but not in normal controls, hospitalized nonschizophrenics and only occasionally in alcoholics. The protein causes hemolysis of rabbit erythrocytes. Factors of nutrition, antibiotics, duration of hospitalization, diagnostic category, etc. are controlled for.

CELLULAR ABNORMALITIES: Several different types of cellular abnormalities in schizophrenia have been described. There have been reports that the schizophrenic's skin contains fewer mast cells and shows a diminished response to injected histamine than does the skin of normals.

Fessel[19, 20, 38] reports that abnormal leukocytes, especially the P-lymphocyte, in the sera of schizophrenic patients can be identified by blind microscopic examination even after possible artifacts of treatment and hospitalization have been controlled for. Attempted replication of the microscopic study finding attributed it to a phenothiazine-induced artifact, not to schizophrenia.[22] Fessel also found the P-lymphocyte in unaffected family members of process schizophrenics. These data point to a genetic contribution of some sort to the etiology of process schizophrenia.

Solomon and Moos[79] attempt to integrate findings of abnormalities in the immune system under the rubric of relative immunological incompetence as follows: Autoimmunity seems to relate clinically and experimentally to relative immunological incompetence; disturbances of autoimmunity are found in agammaglobulinemia, lymphomas, etc. Some schizophrenics have poor immunologic responsivity. There seems to be an elevated incidence of various autoimmune phenomena in the schizophrenias (including antibrain substances). Stress frequently leads to an increase in adrenocorticosteroid production with a concomitant suppression of immunological activity. Emotional stress and disorders of the immune system have been implicated in many of the diseases traditionally labeled "psychosomatic," e.g., rheumatoid arthritis, ulcerative colitis, asthma, thyrotoxicosis, SLE, and others. They suggest that some cases of schizophrenia may reflect a psychosomatic disturbance in the brain analogous to that found in the joints of patients with rheumatoid arthritis.

5. Tissues and Organs

PERIPHERAL TISSUES: There have been reports of abnormalities in fingertip skin and capillary patterns, testes and abdominal viscera in nonparanoid schizophrenics.[3] These studies were done before recent necessary control conditions were employed; replication under such conditions is necessary.

BRAIN: In studies by Kety et al. and Wortis et al., of cerebral blood flow, brain oxygen uptake, and brain glucose metabolism, no differences between schizophrenics and normals could be detected.[46]

Brain tissue changes have been described in schizophrenia, but controls have been inadequate and findings have been inconclusive or conflicting. Wolf and Cowen's review of this literature in Bellak[3] is as follows:

> All the reported microscopic abnormalities [in the brains of schizophrenics] have been challenged as nonspecific by a group of competent histologists and have been attributed to misjudgement of the limits of normal variation, misinterpretation of artifacts, or the uncritical attribution of special significance to casual, coincidental findings.

In a recent article, Feinberg and Evarts[15] review research on sleeping and dreaming in relation to the schizophrenias and other clinical conditions. Using the EEG to distinguish between waking and the four stages of sleep, they employ widely accepted criteria to distinguish between these states. Rapid-eye-movement sleep (S-REM) is associated with low-voltage, fairly rapid, and irregular EEG tracings (stage 1 sleep); slow-wave sleep (S-SW), which comprises stages 2 through 4, is associated with sleep spindles and high-voltage delta activity in a slower rhythm. S-REM is very frequently associated with vivid dreaming; S-SW usually is not.

Feinberg and colleagues studied 22 schizophrenic patients (9 acute, 9 chronic, 4 in remission) and a control group of 10 patients. There were no significant differences between groups for total sleep time, or for absolute or relative amounts of stage 1 sleep. The acutely ill patients showed fewer eye movements during S-REM than did the other groups. The authors conclude that "S-REM mechanisms appeared fundamentally intact in schizophrenia and there was no evidence to implicate a disturbance of S-REM mechanisms in the waking hallucinations of schizophrenic patients."

In contrast, Zarcone et al.[86] report a significantly higher amount and percentage of S-REM in 13 chronic schizophrenic patients who were at or near a state of clinical remission.

Feinberg reports a reduction of stage 4 (S-SW) sleep in his group of 18 actively ill schizophrenic patients, and cites other workers who have similar findings.

From all these findings, Feinberg and Evarts conclude, "Changes in both S-REM and S-SW found in some schizophrenic patients . . . represent a generalized increase in arousal level. . . . However, schizophrenia is neither a necessary nor a sufficient condition for these changes."

A number of investigators have studied the effects of depriving subjects of S-REM by awakening them repeatedly during the night whenever EEG tracings suggest the subject is in S-REM. Most subjects show a compensatory or "rebound" phenomenon during following nights: they show increased amounts of S-REM in amounts proportional to the deprivation during the experimental night(s). Some workers have found little or no difference in the rebound phenomenon between schizophrenic patients and normal controls. Others find that acutely ill schizophrenic patients show significantly less rebound than do controls, and suggest further that the active psychotic process during the day satisfies the same physiological needs which for most people are met only in S-REM.

In any event, the data are still contradictory, the sample sizes small, and the artifacts of treatment and general psychiatric condition only somewhat controlled for. Feinberg and Evarts point out that the visual hallucinations of dreams resemble those of toxic deliria much more than those of the schizophrenias. The relationship of S-REM and the schizophrenias (and within them, acute vs. chronic; active vs. in remission; and hallucinating vs. nonhallucinating) is still unclear.

6. Body Habitus and Somatotyping

Sheldon originally categorized the body types of ectomorphic (tall and slender), mesomorphic (stocky and muscular), and endomorphic (chubby, roly-poly). He believed that the ectomorphic habitus occurs with uncommon frequency in schizophrenic patients. Ectomorphy has been reported to be correlated to paranoid schizophrenia and a better prognosis.[4]

Gerard[26] finds that good performance on psychological tests, by schizophrenics and nonschizophrenics alike, was positively correlated with shorter arm spans, broader shoulders, and smaller wrists; the patient group, in addition, tended to be younger and have a briefer period of hospitalization. Patients with higher androgeny scores have briefer periods of hospitalization and have a lower parasympathetic index. Schizophrenics tended to have smaller chest girth measurements than nonschizophrenics. Schizophrenics have a fine microtremor of the hand and lower skin temperatures than nonschizophrenics have.

The relationship of somatotype and schizophrenia has not yet been settled. Here again, however, the difference between paranoid and nonparanoid schizophrenics on a number of parameters remains; likewise, it is found in parameters of perception and cognitive style.[75] Such a division may be among the first that usefully differentiate between the subtypes of schizophrenia.

Summary

In studies of energy metabolism, findings have been inconsistent. There is equivocal evidence to suggest that a shift from the aerobic cycle to the anaerobic cycle, as shown by chick erythrocyte lactate/pyruvate levels, takes place more readily in schizophrenics than it does in normals. Free fatty-acid metabolism is not abnormal in schizophrenics.

Most recent studies of tyrosine and epinephrine metabolism show no abnormalities when radio-labeled extracts are infused in patients and normal controls. Gjessing feels these metabolic cycles are abnormal in periodic catatonia. The adrenochrome hypothesis is in serious doubt. An abnormal metabolite, 3,4-dimethoxyphenylethylamine, may be present in the urine of schizophrenics. Biogenic amine metabolism is altered during periods of emotional stress regardless of specific psychiatric diagnosis.

Infusions of radio-labeled serotonin are metabolized similarly by schizophrenic patients and normal controls. Serotonin levels in urine seem to be directly related to acute psychic stress but inversely related in blood. Schizophrenic patients may have a defect in transmethylation, shown as an exacerbation of symptoms when loaded with l-tryptophane and l-methionine.

Creatinine, uric acid, and sodium and potassium excretion are related to reaction times in both schizophrenic patients and normal controls.

Studies of adrenal cortical response in schizophrenia are highly contradictory and inconsistent. Evidence of normal, excessive, and diminished adrenal cortical function has been described.

Sex hormones have not been proved abnormal in schizophrenia. There is an interesting correlation of sexual behavior, measured in orgasms per week, and the incidence of first admissions for schizophrenia, plotted by age and sex.

Thyroid abnormalities reported in schizophrenia are probably artifacts of dietary irregularity; such differences disappear with correction of diet.

Among the components of the immune mechanism, radio-labeled histidine is metabolized similarly by schizophrenics and normal controls. The presence of abnormal serum globulins and macroglobulins in schizophrenia has been asserted by some, thought to be artifacts by others. Antigenic and toxic substances in the blood and urine of schizophrenics have been said to produce abnormalities in behavior when injected into experimental animals. Brain tissues of schizophrenic patients may stimulate different antibrain antibody; globulin from the sera of acutely schizophrenic patients when injected into monkey brains produces EEG and behavioral changes distinguishable from injections of sera from chronic schizophrenic patients and other controls. The septal and basal caudate areas of human and monkey brains seem to possess certain unique antigenic properties not found in other areas of the brain. The blood of schizophrenics may contain a heterophile hemolysin not found in normal controls. Abnormal leukocytes, especially the P-lymphocyte, have been described for schizophrenics. Certain methodological weaknesses in such studies demand independent replication before their true worth can be assessed. If the findings hold up, they can fit into a conceptual model of relative immunological incompetence.

Morphological abnormalities of fingertip capillaries, testes, viscera, and brain have been described, but highly inconsistent reports vitiate their importance. Findings in studies of sleeping and dreaming are still equivocal. In studies of body type, ectomorphy has been related to paranoid schizophrenia, and reduced chest girth and a fine microtremor of the hand have been related to schizophrenia generally. The division of paranoid and nonparanoid schizophrenia may turn out to be quite useful in future studies.

GENETIC STUDIES

Introduction

The question of the importance of genetic factors in the schizophrenias has, at its worst, given rise to acrimonious and naïve nature-nurture controversies. Some have attributed the schizophrenias solely to genetic factors, others solely to environmental factors. Both concepts are global and nonpredictive; they have given way to more sophisticated and thoughtful attempts to integrate evidence from several sources.

The major sources of data in deciding on genetic influences have been studies of families of schizophrenic patients, with special interest focused on twins. Other sources have been sociological and psychologically oriented studies of families of schizophrenics. Each of these major areas is important in considering the birthright with which the patient starts life. Genetic makeup, intrauterine influences, and constitution at birth are one kind of birthright, a class of factors that

have both genetic and environmental components. The socio-
economic condition of the family is another kind of birthright, and the modes of parental thinking, feeling, and relating are a third. Even at birth these congenital "givens" can
interact with each other. For instance, suppose a newborn
is a constitutionally active, wakeful, alert, wriggling creature,
and his mother conceives of the model and well-mothered
child as being passive, quiet, and sleeping long hours. Already
there would exist the basis for a good deal of mother-child
anxiety, tension, and conflict. Had the child been fortunate
enough to have been born passive and quiet, in accord with its
mother's preconceptions, or if the mother had been so organized psychologically that she could accept and respond positively to a wide range of neonatal behaviors, the early relationship would obviously have started off on a better footing.
Such an example points to only one of the myriad possibilities
of the interactions of the genetic, constitutional, social, and
psychological forces operant at birth and shifting throughout
life.

General Studies

The investigators whose family and twin data are most
often cited are Rosanoff[66] and Rosenthal,[67-73] of the United
States; Kallman[42, 43] of Germany and the United States;
Shields and Slater[29, 74] in England; and Luxenberger,[55]
Böök,[7] and Essen-Möller,[14] of Scandinavia. Their data are
summarized in Table 9–1.

The two major measures used are morbidity-risk rate
and concordance rate, both expressed as percentages. An
identified schizophrenic patient is called the "proband" or
"index case." Relatives of the proband are rated for psychiatric condition, age, and (often left unreported) sex.

Morbid risk expresses the probability that a given family
member, not a twin, of the proband has or will become schizophrenic by the time he has passed through the age of risk,
thought to be from the ages of 15 to 45 years, for the illness.
Such computations include parameters of first admissions in

TABLE 9–1
A SUMMARY OF FAMILY AND TWIN MORBID RISK AND CONCORDANCE RATES IN THE SCHIZOPHRENIAS

Non-Twin Studies

Proband (Index Case)	Relative	Morbidity Risk Range, Average (in percentages)		
		High	Low	Average
I. General Population				1
II. Both Parents	Child	68[b]	35[f]	
III. Mother	Child	17[e]	16[b]	
IV. Half-sibling	Child			7[d]
V. Full sib, same sex	Sibling	16[b]	4[c]	12
Twin Studies				
I. Dizygotic Twins	Co-twin	27[c]	10[c]	17
II. Monozygotic[a, b, c, d]	Co-twin	94[a]	0[g]	35[g]

[a] Gottesman, I. I., and Shields, J.[29]
[b] Kallman, F. J.[43]
[c] Rosenthal, D.[70]
[d] Shields, J., and Slater, E.[74]
[e] Heston, L. L.[37]
[f] Rosenthal, D.[67]
[g] Kringlen, E.[50]

the general population by age and sex, prevalence in the population, etc.

Concordance rates are used in the twin studies. The proband's co-twin is examined for the presence of schizophrenia; if it is found, the twins are said to be concordant; if it is not, they are said to be discordant; again, these figures are expressed as a percentage.

In Table 9–1, for instance, the morbidity risk rate for the child of two schizophrenic parents ranges from 35 to 68 percent, depending on the investigator. The concordance rates between pairs of male dizygotic (DZ) twins varies from 10 to 27 percent; those for male monozygotic (MZ) twins range from 0 to 78 percent.

The table shows that the more nearly the control case resembles the index case in genetic makeup, the higher the probability that he will become schizophrenic. The morbid-risk rate for a half-sibling is 7 percent; where the index case is a schizophrenic parent, a full sibling, or a dizygotic (DZ) twin, the probabilities range from 10 to 27 percent; for a pair of schizophrenic parents the probabilities range from 35 to 68 percent; for an MZ twin, concordances range from 0 to 94 percent. Meehl[57] has pointed out that the only way to win an even money bet predicting that a given, unknown person is schizophrenic is by finding that he has an identical twin who is schizophrenic. (To this he might have added, find that the unknown person's parents are both schizophrenic, depending on which study is being used.)

There are slight but consistently higher percentages whenever sibling or twin pairs are same-sexed instead of opposite-sexed, and whenever the index case is a female rather than a male.

The accuracy of these figures has been challenged by several authors on a number of grounds; a summary of the major criticisms follows: first are criticisms of case finding and diagnosis. Kallman's sample is drawn largely from a chronically and severely ill state hospital population. In fact, when the concordance rate for MZ twins where the index case is judged to be only slightly or moderately ill (i.e., eliminating the "severely ill" group) is computed, it drops from 86 to 54 percent. Furthermore, because Kallman's interest in finding twin pairs for studying was well known to his colleagues, the possibility that cases brought to his attention were unconsciously biased toward higher concordance rates must be considered.

Even in matters of diagnosis, a good deal of confusion exists. European and American uses of the concept of schizophrenia are different. Kallman, quoted in Rosenthal, puts forth these characteristics of his diagnostic criteria: "Constellative evaluation of basic personality changes, . . . bending curve of personality development, . . . xenophobic pananxiety, . . . loss of capacity for free associations, . . . compulsive tendency to omnipotential thought generalizations." Even though Kallman always employed independent judges to review his diagnoses, interjudge reliability was not studied, and it would seem that consistent application of such criteria to a patient population would be quite difficult. Even if such criteria were consistently applied, whether the group so diagnosed would reliably resemble what others consider to be schizophrenia is open to question.

Morbidity and concordance rates vary also, depending on the investigator and the sophistication of the statistical measures he uses.[71] Hence the figures derived from family and twin studies are at best rough approximations and cannot yet be used as firm data from which to construct and test hypotheses.

Even assuming the figures to be reasonably accurate, genetic, constitutional factors, and environmental heritages have not been adequately separated. Nearly all twins studied were raised together until early adolescence; the major substrates of personality development have already been determined by then, according to psychodynamic theory.

One of the lesser defects has been that the reliability of tests of monozygosity in differentiating MZ from DZ twin pairs has sometimes been found wanting.

Specific Studies—1. Offspring of Schizophrenic Parents

Rosenthal[73] reviews several studies of children born to parents both diagnosed as schizophrenic. Of the 163 offspring studied, 36 (22 percent) had developed schizophrenia; 10 (6 percent) had developed questionable schizophrenia; 42 (26 percent) showed signs of other psychopathology; and the remaining 75 (46 percent) were adjudged normal. He found a morbidity risk of 35 percent (cf. Kallman's figure of 68 percent).

Schizophrenic female offspring succumbed at an average age of 21.1 years; the males at 27.9 years, a statistically significant figure, and opposite to all known curves for first admission by age and sex.[54] In contrast, the age at first admission for their mothers was 37.6 and for the fathers, 36.6, approximately a decade later than the average. Thus Rosenthal is dealing with a group of parent-patients who are unusual in that they were able to marry, conceive families (often there were five or more children), and avoid hospitalization until after the age of 35. He points out that, in assessing the etiology of the offsprings' illnesses, it is difficult to sort out the contributions of a chaotic environment from a chaotic genetic endowment.

In one of the few studies in which environment is controlled for, Heston[37] compares the fates of 47 children separated at birth from chronically schizophrenic mothers with carefully matched controls. He found that the experimental group showed a significantly higher incidence of psychiatric disorder than did the control group. The disorders were schizophrenia (with a risk incidence of 16.6 percent, cf. Kallman's of 16.4 percent), schizoid psychopathology, and emotionally labile neurosis. Interestingly, the experimental patients who did not show signs of disorder were "more colorful, . . . held the more creative jobs, . . . followed the more imaginative hobbies, . . . showed more variability of personality and behavior in all social dimensions." (There is a fine line between genius and insanity, about which Oscar Levant once added, "And I have erased that line!")

Specific Studies—2. Discordant MZ Twins

Studies of MZ twins discordant for schizophrenia help tease out genetic, social, or psychological factors that favor discordance. Most of the twin studies of the 1940s and 1950s drew their index cases from the universe of identified psychiatrically ill persons—patients in clinics or mental hospitals— and the concordance rates thus derived were unnaturally high because of sampling bias. More recent studies carried out from birth records have yielded much lower concordance rates. Earlier, rates of 50 to 90 percent were reported; in 1963 Tienari[83] reported a rate of 0 percent (sic!) for ten consecutive MZ twin pairs, one of whom was diagnosed as schizophrenic.

Pollin *et al.*[63] studied five families, verifying diagnosis and zygosity. They found that the schizophrenic twin differed significantly from his nonschizophrenic co-twin in these ways: (1) He weighed less at birth; (2) the parents, particularly the mother, saw him as vulnerable with imperiled survival; (3) in consequence, he was the recipient of more worry, involvement, and attention; (4) his early development was slower; (5) he tended to perform less successfully and was seen as the weaker and less competent; (6) he was more docile and compliant, less independent, and achieved less autonomy; (7) the relative differences and roles between the twins tended to be persistent and unchanging.

In 1964 Kringlen[50] reported on the families of 8 male MZ pairs, of which 6 were discordant for schizophrenia, and on 12 male DZ pairs, of which 8 pairs were discordant. He gathered data from the twins, their siblings and parents, and from available hospital and ancillary data. From the extensive clinical information at his disposal, he found the following for the discordant pairs:

1. Concordance rates for MZ twins are probably lower than previously reported; using strict Scandinavian diagnostic criteria, such rates range from 0 to 34 percent. The family backgrounds were rich in psychopathology.

2. Premorbidly, the preschizophrenic twin showed significantly more of the following traits than the co-twin: dependency on the mother, neurotic phobias, stuttering, enuresis, sensitivity, introversion, inhibition, gentleness, obedience, and lack of enterprise. (Of the only pair separated in early childhood, the proband had a malignant catatonic schizophrenia; the co-twin "never had neurotic symptoms.")

3. The co-twins were frequently deviant, showing suspiciousness, sensitivity, alcoholism, etc.

For Kringlen's discordant DZ twins, the preschizophrenic twin showed much the same early propensity toward neurotic and overobedient behavior as the MZ pairs, and to approximately the same degree. The author concludes:

That several of the MZ "healthy" partners
deviate from the normal suggests that it is not
the schizophrenia as such which is inherited,
but rather a certain vulnerable personality
structure. The finding that the deviation is
about the same in the DZ group does, however,
speak against this hypothesis.

The general conclusion that can be drawn
from the present study is that genetic factors
do not seem to play as great a role as has been
assumed for the etiology of schizophrenia.
However, the material being small, one cannot
rule out the possibility of accidental influences.[50]

Kringlen[51] later examined Norwegian birth records for
all twin births between 1901 and 1931. Such a study elimi-
nates much of the observer bias where hospital records are
used as the primary source. Of the approximately 50,000 twin
births during that period, only in 144 had one or both twins
been hospitalized for schizophrenia (using the strict Scandinavian definition) or schizophreniform psychosis. Of the
55 MZ pairs, 14 (25 percent) were concordant; for the 89 DZ
pairs, 9 (10 percent) were concordant.

Rosenthal,[71] in examining discordant and concordant
male twin pairs, says,

There is almost a total absence of schizophrenia in the families of the discordant twin
pairs, but the illness occurs in about 60% of
the families of the concordant twin pairs. The
affected discordant male twins tend to have a
later age of onset and more favorable outcome
than the concordant male twins. The former
tend to be of the paranoid subtype, the latter
catatonic. Of the discordant male twins, the
one who does not become ill tends to have the
better premorbid social and sexual history, and
the twin who does become ill tends to have a
better premorbid adjustment than do the con-

cordant twins. It is concluded that, biologically speaking, at least two broad groups of schizophrenia are differentiated by this method of analysis: in one, the genetic contribution is absent or minimal; in the other, the genetic contribution is probably considerable.

An attempt to integrate genetic and constitutional contributions into what is primarily an experimental- or learning-oriented hypothesis on the origins of schizophrenia is made by Singer and Wynne.[76, 85]

GENETIC HYPOTHESES: Monogenic and polygenic hypotheses have been generated to account for these findings. The monogenic hypotheses assert that the appearance of schizophrenia is governed by a single gene; the polygenic theories implicate multiple genes.

MONOGENIC HYPOTHESES: These assert that the gene responsible for schizophrenia is dominant, with or without complete penetrance, or that it is recessive, with or without complete manifestation in the homozygote. The logical propositions and the corresponding genetic configurations that stem from these views is given below and in Table 9–2.

Proposition A.—Schizophrenia is a monogenic trait carried recessively. It will be manifested by all persons homozygous for the condition and none who are heterozygous, and in all offspring where both parents are affected.

Proposition B.—Schizophrenia is a monogenic trait carried dominantly. It will be manifested in all persons heterozygous or homozygous for the condition and in all offspring of the homozygote.

Proposition C.—Schizophrenia is a monogenic trait carried by a recessive gene that only incompletely manifests itself. The trait will be manifested by some persons homozygous for the condition and none who are heterozygous.

Proposition D.—Schizophrenia is a mono-

TABLE 9–2

GENETIC CONFIGURATIONS CORRESPONDING TO
PROPOSITIONS IN THE TEXT

Notation

GENOTYPES	PHENOTYPES
A = Normal gene	N = Normal
a = Schizophrenic gene	X = Affected

For incomplete manifestation (= incomplete penetrance)
a_m = Manifested trait a_o = Unmanifested trait

Genotypes	*Phenotype*	
	Proposition A	*Proposition B*
AA	N	N
Aa	N	X
aA	N	X
aa	X	X

	Proposition C	*Proposition D*
AA	N	N
Aa_m	N	X
Aa_o	N	N
$a_o a_m$	?X	X
$a_o a_o$	?X	?X
$a_m a_m$	X	X

genic trait carried by a dominant gene that is
only incompletely penetrant. It will be shown
by some persons heterozygous for the condition
and all persons homozygous for the condition.

Propositions A and B can immediately be discarded because they have been contradicted by available evidence. The
observed morbid-expectancy rate for children of schizophrenic couples, 35 percent, is far less than the 100 percent
figure dictated by Proposition A.[73] Similarly, Proposition B
dictates that 50 percent of the offspring of one schizophrenic
parent heterozygous for the condition, or 100 percent of the
offspring of one schizophrenic parent homozygous for the
condition, should be schizophrenic; the actual morbid-risk
rate is about 16 percent.[37] Propositions A and B also demand

that concordance rates for MZ twins should be 100 percent; these rates, in fact, vary from 0 to 91 percent.

Proposition C has been proposed and discussed by several investigators, among them Böök,[7] Kallman,[42] Slater,[77] and Gregory. Böök postulates that the affected gene, largely recessive, manifests itself in all homozygotes and in about one in five heterozygotes. Slater uses this concept in standard equations of population genetics and calculated expected gene frequencies and manifestations of the trait in parents, sibs, and cousins of schizophrenics. He compared the expected frequencies with those observed and concludes:

> When one takes into account the magnitude of the statistical errors to which all these estimates are liable, it is seen that they are all readily compatible with a gene frequency of about 0.015, and a manifestation rate in the heterozygote of about 0.26. At this point, all but three percent of schizophrenics are heterozygous.[77]

Slater feels that these findings lend support to Böök's hypotheses.

Gregory,[30] using similar statistical models concerned with the same types of data, examines three hypotheses that represent a combination of Propositions C and D, and concludes: "The present writer is now convinced that, even when modified by various degrees of penetrance and expressivity, no monogenic hypothesis is compatible with all the data recorded."

A monogenic theory, furthermore, demands a certain rate of mutation of the responsible gene if the incidence of schizophrenia is to be kept steady in the population over time. Erlenmeyer-Kimling and Paradowski[13] point out that the mutation rate necessary by a monogenic theory for schizophrenia is about 3 to 5×10^{-3}; general estimates of gene mutability in human beings are on the order of 10^{-5}. They feel that the former figure is too high to be reconciled with the latter.

THE POLYGENIC THEORIES: These theories dictate that some combination of two or more genes is required for the appearance of schizophrenia. In one such theory, Karlsson[44] suggests that two genes are responsible, one dominant, the other recessive.

Other theories propose that there are both genes that incline toward the appearance of schizophrenia in the carrier and other benign, modifying genes that protect against its expression. These protective genes may carry with them special survival advantages for the carrier, in a manner analogous to the carriers of the gene of sickle cell anemia's being protected against malaria. Such genes are sufficient to maintain the gene pool in the population even in the face of the distinctly lowered reproductive rate of schizophrenic patients. This latter view has been proposed by Huxley *et al.*[41] and discussed by Erlenmeyer-Kimling and Paradowski,[13] Baldessarini and Snyder,[2] and Rosenthal.[71]

Erlenmeyer-Kimling and Paradowski state,

> Viewing schizophrenia as a genotypically heterogeneous collection of conditions would allow a significant role to be assigned to recurrent mutation while not excluding the possibility of favorable selective properties rooted in immunological advantages.[13]

The evidence for survival advantages is slender, indeed, if there is any, to the carriers of the hypothesized genes that both induce toward, and protect against, the schizophrenias. Nevertheless, Heston's finding of greater diversity and richness of life style of children separated in infancy from schizophrenic mothers demands that further investigation be done in this area.

Summary of Genetic Studies

The question, "Are the schizophrenias hereditary or environmental?" is a naïve and unanswerable question. Questions such as "How much do genetic, constitutional, social, and psychological factors contribute to the different kinds of schizophrenia?" are much more to the point, and these questions are only beginning to be answered.

There is considerable evidence to suggest that the closer in consanguinity to a schizophrenic patient a person is, the greater the likelihood he will develop schizophrenia. The likelihood is slightly increased if one is of the same sex as the index patient, or if the index patient is a female.

The reported probabilities vary widely and reflect artifacts in case finding, diagnostic criteria and reliability, choice of statistical tests, insufficient separation of genetic and social heritages, unreliability of tests of zygosity in twin studies, and other factors. Hence the reported figures must be taken as suggestive rather than established.

Children of schizophrenic mothers, raised away from the mother, show a morbid-risk rate of 16 percent, compared with a rate of about 1 percent for children of nonschizophrenic mothers, also raised apart. If children of schizophrenic mothers did not become schizophrenic, they showed a higher incidence of psychopathology and more interesting, varied, and creative lives than did the control-group subjects.

In two studies of MZ twins discordant for schizophrenia, investigators found that the premorbid adjustment of the afflicted twin, as compared with his co-twin, was poorer and marked by greater parental concern, slower development, greater docility, dependency, sensitivity, introversion, and inhibition. The incidence of schizophrenia in families of discordant MZ twins is lower than in the families of concordant MZ twins, a fact suggesting a greater genetic contribution in the latter.

Monogenic and polygenic hypotheses have been proposed to fit the observed data. Within these hypotheses, varying degrees of dominance, recessivity, penetrance, and manifestation have been invoked. Of the monogenic theories, models of simple dominance or recessivity with complete penetrance do not fit the data and can be discarded. More complex models also do not yield a good fit, and in their present form are not sufficient. Furthermore, monogenic theories demand a rate of genetic mutation that far exceeds the rate generally observed.

Polygenic theories, some of which posit benign modifying genes that protect against the appearance of schizophrenia in carriers, have also been advanced. Supporting data for these theories is still equivocal at best.

In summary, Shields and Slater say:

> On this basis [genetic studies], some 70% of all persons carrying an adequate genetical predisposition to schizophrenia would not fall ill, leaving therefore a considerable margin for the operation of environmental factors.[74]

Rosenthal says:

> If we keep in mind that what is called schizophrenia is probably not a unitary disease, biologically speaking, that sampling procedures must be exceptionally rigorous, that criteria of diagnosis must be specified in reliable detail, that rating and testing procedures should be liberally employed, that future research should be hypothesis-oriented and that both hereditary and environmental factors are probably contributing in varying degree to different types of the disorder, we may only now be on the threshold of discovery with respect to the basic issues surrounding the origin and transmission of schizophrenic behavior.[71]

10

Methodology and
a Theoretical Model

INTRODUCTION

It is clear that, in spite of the enormous volume of research that has been done in the schizophrenias, answers are still few, questions many. The current and future literature will provide attempts at answering the questions, but the literature must be read carefully and critically if the valuable articles are to be separated from the worthless. Many efforts in the past have been weakened because of a lack of attention to methodological rigor, and there is no reason to believe that such defects will be universally remedied in the future.

Studies should be examined as closely for what they do *not* say as for what they *do* say. The critical reader should be cautious in accepting the results of research where such things as diagnostic criteria, controls for observer bias, control groups, etc. are not spelled out in detail.

In the material that follows, as an aid to critical evaluation, I have gone over the studies reported in the preceding three chapters and attempted to identify the most common and relevant sources of error that have appeared. One of my colleagues, on looking over the next section of this chapter, thought that much of the material was painfully obvious and wondered if it needed saying. Obvious though much of it may be, many of these errors still appear in published reports. It still needs saying.

METHODOLOGICAL CONSIDERATIONS

Observer Bias and Control Groups

There is a number of potential sources of error that should be avoided in any study of the schizophrenias, whether the study be oriented to psychological, familial, biochemical, genetic, or sociological factors. These sources include observer bias and lack of controls.

Any observer who has a hypothesis about the presence or absence of a given factor or substance in a schizophrenic patient's background will be influenced in his assessment if he knows whether the data he gathers are from a schizophrenic patient or from a control. Researchers are human and share the human propensity to see what they want to see, no matter how scrupulously they may try to avoid bias. The tendency toward bias can be counteracted only by setting up experiments in which the person who collects and evaluates the data does not know the source of the data. The double-blind method of experimental design is as important to psychiatry as it is to pharmacology. The person who rates the EEG tracing, the family Rorschach protocol, or the fluorescent serum antibody sample simply must not know the source of his data.

Admittedly, this stricture will not always be easy to follow, and there will be situations where it is impossible to follow; allowances must be made for such circumstances, especially if the investigator is in an early, descriptive (as contrasted with a hypothetico-deductive) phase of his work. Regrettably, however, there are a myriad of studies already reported where building in such a safeguard would have been easy, and it just simply was not done.

Control groups are a necessity if results are to have meaning. The groups should be composed of subjects who are also likely to vary on the given parameter being studied. If only the experimental group varies in the predicted direction, and none of the control groups does, the investigator may become increasingly confident that his results mean what he thinks they mean. One of the most conspicuous examples of lack of adequate controls is found in the area of metabolic and physiological research, as discussed in Chapter 9. Nearly every compound, substance, or process studied is one likely to be affected by emotional stress per se, whether the patient undergoing the stress is schizophrenic, depressed, manic, or merely caught in a turbulent life situation. *Yet very few studies included a control group of emotionally distressed nonschizophrenic persons!* Without such a group, it is impossible to say whether deviation from normal is associated with schizophrenia or is merely a concomitant of emotional stress.

For this criticism, however, it would be unfair to single out workers studying metabolism and physiology. The need for adequate control groups exists just as much for the psychologist, psychiatrist, geneticist, and sociologist as it does for the physiologist. Again, the investigator involved in early, descriptive work may be excused a lack of controls (it may be so early in his work that he would not quite know what he was controlling *for*), but once his findings have led to testable hypotheses, control groups must be included in the test procedure.

The choice of what kind of, and how many, controls to employ in a given experiment is a challenge to the sophistication and imagination of the researcher. In retrospect it seems absurdly simple to think that coffee consumption might be related to catechol amine metabolism and to control for this factor; at the time, it was an imaginative step. Currently, controls for dietary factors are built into all worth-while metabolic studies; the need for this kind of control was not always apparent.

Case Finding, Diagnosis, and Classification

One of the major difficulties in research in the schizophrenias has been the disparity in the use of the concept of schizophrenia. What is "schizophrenia" in an American state hospital may be "schizophreniform psychosis" in Scandinavia, and a "psychoneurotic dissociative reaction" in a private sanitorium where diagnoses may be applied more delicately. Yet the criteria for making the diagnosis have been spelled out in elegant detail by Bleuler, who sees the schizophrenias as being a symptom-syndrome in which several aspects of disordered mental functioning must be present to justify the diagnosis. *Research workers reporting on the schizophrenias should adhere to Bleuler's criteria, and so state, or identify explicitly any departures from his criteria.*

Premorbid adjustment, precipitating stress, acuteness of onset, and duration of clinical course have all been studied. Several seemingly unitary concepts, such as "process-reactive," "schizophreniform psychosis–true schizophrenia" and "acute-chronic," in fact contain within them two or more parameters and thus make precise use of these terms difficult, as discussed in Chapter 2. It would be well to separate out and identify all these hidden parameters, and to rate each patient studied on each of them.

The parameters listed below are important in evaluating the meaning of research results. Each should be evaluated, preferably by a relatively objective and public set of criteria:
1. *Precipitating stress*
2. *Quality of premorbid adjustment*
3. *Presence of confusion, delirium, and disorientation on admission*
4. *Length of onset, e.g., less than three months, between three and six months, between six months and a year, greater than a year*
5. *Duration of first and subsequent episodes in terms of*
    a. *Presence or absence of symptoms of the schizophrenias*
    b. *Presence or absence of social recovery*
    c. *Proportion of time in hospital vs. out of hospital*
6. *Age at first admission*
7. *Sex*

Family Studies

The major findings in studies of families of schizophrenics, as reported in Chapter 7, fall into three categories, as follows: (1) abnormalities in communication patterns and transaction styles; (2) peculiarities in role structures and relationships; and (3) familial psychopathology.

Two kinds of data only occasionally reported in such family studies are those of (1) family pedigree for mental illness, and (2) suggestions of neurological defects, subtle or overt, in family members. Such data should be carefully gathered and reported in the future. For example, it may turn out that families of schizophrenics that have a high incidence of mental illness in their pedigrees will demonstrate substantially more (or less) pseudomutuality and rigidity of role structure than do families that have a low incidence.

Goldfarb,[2] studying childhood schizophrenics, found that when the child demonstrated "soft signs" of neurological defect, the degree of familial psychopathology was lower than when he did not. Similar findings may prove true for adult patients: in a study of discordant monozygotic twins, Pollin[9, 10] found suggestions of such "soft signs" in an appreciable portion of his index-patient sample.

For controls, there should be famiiles of chronically, psychiatrically ill nonschizophrenic patients whose age (both current and at admission), sex, social class, degree of impairment, premorbid adjustment, and length of hospitalization match the experimental (i.e., schizophrenic) group's. Whenever possible, data obtained from either experimental or control groups, e.g., psychological test protocols, transcriptions of tapes of interviews, social histories, etc., should be rated "blind" by independent raters.

Social Class

Inexactitude of measurements and reports is perhaps more evident in studies of social class and the schizophrenias than in any other area of study. Dr. Kohn points out many of these deficiencies in Chapter 8. Future studies would be considerably enhanced if the authors were strict and explicit about their diagnostic criteria, about employing the parameters implicit in the concepts of "process-reactive," "acute-chronic," etc., and about the incidence of other forms of psychiatric and organic illnesses encountered in the sample populations.

The definitions of "social class" are many and varied. Most of them rely on some combination of the following in either the patient or his parents: income, education, occupation, place of residence, and indices of power and prestige. Which combination of these factors is used varies from one study to the next; thus comparison is made difficult, if not impossible. These data should be made explicit to facilitate comparability of studies.

Many studies indicate that the incidence of the schizophrenias is highest in the lowest social classes, particularly in central city areas, in *large cities*. This relationship tends to disappear in cities of a population under 100,000. Therefore future epidemiological studies must be explicit about the nature of the community (population, density, etc.) of the sample population.

Even admitting the preponderance of evidence of a high incidence of the schizophrenias in the lower social classes of large cities, the interpretation of this evidence is far from certain, as Dr. Kohn points out. Tests of the "drift" hypothesis have yielded equivocal results. Certainly one needs to know the *father's occupation* to know whether the patient was born to a lower-class existence or drifted down to one as he got older. Preliminary findings suggest that for some patients the former is true, for others the latter, and that no single "drift" hypothesis can account for all the findings. Once again, the need to see the schizophrenias (and their socio-environmental origins) as diverse becomes evident.

Study of admission records of psychiatric facilities will not give adequate data because a number of mentally ill persons never get to such facilities. In San Francisco, the Chinese community is remarkably reluctant to expose problems of emotional illness to local hospitals; estimates based on hospital admission records of the incidence of the schizophrenias in that population would be mistakenly low. The only alternative is to study a community in its own setting, though this approach has its difficulties and drawbacks.

Most studies have measured *prevalence* (the number of cases of illness in the population at the time of study) rather than *incidence* (the number of new cases per 100,000 per annum). Such data perforce emphasize the chronic, severe, and debilitating instances of illness and neglect briefer and milder episodes. *Repeated* studies of the same population to pick up new cases as they arise is the best way of establishing *incidence* figures when they are desired.

Other factors that should be specified in future studies are those of the degree of social integration of the community from which the population is drawn, the degree of ethnic similarity to the surrounding community, and the incidence (or prevalence) of the schizophrenias in the parents and grandparents of the index patient.

For such studies, samples should be drawn from all social classes. The circumstances of the family at the time of birth of the index patient and during the months preceding his overt mental illness should be examined. Only in this way can the stresses of environmental forces be evaluated with respect to the schizophrenias. Stress is not uniformly distributed in the lowest social classes; one family may have more misery than another. Only by studying differential stress in families of the same social class can the investigator begin to tease out the specific factors of environment that are correlated with the appearance of the schizophrenias.

Metabolic, Physiologic, Anatomic, and Genetic Studies

For metabolic, physiologic, and anatomic studies, a number of controls are necessary if results are to be meaningful. The "process-reactive" and "acute-chronic" distinctions have already been made.

Emotional state must be controlled for. In any study, there should be a group of emotionally calm and emotionally agitated schizophrenic patients. There should also be groups of calm and excited psychiatrically ill nonschizophrenic patients. Whether a patient is paranoid or nonparanoid affects certain findings; this distinction must be kept in mind.

Effects of hospitalization and treatment must be controlled for. If the patient is on a phenothiazine treatment, his control should be too. Diet, ECT, and prolonged institutionalization must be equated between groups. Exercise and physical condition should be controlled for.

Though premorbid adjustment is implicit in the process-reactive concept, it deserves special mention. One may speculate that patients whose premorbid adjustment was poor will demonstrate patterns of metabolism and physiology different from those of patients whose adjustment was good. Similarly, patients whose family histories show a high incidence of schizophrenic illnesses may be different biologically from patients whose families show a low incidence. To the extent that there is a genetic-metabolic predisposition to a form of schizophrenia in certain patients, it is crucial to try to segregate such patients from the universe of all schizophrenic patients and to study them in depth. Premorbid adjustment and family history would appear to be two of the most useful indices of identifying such a biological predisposition.

In genetic studies, a search of birth registries, in the manner of Kringlen and Tienari,[7, 13] is much to be preferred to a search of rosters of clinics or hospitals, as Kallman[6] and others have done.

Heston's[5] study of infants separated at birth from schizophrenic mothers, compared with a control group, is one most imaginative step in separating hereditary and environmental factors. Another possibility is the study of children adopted into families who show the kind of characteristic communication patterns and role structures described in Chapter 7, provided, of course, that one obtained data on the incidence of mental illness in the natural parents as well. Monozygotic twins discordant for schizophrenia, reared together and/or separated in early life, are a rich source of data for testing genetic hypotheses.

A THEORETICAL MODEL

Among schizophrenic patients, differences are greater than similarities on a number of parameters. These parameters include the following: age of onset; premorbid adjustment; precipitating stress; confusion and delirium on admission; length of onset; duration of first and subsequent episodes; clinical course; family patterns of communication, transactions, role structures, and psychopathology (including preceding generations); social class; organization of community of residence; emotional agitation; types of treatments and their effects; abnormalities of amine metabolism, immunological system functioning, and other possible physiological indices; and genetic background.

Such differences make it wise to consider the schizophrenias as a final common pathway, the resultant of interaction of biological, emotional, familial, and social factors, as Meyer, Bellak, and others have stressed.[1,8] Muncie cites Meyer's point that there are for human beings, as for any other creature, only a limited number of patterns in the behavioral repertoire available; for human beings, schizophrenic behavior is one of them.[8] The fact that schizophrenia is found in all cultures and with roughly the same incidence (though with some interesting variations) suggests that the propensity for schizophrenic behavior is as much a part of our human heritage as the capacity to walk upright, achieve intellectual and physical control of our surroundings, etc. Yet the fact that not all persons (in fact, only about 1 percent of them) respond to life experiences with schizophrenic behavior suggests that there is a good deal of difference in individual susceptibility to this mode of behavior. It is precisely in trying to elaborate a model that will help define the factors leading to this differential susceptibility that the findings reported above must be placed.

Handlon[4] proposes the following model:

> Schizophrenia is a class with several members, each member having single or multiple causes which are not necessarily unique to that member.

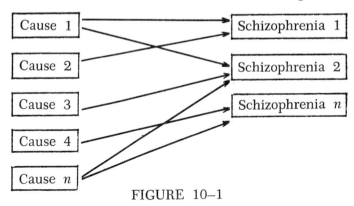

FIGURE 10–1

He then explicates the several various logically possible combinations of necessity and sufficiency that stem from this model.

It has been traditional to equate the various types of schizophrenia, the schizophrenias 1, 2, . . . n of Handlon's model, to the clinical subtypes, e.g., catatonic, hebephrenic, paranoid, etc. In recent years, distinctions such as acute-chronic, reactive-process, and paranoid-nonparanoid, have come into use. In the past, the fact of being schizophrenic has been made the independent variable, and the abnormality in physiology or heredity has been the dependent variable. The studies reported on in this book have largely taken this form: "Once it is established that we have a group of schizophrenic patients, we will examine for such-and-such a defect." Results for the most part have been inconsistent and contradictory, as one would expect if the schizophrenias are a heterogeneous group of disorders.

It would make more sense to make a psychological, familial, socioenvironmental, physiological, or genetic abnormality the independent variable instead. Schizophrenia "X" might be defined as "those clearly schizophrenic patients who show a defect in transmethylation in handling loads of methionine"; schizophrenia "Y" as "those schizophrenic patients who have a schizophrenic mother (and/or father and/or sib, etc.)," and so on.

Such a formulation would be analogous to definition of types of mental deficiency, where mental deficiency "X" is "those patients who show PKU," mental deficiency "Y" is "those patients who show signs of Down's syndrome," and so on. For each of these types, more nearly specific etiologies, and where possible, treatments, have then been determined.

Other criteria for defining types of schizophrenia include the following: defects in the immune system, distorted parental modes of thinking and relating, and poor premorbid adjustment. These criteria are not mutually exclusive, of course; the patient with poor premorbid adjustment may also have a defect in transmethylation.

Rosenthal[12] summarizes three major current theoretical positions on the contribution of hereditary and environmental factors to the schizophrenias; he names these the Monogenic-biochemical, the Diathesis-stress, and the Life Experience approaches.

The Monogenic-biochemical approach holds that a single inherited mutant gene is responsible for the later appearance of schizophrenia, through the pathway of an inborn error of metabolism in a manner similar to PKU. Variability of penetrance is used to explain the fact that not all persons with the genotype demonstrate the illness. Schizophrenia is seen as a unitary phenomenon in which environmental factors, either predisposing (in childhood) or precipitating (in adulthood) are of little import.

The Diathesis-stress approach asserts that potential schizophrenics are born with a variety of predispositions to develop a variety of the schizophrenias, and that the genetic contribtuion is polygenic, in a manner similar to the multiple determinants of adult intelligence. Thus normally adaptive stress-response systems in the adult may go awry.

The Life Experience approach says that some combination of unfortunate early life experience (e.g., maternal deprivation, an irrational environment, etc.) and current life stresses (e.g., adolescence, marriage, childbirth, job loss, etc.) conspire to produce the appearance of illness.

The Diathesis-stress position is the one most nearly consistent with the heterogeneity of findings in genetic, metabolic, and psychological studies in the schizophrenias. The other two are amplifications of the single-mindedly genetic and environmentalist points of view, respectively, the limitations of which have already been commented upon.

Hamburg and Lunde[3] have applied a logic similar to the Diathesis-stress point of view in a recent review of thyroid disease:

> There is growing evidence that incomplete defects in thyroid hormone synthesis occur in adult heterozygotes who develop simple goiter without clinical hypothyroidism. For example, a partial deficiency in the enzyme dehalogenase has been discovered in the relatives of goitrous cretins, some but not all of whom had goiters. Heterozygotes, having a partial defect, are able to maintain normal thyroid function under usual conditions but develop goiters when faced with extraordinary stresses. Iodine deficiency, pubescence, and pregnancy are the best-known situations of this kind. Psychological stresses might well be added to the list.[3]

In the studies of inborn errors of metabolism, where there are genetic alterations of normal enzyme systems, the result is either a build-up of precursors preceding the block (as the phenylalanine in PKU), or use of alternate or abnormal metabolic pathways of degradation, with the appearance of qualitatively and quantitatively abnormal metabolites in blood and urine.

A hypothetical example synthesizes Handlon's multifactorial model, Rosenthal's Diathesis-stress model, Hamburg's analysis of thyroid dysfunction, redefinition of dependent and independent variables, and the possible positive findings reported in this book.

Let us define hypothetical schizophrenic patients as follows: This is the group of clinically schizophrenic persons who have a schizophrenic mother, whose family styles of thinking and relating are distorted, whose premorbid adjustment was marked by retreat and withdrawal from human contacts, and who demonstrate a defect in transmethylation. In addition to these clinically demonstrable phenomena, we assume that the defect in transmethylation is genetic, that the patient is heterozygous for the condition and shows it only when there is depletion of his enzymatic reserve, in the manner of the thyroid heterozygotes.

In such a group of schizophrenic patients, the following train of events may be operative:

1. Adolescence brings with it a new set of hormonal and interpersonal stresses requiring new social and sexual integrations to be made.

2. Because of longstanding difficulties in interpersonal relationships, these stresses result in chronic and severe anxiety and social withdrawal.

3. The anxiety results in increased metabolism of tyrosine, epinephrine, and related compounds.

4. Because of genetic defects and hence lowered enzymatic reserve, there is a shift in such metabolism toward pathways that produce high levels of abnormal isomers.

5. These abnormal isomers either pass more easily through the blood-brain barrier, or their presence there, even in small quantity, affect brain function in such a way that they cause the symptom picture of schizophrenia.

6. The fact of being schizophrenic, with heightened sensitivity to rebuff, ridicule, and fear of close relationships, serves as a new and persistent source of emotional stress and helps to maintain the abnormal metabolic chain of events.

7. Administration of a phenothiazine interrupts the anxiety and causes a diminution of tyrosine metabolism to premorbid levels. Abnormal pathways no longer are used because the limited levels of normal enzyme activity are sufficient; the symptom picture clears.

8. On reduction of phenothiazine, anxiety recurs, and with it the reappearance of altered metabolism and the clinical picture of schizophrenia.

9. Effective psychotherapy enhances the patient's capacity to make profitable and enjoyable interpersonal contacts. Such contacts no longer evoke intense anxiety and concomitant increased epinephrine metabolism; abnormal enzymatic pathways are not needed, and remission persists in the absence of phenothiazines.

In summary, then, it would be wise to see the schizophrenias as a final common pathway reflecting the interaction of biological, emotional, familial, and social factors; they are therefore a heterogeneous group of disorders even though they may appear clinically similar. Any model that would hope to improve understanding of the etiologies of the schizophrenias must reflect this complexity. Such models have been proposed by Handlon,[4] Rosenbaum,[11] and Rosenthal.[12] Rosenthal's Diathesis-stress approach is analogous to that used by Hamburg in a review of thyroid disease in homozygotes and heterozygotes for partial and complete enzyme dehalogenase deficiency. The model proposed is one that integrates a genetic defect, childhood stress, current anxiety in interpersonal adjustments, altered metabolism of tyrosine and its derivatives,* and response to phenothiazines and psychotherapy.

* Abnormalities in tyrosine metabolism are only one set of biochemical defects currently under study. In the next several years other kinds of defects may prove to be as, or more, important.

11

Three Psychodynamic Fomulations

Freud, Jung, Sullivan, and their followers have all made important contributions to understanding the psychological and metapsychological phenomena of the schizophrenias. Certain aspects of these points of view are summarized in this chapter.

FREUD AND PSYCHOANALYSIS

Ego and Superego Functioning

In normal and neurotic persons, the functions of the ego in maintaining psychic equilibrium are many and varied. The ego must mediate stimuli and impulses arising from several sources: external reality, the body (proprioception), the unconscious (id and unconscious superego), the preconscious, and the conscious superego. Perhaps the most important of the ego's tasks is the reduction of irrelevance and the amplification of the salient. External reality is filled with stimuli; if each stimulus were attended to and responded to, goal-directed behavior would become impossible, and the organism would be reduced to a psychological equivalent of Brownian movement. Similarly, the unconscious never sleeps, as Freud demonstrated in "The Psychopathology of Everyday Life";[7] again, the ego must exercise great selective powers.

The ego performs these functions with superb suavity in normal persons; in fact, one is only occasionally aware

that the work is going on at all. It is only when ego functioning is disturbed or breaks down seriously, as seen in the schizophrenias, that the need for good ego functioning, often taken
for granted, becomes evident.

Much of the ego's work takes place through the mechanisms of defense. The kind and degree to which the various
defense mechanisms are employed are an index to the relative health (adaptiveness) or sickness (maladaptiveness) of
ego functioning. Of these mechanisms, described in excellent
detail in Anna Freud's *The Ego and the Mechanisms of Defense*,[6] those most commonly used by normal persons are
repression, suppression, sublimation, and reaction-formation.
Certain other mechanisms of defense are less adaptive; i.e.,
they seriously distort reality, and/or they severely compro-
mise the organism's flexibility of response to stimuli. Among
these more maladaptive defenses are those of projection,
massive denial, primitive incorporation, magical and obsessive thinking, and compulsive rituals of doing and undoing.
Many of these latter defenses appear in exaggerated form
in the schizophrenias.

The single most important defense is that of repression.
The ego's barrier of repression against the unconscious protects most people from possible irruptions into consciousness
of the primitive, primary process thoughts, drives, and impulses described in detail in Chapter 4. The ego and its barrier
of repression did not exist at birth; it derived from id during
the first several years of life. Said Freud, "Where id was,
there ego shall be. It is a work of culture—not unlike the
draining of the Zuider Zee."[8] With the regression of schizophrenia, the once nearly impenetrable barrier of repression
(an impenetrability well known to every psychoanalytic patient who has spent hundreds of hours trying to know better
his own unconscious), often sadly crumbles. The moat is
empty; the bridge is down; the sentinels fail to stand guard.
The unconscious storms into consciousness, and the walking
dreamer of Jung is to be seen. The patient is tormented both
by strong id impulses as well as simultaneous strictures
against them that come from a punitive superego.

The superego of the schizophrenic is far different from its later derivatives in healthy adults. The superego of the 5-year-old is relatively unsubtle: things are either good or bad, and there is little, if any, middle ground. In contrast, in healthy adults, the conscious superego has evolved in the direction of an ego ideal that balances, weighs, and thinks; sexuality, aggression, and the other strong emotions are neither good nor bad; rather, their goodness or badness depends on the situation. To paraphrase Freud, where once was the primitive superego of the child, there shall be the ego ideal of the adult. For the schizophrenic, the superego lacks this flexibility of judgment and condemns harshly. Stephen J.'s voices constantly reminded him that he was a "bowel eater"; and Sylvia T.'s psychotic thoughts punished her when she feared the desertion of her husband and the loss of her baby.

At the same time that the schizophrenic patient's ego is dealing with irruptions from the unconscious, its abilities to attend to and respond to external stimuli are severely impaired. Events are not perceived, because of preoccupation with unconscious processes (autism), or they are misperceived (e.g., did Sylvia T.'s lighting of a cigarette cause me to be paged?). Relationships with others are misconstrued (e.g., George M.'s runaway to protect me from electrocution, Chapter 4).

The simultaneous failures of repression and of reality testing lead to a paradoxical state: the schizophrenic may be amazingly conversant with his own unconscious, yet startlingly ignorant of simple social reality. The very patient who may be able to elucidate his oedipal conflicts in fine detail may not realize that it is good form to be clean-shaven and neatly dressed when going for a job interview.

The ego defects are never total; there are always surviving intact islands of ego. Even severely deteriorated patients, such as Naomi N., are able to feed themselves, clothe themselves, ask for cigarettes, etc., even though they may go about it in rather bizarre ways. One chronic paranoid schizophrenic patient, a former jazz musician hospitalized for a decade, would impulsively go to the piano from time to time and play excellent music, ending his playing as abruptly as he had started. Another chronic patient, formerly a mathematician, presented a sad picture of dilapidation, yet he worked out complicated mathematical equations on the backs of envelopes or on scraps of paper; many of these were valid scientifically according to mathematicians who examined them.

A table of normal ego functions and their disturbances found in the schizophrenias is presented in Table 11–1.

TABLE 11–1

NORMAL AND DISTURBED EGO FUNCTIONS

(Bellak's[3] adaptation of Beres[4])

Ego Functions	*Disturbances*
I. Relation to Reality	I. Disturbances in Relation to Reality
A. Adaptation to reality	A. Disturbances in adaptive capacity
1. Differentiation of figure and ground	1. Inappropriate behavior with subjective or objective difficulties
2. Role playing	2. Inability to cope with deviations in normal routine
3. Spontaneity and creativeness; regression in the service of ego	3. Failure in social adaptation; rigidity
B. Reality testing	B. Disturbances in reality testing
1. Accuracy of perception	1. Projection, rationalization, denial, and the distortion of reality by hallucinations and delusions
2. Soundness of judgment	

TABLE 11–1 (*continued*)

Ego Functions	Disturbances
3. Orientation in time, place, person	
C. Sense of reality	C. Disturbances in sense of reality
1. Good "self boundaries"	1. Feelings of estrangement and lack of spontaneity
2. Unobtrusiveness of ordinary functioning	2. Excessive feelings of *déjà vu*
	3. Oneirophenia
	4. Cosmic delusions
	5. Confused body images
	6. Intrusion of self as subject or object
	7. Physiological manifestations
II. Regulation and Control of Drives	II. Disturbances in Drive Control
A. Ability to engage in detour behavior	A. Conduction and habit disorders (temper tantrums, nail biting, etc.)
B. Frustration tolerance (neutralization of drive energy)	B. Accident proneness
C. Anxiety tolerance	C. Excessive impulsivity
D. Integrated motility	D. Tension states
E. Tolerance of ambiguity	E. Catatonic and manic excitement
F. Sublimation	F. Psychomotor slow-up of catatonia and depression
	G. Lack of, or incomplete acquisition of, control of excretory functions
	H. Physiological manifestations

TABLE 11–1 (*continued*)

Ego Functions	*Disturbances*
III. Object Relations	III. Disturbances in Object Relations
A. Capacity to form satis-factory object relations	A. Psychotoxic and psychic deficiency diseases (in infancy)
B. Object constancy	B. Narcissism, autism
	C. Symbiotic relationships
	D. Anaclitic relationships
	E. Hypercathexis of the self; ambivalence, fear of incorporation, sado-masochism
IV. Thought Processes	IV. Disturbances in Thought Processes
A. Selective scanning	A. Thinking organized and compelled by drives
B. Ability to avoid contamination by inappropriate material or drives	B. Preoccupation with instinctual aims
C. Good memory	C. Autistic logic
D. Sustained ability to concentrate	D. Loose and "nonsensical" types of associative links
E. Abstracting ability	E. Distortion of reality
	F. Lack of referents in time and place, anthropomorphism, concretism, symbolism, syncretism, etc.
	G. Magic thinking
V. Defensive Functions	V. Disturbance in Defensive Functions
A. Repression (as a barrier against external and internal stimuli)	A. Emergence of primary thought process
B. Sublimation, reaction formation	B. Overreaction to stimuli
C. Projection	C. *Déjà vu* experiences

TABLE 11–1 (*continued*)

Ego Functions	Disturbances
D. Denial, withdrawal, and other defenses	D. Lack of drive control
	E. Frightening hypnagogue phenomena
	F. Increase in parapraxes
	G. Impairment in emotional control
VI. Autonomous Functions	VI. Disturbance in Autonomous Functions
A. Perception	A. Corresponding impairment of these ego functions
B. Intention	
C. Intelligence	
D. Thinking	
E. Language	
F. Productivity	
G. Motor development	
VII. Synthetic Function	VII. Disturbance in Synthetic Function
A. To unite, organize, bind, and create—the ego's ability to form Gestalten	A. Tendency to dissociation
B. Neutralization	B. Inability to tolerate change or trauma
C. Sublimation	C. Inability to bind psychic energy
D. Somatic "homeostasis"	

Psychosexual Development

In normal persons, the level of psychosexual development is more or less at the genital stage, with elements of fixation or residua from the preceding oral, anal, phallic, and latent periods still remaining. During the phallic period, which separates the pregenital from the genital stages of development, a number of important developmental events take place. First, the ego's barrier of repression against the unconscious becomes well developed. Second, because of the oedipal conflict and its resolution, a firm sense of gender-role identity emerges. Though there is now considerable evidence to suggest that gender-role identification, or conflicts about it, is already quite apparent by the age of 2½ or 3,[31] the coalescence of the many disparate elements of gender identification takes place during the phallic stage.

Among these various elements are (1) awareness of sexual anatomy and functioning; (2) renunciation of the parent of the opposite sex as an ideal love object; (3) identification with the parent of the same sex; (4) a sense of masculinity or femininity and (5) a change from primary narcissism to secondary narcissism and the beginnings of true mutuality in relationships.

In the profound regression often seen in the schizophrenias, the patient functions primarily at a pregenital level, and thus many of the developmental accomplishments of the phallic stage are lost or are present only in rudimentary form. Knowledge of sexual anatomy and functioning may be scanty and unreliable; patients may be literally truly unsure whether they are men or women. In Draw-A-Person tests, the figures may either show no sexual apparatus at all or else characteristics of both sexes. As McAlpine and Hunter[21] have pointed out, the fear that many paranoid patients have, expressed in delusions and hallucinations, that they are homosexuals, or being transformed into the opposite sex (as seen in Freud's famous case of Judge Schreber), may be due to such sexual confusion. This confusion may complement Freud's famous formulation of the role of latent homosexuality in genesis of paranoia in males, i.e.,

1. "I love him." (Ego-alien; repressed and through reaction-formation converted into . . .)
2. "I hate him." (Also ego-alien, and converted by projection into . . .)
3. "He hates me." (And, by generalization, to . . .)
   "They hate me."

These matters of sexual confusion are complicated, in Western society certainly, by the confusion between emotional intimacy, physical intimacy, and lust, as Sullivan has pointed out.[33] By emotional intimacy, I mean the kind of close sharing of feelings that can take place between close friends, husband and wife, psychiatrist and patient, etc. By physical intimacy, I mean the kind of comfort that can be gained by two bodies touching, such as when two friends embrace, or a parent cuddles or roughhouses with a child. By lust, I mean the powerful orgasmic urges for sexual discharge, characterized succinctly in the slang terms "horniness" or "having hot pants," which may have little or nothing to do with intimacy.

At life's best, all three of these needs are combined in a love relationship between a man and a woman. The popular media, in fact, present them as a package deal, but life only occasionally conforms to the popular media, and most persons learn that there are situations where one or two of these needs can be satisfied but not the other(s). For the schizophrenic, it may be extremely difficult to separate the wish for emotional and physical intimacy—the wishes to be held, cuddled, and comforted—from lust. Thus he may assume that if he has wishes for emotional intimacy with a man, he must therefore be a homosexual. Furthermore, there may be powerful unconscious wishes to incorporate the father's strength by incorporating his organ of strength—his penis (or his right arm, as seen in the case presented in Chapter 4).

The normal renunciation of the parent of the opposite sex as the ideal sexual object, and identification with the parent of the same sex is difficult for the schizophrenic patient. The studies of gender-role functioning between parent and child in the families of schizophrenics is described in some detail in Chapter 7; suffice it to say here that these normal resolutions are often far from complete in the developing preschizophrenic, and crumble away entirely under the stress of overt psychosis. Such conflicts have been documented in detail by Alanen.[1, 2]

Freud described the state of narcissism present at birth

as "primary narcissism," in the sense that there was no difference perceived between "self" and "not-self." It is a state of
perfect solipsism. By the age of 5, however, there is a firmly
differentiated concept of "self" and "not-self." Yet a large
proportion of the child's drives and motivations are self-centered, a series of messages to the world of the sort: "Take
care of me; feed me; look at me; make the universe revolve
around me." This latter differentiated absorption with the self
Freud termed "secondary narcissism." With the regression to
pregenital levels in schizophrenia, primary narcissism makes
a reappearance, and the sense of individuality, of self vs. not-
self, often becomes blurred.

What appears, then, are conflicts that are more from the
oral and anal periods than from the phallic or later periods.
The oral conflicts revolve around nurturance, cannibalism,
feeding, being taken care of, and fears of starvation, abandonment, and death through neglect or of being engulfed because
of projected cannibalistic fantasies. Naomi N.'s chattering,
recorded in Chapters 1 and 3, is almost exclusively on this
level. The anal-stage conflicts revolve around dominance and
submission, aggression and control, locomotion and inhibition, and dirtiness and cleanliness. Most compulsive rituals
and obsessive thoughts are attempts to defend against these
conflicts, as shown by the wooden-soldier behavior of Stuart
M. (Chapter 1). In contrast to the obsessive-compulsive
neurotic, the thoughts and rituals of the schizophrenic are
archaic and primitive and defend against almost entirely
autistic wishes and fantasies.

I have gone on at some length about these pregenital
phenomena because they may often be masked by pseudo-
genital thoughts and behavior, and the student beginning his
acquaintance with schizophrenic patients may be misled. The
patient who becomes promiscuous as his psychosis becomes
apparent is most probably *not* interested in heterosexual union
per se, but is engaged in a desperate search for reassurance
that he or she is lovable as a human being, or that he must
still be a man because his penis functions or a woman because

her vagina functions. It is often tempting for the inexperienced interviewer to read a sexual (i.e., phallic-stage) meaning into schizophrenic behavior, especially with patients of the opposite sex, but the simple fact of the matter is that most of the severely ill patients are functioning primarily on a pregenital level and are best understood as such.

Metapsychological Considerations

Psychoanalytic attempts at etiological explanation for the profound regression seen in schizophrenia have become more sophisticated in recent years. Originally, the traditional concepts of intense overfrustration or overgratification early in life were invoked: the patient was either so extremely frustrated or so symbiotically gratified in the first two or three years of life that a serious arrest of psychosexual and libidinal development took place, and the ego derived from such imperfect beginnings had little capacity to endure the stresses of later life. Though there may well be truth in such concepts, they are difficult if not impossible to document or test.

Szasz,[49] in a metapsychological article that specifically avoids questions of etiology, puts forth a number of ideas about early defects in object relations as a precursor to later schizophrenic phenomena. Many of his concepts derive from the works of the British school of object relations, especially those of Klein[20] and Fairbairne.[5] For the proper physical growth of the child, Szasz notes, food must first be acquired and ingested; then it must be broken down and assimilated. Thus each normal child builds up a reservoir of stored internal objects, starting from the moment of birth; as ego development proceeds into the third and fourth year, these objects may become introjected identifications, that is, rather well-differentiated representations of other objects.

Szasz points out that many schizophrenic breakdowns occur in the face of object loss or the need to establish new object contact. In normal persons faced with loss of an external object, the store of internal objects is called on to provide psychological sustenance, just as the tissues provide sustenance during periods of starvation. (In fact, it is often the internal representation of the lost person that is called forth, and the mourner unwittingly imitates traits, mannerisms, or expressions of the absent person.) For the schizophrenic, suggests Szasz,[50] "the occurrence of a schizophrenic break in the face of the loss of an external object might be regarded as evidence of a lack of 'stored objects'. . . ."

Szasz contrasts the response of the neurotic patient and the psychotic patient to psychotherapy. The development of the transference neurosis of the neurotic is slow; it is "the patterning by the ego of a relationship to an external object on the model of a pre-existing relationship with an internal object."[49] As mentioned in Chapter 4, on phenomenology, and Chapter 14, on psychotherapy, the schizophrenia patient is often *unable to avoid* immediate and intense transferences to the therapist. Szasz would attribute this phenomenon to the relative deficiency of stored objects on which to pattern a more differentiated transference reaction. Such an immediate transference he terms a "model relationship," for which the prototype is the "small child vis-à-vis his mother, father, and older siblings."

Szasz speculates that there are two important forms of human learning, "model" and "transference." The former corresponds to learning by "identification," e.g., a child learning his mother tongue; the latter implies "abstraction, comparison, and logical discrimination." Though both types of learning take place throughout life, the model or identification mode must precede the transference mode: one cannot use language for effective communication until one has learned the language; one cannot show subtlety and discrimination in human relationships until there is an adequate store of internal objects. Adult social functioning requires a certain knowledge about the other person's emotional and social needs. Szasz[51] points out that such knowledge "is based on previous human relationships of a more or less similar nature, which serve as models for later relationships. The lack (in schizophrenics) of such internal models (objects) explains the difficulties which arise with the need for human relationships at a later time."

He considers the schizophrenic patients' primary need in therapy, then, to be a need for a good external object (the therapist) whom the patients may introject to compensate for their own lack. He points out further that many therapists, known to be skilled in work with such patients, vary widely in their techniques and their interpretations (e.g., from the forceful intrusion of John Rosen to the motherly acceptance of Gertrude Schwing), but the therapists share the central characteristic of making themselves available for introjection by the object-hungry patient. The implications of this notion are amplified on in the chapter on psychotherapy.

There is extensive evidence to suggest that the deficiency of internal objects (Szasz sees these as central to the psychology of schizophrenia) is, in fact, a reflection of a real lack of available objects in the early years of life. Searles,[30] in describing the parents of schizophrenics when the patients were young, says:

> The mother is a typically deeply anxious, precariously integrated person whose chronic anxiety is probably intensified in her dealings with her young infant by reason of the symbiotic relatedness—with its concomitants of mutual incorporation and poor definition of ego boundaries—which the infant needs, and therefore strives to establish with her. Thus, in the relationship with the infant, her own personality disorganization is probably even greater than usual.

Later Searles says:

> Thus we can understand how fragmenting it is to his (i.e., the preschizophrenic's) personality for him to have, as often happens, a be-

wildering succession of mothering figures, or
many changes in residence, or for him to be
exposed to intrafamilial relationships or
marked dissension. He cannot incorporate usefully the personality ingredients of two parents
whose interpersonal relationship with one another is a very poorly integrated one—parents
who seem (in some instances when one interviews both together) to function almost without
any cordination at all, even an antagonistic
one. Thus, at an intrapsychic level in the child,
introjections from the mother cannot be well
integrated with introjection from the father.

Thus Szasz talks about a deficiency in stored, internal
objects as a central part of the psychology of the schizophrenic
patient and his current object relations, and Searles suggests
that the deficiency results from the unavailability in early
life of suitable objects capable of being introjected. Searles'
suggestion (1959) came before many of the family studies
reported in Chapter 7 had been published, but they certainly
support his thesis. There can hardly be a surplus of available,
healthy objects for introjection in families marked by a predominance of pseudomutuality, marital schism and skew, excessive rigidity or chaos of role structure, and a predominance
of psychosis, severe neurosis, and other forms of significant
psychopathology!

In an article that relates clinical findings to psychoanalytic theory, Alanen[1] examines the implications of disturbed family interactions at four stages of ego development.
The earliest defect in ego development is "the defective initia-
tion into important object relationships, above all in that with
the mother," especially where the parents have been remote
and lacking in emotional contact with the child. Such a defect
may be present in adults "who have been strikingly withdrawn even before their manifest psychological breakdown."

At a second level, in contrast, there are families where
one or both parents are pathologically possessive of the child

and maintain a symbiotic relationship with him years beyond the time such symbiosis is appropriate. Such parents use the child for their own needs; he must sacrifice his own ego development for the parents. These are families marked by high levels of pseudomutuality. Alanen suggests that patients from these families, unlike the aloof and hard-to-reach patients from families with remote parents, can readily enter into a therapeutic relationship, provided that the therapist is able to allow the patient to reconstruct a symbiotic mode of relating.

Alanen then points out, "The third point of pathological ego development in schizophrenia . . . is the lack of healthy patterns for ego mastery and personality integration in the families. . . ." It is here that Lidz's findings of familial irrationality and lack of clarity about personal and gender-role identification, presented in detail in Chapter 7, would best apply.

His fourth point of pathological ego development is the lack of opportunity in the family for "role-taking and identity formation in the family and in the life environment in a broader sense." Here the patient is deprived of the opportunity to learn the social skills that would help him adjust in the extrafamilial community. The family boundary-maintaining system, the "rubber fence," serves to insulate the patient-to-be from potentially ego-strengthening influences available in the surrounding community.

In summary, then, Szasz views the schizophrenic patient as having a basic deficiency of stored internal objects from the past on which he can pattern a differentiated response to objects available in the present, can employ a "transference mode" of interpersonal learning. Searles' evidence suggests that, in the schizophrenic patient's childhood, the parents rarely behaved in a sufficiently stable, predictable, or relatively anxiety-free way; thus they were unavailable to the child as useful objects of incorporation. Alanen, in the light of recent family studies, points out in what way disturbed family interactions provide grave impediments to healthy or adaptive ego development.

JUNG AND ANALYTICAL PSYCHOLOGY
by John Weir Perry, M.D.

C. G. Jung's first published work was a study of the structure and functioning of complexes in the psychology of schizophrenia; it provided the occasion for his association with Freud. His second major work was on symbolic content in schizophrenia, and it occasioned his break with Freud. These early studies were based on psychopathology; later researches led Jung to his formulations about healthy personality development, thereafter his predominant interest, though he came back to researches in the schizophrenias repeatedly. Jung's approach has become known as *analytical psychology*.

BASIC CONCEPTS

A number of Jung's basic concepts will be described before we come to their application to the schizophrenias. The most important of these concepts are the following: archetypes and imago; complexes; ego consciousness; and collective and personal unconscious.

Archetypes and Imago

Archetypes are innate propensities to represent the typical emotional experiences of man in typical universal forms, composed of emotion and image.[11, 13] They are instinctive in that they are innate readinesses to respond to specific constellations of inner and outer conditions. They have a mythological cast and aura. For instance, a withholding and destructive mother is a common phenomenon in the emotional lives of children, a phenomenon so regularly repeated through the generations that it has become "coded in" the germ plasm, and has given the child a "readiness" to apperceive the mother in such a moment as "witch," and simultaneously to feel a specific kind of chilling fear. Out of this encounter is formed a parental *imago*, made up of the

John Weir Perry, M.D., is Assistant Clinical Professor, University of California Medical School, San Francisco, and Director of Studies, C. G. Jung Institute, San Francisco.

combined impressions of the personal and the archetypal negative mother.

Complexes

A *complex* is an emotionally toned grouping of representations and associations around such a nuclear imago;[15] it results from an often repeated and highly charged encounter of the type that gave rise to the original imago. The emotional tone is provided by the archetype, the "affective root" of the complex; hence the unconscious is regarded as the "emotional psyche" and is experienced in the form of its constituent complexes. Complexes tend to become and to remain *autonomous*, i.e., independent of the ego. Though the ego may be aware of the existence and effects of such autonomous complexes, it is powerless to prevent their activity. Each complex has its own emotional coloring (affect) and energic charge, and comes into play as a part-personality with considerable inner cohesion.

Ego Consciousness

The representative in consciousness of the psychic organism is the *ego*. It is the *master complex* and acts as the carrier of the sense of identity as it gradually develops into its fullness of experience. The development of personality is a spontaneous process whose aim is the broadening of the ego's scope of awareness and the differentiating of its own unique individuality. Like other complexes, the ego has its roots in an archetypal foundation, the *self* or *central archetype*. By its activity the raw materials of ego development are activated in the unconscious and come into the ego's experience at the appropriate times by way of the emotional life. This is the work of the *individuation process* of which Jung made extensive observations.

Collective and Personal Unconscious

The distillate of generations of universal human experience represented publicly in myth, symbol, and legend is represented privately and individually by the *collective unconscious*, with its archetypal contents.[17] As personal experience interacts with the collective unconscious, autonomous complexes are produced; they provide the contents of the *personal unconscious*.

Just as the ego is the governing center of consciousness, Jung found that there existed an unconscious counterpart, an unconscious source of integrative activity that he termed the self.[14] The *self* is, itself, an archetype and occupies a central position in Jung's views of the dynamics and genetics of psychological development.

From his early work on word association tests, Jung recognized that children derive their problems from the psychology of the parents.[10] The tests revealed that, to a great extent, unconscious autonomous complexes in the parents formed similar complexes in the child. The Jungian theory of genesis of these emotional components of the unconscious rests on this ground,[12] not on the fate of the instinctual drives toward the parents as objects. For example, the negative mother's mood of withholdingness may emanate from a complex based on the archetype of the witch mother. The child at these times experiences both fear of abandonment and the mother's emotion; she thus develops within herself a replica of the mother's witch complex, and may be found in certain moods doing what the mother had done, even sounding like her.

APPLICATIONS TO THE SCHIZOPHRENIAS

Unconscious Complexes

In his classic study based on both clinical observations and word-association-test data, "The Psychology of Dementia Praecox" ('07),[9] Jung notes that the objective signs of affect are stronger and more distorted in the schizophrenic than in the normal or neurotic subject, an indication that there is an unconscious pathological content. At the outset of the disorder, one finds the presence of strong emotion, indicating the activity of a complex having a causal role in the genesis of the syndrome. The subject, unable to free himself from this complex, increasingly associates only to it. Under the spell of this insuperable complex, the subject gradually loses interest in reality. The inevitable outcome is an extensive destruction of the personality.

In a detailed analysis of the productions of a typical case of deteriorated paranoid schizophrenia, Jung formulates a characteristic division of the affective and ideational material into three predominating complexes. Consciousness may be dominated by the "complex of grandeur," a systematic creation of a wish-fulfilling fantasy as a substitute for a life of emotional privation and a depressingly wretched family environment. Unconsciousness is then found dominated by a "correcting," contradictory "complex of injury," of which split-off fragments enter consciousness in the form of hallucinations. The relation of these may be reversed in other cases, the former unconscious, the latter conscious. The third in the triad is usually represented in a voice that speaks for a "correcting," "ironical," "semi-normal ego-remnant," looking on and commenting on the futility of these pathological fantasies and mocking them. This complex in some cases dominates the conscious field, leaving the other two as mutually contradictory complexes in the unconscious.

In a detailed account of a series of therapeutic interviews and accompanying drawings of a catatonic woman, Perry[25] demonstrates how consistently the imagery focused on the theme of a symbolic center and a quadrated circle. He concludes that the schizophrenic process is one of dissolving and then reorganizing the self in the image of the "central archetype." An array of comparative symbolic material drawn from various cultures is presented to verify the nature of this image.

In a final pair of papers in his late years, Jung turned his attention to the events in the unconscious in the disorder; the disintegration of complexes themselves; and the stirring of affective foundations. He observes[18] that the schizophrenic complex differs from the normal or the neurotic one in that it "is characterized by a peculiar deterioration or disintegration of its own ideational content, leaving the general field of attention remarkably undisturbed. It looks as though the complex were destroying itself by distorting its own contents and means of communication," and it devours its own energy drawn from its own contents rather than from other mental processes. This self-destruction of the complex "manifests itself . . . in a disintegration of the means of expression and communication" and also in an inadequacy of its affectivity. Its "emotional values seem to be illogically distributed or absent, disintegrated in much the same way as the disturbed psychic elements."

In his last paper[19] Jung points out that the affective concomitants of the complexes differ from the ordinary only in that they have far more devastating consequences and in that they form the symptoms specific for schizophrenia, creating the neologisms, perseverations, stereotypies, etc., all signs of the violence of the affect. This affect runs in courses that are not visible to the observer, and produces instead the apathy characteristic of the disorder. Hence the complexes become random and chaotic, and characterized by archaic associations akin to mythological motifs, pointing to the fact that the biological foundations of the psyche are deeply affected. The ordinary compensations thus remain stuck in archaic forms.

Ego Functioning

In its reciprocal relation to the ego consciousness, the unconscious performs a compensating and balancing function. In normal and neurotic personalities, development is never so one-sided that this "corrective" influence goes without effect. In the abnormal case, there is a characteristic refusal to recognize and a resistance against this compensating influence, and a renewed emphasis upon the one-sidedness. What should be the beginning of a healing process comes in a form unacceptable to the ego, and is then experienced as a criticism that is projected out onto the surroundings. The pairs of opposites are torn asunder and a state of division ensues, in which the unconscious obtrudes violently into the field of awareness.

Jung[16] sets forth his fullest formulation of the disorder in a paper published in 1939. Bleuler, who had worked with Jung, had divided the symptomatology into primary and secondary groupings, the latter being the familiar groupings of psychological origin; the primary groupings he had found to consist of a fundamental disintegrative disturbance of the association processes, attributable to an organic cause. Jung attacks here the problem of the primary symptoms, and finds in Janet's concept of the *abaissement du niveau mental* the basis of a truly psychogenic formulation of the root of the schizophrenic process. This "lowering of the level of consciousness" Jung makes into an energic concept, in which the activation of the affects induces a shift of psychic energy, leaving the ego consciousness weakened relatively to the now strengthened unconscious. The effects of this shift were all observations drawn from the word-association studies, which he recapitulates: "The *abaissement* (1) causes the loss of whole regions of normally controlled contents; (2) produces split-off fragments of the personality; (3) hinders normal trains of thought from being consistently carried through and completed; (4) decreases the responsibility and the adequate reaction of the ego; (5) causes incomplete realizations and thus gives rise to insufficient and inadequate emotional reactions; and (6) lowers the threshold of consciousness, thereby allowing normally inhibited contents of the unconscious to enter consciousness in the form of autonomous invasions." The ego thus becomes increasingly hampered, losing ground to the activated unconscious. When emotional stress then brings the *abaissement* to a critical point, the personality splits up into complexes, and the ego appears as only one among these, with no superior energy charge and thus no mastery.

In a series of articles, Metman[22, 23, 24] describes several types of ego in the genesis of schizophrenia. He finds the essential pathogenic complex to be an "infant-mother-self identity," representing an arrest at a presexual level. Metman visualizes three phases of life, the middle one being the time of acceptance of the demands of adulthood, sexual maturity, parenthood, and the responsibilities of one's position in the social world; the schizophrenic tendency is to keep these demands remote and confused and thus to avoid the meaning of this part of life. In the fantasy imagery are seen the magical means used to bypass it by soaring above it.

Metman finds four main types of ego formation in his cases: (1) the "rudimentary ego," constantly being overwhelmed by the fear of experience and fleeing from danger by scattering itself, thus playing the inferior role; (2) the "ego-substitute," rising above the painfulness of experience by identifying with the archetype of order, thus playing the superior role; (3) the "pseudo-ego," fascinated by the safety that normal people seem to find in the generally accepted conventions of the cultural canon; and (4) the "incipient ego," which senses in any such safety a greater danger, that of stagnation; like the "Trickster" figure, he makes a mockery of the generally accepted conventions.

From case material, Perry finds[26] the dynamic focus of acute schizophrenic process to be the self-image, composed of two interrelated systems: a personal and an archetypal one, the former damaged and debased, and the latter compensatory and exalted but representing the lost potential of the personality's self-esteem and strength. Both find their origin in the earliest love-bonds, chiefly with the mother. The distortions of the self-image by the mother's unconscious projections onto the child he calls "central injuries,"[27] inasmuch as they involve the central archetype, the powerfully dynamic core and containing structure of the most significant love-bonds. The consequent withdrawal of feeling, due to a distrust of acceptance and to an expectation of hurt, is seen by Perry as the factor that starts off the disorder and its energic imbalances which Jung formulated as the *abaissement du niveau mental.* This is an unstable and anxious state, and needs only the occurrence of some emotional episode involving the self-image to set off an activation of the archetypal self-image, the central archetype, which then overwhelms the ego consciousness.

There are three major phenomena in the process.[28] There is fragmentation, not only of the ego-conscious but, more notably, of the autonomous complexes: their associations become scattered and their affective cores appear as the play of archetypal myth forms disconnected from the problems of the personal emotional life. A second feature is the marked tendency of the ego to identify with any activated unconscious content happening to prevail at any moment, especially the mythological. The third is the extraordinary disproportionate energic charge of the archetypal images and processes when they are activated in the acute disorder, making them flood the field of awareness with their contents; this charge seems due to the activation of the central archetype. The paranoid process then seems to be based on the patient's proclivity to hold on to his grossly inflated archetypal identification, and his mortal terror of the activity of the archetypal process that sets out to dissolve and recreate this imbalanced and deeply cloven self-image, a process that expresses itself in terms of being destroyed by a hostile insurrection from an opposition.

In a review of therapy with various kinds of schizophrenic cases, Perry[29] found a group of a dozen cases in which a reconstitutive process could be discerned in the archetypal imagery. It recurred enough to be identifiable as a syndrome, recognizable by the content of the patients' preoccupations. The greater part of the imagery could be grouped under ten headings:

1. Location at a world center
2. Death and afterlife
3. A return to the beginning of time
4. A cosmic conflict or battle

5. A threat from the opposite sex
6. An apotheosis as supreme ruler or savior
7. A sacred marriage
8. A new birth or rebirth
9. A new society
10. A quadrated world

This same image sequence can be found in the central myth and ritual form of archaic urban civilizations, namely, in their annual New Year Festival of renewal of the kingship, the kingdom, and the world. The death and renewal symbolism belongs to the class called "rites of passage," a motif that seems to accompany the shift from one stage of development to another. In each stage of the emotional life of the self as it evolves there is a principal love-bond that contains the central archetype as its dynamic core in this order: mother and child; mother and son-lover; father and son; peer group and youth; lovers; parental couple. Each such love-bond has its characteristic archetypal representation. The recovering schizophrenic patient, emerging from deep regression, often recapitulates these stages. Thus the patient is working consistently on the reorganization of the self-image from its earliest stage, holding the central archetype always at its focus.

SULLIVAN AND THE INTERPERSONAL VIEW

Harry Stack Sullivan worked extensively with schizophrenic patients throughout his entire professional career. At Shepard and Enoch Pratt Hospital and Chestnut Lodge, both in Maryland, he began to formulate his ideas on psychiatry in general and on the schizophrenias in particular; he presented a great part of his material as lectures at Chestnut Lodge and to the Washington (D.C.) School of Psychiatry. Many of these lectures were published in books.[32, 38, 39, 48]

Sullivan's writing varies from being obscure and almost impossible to fathom to being lucid, witty, and stimulating. *Clinical Studies in Psychiatry*[39] is one of his most lucid and useful works; the chapter on hysteria is in parts hilarious.

The material on the schizophrenias is more sober, because Sullivan was profoundly affected by the sense of tragedy, futility, and despair that permeates the existence of the schizophrenic patient.

Sullivan felt that the theory and terminology that he had learned during his psychoanalytic training was not adequate to describe psychological growth and development in *interpersonal* terms. He saw psychiatric health and illness as the result of continuous interaction, from birth on, between the individual and significant others in the environment, and he evolved a theory and vocabulary that reflected this emphasis. In his formulations, he tried to avoid what he felt were many of the questionable highly abstract and inferential statements of orthodox psychoanalysis and to replace them with more directly observable phenomena. He also espoused the *participant-observer* mode of interviewing and therapy, one in which the therapist is actively involved in the interview, in contrast to the more passive and remote posture of traditional psychoanalysts.

Many of Sullivan's ideas and techniques have become amalgamated into contemporary psychiatric training in the United States, as have many of those of psychoanalysis. To my mind, the differences between these two points of view, as they are currently practiced, become increasingly hard to detect. What to Freud was "unconscious" was to Sullivan "out of awareness"; what to Freud was "transference neurosis" was to Sullivan "parataxic distortion," and so on. Admittedly, there are definite points of difference, but I think that they are less important than the points of congruence and complementarity.* One most important emphasis of Sullivan's is that human development always takes place in the context of social learning and reinforcement, and that mental illness

---

* Sullivan's view of such comparisons:[34] "I surmise that there is some noticeable relationship, perhaps in the realm of cousins or closer, between what I describe as the personification of the self and what is often considered to be the psychoanalytic ego. But if you are wise, you will dismiss that as facetious, because I am not at all sure of it; it has been so many years since I found anything but headaches in trying to discover parallels between various theoretical systems that I have left that for the diligent and scholarly, neither of which includes me."

arises from a failure in interpersonal relationships. First, there will be a brief review of some of Sullivan's concepts that are most relevant to understanding the schizophrenias; then these concepts will be applied directly to the illnesses.

Referential Processes

In normal adults, thought and speech usually *refer* to some object or event that can also be perceived by someone else, hence the term *referential processes*. If I say to another, "See that car over there," or "It's lunchtime; let's eat," the other person can agree on the percepts; the percepts are capable of *consensual validation*, to use another of Sullivan's terms.

Such precise, highly refined use of referential processes is the product of acculturation and learning; in childhood, in contrast, there are, according to Sullivan,[40]

> . . . the referential operations of very early life
> in which there is no precise delineation of what
> is itself unknown or very dimly realized; such
> a state of mind might be described as a vague
> and global feeling of unutterable turmoil.

There is little mental capacity to connect percepts, images, sounds, ideas, or other aspects of private mental life with what is going on in the environment. In the early years of life, with the beginnings of speech, and the thought patterns underlying it, there are increasing attempts to relate thought and event, but these attempts are for the most part private, idiosyncratic, and incapable of clear comprehension to another person. When adults communicate in these ways, it is referred to as "autistic."

As intellectual growth takes place, the degree of correspondence between thought and speech to life events improves, and, by adolescence, the world of private thought and speech of infancy has largely been relegated to the world of out-of-awareness, except perhaps for reverie and hypnogogic states ("brown studies," as Sullivan likes to call them), and dreaming. Again the parallels between Sullivan's terminology and concepts and those of psychoanalysis should be apparent: "early referential processes" corresponds in many ways with "primary process thinking."

The Self-System

During the early years of life, the infant comes to have some sense of self, of being different from those who are around him. In particular, he grows to learn that some of his behaviors evoke pleasurable responses from other persons; these behaviors become organized around the personification of "good-me." Those that evoke unpleasant, mildly to moderately, i.e., anxiety-provoking, responses become organized around "bad-me"; those that evoke intensely anxiety-provoking responses become partitioned into (rather than organized into) "not-me"; these concepts are discussed more fully in Chapter 4.

"Good-me" and "bad-me" are available to the *waking, conscious self* (one of the three components of the tripartite self-system, the other two being the *rest of the personality, "not readily accessible to awareness,"* and *sleep and the mental functions that take place in it*). The self-system comes into being as a series of mental operations whose unifying theme is that they serve to avoid anxiety (in other words, to diminish insecurity) and to seek after interpersonal gratification.

Through the apparatus of the self-system, the referential processes, at first private and preverbal, become more and more highly refined and effective in communicating meaningfully with others. The contents of awareness become increasingly germane to satisfying social interaction, and things that are either irrelevant or inimical to the pursuit of satisfaction and/or the avoidance of insecurity tend to be placed out of awareness by the various *dynamisms of dissociation*.

Dissociation and the Dynamisms

There are many impulses, impulse systems, and tendencies that, if they entered awareness, would cause the self to experience considerable anxiety and insecurity or a sense of being deflected from goals. The evidences that many of these uncomfortable or irrelevant matters are never experienced consciously, never enter awareness, led Sullivan to the concept of *dissociation* and *dissociative processes*. Dissociation in this usage is a general term, under which several more specific *dynamisms* are grouped. He points out that the *suppression* and *repression* of psychoanalysis were particular, highly motivated forms of dissociation, and not to be made synonymous with his more general term.[44]

In many instances, the dissociative processes can be most adaptive. The dissociative processes of the self system generally work smoothly and suavely; some of the dynamisms, in descending order of adaptiveness, that help accomplish the dissociation are those of *selective inattention, sublimation, obsessive substitutions, automatisms* and *fugues*, and *projection*. When large complexes of impulses must constantly be kept out of awareness, a good deal of psychic energy is bound up in maintaining the dissociations in the interests of avoiding anxiety and maintaining interpersonal security, and if these dynamisms fail to operate smoothly, mental illness appears.

SELECTIVE INATTENTION: The term describes the phenomenon of restricted awareness of mental events. If we were to perceive and respond to every stimulus coming from without or within, we would be so overwhelmed by stimuli that we would be unable to will meaningful behavior. Much "noise" automatically gets filtered out. Sullivan cites this example:

> I have literally been so much of a scientist as to stick a pin into a very, very dear friend of mine (a marksman about to shoot at a target). And sure enough, as I had expected, it was only after having fired that he reached around to the injured area and gave me the devil. Literally, on the rifle range, things are suspended from any disturbance of one's consciousness until it is time to notice them.[42]

For most people, selective inattention is a useful dynamism. It helps with the business of living. When, however, people are unable to attend to important data about their own functioning because of highly motivated unconscious needs *not* to be aware of something, serious failures in perception can result. Such instances resemble what psychoanalysts would call "repression and denial." It is common, for example, for patients in observed group therapy to "forget" that they had been told that they would be observed through the one-way mirror, or for patients in brief psychotherapy to "forget" that the number of sessions was limited to eight, etc. Sullivan[43] cites the example of a young man who complained of a series of unrequited love affairs; he never allowed himself to see, until forced to, how he had always related to the young woman in question in such a way that he alienated her.*

SUBLIMATION: Sullivan defines sublimation as "the unwitting substitution of a partial satisfaction was social approval for the pursuit of a direct satisfaction which would be contrary to one's ideals or to the judgment of the social censors and other important people who surround one."[41] He cites as example that we automatically seek out a bathroom when we need to eliminate, never pondering for a

---

* There is one more example of Sullivan's[35] that I must present, not because it is absolutely germane to my thesis, but because it is an example of Sullivan at his amusing best, one which I want to share with the reader. It deals with a circumvention of selective inattention: "There is a drugstore at which I frequently have to purchase this and that; and during the war years it had among its clerks at the soda fountain a person who, I am quite sure, would be shown by intelligence tests to be a low-grade moron. Not only was he quite lacking in intelligence, but also—in which I sympathize with him, as I do with everyone who deals with the public—he showed a very rare collection of hostilities to the customers, so that whatever you asked for, he would dutifully, when he got around to it, bring you something else. Having suffered from this repeatedly, I was extremely unpleasant on one particular occasion and said, 'What is that, huh?' And he said, 'Water. Didn't you ask for it?' And I said, '*Get me what I asked for!*' Whereupon the poor bird tottered off under the unpleasantness and got me what I had asked for. But the great joker is that the next time I saw him he grinned at me and immediately got me what I asked for. Now, that humbled me, because his [selective] inattention was not as complete as I had thought. He profited from an unpleasant experience, and, by God, that's more than some of us do."

moment the fact that we have relinquished the childhood pleasure of defecating when and where we wanted.

He further emphasizes the *unwitting* manner in which sublimation operates, that the partial frustrations resulting from sublimation do not accumulate, and that they are discharged in symbolic operations during sleep and dreaming. It would appear that Sullivan's and Freud's uses of "sublimation" are virtually identical.

THE OBSESSIONAL DYNAMISM: Early in life one can learn that there are certain verbal rituals, many of them magical or unrealistic in nature, that one can go through in order to avoid insecurity. The 5-year-old who has hit his baby sister may be told to tell her he is sorry (he isn't, at all), when she doesn't have the slightest idea of what he is talking about, and he knows it. Nevertheless, going through the verbal ritual of "I'm sorry" considerably lowers the level of parental disapproval. Furthermore, the words themselves have a highly private or autistic meaning to the child (how many 5-year-olds have a firm notion of what adults mean by the concept of being sorry?); thus the verbal rituals of the obsessional adult may have only approximate resemblance to the meaning others would ascribe to the words, and serve more in the interests of warding off anxiety than as an attempt to communicate ideas.

PROJECTION: This dynamism is discussed in detail in chapters 3 and 4.

The Self-System and Dynamisms

Sullivan points out that in schizophrenia early types of referential processes obtrude into waking life. He says,[41]

> Now the schizophrenic is, so far as I can discover, essentially characterized by the fact that his self-system has lost control of awareness, so that it cannot exclude these earlier referential processes and restrict awareness to late, highly refined types of thought . . . the self is in such a critical position that these

much earlier types of mental process receive
more or less the same clear representation in
awareness that they did in late infancy or early
childhood.

Thus does Sullivan, like Freud and Jung, see schizophrenia as a regression to earlier, more primitive types of
thinking, a kind of awareness available to most people only
during dreaming or while in reverie states.

With the breakdown of dissociative processes and the
subsequent incursion of primitive thoughts into awareness,
the distinctions between the parts of the tripartite self-system are effaced. The boundary between the *waking, conscious
self* and the *rest of the personality* becomes blurred. The
sense of self, the ego boundaries, merges with the entire
personality. Selective inattention, that dynamism which
protects the *self* from having to deal with all external stimuli,
no longer functions properly. Likewise, the dynamisms of
sublimation and *obsessionalism* fail as ways of avoiding
anxiety and maintaining the possibility of satisfaction; new
ways must be found. Often the new way is a heightened use
of obsessionalism, but one that has become more and more
autistic and remote from dealing with real-life situations,
such as Vivian's endless rituals of cleaning the kitchen and
bathroom and the ideational component that accompanied
her activities.

Abhorrent cravings[36] may make an appearance as dissociation fails. He cites the case of an adolescent boy who
was picked up by a homosexual who performed fellatio on
him. The next day the boy found himself unwittingly in the
same neighborhood and thus could no longer conceal from
himself the fact that he wanted to continue the experience.

. . . when it burst upon him this way, it was
attended by all sorts of revulsions and a feeling
that it would be infrahuman, and what not, to
have such interests. And he arrived at the hospital shortly afterward in what was called schizophrenic disturbance.[36]

Should the abhorrent cravings persist and precipitate a change for the worse, a situation of panic ensues, a state of brief, complete disorganization. Whether or not preceded by abhorrent cravings and a state of panic, the initial disorganization may be followed by the mystifying emergence into awareness of *early referential processes,* many of which had been buried within the *not-me* components of personality, thus seeming to the patient to be bizarre, uncanny, inexplicable, and often terrifying. The patient can frequently no more explain to himself or others what is going on than can the 2½-year-old child make comprehensible his private world. Still, if he is able to connect his experiences

> . . . with the main trends of personality development, then we would have achieved the integration of a previously dissociated motivational system with the rest of the personality; and there would then be none of this dreadful spectacle of the schizophrenic way of life, with its exceedingly ominous probable outcomes.[36]

Sullivan, like Jung and Freud, was impressed with the similarities between dreams and the schizophrenias. He describes the situation where a nonschizophrenic patient recounts a terrifying dream and re-experiences the uncanny emotion or terror of the dream:

> The psychiatrist is literally seeing a mild schizophrenic episode right there in the office. In the same way, any of us who have difficulties in asserting our knowledge of reality on awakening from certain types of unpleasant dreams are, at least for a few minutes, living in a world completely of a piece with the world in which schizophrenics live for hours.[37]

Catatonia as the Essential Schizophrenic State

Sullivan felt that catatonia is the essential schizophrenic state, one which may progress into a hebephrenic or paranoid outcome.[45] With the "extravasation of meaning over a great many things from which meaning had long since been withdrawn as a result of previous experience—if it ever was there —as an outstanding characteristic of schizophrenia," there often comes a feeling of urgency, a feeling that things should be understood, grasped, and responded to. But the schizophrenic cannot explain what the urgency is about, what causes it (in the sense that the phobic neurotic can identify the situation that causes him fear), because the urgency stems from feelings and percepts first sensed at a stage of life when *words could not describe them*. Sullivan suggests that a gifted schizophrenic, on being asked, "What is this urgency for?" might respond,

> "Well, we are really a little interested in getting back to being human beings. It seems quite imperative. I guess that must be what you are talking about." In other words, the urgency is to get together again, to have the world remain, you might say, at peace instead of undergoing the unearthly intrusions and extrusions and divagations and one thing and another that the rest of us experience in our nightmares.[46]

STUPOR: The urgency drives the patient toward some action, though he is, of course, not exactly sure what he should do. But his actions frequently miscarry, and this suggests to him that he is indeed crazy. When the patient sees that his action has not carried him closer to a goal, and in fact may have done nothing but make him look crazy in the eyes of others, it ". . . ties up the skeletal activity in the fashion which we call stupor. Incidentally, this stupor is a very active postural business, and anything but the inhibition of all postural tensions."[46]

Because of the prevalance of early (rather than refined) referential thinking, however, the patient does not attribute this inhibition of motion to himself but rather to outside forces that he senses impinging on him; ". . . it is that a

power, some great cosmic force, ties up the muscles and pre-
vents action."

EXCITEMENT: Though stuporous, the sense of urgency
is still present, and sometimes, from the stupor, the conviction of being under the influence of cosmic forces changes
to the conviction that *the patient himself is the power, the
cosmic force.* The stupor gives way to excitement, and the
patient reveals through gesture and speech his identification
with the magical thoughts and rituals with which the power
is invested. "Many a catatonic has said things which equalled
in every sense the alleged import of the spells cast by our
medieval wizards over the Devil. . . ."

HEBEPHRENIC AND PARANOID OUTCOMES: If the patient's
life experience prior to his schizophrenic episode has been
lacking in *any* truly intimate relations with another human
being, the type of friendship such as having a chum during
preadolescence, he is highly vulnerable to a state of abject
despair, a state of complete loss of hope for rewarding relationships in the future (as contrasted to *demoralization,*
which at least contains the hopes of remoralization at some
future time). The despairing catatonic may then quickly lose
". . . a great many of the recent additions of the self. In other
words, there will be a strikingly regressive course in which
social habits, communicative utilization of speech, and so
on, will be lost very swiftly; and the gross picture of the
hebephrenic will manifest itself." Sullivan felt that all the
hebephrenic patients he had ever studied closely had been
catatonic before they had become hebephrenic.

In contrast, patients who *had* had at least some acquaintance with friendship and intimacy did not relinquish recent
social learning nearly so readily and were more likely to maintain a (relatively nonregressive) catatonic state.

During catatonic stupor, the mechanism of projection
may come to offer the patient an explanation of his distress
in which he is blameless. His interpersonal failures are no
longer his fault, are no longer a reminder of his interpersonal
clumsiness, but are instead the result of others' malfeasance.
He emerges from his stupor with a paranoid delusional sys-

tem, more or less elaborated, which further protects him from the anxiety of low self-esteem. Such patients, suggests Sullivan, may have been brought up in families where blaming and scapegoating were favorite pastimes and who were, therefore, at times of discomfort, predisposed to look outward rather than inward to find the causes.[47]

Sullivan's Impact on Treatment

It would be presumptuous of me to think I could list here, in this brief space, the full impact of Sullivan's thinking on the treatment of schizophrenic patients. I will emphasize one major point, however, a point elaborated on in Chapter 14. That chapter, in fact, owes a great debt to Sullivan, his colleagues and students, some of whom in turn became my supervisors and teachers.

Perhaps Sullivan's greatest contribution was his constant view of the schizophrenic patient as a human being who had been cheated, early in life, of many of the opportunities for social learning and satisfaction that could have enhanced his later success as a person. Such a view, coming as it did, when many psychiatrists saw schizophrenic patients as a species apart, was important in establishing a humane and rational approach toward treatment.

Perhaps Freud, Jung, and Bleuler helped at least partially to unravel the mysteries of the schizophrenic's communications, but Sullivan's was the more important influence in applying these understandings to treatment of the patient.

By seeing human growth as the outcome of interaction between two (or more) people, Sullivan's developmental theory also has had profound implications for psychotherapy. Rather than viewing the patient as a repository of interesting psychopathology, to be analyzed, the therapist must be willing to enter into a real relationship with him in an attempt to understand just what deficiencies of life experience led to a schizophrenic outcome, and in the hope that such contact can make the patient more successful in his future attempts at finding interpersonal security and satisfaction.

Section Three

TREATMENT

12

Somatic Treatments

INTRODUCTION

Over the centuries physicians and others have done things to the bodies of schizophrenic patients. They have bored holes in their heads to let the demons escape; they have cut into their brains to interrupt impulses; they have thrust them into pits of snakes to scare them back to sanity; they have purged them with vapors, liquids, and colonic irrigations; they have sprayed them and bathed them; they have induced fevers in them; they have fed them and injected them with drugs and medicaments; they have passed electric currents through their brains; they have put them into comas. The justification for these treatments has alternately been medical, religious, political, or based on folklore and superstition.

In our century, many of the barbaric and inhumane practices have disappeared, though they are by no means gone entirely. The modes of treatment now in use are powerful; when applied more as an expression of frustration of the healer than as a compassionate attempt to help the patient, they can still be inhumane. Only forms of treatment still enjoying some psychiatric respectability will be described in this chapter.

In the 1930s and 1940s, electroconvulsive therapy, insulin-shock therapy, and psychosurgery were the predominant methods of somatic treatment. With the advent of the phenothiazine drugs in the 1950s, use of these older methods has fallen off sharply. This chapter discusses, in order, drug therapy, electroconvulsive therapy, insulin shock therapy, psychosurgery, and miscellaneous other somatic treatments.

Though the somatic therapies are presented here in a section separate from the milieu and psychotherapies, the reader should keep in mind that such division is artificial and for purposes of explication only. The various modes of treatment should be offered in concert, as the condition of the patient warrants.

DRUG THERAPY

by Leo E. Hollister, M.D., and
C. Peter Rosenbaum, M.D.

We are in the phenothiazine era. This group of drugs dwarfs all others, past and current, in importance in the treatment of the schizophrenias. For centuries men had searched for drugs that would have a beneficial effect on the symptoms of the schizophrenias, with indifferent success at best. Sedatives and hypnotics made schizophrenic patients sleepy, as they did anyone else, but they had little effect on the symptom complex proper and were useful only to take the edge off extremes of tension, anxiety, and restlessness.

In 1952 French scientists found a group of antihistaminic drugs, the phenothiazines, whose sedative and tranquilizing effects (common side effects among antihistamines) outweighed their primary effects.[5] The first, and still best known of the drugs, chlorpromazine, seemed to exert a remarkably beneficial effect on schizophrenic patients. Such knowledge spurred research on this family of drugs at an almost frenetic pace during the following years; the family

Leo E. Hollister, M.D., is Associate Chief of Staff, Veterans Administration Hospital, Palo Alto, California.

of phenothiazines has firmly established itself as a major mode of treatment in the schizophrenias.

The tranquilizing effects of some of the rauwolfia compounds also became known in the early 1950s. After a brief popularity, it soon emerged that rauwolfia compounds could produce profound depressions, both of blood pressure and of mood; these serious side effects have virtually eliminated them from the treatment of the schizophrenias, in favor of the safer and more effective phenothiazines.

The phenothiazine drugs share a common basic nucleus; they differ only in the nature of the side chain structures substituted at position R_1 and by the small group substituted at position R_2, as shown in Figure 12–1.[29] The chain structures

Figure 12–1.

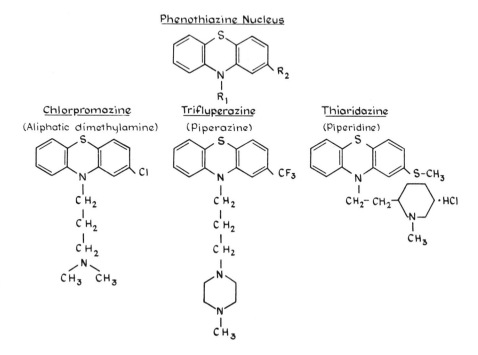

substituted at R_1 are of three types: (1) an aliphatic, straight, three-carbon chain; (2) a straight, three-carbon chain with a piperazine ring; and (3) a chain with a piperidine ring.

The substitutions at positions R_1 and R_2 cause variations in the potency of these drugs and in their numerous side effects. Some of these variations are summarized in Table 12–1.[2]

The fact remains, however, that these drugs are more similar than different in their effects. Promotional literature from pharmaceutical houses has exaggerated the differences; but the practitioner is better served by becoming extremely familiar with one or a few of the drugs than by attempting to learn all the minutiae of the primary and secondary effects of each of the drugs. There is considerable variation, furthermore, between patients receiving the same drug; these differences must be attended to just as diligently as to the alleged differences in the drugs themselves.

In Table 12–1, the potency of each drug has been rated on comparison to 100 mgm of chlorpromazine, orally administered. Injectable forms of these drugs are at least twice as potent as oral forms.

The phenothiazines have several major uses. They appear to have a primary effect on the psychotic process itself; thus they are referred to as "antipsychotic drugs," rather than "tranquilizers," with the implication of mere sedation or chemical restraint.[2, 4] Still, their ability to ameliorate the symptoms of the schizophrenias may be nothing more than that. As yet no evidence supports a curative action on a set of disorders whose causes are unknown.

Another use of these drugs is to make patients accessible for psychotherapy and milieu therapy who otherwise have been too agitated, remote, or withdrawn to participate. Silvia T.'s confusion, agitation, and disorientation on admission made it almost impossible for her to attend to the efforts of her therapist and the ward staff to help her; furthermore, her disorganized and pathetic trips off the ward to look for her husband in his laboratory caused unnecessary embarrass-

TABLE 12–1

COMPARISON OF THE PHENOTHIAZINES AND RELATED DRUGS

DRUG NAME		Equivalent Dose to 100 mgm Chlorpromazine mgm	EFFECTIVENESS (Suggested for acute, chronic, or both)	SIDE EFFECTS AND COMPLICATIONS
Generic	*Proprietary*			*Approximate Incidence*
Phenothiazines				For the phenothiazines as a group, the current information is as follows:
Chlorpromazine[a]	Thorazine	100	Acute	(In percentages)
Triflupromazine[a]	Vesprin	25	Acute	
Thioridazine[b]	Mellaril	100	Acute	
Aceto phenazine[c]	Tindal	20	Acute	Central nervous system reactions 1.0 to 10.0
Carphenazine[c]	Proketazine	20	Chronic	Allergic or toxic reactions:
Prochlorperazine[c]	Compazine	20	Chronic	Jaundice and agranulocytosis 0.01 to 0.1
Thiopropazate[c]	Dartal	8–12	Unknown	Photosensitivity, especially with chlorpromazine 0.1 to 1.0
Perphenazine[c]	Trilafon	8–12	Chronic	Autonomic reactions 1.0 to 10.0
Trifluperazine[c]	Stelazine	5	Chronic	
Fluphenazine[c]	Prolixin Permitil	2.5	Chronic	
Nonphenothiazines				
Chlorprothixine	Taractan	40	Acute	
Thiothixine	Novane	2–4	Acute	
Haloperidol	Haldol	1–2	Both	

Adapted from Caffey et al.[2]

[a] Aliphatic side chain.
[b] Piperadine side chain.
[c] Piperadine side chain.

ment to all concerned. Chlorpromazine was remarkably effective in helping her to establish contact and to control these symptoms. There still remain some therapists for whom the art of psychotherapy, unadulterated by pills, is so sacred that they are reluctant to start schizophrenic patients on drugs. Their number, fortunately, is decreasing.

For many patients, such as Silvia T., the drugs serve as a crucial interim factor in helping them work out a constructive resolution of the personal stress that precipitated the psychotic episode; the dose of the drug can be gradually decreased as resolution proceeds and the psychosis clears. Other patients, however, become increasingly psychotic again as their medication is reduced.[7] Certain patients in recent studies were acutely disturbed on admission and treated with high doses of phenothiazines. These doses were reduced to maintenance levels as the patients improved, and the patients were discharged to the care of their family physician. The family physician weaned the patient from his medication, and the patient became more psychotic, finally requiring readmission to the hospital, where he was again treated with relatively high doses. From this experience with "ping-pong schizophrenia" it became apparent that these patients should be kept on maintenance doses of phenothiazines for years, perhaps life, with dose levels being increased during times of acute personal stress, much as the diabetic is maintained on insulin for life, with doses being increased during physiological stress.[7, 21, 24]

Dosage

There is an enormous range of response from patient to patient to a given amount of a phenothiazine. A small, relatively calm patient may do quite well on 100 mgm of chlorpromazine a day; a large, excited patient may require doses from ten to 20 times as large, at least until disturbed behavior is controlled. Furthermore, it is virtually impossible to predict in which patients the predominance of side effects will outweigh the primary effects. In general, for the acutely disturbed patient, we would suggest starting the patient as rapidly as possible on the drug as is consonant with safe medical practice, titrating dosage against the appearance of the desired primary or undesired secondary effects. For chlorpromazine, 400 to 800 mgm per day orally, or half that amount I.M., is a reasonable starting dosage; doses should be divided over six-hour periods so that no single dose produces excessive degrees of somnolence, hypotension, or other undesirable side effects. Proportionate strengths of other phenothiazines may be determined from Table 12–1. Oral chlorpromazine usually takes from about 15 to 30 minutes to become noticeable, with the peak at about three hours. Sedative effects may precede antipsychotic effects, often by hours or days. If the desired effect does not occur in that time, an additional dose can be given. Specific dosage recommendations on manufacturers' package inserts should be consulted before prescribing the drug.

Once control of symptoms has taken place (the gusher has been capped, as it were), dosage levels can be gradually reduced to maintenance levels; these again are determined more by the response of the patient than by any predetermined formula. In all, the strategy is similar to that of managing a diabetic in coma.

The drugs come in a great multitude of forms: short-acting pills, long-acting pills, elixirs, short- and long-acting injectible forms, etc. Each has its uses; the reliability or recalcitrance of the patient to take medication is the usual determining factor. Injection sites often remain painful for days and are sometimes prone to abscess; oral forms should be used when possible.

Effectiveness

A number of well-controlled studies have proved beyond a doubt the effectiveness of the phenothiazines in treating schizophrenic patients. Large-scale studies in which phenothiazines have been compared to placebo, phenobarbital, and reserpine demonstrate significant superiority of the phenothiazines.[2, 3, 4, 12] Patients treated with phenothiazines showed, on the average, a drop in total morbidity scores (an index of observable psychiatric symptomatology), of one third after four weeks of treatment and of one-half after 12 weeks; controls at 12 weeks showed a drop of less than 10 percent. In another study of nearly 600 patients followed for three years, ". . . two out of three were released within nine months; almost a third were released in four months. Ten percent are clearly therapeutic failures as they remained hospitalized continually over the three-year period."[12]

Within the phenothiazines are any compounds significantly more effective with one type of schizophrenia than with another? Most clinicians prefer to use the piperazine derivatives in chronic patients and the aliphatic or piperadine derivatives in acute patients when their greater sedative action may be of especial value (see Table 12–1).[2] However, despite statements to the contrary, there seems to be little, if any, difference in the effects of the derivatives on the clinical subtypes of the schizophrenias. Some evidence indicates that paranoid schizophrenia may respond slightly better than nonparanoid. However, as Hollister has commented:

> It is commonly assumed that those drugs with highest sedative activity, such as chlorpromazine, thioridazine and the like, are preferred for acute or disturbed patients, while those with less sedative action effects may be better for chronic, withdrawn patients. It makes some sense, but the actual data to support this contention are not great.[11]

Side Effects and Complications:

1. CENTRAL NERVOUS SYSTEM: Sleepiness is a frequent side effect of chlorpromazine, especially during the first few days of its administration. For the acutely disturbed patient, this may be more of a blessing than a curse. Most newly admitted patients simply have not had much sleep in the days preceding admission, and the restorative powers of a few

good nights' sleep are not to be underestimated. "Sleep that knits up the ravell'd sleave of care" is as true for psychiatric patients as for anyone else. Phenothiazines potentiate the effects of barbiturates and alcohol; the restless patient who is on a phenothiazine may well benefit either from increased doses of chlorpromazine at bedtime or by the addition of about one-half of a normal dose of barbiturate to help him get to sleep. The somnolence induced by chlorpromazine usually wears off after a few days; if it is unpleasant, patients may be persuaded to continue on the drug on the expectation that this side effect will largely disappear.

An extrapyramidal syndrome, closely resembling Parkinson's disease, occurs most frequently with the piperazine derivatives. Patients so afflicted demonstrate muscular rigidity, especially in the expressive masculature of the face, a slowed, shuffling gait, clumsiness, and drooling. These symptoms can often be controlled by reduction of dose or by the addition of anti-Parkinsonian drugs, such as trihexyphenidyl HCl (Artane) or benztropine methanesulfonate (Cogentin), in doses of from 2 to 8 mgm per day.[2]

The anti-Parkinsonian drugs themselves can produce such anticholinergic side effects as dryness of the mouth, blurred vision, etc. Once Parkinsonian symptoms are controlled, the anti-Parkinsonian drugs may be reduced or even discontinued, even though the patient remains on his previous dose of phenothiazines. Anti-Parkinsonian drugs should be discontinued gradually in order to avoid withdrawal symptoms.

Occasionally muscular dystonia, especially in the form of a spastic torticollis, appears. The offending phenothiazine should be stopped; the patient should be treated with intravenous caffeine with sodium benzoate, 0.5 gm, or a parenteral anti-Parkinsonian drug or phenobarbital. The most serious possible complication of the dystonic syndrome is choking caused by involuntary constriction of the muscles of the tongue and throat; utilization of an endotracheal tube may be called for.[2]

Diffuse motor restlessness, akathisia, may occur. The patient moves about as if tormented, wants to control his movements, but cannot. Reduction in dosage, change to another phenothiazine, or administration of phenobarbital may all be helpful in treating akathisia.[2]

The phenothiazines as a group tend to reduce seizure threshold and produce EEG slowing. If seizures occur or threaten, phenobarbital may forestall further episodes; again, reduction of dose or change to another phenothiazine is indicated.

2. ALLERGIC OR TOXIC PHENOMENA: These phenomena tend to occur within the first six weeks if they are to occur at all, tend not to be related to dose, thus resembling hypersensitivity phenomena, and are more frequent with chlorpromazine than with the other drugs. Early signs of leukopenia or cholestatic jaundice can be detected by taking the temperature accurately once daily and by weekly total white blood cell counts and such hepatic function tests as the serum glutamic pyruvate transaminase (SGPT) measurement for the first eight weeks of treatment. The drug should be stopped when these or other signs of hypersensitivity occur. Patients with photosensivity should be kept out of the sun.

3. AUTONOMIC NERVOUS SYSTEM: Hypotension is the most frequent autonomic complication of the use of phenothiazines; chlorpromazine is especially prone to produce this effect. For young adults in good health, a bothersome orthostatic hypotension occurs; the patient should be helped to rise slowly and carefully from chair or bed. As with somnolence, this symptom usually disappears after a few days.

These drugs should never be given intravenously; they may cause a hypotensive crisis that in turn may induce a coronary thrombosis or stroke in the predisposed patient. Severe hypotension may be treated with intravenous levarterenol.

Adrenergic suppression and the anticholinergic effects of these drugs cause many symptoms that are bothersome and in some instances dangerous. All can be controlled by lowering the dose or stopping the drug and starting conventional medical treatment for the specific condition. The conditions that are primarily bothersome are those of tachycardia in otherwise healthy patients, blurred vision,* dry mouth, nasal congestion, diarrhea, and, in males, with thioridizine, inhibiton of ejaculation. Potentially dangerous conditions are aggravation of glaucoma, paralytic ileus, oral infections, peptic ulcer, and fecal impaction.

4. METABOLIC AND MISCELLANEOUS EFFECTS: Other side effects that have been reported have been gain in weight, edema, estrogenic effects such as lactation, menstrual irregularities, and false positive pregnancy tests; in addition, teratogenic effects and abnormal pigmentation of the cornea, lens, and retina have been noted. Recent work has shown that long-term administration of phenothiazines leads to these serious eye complications more frequently than was previously believed. Hence regular ophthalmologic examinations are important for the patient who takes these medications over long periods.

EKG changes have been reported; thioridizine has been reported to produce flattened T-waves, which in turn are suspected to lead to a greater susceptibility to premature ventricular contractions and ventricular fibrillation. Such changes have been suspected (but not proved) to be important in instances of sudden death of patients who are on high dosages; such changes are rarer for patients on lower dosages.

Chlorpromazine is *not* excreted in substantial amount in the milk of nursing mothers and therefore may be used in postpartum psychoses without fear of poisoning the baby.[1]

Mode of Action

One is always safe in saying that the precise mode of action of a drug is at best partially known and that all

* "Blurring of vision can be managed by the concomitant administration of neostigmine bromide 10 to 15 mgm per day, the use of physostigmine in 0.1 percent ophthalmic solution once or twice daily."[2]

theories are subject to change. Such is true of the phenothiazines, where a number of theories have come and gone over
the past decade.

Fundamentally, there are two major approaches to the
problem, electrophysiologic and biochemical. Electrophysio-
logical evidence suggests that these drugs act on three major
integrating systems in the brain: the reticular formation, the
limbic system, and the hypothalamus.[10] The reticular formation sits astride all sensory input and is believed to modulate
incoming messages. When this modulation is decreased, sensory input is increased, and it becomes more difficult to sort
out relevant from irrelevant messages. Evidence from a number of quarters suggests that some sort of "hyperstimulation"
may be working in schizophrenics; phenothiazines are believed to alleviate the schizophrenic symptoms by reducing
the flow of incoming messages. The limbic system is believed
to provide emotional coloring to messages, and the hypothalamus may be construed as the effector organ, which
evokes bodily responses to emotion-arousing messages. Obviously, decreasing the activity of these systems might be expected to be beneficial for patients with emotional disorders
such as schizophrenia.

On the biochemical side, the most widely believed current theory is that phenothiazines decrease the permeability
of membranes around the synaptic clefts in the central nervous system.[28] This action is probably strongest at adrenergic
synapses mediated by the neurotransmitters, norepinephrine
and dopamine. Such a decrease in permeability might have
the combined effects of impairing the release of these trans-
mitters to the synaptic space and impairing their reuptake
by the neurone, thereby exposing them to excessive catabo-
lism by the enzymes monamine oxidase and catecholamine
0-methyl transferase. The net result would be decreased
central adrenergic transmission, which, if effective in the
anatomical areas mentioned above, would have the effects
described. The decrease in membrane permeability may be
dependent on a physicochemical property of phenothiazines

in being strong electron donors and thereby being able to attach readily in monomolecular layers to membranes.

Other Drugs

Three nonphenothiazine drugs, chlorprothixine, thiothixine, and haloperidol, are marketed and effective; in most respects they resemble the phenothiazines. A number of other nonphenothiazine drugs is being tried experimentally.

Periodically, claims are revived by the Saskatchewan group for nicotinic-acid therapy of schizophrenia.[26] Unfortunately, few other investigators have attempted to replicate this work, principally because the assertions made by the proponents change periodically, including the suggestion that nicotinic acid is therapeutic also in treating alcoholism and senility. The rationale for the use of nicotinic acid or niacinamide derives in part from the well-recognized pellagrous psychosis, specifically alleviated by these vitamins, and, in part, from the transmethylation hypothesis of schizophrenia. In brief, this hypothesis postulates an overly active methylating system in schizophrenics that could produce endogenous psychotogens resembling mescaline from normally occuring catecholamines. As nicotinic acid is a strong trap for methyl groups, it should protect against this abnormality. Within the past year or two, diphosphopyridine nucleotide (also known as DPN, or by an alternate name, nicotinic adenine dinucleotide, NAD) has been claimed to be curative for schizophrenics even after a short course of treatment. Before this study could be published, data was presented by another observer refuting this claim, which is rather typical of the whole story. In short, the claims made for nicotinic acid appear to be based on tenuous hypotheses and poorly controlled data. On the other hand, they have not yet been clearly refuted.

ELECTROCONVULSIVE THERAPY

Electroconvulsive therapy (also called ECT, electroshock therapy, EST, shock treatment, and, euphemistically,

Cerletti treatment) was first used as an artificial form of epilepsy in treating the schizophrenias. An observation of many years' standing (and now invalidated) held that epileptic patients showed a lower incidence of schizophrenia than did the general population; perhaps, therefore, the experience of having seizures provided some kind of "immunity" against schizophrenia. Accordingly, in the early 1930s, certain workers attempted to induce artificial seizures in the hope that these would confer the same "immunity." The first attempts by Meduna used chemicals, first camphor and later metrazol. In 1938 Cerletti and Bini first sent an electric current through the head of a schizophrenic patient in an attempt to induce a seizure.[25]

This technique quickly became popular and in the 1940s and early 1950s it was routine in a majority of state and private hospitals to administer a course of 20 or more ECT's to newly admitted schizophrenic patients. Part of the popularity must be attributed to the hope induced in the physician that at last he had a treatment that would do *something* and thus reduce his sense of frustration.

With the discovery of the phenothiazines in the 1950s, there has been a corresponding decline in the use of ECT in the treatment of the schizophrenias, though it is still recognized as the treatment of choice in certain kinds of depression. Nevertheless, there are still points in a schizophrenic illness where ECT can be useful, even if the day of its routine application has passed.

Technique of Administration

ECT and the drugs that modify its effects must be administered extremely carefully if serious complications are to be avoided. The material represented below is by no means to be taken as a guide for the administration of ECT; to learn this technique one must work under the close supervision of an experienced practitioner and read works of recognized authorities.[16] This material is presented primarily to help the reader get a general picture of the techniques and risks of the use of ECT.

Though there have been many variations of technique over the years, the most common method now is to use certain premedications to allay anxiety and to decrease the incidence of such complications as cardiac arrhythmia and fractures. On the day of treatment, breakfast is withheld. Atropine sulphate is given 45 minutes before treatment to decrease bronchial secretions and reduce the likelihood of a vagus-induced cardiac arrhythmia. Medium-acting barbiturates are given to severely anxious patients orally half an hour before the treatment, to allay anxiety and promote relaxation. A muscle relaxant, commonly succinylcholine 20 to 80 mgm, is administered intravenously from 25 to 30 seconds before the treatment to diminish the risk of fractures during the convulsion.[14, 15]

For the treatment itself, an alternating electric current of 70 to 150 volts and 300 to 400 milliamperes is generated by a standard machine (the "shock box"). Electrodes are placed bitemporally, and the current is passed through the patient's brain for 0.1 to 1.0 second. Routine treatments for possible sequellae of a convulsion are always kept available; these include tongue depressors, endothracheal tubes, and a CO_2–O_2 inhalant for delayed resumption of respiration.

Indications and Results of ECT

Patients in an acute manic or catatonic excitement run the risk of death through exhaustion and cardiovascular collapse. They must be slowed down as a life-saving measure. They frequently are relatively refractory even to large doses of sedative drugs. For such patients, several ECT's in a single day may be necessary.[17, 25]

Patients having a first, acute schizophrenic break who are treated with ECT show a remission rate during the first six-month period approximately twice as great as do untreated patients, but no greater than patients treated with phenothiazines. However, the rate of relapse and readmission is just as high in the two groups, and the benefits of ECT disappear with a two-year follow-up. Thus, in view of the possible complications of ECT, it remains debatable whether the advantages outweigh the disadvantages of its use during acute schizophrenic episodes. Patients who are paranoid during an acute episode may derive the greatest benefit.[25]

The remission rate with ECT (as with other treatments) drops with repeated episodes of illness or with a chronic first episode. Attempts to predict which patients would benefit from ECT by measuring pretreatment response to injections of methacholine and epinephrine have been equivocal at best.[6, 9, 20] In general, catatonic patients in stupor respond better than do simple, hebephrenic, pseudoneurotic schizophrenics or paranoid schizophrenics whose illness began after the age of 40.

It would appear, then, that the only clear indication for the use of ECT in schizophrenic illnesses is to curb an excited patient's activity; it may also have some use in acute first episodes and for catatonic patients in stupor, but relapse rates for these latter two conditions have been quite disappointing.[16, 29] It may also be useful in treating combative patients in poorly staffed state hospitals.

Side Effects, Complications, Contraindications, and Risk

As noted above, the major physical side effects are those of fractures and cardiovascular collapse.

Compression fractures of the thoracic spine are most frequently encountered; those of the long bones, e.g., humerus, tibia, fibula, are rarer. The spinal compression fractures are relatively innocuous in terms of disability or pain; those of the long bones are, of course, serious. In one study,[14] the incidence of vertebral fractures was 7 percent in patients not receiving a muscle-relaxant; there was none in a matched group for whom succinylcholine was part of the treatment. Severe osteoporosis in the elderly may be a contraindication for ECT, but most schizophrenic patients are in young adulthood and would not be likely to be suffering from this condition. Succinylcholine itself is a potent drug, and some hospitals think that its disadvantages outweigh its advantages.

The most frequent fatal complications are found in the

cardiovascular system. Lewis and colleagues[19] found evidence
of cardiac arrhythmia in 16 of 21 patients receiving a total
of 220 ECT's. These arrhythmias occurred in 47 percent of
the treatments; 65 percent of the arrhythmias were judged
mild or moderate; the remainder were severe or very severe.
There were no fatalities. Generally, the presence of an aortic
aneurysm, a recent (i.e., within the preceding six months)
myocardial infarction, and severe hypertension are contraindications for ECT.

Many other conditions, once thought to be adversely affected by ECT, have turned out not to be. Thus there is no
increase in the average risk for ECT in patients who have
the following diseases or conditions: pregnancy, tuberculosis,
extreme youth or old age, or spinal arthritis.[16, 25]

Risk with ECT is low; fewer than one in 1000 treatments
result in death.[16] In one study[23] there were four fatalities in
20,000 treatments, a ratio of 1:5,000; the authors state,
"... one 21-year-old female has had a total of 320 treatments
with no premedications and no complications of any sort."

ECT produces temporary, organic mental deficits. Primary among these are retrograde amnesia for the period
preceding the ECT, confusion, emotional dullness, and occasional postshock excitement.[16, 25] Depending on how many
treatments the patient has had in the preceding days or
weeks, these symptoms clear in hours or days. There is no
firm evidence of permanent mental impairment as the result
of ECT; brain damage, similarly, has not been found on
autopsy neuropathological studies of patients who had had
extensive ECT while living or in sacrificed experimental
animals.

Mode of Action of ECT
    No one knows.

INSULIN-SHOCK THERAPY

Insulin-shock therapy (IST), also known as insulin-
coma therapy (ICT), was introduced in the treatment of the
schizophrenias by Manfred Sakel (who noted the therapeutic

effect of accidental hypoglycemia when insulin was given as
an appetite stimulant), in the early 1930s, and it enjoyed
considerable popularity in the two decades that followed. In
the United States, use of IST has declined dramatically since
1952; as a result, this section will be brief. Readers interested
in the details of the indications, contraindications, and techniques involved in IST are referred to standard texts.[13, 25]

Sakel's technique, largely unchanged, is to give the patient sufficient insulin to induce hypoglycemic coma, shown
by areflexia of knees and cornea, lasting minutes during the
first treatments and an hour or more later. The comas are
induced from three to five times a week; a course of treatments lasts eight to ten weeks. Coma is terminated with oral
or injected glucose. Convulsions, either as the result of hypoglycemia or induced with ECT during coma, enhance results;
such combined treatment does not seem to be more hazardous
than IST alone.[13, 17, 25]

The procedure is risky; prolonged or irreversible coma
with resultant brain damage or death is most to be feared.
The mortality rate is about 1 percent, making IST more than
ten times as dangerous as ECT.

As with all other treatments for the schizophrenias, IST
is most effective with acute, first-break patients, and becomes
decreasingly effective with repeated psychotic episodes or
with chronicity. Nevertheless, it seems to be more effective
than no treatment at all. In a study reported by Patterson[27]
three matched groups of patients were treated; two with
insulin and one with "spansulin" (an inert placebo carefully
colored and dispensed to ward personnel with the explanation that it was a new form of long-acting insulin). Of the
two groups receiving insulin, one was discharged from the
hospital before the study, thus comprising a retrospective
control group, and one was in the hospital at the time of the
study, as were the patients receiving "spansulin." The patients were matched for age, sex, diagnosis, length of illness,
and several other important parameters. All intergroup differences were insignificant except length of illness, which

for the "spansulin" group was 14 months, for the insulin groups, 28 months. If anything, this difference would bias the results in favor of better posttreatment findings in the "spansulin" group. Nevertheless, more than 60 percent of both insulin groups were discharged, and remained out of the hospital during the criterion period; for the "spansulin" group, only 29 percent had been discharged. Thus the suggestion is that IST can cause measurable improvement in chronically schizophrenic patients. Insulin and chlorpromazine were compared for their effects on chronic schizophrenic patients by Markowe and colleagues.[22] They found no differences in discharge rates between groups of patients treated with either drug.

PSYCHOSURGERY

Men have attempted for centuries to alter behavior, schizophrenic or otherwise, by altering people's brains; primitive trephining operations ("burr holes") on ancient skulls have been found in excavated ruins. Moniz, in 1933, and, later, Freeman and Watts have attempted to put such treatment into a more scientific framework; this work is reported in detail in standard texts.[8, 25] As with ECT and IST, the peak of enthusiasm for this method was reached during the 1930s and 1940s; since then it has largely fallen into disuse.

The major principle behind such surgery was to interrupt certain cerebral nerve tracts or radiations, especially the thalamofrontal radiation; these almost always impinged on frontal-lobe cortical functioning. "Prefrontal lobotomy" was among the earliest and most famous of such operations. Numerous variations of operative site and technique have appeared since then, none showing clearly superior results.

As with IST, this procedure is hazardous. Freeman[8] estimates postoperative mortality at from 1 to 3 percent, and postoperative seizures (of which 75 percent can be controlled medically) at from 1 to 30 percent.

At its most favorable, the results of such surgery are a relative or total loss of schizophrenic symptomatology and a

concomitant gain in social functioning. Sometimes there is
a desirable abatement of hostility, tension, incontinence, and
other forms of behavior that make patients difficult to manage in the hospital. Discharge rates of operated patients
seem strikingly similar to those for other forms of treatment:
two of three acute patients will be discharged; only one of
ten patients hospitalized ten years or more will be discharged.

Not even the most vigorous proponents of psychosurgery
claim, however, that operated patients are "good as new."
Almost inevitably after surgery, the immediate changes are
those of the "reverse Boy Scout Syndrome." Patients become
sloppy, thoughtless, unheeding of conventional customs of
dress, language, and behavior. They require diligent care and
retraining by staff or family and have to be watched over
much as one watches over a retarded child. Psychosurgery,
admits Freeman, ". . . reduces creativity, sometimes to the
vanishing point."[8] That this cure may be worse than the disease is shown by the statement of one husband of a lobot-
omized wife, quoted in Redlich and Freedman:[29] "She's not
driven by all the devils of hell anymore, but she has become
so sloppy and smelly!" Symptoms of confusion and memory
loss also are frequent in the immediate postoperative period.
These complications tend to improve with time, but they
rarely disappear completely.

Psychosurgery should be held as the absolutely last resort in the treatment of patients who have been refractory
to *all* other types of treatment for many years, and whose
existences are marked by great pain, anguish, and tension,
not only for themselves but for those who take care of them.

OTHER SOMATIC THERAPIES

The most familiar restraint is the strait jacket, so be-
loved by the cartoonist. Restraint is often mechanical; canvas
and leather straps, belts, and suits are used in combination.
Sometimes it is personal: several people will wrestle an
agitated patient down and hold him down until he has re-

gained control or has otherwise been restrained. (Sarcastic mention exists of the use of large doses of phenothiazines as "chemical restraints" or "chemical lobotomy.") Cold, wet sheet packs have also been used. The fact of the matter is that patients who go out of control frighten themselves and frighten everyone around them, are dangerous to themselves and others, and need to be restrained. Restraint should be brief and end as soon as the period of acute danger seems to have passed.

The acutely agitated patient needs sedation; sedatives such as amobarbital and secobarbital work well. Their dosages should be reduced for patients already receiving phenothiazines. Similarly, warm tub baths are a universal way of inducing comfort and serenity.

SUMMARY

Though the advent of the phenothiazines has put older forms of somatic treatment, such as ECT, IST, and psychosurgery into eclipse, the eclipse should not be total. Of the various somatic therapies in the schizophrenias, phenothiazine drugs are the treatment of choice. If, and only if, they are dangerous or ineffective, or if getting the geographically remote patient to take his medication is difficult, should other forms of treatment be used.

Of the other forms, ECT is by far the least dangerous and frequently the most effective. It is particularly useful, and may in fact be life saving, in cases of acute mania and acute catatonic excitement. It is also especially useful for patients, refractory or hypersensitive to phenothiazines, who are having their first schizophrenic episode or who are in a catatonic stupor. Kalinowsky,[17] a vigorous proponent of ECT, suggests, "It is, therefore, our strong conviction that every patient who does not remain symptom-free after two or three months of pharmacotherapy should receive the benefits of shock treatments."

If, after one to two years of combined drug, ECT, and milieu therapy, there is not a substantial response to treat-

ment, IST, with or without ECT, should be seriously considered. By this time the patient would seem to be headed for a
lifetime of chronic illness and hospitalization, and the risks
of IST to interrupt this career are justified.

Finally, if the patient has been continuously ill for several years, and especially if he is in torment, psychosurgery
should be considered. Without psychosurgery, the patient is
virtually doomed to a lifetime of tragic disquietude; with it,
there is a small chance of surcease.

Barbiturates, restraints, and warm baths may be useful
for the acutely disturbed patient.

13

Milieu Therapy

by DAVID N. DANIELS, M.D

INTRODUCTION

This chapter deals with environmental therapies of schizophrenia—therapies utilizing the milieu or setting per se as the curative agent.

Despite favorable trends in reducing the number of hospitalized patients, approximately 500,000 persons in America are hospitalized in mental hospitals,[39, 56] one half of whom have schizophrenia or related disorders.[55] The total direct and indirect costs of mental illness recently have been estimated at a staggering 20 billion dollars.[20] Because the chronically hospitalized patient and, more recently, the relapsing "revolving-door" patient remain, in my opinion, the most pressing problems of rehabilitative psychiatry, I shall give some special emphasis to the mental hospital milieu. However, because there are indications that the community itself can and perhaps will become the basic milieu for the treatment of the schizophrenias,[41, 45, 55] I shall also discuss environmental therapies outside the hospital milieu.

Dr. Daniels is Assistant Professor of Psychiatry, Stanford University School of Medicine, and Consultant in Psychiatry at the Palo Alto Veterans Administration Hospital.

The author wishes to acknowledge the contribution of Mary M. Shapiro, A.B., in the preparation of this chapter.

The history of sequestering psychotic people away from others is long and checkered, and not one to reassure us about man's humanity to man.[1] Yet waves of humanism in the handling of mental patients have been interspersed among the troughs.[9] For example, "moral treatment"—the humane, benevolent, and "hopeful-environment" treatment of mental patients—attained remarkable acceptance and results in the period from 1820 to 1860, following the contributions of Pinel, Tuke, and others.[85]

The most recent wave of humane treatment has resulted from a growing interest in, and knowledge of, ego psychology, field and role theory, and social-cultural theory.[21, 70, 85] In fact, since World War II the growth of social psychiatry, especially milieu hospital treatments, has resulted in what has been termed the "third revolution in psychiatry."[7, 70] Hopefully, this most recent wave of humane treatment will be sustained through the light of knowledge and not be dependent on the "soul" or good will of man alone. For it is precisely this increase in knowledge about emotional disorders, hospital social systems, and milieu treatments that can come to differentiate present milieu therapy from previous "moral treatment."

This is not to say that a well-marked path of knowledge about milieu treatment exists. There is as yet very little clear evidence for the specific effectiveness of any particular form of hospital treatment of schizophrenia,[33, 34, 68, 78] except some evidence of the success of supportive programs in association with phenothiazines.[53, 77] The contradictory nature and sparseness of the evidence are partly due to the lack of rigorous experimentation and the failure to stratify patients into different groups according to specific criteria and characteristics, e.g., into schizophrenic and nonschizophrenic groups, into chronic and acute groups. For instance, there are conflicting data regarding the relative importance of social-behavioral factors (e.g., ability to work, maintaining a home) and psychiatric symptoms (e.g., delusions and bizarre behavior) in determining discharges and readmissions.[24, 40, 68,

[72, 74, 88] Similarly, Miller[66] reports lower readmission rates for discharged patients living with families, whereas Carstairs[10, 12] reports that schizophrenic patients fare worst in family settings.

But this scarcity results to some extent from the lack of attention given to the potential curative effect of specific components of the treatment setting per se. Such nonspecific effects as change in attitude of hospital personnel, renewal of enthusiasm and hope, the belief in human capacity and dignity, and cessation of abuses—i.e., the old "moral treatment"—could alone account for the increased discharges of hospital patients that are in fact occurring.[51, 66, 88] In general, milieu treatment has been viewed as supportive of more specific "real" treatments, such as individual and group psychotherapy or somatic therapy; the milieu is believed to provide a conducive atmosphere for therapy but not to be therapy per se.[23, 69] This belief about milieu therapy is not difficult to understand, because psychiatrists and other mental health professionals come from clinical backgrounds and have very little training in organizational theory, development, and management. The relevance of human social organization to adaptation and ego function has not been adequately appreciated.

This chapter is divided into seven sections or topic areas followed by a chapter summary. The first section discusses the noteworthy relevance of human social organization to ego function and to adaptation. The second section discusses the characteristics of the mental hospital as a social system. The third section considers the nature of the ego dysfunction and socially disordered behavior in schizophrenia that the milieu must be organized to correct and to restore. In this section I distinguish among three functional subgroups of schizophrenic disorders. In the fourth section a general theoretical model for milieu therapy, entitled intentional social-system therapy, is put forth. Finally, the last three sections discuss the specific therapeutic organization of milieus that can lead to repair of the kinds of ego impairment and socially disordered behavior seen in schizophrenia. Thus the fifth section describes specific examples of milieu therapies both in hospitals and in extrahospital environments; the sixth section enumerates common problems encountered in milieu therapies and offers suggestions for their solution; and the seventh section presents speculations about the future of milieu therapies.

SOCIAL ORGANIZATION, EGO FUNCTION, AND ADAPTATION

Our existence depends in large part on the adaptiveness of our social environment, especially our family and communal grouping. We must obtain our gratifications, identity, and validation of actions through our social environment. In fact, our social organization is itself a collective coping mechanism. Our very survival is rooted in cultural as well as biological evolution.[22] Even our biological evolution has uniquely endowed us for complex communal living. The ego abilities of higher intelligence, self-awareness, symbolization in the form of language, and plasticity and flexibility; the upright posture; prehension; the vocal apparatus; the extremely long period of nurturance of the young; and the prolonged maturation process—all these biological characteristics favor and allow for rich, changeable, and complex adaptation through communal organization.[27] It is little wonder that Goldschmidt[47] has written that man's culture— the sum total of his communal living that is transmitted from generation to generation—is "man's way." He further points out that man's needs are served best by the group, even though individual and group needs may conflict at times. Goldschmidt goes so far as to postulate a biologically based drive that he calls the need for positive affect—each person's craving for response from his human environment. Certainly studies of human infants suffering from institutional deprivation[79] and Harlow's[52] dramatic studies showing that monkeys deprived of social contact lack even basic sexual and mothering behaviors indicate the importance, even the absolute necessity, of social and affective contact in development. There is also impressive evidence from naturalistic studies of many species that social organization serves as an important adaptive mechanism in species' survival.[26, 76]

Although quite clearly man's ego growth and function and his adaptation are crucially influenced by the social environment, we as mental health professionals often have failed to recognize the potential of a planned or designed environment for the recovery of mental patients. The changing of the disturbed or disordered person requires more than direct treatment of his individual characteristics. In order to change and grow, man must have situations that provide some stress and challenge yet also opportunity and support, which are basic to education at all ages. The social system with which he interacts—the mental hospital, in the case of most treated schizophrenic patients—must be structured to facilitate change and growth. But what is the nature of mental hospital organization? In what ways, if any, is a hospital organized to facilitate restoration and promote growth? In order to answer these and related questions, I turn now to a discussion of the very milieu, the mental hospital, that society has created to restore disturbed and disordered people to productive lives.

THE SOCIAL ORGANIZATION OF MENTAL HOSPITALS

Because the mental hospital remains a primary environment for the treatment of schizophrenia, knowledge about the characteristics of mental hospitals is indispensable for anyone wishing to understand or engage in milieu therapy. A great deal has been written about mental hospital social systems during the last two decades and about their potential as therapeutic environments.[14, 17, 21, 25, 29, 46, 50, 75, 81, 82, 86] Yet the greatest single error of mental health professionals engaged in milieu therapy is the failure to understand clearly the nature of mental hospitals as complex organizations—their goals, structure, and impact on patients and staff members alike.

First, mental hospitals have several goals or objectives that frequently are contradictory and conflicting. These objectives include maintaining the institution per se quite apart from any other consideration, treatment, care, and protection of persons unable to provide for themselves, and incarceration of persons with objectionable behavior that is identified as mentally disordered. Sometimes research, training, and mental health education are also objectives. The hospital administration commonly is concerned with running an efficient bureaucratic organization; the clinical personnel, however, are more concerned with a variety of treatments or procedures aimed at returning patients to the outside community, hopefully as "cured," and usually without consideration of specific cost factors. Similarly, conflict about the objectives of incarcerating disturbed people, treating them, and simply protecting the helpless may occur. What is more, good patient care should not be equated with good treatment. Good patient care may be a requisite for good treatment, but it is not identical with it and may encourage institutionalization. In fact, all the various objectives are at one time or another in conflict with one another. As a result of these conflicts patients can become, in effect, sacrificial pawns, the least important object in the system rather than its subject. In order to be effective, one needs to identify clearly what the objecives are and in what order of priority they are at any one time in any particular institution, e.g., when and where some treatment goal is secondary to an administrative objective.

Second, the structure of the mental hospital reflects these divergent and conflicting objectives. Treatment staff members frequently have two lines of authority, one associated with a treatment team (ward), and the other with the administrative chain of command. For instance, nurses, the most seriously affected group, must divide loyalties and reconcile differences between the treatment team of which they are members and the nursing service administration. Disturbances in patients' behavior frequently are associated with conflicts among staff members, particularly covert or unrecognized conflicts.[81] Of even greater importance because of its potential effect upon patients is the fact that mental hospitals are mobility-blocked, opportunity-closed social systems. On the one side is the staff, and on the other, patients. Traditional hospital structure emphasizes the "we-they," superordinate-subordinate relationship between staff members and patients.

Third, the distance and difference between patients and staff members are highlighted further by the patients' total institutionalization status, 24-hour-a-day residency status in an institution that meets all one's survival needs at the price of "mortification" of the self.[46] Thus, while providing total life maintenance, security, and protection for patients, the hospital tends also to regiment, take responsibility for, and assume control over patients (and may be instructed to do so by the courts). For the person who has found living outside the hospital very distressful and full of failure, the radically different norms, the relative dehumanization, the regimentation, and the dependency of hospitalization do not seem to be an excessive price to pay in exchange for the security, stability, and protection provided by the hospital.[24] This interaction between the patient and the hospital environment is a process that can occur unwittingly and without intent.

Thus in many respects the traditional hospital milieu, including many so-called therapeutic communities, paradoxically represents the antithesis of what we know creates human growth and development. Although this indictment of mental hospitals is general, it is not applicable equally to all institutions and settings. Furthermore, the characteristics described concerning the mental hospital are not exclusive to mental hospitals. Other treatment settings can be equally antitherapeutic, e.g., home-care programs, day-treatment centers, halfway houses, sheltered workshops.

But before I can discuss the therapeutic organizations of hospitals and other milieus, a review is necessary of the kinds of ego dysfunction and social disorder that the hospital milieu is attempting to correct.

EGO DYSFUNCTION AND DISORDERED
SOCIAL BEHAVIOR

The diverse and far-ranging phenomena present in schizophrenia and the interaction of biological, psychological, interpersonal, and social forces in producing schizophrenia are discussed in other chapters. From the standpoint of milieu therapies the schizophrenic phenomena will be viewed as primarily disorders in ego function and social behavior. My general statements about the nature of the schizophrenic disorders that the treatment environment must be organized to correct fit somewhat better with a description of chronic patients, people who in number and need constitute the major problem for milieu therapy. Here these disorders will be reviewed briefly.

The Ego Dysfunctions

The schizophrenic shows deficits in his executive ego functioning[21]—the ego abilities regarding perceiving, organizing, and judging the environment. He shows serious disturbances in the logical thought processes and has associated problems in identifying and differentiating thoughts, actions, and objects, one from another. His distractability and fragmented thinking often are reflected in an inability to organize tasks and to rank events according to order of importance. His decision-making may reflect failure to anticipate the outcome of events and consequences of action. He frequently is unable to fit behavior to the varying demands of particular situations, i.e., to show behavior appropriate to cope with environment demands. In addition, he has few or poorly differentiated internalized objects, ego sets, and roles on which to base action.[21] Having a lack of stored objects, he is at the mercy of objects in the here and now; he is a prisoner of the present or of his fantasies. He has a poverty of meanings in action and hence ways to validate himself.[4] He has poorly differentiated ego boundaries and hence a very poor sense of self in relation to others, plus an excessive amount of denial or "not me" and low self-esteem. Not uncommonly this kind of disorder is manifested by "regressed" behavior, loss of interest in life, and withdrawal.

Given these executive ego-function deficits,* it is little wonder that the schizophrenic has disturbance in the synthetic or conflict-born ego functions, those concerned with the mediation and integration of drive, emotion, thought, and action. Not being able to regulate sensory input, he may not be able to regulate impulse control, gain satisfaction through interpersonal relations and acceptable social pathways, or relate to others as objects in their own right. The give and take of relationships may be disordered, and relationships curtailed or "narcissistic." Motivation as a positive life force often is lacking or aborted into immediacy motivation. He often comes to experience himself as a tormented recipient of forces and actions beyond his control and therefore helpless to change his situation.

Socially Disordered Behaviors

Associated with the ego dysfunctions are the socially disordered behaviors. A limiting factor on the community acceptance of schizophrenics is family and public tolerance for "sick" or socially disordered and unacceptable behavior.[40, 88] These behaviors include noncooperation occasionally manifested in violent behavior, eccentric and bizarre behavior, delusions and hallucinations, withdrawal and loss of interest in life, and failure in self-care or self-support.

The schizophrenic, particularly if he has a long history of "illness," frequently lacks residential stability or adequate living accommodations. He may have a long or checkered history of institutionalization in some form of ghetto, hospital, or prison. He has frequently lost or alienated his family, spouse, or other human resources of support and help, people that he could lean on or count on to help out in time of need.[22, 72] He frequently has a poor and worsening employment history. If employed, he is likely to occupy a low-status,

---

* See also Chapter 11, Table 11–1, for further discussion of ego function and dysfunction.

unstable, poor-paying job. In some combination his residential, human, employment, and financial roots are withered or lacking. He often becomes a misfit, a person alienated and disaffiliated from the mainstream of society.[22] Thus he is in truth both a psychologically and socially disordered person.

Functional Subgroups of Schizophrenics

Most importantly, any statement concerning the nature of schizophrenic disorders must account for the diverse range of phenomena and the number and severity of the phenomena present in each case. Any general statement about schizophrenia is most certainly incorrect if applied monolithically. In particular, three broad functional subgroups must be distinguished.

1. ACUTE-REACTIVE: Here the person is likely to have mainly disturbances in the synthetic-mediative ego functions (except in the initial phase when the undergirding executive ego functions also are impaired), high environmental stress, a precipitating life crisis or event(s), relatively high motivation, identifiable interpersonal-psychological events associated with the psychosis, and little history of prolonged institutionalization. He is less likely to have serious severing or permanent rupture of the sustaining network of interpersonal relationships and roots in the environment.

2. CHRONIC-PROCESS: Here the person is likely to have mainly disturbances in the executive ego functioning, low environmental stress, a minimal precipitating life crisis, inability to cope with "minor" stresses, low or immediacy motivation, and a history of prolonged or steady-stay institutionalization (i.e., he is overinstitutionalized). Subsequently, he is likely to have serious severing of adequate roots in the environment and of interpersonal relationships on which he can depend.

3. CHRONIC-REACTIVE: Here are the host of people who do not fit nicely into the other two subgroups. Like the chronic-process schizophrenic, he is likely to have poor and

few roots in the community and at best a number of unstable interpersonal relationships. He tends to alienate himself through poorly organized, impulsive, immediacy-oriented behavior, rather than to become alienated subsequent to long periods of hospitalization. He is underinstitutionalized, i.e., he shows a "revolving-door" rather than steady-stay type of hospitalization. He never stays long enough anywhere to become institutionalized. He tends to overreact to minimal environmental stress and minor crises with some form of self-destructive behavior. He is less likely to have the classical thought disorder of chronic-process schizophrenia or the extent of cognitive dysfunction, yet his ability to perceive, organize, judge, and act on stimuli is seriously disordered.

These factors indicate a need for specificity in planning treatment settings and in selecting patients appropriate for particular settings. These factors are important because they point clearly to a need for different basic types of treatment milieus, an issue that will be discussed at length later in this chapter.

Considering the nature and extent of the disorders of the schizophrenic, which are listed above, it is little wonder that this person who has experienced life as full of failure and pain gravitates toward or is impressed into a mental hospital. In the hospital, as discussed above, he is provided with a protective, stable, relatively secure environment, something that he may not have in the outside community. That the characteristics of mental institutions amplify and confirm his ego dysfunction and socially disordered behavior —his weakened roots or ties in the outside world, his alienation, his already poor self-concept and low self-esteem, his low or immediacy motivation, his difficulty in maintaining interpersonal relationships, his ineffectual coping strategies, and his cognitive dysfunction—is but a by-product of a mutual contract between the patient and the institution that sustains and preserves both. In light of this amplification and confirmation of weaknesses and disorders, it is not surprising that the reported findings of psychiatric hospitalization are so poor and contradictory and that little beyond the sheer amount of hospitalization has been predictive of outcome.

From yet another perspective, the perspective of human growth and change, the marriage between the patient and the institution is the antithesis of all that constitutes a restoration process. For people grow, change, and strengthen when their milieu provides opportunities and challenges, meaningful tasks and roles, the power to make decisions, group membership, interdependence and support, incentives and rewards for successful performance, and an organizational structure that is open to upward mobility. In addition, the more chronic patients must become affiliated with the mainstream of society, adopt its norms, develop roots in it, and be sustained by the gratifications it offers.

The hoped-for goal is that the schizophrenic will expand and develop his ego functioning and social ties to the end of becoming an accountable, participating, and reasonably satisfied citizen. If he is to achieve this goal, the treatment setting, institution or otherwise, must be constructed to facilitate ego growth and normative social behavior. Such a construction should be the logical outgrowth of theoretical concepts that would foster the achievements of these goals. I shall now present a theoretical model, based on these concepts, that encompasses a range of therapeutic milieus and then shall consider details of designs based on the theoretical model.

INTENTIONAL SOCIAL SYSTEM THERAPY

Although there are numerous milieu programs for the treatment and rehabilitation of the mentally disordered, relatively little attention has been given to the formulation and testing of theoretical models on which these programs are based.[23, 34, 59] Indeed, the failure to specify the elements of the therapeutic process constitutes a serious impediment to progress in milieu therapies and institutional psychiatry in general. There is great need to clarify what elements of a milieu are therapeutic for various kinds of people.

Better works on this subject include the following: Vitale[85] has an excellent short summary of the development and nature of the therapeutic community concept. Clark,[18] Jones,[58] and Kraft,[60] all of whom have extensive experience with the therapeutic community approach, have written recent articles on the concepts and practices of the therapeutic community. Although these three authors provide descriptive and expository discussions, they fail to provide evidence for the success of the therapeutic-community approach or a systematic presentation of theory. Most frequently writers fail to recognize the importance of the components of the organizational structure as curative agents. Coming from clinical heritages, they generally tend to overemphasize the relationship between people as being the curative agent and to see the milieu as producing merely a "therapeutic atmosphere." Clark[17] has also written a highly readable historical and practical volume emphasizing the role of the physician in milieu therapy. Cumming and Cumming[21] give an extensive, clear, and systematic discussion of the relationship between the design and practices of curative social environments and ego and role theory. In another work, Edelson[31] discusses the relation of ego, adaptation, and the hospital social environment. Finally, Rapoport's[70] descriptions of the phenomenon of oscillation, the distinction between treatment and rehabilitation concepts, and systematic observations are among the many contributions he has made resulting from his study of Jones's[57] therapeutic community at Blemont Hospital in England. Elsewhere Daniels and Rubin[22] report in detail an analytical study and theoretical statement concerning the community meeting, an important component of the therapeutic community.

Fairweather's[34, 36, 73] approach, to be discussed later, complements the therapeutic-community approach with a social system therapy based on heterogeneous, autonomous, patient-led task groups functioning both within the hospital and in the outside community. With chronic and poorly motivated groups the importance of generating peer-group tasks to enliven the group processes and provide incentive and hope cannot be overemphasized.

The information from the preceding sections provides a background against which to present a general model for milieu therapies. This information indicates that a model must fulfill a number of requirements in order to attain the goals of improved ego functioning, more stable and satisfying relationships, better sense of personal well-being, and some form of self-supported community living.

1. It should recognize the importance of human organization to man's adaptation, to his need for relatedness, and to his ego growth and function. Hence the model requires careful attention to the elements in human social systems.

2. It should be organized to repair, restore, and increase function in both the executive and synthetic spheres of ego function manifested in schizophrenia.

3. It should be cognizant of, and avoid, the damaging process of institutionalization associated with any prolonged hospitalization. In this regard the model should reflect as nearly as possible the norms and expectations of outside living.

4. It should provide means to meet the social-environmental needs of many schizophrenics, especially those who have unstable ties or have lost their ties in community life.

5. It should be able to treat the heterogeneous population present in most treatment milieus.

As a social-system model its adequacy will be reflected in its ability to represent a synthesis of relevant theories of behavior, specify the components of the system and their effects, respond flexibly and promptly to varying situations and changed demands, and provide comprehensive care with continuity and efficiency.

The model presented here, called intentional social-system therapy,[22] attempts to meet these criteria. It is a synthesis of principles drawn from ego psychology, social-adaptation theory, role theory, and organizational theory. In this context the therapeutic-community approach is seen as just one possible planned design for "therapeutic living," one possible plan for an intentional social system.

Intentional social system therapy is a social-psychological milieu treatment that utilizes the group context, frequently a living-together group (e.g., a ward community), as a method to induce social recovery and individual growth and adaptation. It is based on the concepts of man as an adaptive being who survives through both his group or organizational living and his ego functioning and their interaction. The theory postulates that man through his communal living must obtain gratifications, develop his identity and his capacities, and find validation and confirmation of his being. Patients are viewed as people with serious adaptative disturbances in some combination of both executive ego functions (so-called autonomous, conflict-free sphere of the ego) and synthetic ego functions (so-called conflict-born, ego defense, and mediative sphere of the ego). These disturbances are manifested by disordered social-role behavior and various psychological symptoms. The intentional social system attempts to develop, facilitate, and utilize a combination of both the organization structure and approaches to the individual as the means of repairing ego damage, especially impairments in social-role functioning.

In more specific terms the elements of an intentional social system are as follows:

1. Real tasks, ordinarily in the form of group or community maintenance functions, but sometimes in the form of specific peer-group tasks, e.g., real work situations that require a division of labor among members, interdependence, and group rewards. Arranging for interdependence and division of labor through group tasks is crucial in working with, and increasing the participation of, poorly motivated and chronic patient groups. The tasks need to reflect the comprehensive range of services to the population being served.

2. An organizational structure that is hierarchical yet neither mobility-blocked nor strictly superordinate-subordi-

nate. Such a structure provides for participation in decision-making by all the group members, graded responsibility, accountability, and a series of challenges to the participants ranging from problems of everyday living to naturally occurring crisis situations (sometimes referred to as a series of controlled crises).

3. Meaningful roles, approximating those required for general living in the mainstream of society, that have specified duties and obligations that must be carried out to make the intentional social system function. A variety of meaningful interdependent roles encourages individual growth through role-modeling behavior (showing the other person how to do it) and through "going through the motions" of trying new behaviors and roles.

4. An ideology and value system that espouse the capacities and assets of man rather than his liabilities and defects, the individual responsibility of man as basic to human social function and dignity rather than control and regimentation, flexibility rather than rigidity, human growth through living-learning experiences rather than *in situ* insight, humanistic attitudes (understanding, warmth, respect, consideration, encouragement, hope, and support) rather than dehumanism, the helper-therapy principle rather than passive compliance, and a model of patients as more socially disordered rather than diseased "sick" people.

5. Codes and policies governing the social behavior of members and ideally determined by them in accordance with general standards of the community at large.

6. The use of social pressure, the compelling and impelling force to conform and perform, which arises around potentially disruptive situations and threats to the social system.

7. The close scrutiny, confrontation, and examination of the actual roles and behavior and their consequences in the here and now, all of which develop self-awareness, a sense of reality, responsibility, and more satisfactory interpersonal relationships and reduce or modify conflicts in the synthetic-mediative sphere of the ego. These pro-

cedures may occur in a variety of individual and group encounters both formal and informal. However, it should be recognized that overstimulation and excessive confrontation may make the chronic patient worse.[88]

8. Regularized assessment as a core treatment component, such assessment to include evaluation of outcome on both "hard" and "soft" data criteria; the relationship among patient, program, and outcome variables; and cost-benefit analysis. This assessment should involve a regularized review and planning procedures that utilize the feedback of machine-analyzed data concerning program effectiveness and individual patient progress. This type of assessment keeps the system responsive to needs, facilitates constructive change, and points up areas of deficiency as well as strength in program design and operation.

A milieu program through the use of these elements becomes a problem-solving, supportive, self-maintaining social system—an intentional community. In such a milieu both executive and synthetic ego disturbances can be corrected, and better social living implemented. Patient change can occur from without to in (direct social change followed internal reorganization) as well as from within to out (internal reorganization followed by social change).

In order to distinguish further this theoretical model for the delivery of services, a tabular comparison with traditional milieu treatments follows. Although these differences are presented in polar fashion, they should not be considered as mutually exclusive or as absolute differences.

TABLE 13–1

INTENTIONAL SOCIAL SYSTEM MODEL	TRADITIONAL MODEL
Structure	
Opportunity-open nonblocked integrated structure. Power distributed among patients and staff members. More democratic. Patients involved in delivery of services. Staff roles more indirect and consultative.	Mobility-blocked, superordinate-subordinate system between the staff and patients. Power in the staff. More authoritarian. Patient receives services. The staff delivers direct-treatment services.

Concepts Concerning Change of Behavior

Patient socially disordered and responsible. Emphasis on action and adjustment. Etiological interest relatively low. Change in social behavior leads to psychological and personality change. Restoration and employment hand in hand. Group oriented.	Patient mentally sick and not responsible. Emphasis on curing underlying disorders and insight. Etiological interest high. Psychological and personality changes lead to changes in social behavior. Restoration followed by discharge and employment. Individually oriented.

Attitude toward Patient

Emphasis on patient's undeveloped or atrophied potential strengths and abilities (eugenic model). Emphasis on high instrumental performance.	Emphasis on patient's current weakness and liabilities (psychopathology model). Emphasis on developing understanding.

Evaluation

Core program component. Effectiveness analysis part of treatment.	Considered "Research." Separate from treatment program functions.

Focus

Group processes and tasks considered important. Social system and task groups as curative agents per se. Problem solving and crisis resolution emphasized.	Individual and dyads and individual goals considered important. Social system support to therapy. Understanding and conflict resolution emphasized.

From this comparison it can be seen that in intentional social-system therapy the patient potentially can play a much greater role in the delivery of services of which he is usually the recipient. Furthermore, the model provides a more balanced utilization of the three basic elements of organizational development—the "people" component, the structural component, and the technological component.

Many hospital and extrahospital systems similar in principle, but differing as to arrangement, numbers, and types of specific components, are possible. In the section that follows, several examples of milieu therapies that meet at least some of the requirements of an intentional social system or are of special interest are discussed.

MILIEU THERAPIES

A plethora of milieu therapies have been reported in the past 20 or so years. Those therapies reported include inpatient milieu therapies, especially the therapeutic community;[19, 23, 31, 57, 69, 73, 80, 87] day-night psychiatric programs;[5, 11, 37, 42, 61, 90] halfway houses;[5, 15, 38, 48, 63] foster-home and family-care services;[28, 67, 84] sheltered workshops;[6, 12, 16, 30, 43, 54] and comprehensive community mental-health services.[45]* Unfortunately, most reports are descriptive only. Even when specific outcome data are cited, experimental designs (e.g., use of controls, matched and/or randomized samples, stratified samples, comprehensive outcome criteria) are a scarce commodity.[23] Many authors lament the lack of definitive research.[21, 35, 59, 74, 75] In contrast, enthusiastic claims and advocacy are abundant. The unfortunate result is a baffling array of contradictory information.

I shall here attempt to provide some degree of clarity to the confusing information by presenting short descriptions of selected milieu programs—those social-system programs pointing in an important direction, showing some success, and providing evaluation. These descriptions will include the population served, nature of the program, results, and significance. Examples are drawn from hospital- and community-based programs. In addition to these examples, other representative programs of interest are mentioned. Milieu therapies focusing primarily on children, adolescents, and nonpsychotics and treatment modalities other than the milieu are excluded, except for the Louisville home-treatment program.

Because the rubric "the therapeutic community" is sub-

* Useful selected reference lists in these various topic areas are published by National Clearinghouse for Mental Health Information, National Institute of Mental Health, 5454 Wisconsin Avenue, Chevy Chase, Maryland 20015.

sumed in this chapter under the general concept of an intentional social system, examples of the therapeutic community as generally espoused are omitted. Representative reports describing therapeutic communities with chronic and/or acute patients appear in the bibliography. Jones's[70] original concept of the therapeutic community was based on an ideology of democratization, permissiveness, communalism, and reality confrontation. To this ideology multi-directional open communication, patient participation in management functions, and flattening of the authority pyramid often have been added. In addition, the community or large group meeting is a nearly ubiquitous component of the therapeutic community.

Hospital Based Systems

1. THE FOUR-STEP PROGRAM: Fairweather[34] developed a hospital social system based on heterogeneous, autonomous, patient-led task groups of from 12 to 16 patients. His controlled experiment, conducted at a Veterans Administration Hospital, included acute and chronic, psychotic and non-psychotic patients who for the most part had marginal social adjustment. The patient task groups were responsible for the progress of their members toward recovery. Each member of a group moved through four steps of differential privileges (money and passes) according to his behavior and progress. Recommendations for all decisions concerning individual patients were made by the group to the staff via a system of notes. The staff then voted on these recommendations and rated the entire group on the quality of its recommendations. If the staff judged the group's proposals and decision-making regarding its members inadequate, it moved the entire group back a step or two, thus limiting the members' privileges.

The program was quite successful as long as the patients remained in it. Compared with the active control (a therapeutic community), the four-step-program patients showed heightened social activity, high morale, more positive attitudes, and shorter hospitalization. After discharge they temporarily had more employment and returned to the hospital at a somewhat slower rate than did the control patients.

The four-step program makes several important contributions. It shows that markedly chronic patients, including schizophrenics, can contribute to their own recovery, that social-system organization is an effective treatment per se, and that chronic alienated patients need self-maintaining group living outside of hospitals—a finding that led to Fairweather's community lodge discussed below.

2. THE SOCIO-ENVIRONMENTAL TREATMENT PROGRAM: Sanders[74] initiated several experimental programs with chronic schizophrenics (average hospitalization was more than eight years) at the Philadelphia State Hospital. The major components of what he called socioenvironmental treatment programs were the social living situation (a therapeutic community), the interaction activity program, and intensified group activities (e.g., group therapy and patient government). These components were structured according to the intensity of interaction required.

The programs showed that social interaction related to intensity of social structure, that differently structured experimental programs helped some subgroups more than others (a finding also reported by Wing[88]), and that patients receiving the socioenvironmental treatments had somewhat better community adjustment.

The significance of the work by Sanders and his associates is in the effort to manipulate experimentally the therapeutic social system, in the differential effect on patient subgroups, in the more favorable effect of task-centered activities over discussion-centered activities, and in the deliberate effort to report and change the institutional resistances to a socioeducational model of treatment.

3. TOKEN-ECONOMY PROGRAMS: Ayllon and Azrin[3] pioneered a form of intentional social-system therapy with chronic psychotic patients, based on the principles of operant conditioning. The program operated by Ayllon and Azrin

at the Anna State Hospital, Illinois, compared female patients before, during, and after a series of experiments wherein the patients earned tokens by performing personal grooming, ward maintenance, and hospital industry assignments. With the tokens the patients could purchase privacy, off-ward passes, social interaction with staff, extra religious services, recreational opportunities, and commissary items.

In terms of in-hospital outcome, the only outcome reported, the results were dramatic. Approximately 80 percent of the patients performed the token-reinforced tasks (behaviors). Of interest is the fact that in one experiment patients used tokens almost exclusively to purchase privacy, off-ward passes, and commissary items. Only 30 of 23,560 tokens were used to purchase staff consultation, and even fewer, 19, to purchase recreation. The primary limitation of the token system was that some patients had lost almost all behaviors that could be rewarded through the intermediary of the tokens.

Because many chronic patients respond poorly to the usual social reinforcements provided by therapeutic communities and psychotherapies, the behavioral reinforcement afforded by token economies may offer a vital link to improvement. Translation of these programs into more independent living situations are being tried.[2] Finally, these programs may have applicability to the mentally retarded and to other groups.

Community Based Systems

1. THE COMMUNITY LODGE PROGRAM: Using the findings of his earlier four-step program, Fairweather[36, 73] initiated a community lodge for similar chronic and marginally adjusted VA Hospital patients. The men lived together autonomously in community housing and ran a janitorial service. The only direct staff coverage was provided by a psychologist.

About 69 percent of the lodge members remained out of the hospital at least six months, whereas 47 percent of the matched control group never left the hospital during the first six months of the follow-up period. Similarly 53 percent of the lodge group worked full time; 82 percent of the control patients did not work at all.

Fairweather and his associates' dramatic experiment demonstrates the potential of interdependent group living and task groups as curative agents and shows the capacities of mental patients to be greater than usually thought. The work of these investigators indicates that it is possible to design intentional communities to meet the needs of various patient subgroups.

2. PARTIAL-CARE SYSTEMS: The great number and variety of programs that are intermediate between total hospitalization and outpatient therapy, and the primarily descriptive nature of the reports of these programs make selection of a particular program for description difficult. Modern-day systems of partial care had developed in the U.S.S.R., Canada, and Great Britain before the United States got into the act.[13, 71] Some of the better and more well-known programs in America are Altro Workshops,[6] CHIRP at Brockton VAH,[43] Fountain House,[38] Rutland Corner House,[63] and The Quarters.[48]

The components of these various systems and the populations vary greatly. In general, the components involve some combination of the following: (1) transitional or potentially permanent living facilities, such as halfway houses (both in place of and after hospitalization), "satellite" apartments dispersed in the community, day hospitals, night hospitals, weekend hospitals, work villages, foster or family care homes (in this regard the programs at Gheel[28] and Aro Hospital in Nigeria[62] are notable); (2) protected work settings, such as sheltered workshops (in and out of hospitals), industries, and hospital-based work-for-pay programs; (3) specific treatment and rehabilitation services, such as group therapy, vocational counseling, and family therapy; (4) and social-rehabilitation activities, such as social clubs, self-help recovery groups, occupational therapy, and recreation activities.

These partial-care systems demonstrate a number of important factors: (1) that hospitalization can usually be circumvented entirely or greatly shortened; (2) that institutionalization can be reduced or prevented; (3) that acute as well as chronic patients can benefit; (4) that continuity of care is important, especially while patients are making the transition from the hospital to the community; (5) that socialization or resocialization can be accomplished better in the community; and (6) that nonprofessionals can operate these systems as well as, if not better than, professionals (the Synanon communities are a notable example, even though few schizophrenics are "treated" in Synanon settings).[44, 89]

Nonetheless, certain cautions need to be pointed out. The claims made are frequently undocumented. The extent of systems orientation, e.g., patient involvement in management positions and decision-making, varies considerably. The danger of substituting one form of chronic institutionalization for another does exist and can go unrecognized.[8, 32] Also, the iatrogenic effect on families of having seriously disabled people in the community is rarely mentioned. Grad and Sainsbury[49] have pointed out the potentially detrimental effect on family function that can result from keeping disturbed individuals at home.

3. THE LOUISVILLE HOME TREATMENT PROGRAM: Although this program is not a milieu therapy per se, it demonstrates a number of crucial issues so thoroughly that it requires description. Pasamanick[68] initiated an experimental program as an alternative to hospitalization, consisting of phenothiazine therapy, public health nurses making home visits, and backup psychiatric consultation and management.

The study followed three randomly selected groups of schizophrenics: a drug-home care group, a placebo-home care group, and a regular hospital group. These were severely disturbed, marginally functioning people. Yet the results regarding hospitalization showed that only 22.8 percent of the drug-home care group and 65.9 percent of the placebo-home care group required some hospitalization and that the proportion of time at home was 90.2 percent for the drug-home care group, 80 percent for the placebo-home care group, and 75 percent for the hospital group. The psychiatric status of all three groups showed improvement.

Thus this study indicates that home care can work, that phenothiazines are effective in preventing hospitalization, and that home care is at least as effective in altering psychiatric disabilities and symptoms as are hospital programs in the community. Besides showing that severely disturbed people can be treated, the Pasamanick study is important in other respects. It documents the altogether too frequent biases of professionals, administrators, and families concerning empirical innovations (even though this type of program was not without peers).[65] Also the study was well thought out, controlled, and clearly reported.

Comprehensive Systems

1. THE FORT LOGAN MENTAL CENTER: Located in Denver, Colorado, on the site of an old U.S. Army fort, the Fort Logan program started from scratch in 1961.[45] The Center offers a system of services ranging from inpatient milieu therapy through partial care to outpatient follow-up. Each of the Center's treatment teams serves a specific geographical catchment area and is responsible for continuity of care for both acute and chronic patients. Features of interest are the relative importance assigned to research; the group orientation, which extends to the absence of formal individual psychotherapy; the attractive and functional architecture; the integration of female and male patients; the emphasis on real work for pay as a core treatment component; and employment placement and follow-up.

This comprehensive system has resulted in only a small proportion of patients in full inpatient status (approximately 15 percent) at any one time, and an average total duration of treatment of 122 days, including out-patient follow-up care. Nearly 60 percent of the patients are judged psychotic.

Fort Logan is significant because it is a good example of

the Community Mental Health Center concept* and because of its milieu approach to comprehensive care. A number of other programs offer a similar range of comprehensive services.

2. DANN SERVICES: Daniels[22] and associates initiated an intentional social-system program with a chronic but fairly heterogeneous group of Veterans Administration patients (approximately one third were schizophrenics) wherein a hospital ward was organized into a nonprofit corporation (Dann Services, Inc.) with three divisions—an employment division, an industries division, and a housing division. This on-going program is comprehensive. The patients participate in multiple levels of the organization, including management and therapy.

Although evaluative data cover the time before community housing was developed, they showed significant favorable results when compared with an active and independent control program to which patients had been assigned directly from the admissions office on a random basis. Eighteen-month follow-up showed 37 percent less accumulated rehospitalization for the Dann Services program; better work outcome (e.g., 143.9 compared to 113.5 equivalent eight-hour days worked on the average during the first 360 days after discharge, and 275.7 compared to 125.7 days worked on the first full-time job); and total cost savings of $3.30 per patient-day, of which $1.28 was direct savings to the hospital. On the other hand, patients in the control program reported less tension and depression, a fact which could be attributed to somewhat lower expectations and stress.

The significance of this novel program lies more in its future potential than past achievements. For the Dann program shows that patients can play much more important roles in the curative process, including the delivery of specific

* The Community Mental Health Center model consists of four essential elements—inpatient, part-time hospitalization, 24-hour emergency outpatient, and consultation services—and five supplementary elements— transitional and aftercare, rehabilitation, training, diagnostic, and evaluation services.

psychiatric and rehabilitative services. It shows that the potential performance and capability of patients are frequently seriously underestimated. Finally, this program significantly contributes to the advancement of milieu therapy design.

Many of the workers cited above report common problems associated with, or generated by, milieu therapy programs. In the next section I shall summarize some of these common problems.

COMMON PROBLEMS IN MILIEU THERAPY

This section constitutes a guide to a number of common problems, dilemmas, and pitfalls encountered in milieu therapy; it also provides prescriptions or "helpful hints" for their solution. I have categorized these problems somewhat arbitrarily into those concerning models and concepts; roles associated with these models; structure and its specificity, with special references to patient type and to the community meeting; process; psychotherapy in milieu settings and assessment.

Models and Concepts

1. INTERPERSONAL-PSYCHODYNAMIC VERSUS SOCIAL-BE-HAVIORAL MODELS: Clinical behavioral scientists conducting milieu therapies hold to two basic world views regarding schizophrenic disorder and its treatment.* One is the interpersonal-psychodynamic model, wherein psychiatric disorders are viewed in disease- and psychopathology-oriented terms and in psychological terms. This model emphasizes treatment either in somatic or psychotherapeutic terms and views change as resulting from some internal reorganization, i.e., insight or physiological change, from which alterations in social behavior result. The second basic view is the social-behavioral consequences model, wherein disordered behavior

---

* There are those who view schizophrenic disorders in primarily medical-somatic terms. These adherents are not discussed here because, in general, they do not advocate specific milieu approaches.

is viewed in social-field and behavioristic terms. This model emphasizes rehabilitation (rather than treatment) in either social-reinforcement or behavioral-reinforcement terms and views change as occurring from without to within, i.e., "out-sight" followed by some internal change. In addition, there are differences within the two positions about the relative emphasis on interpersonal versus intrapsychic approaches, and, on the other hand, about social reinforcement versus behavioral-reinforcement approaches. A major problem is that adherents of these two conceptual models frequently defend their views tenaciously, when in fact neither is mutually exclusive. The appropriateness of each model depends on the type of patient population treated and each model's efficiency for the particular setting and situation at hand. Recognizing the complementarity between these models and being able to specify their differing applicability to specific patient groups in particular situations are of crucial importance to favorable outcomes and solution of the dilemma of selecting an appropriate model. Now is the time for an approach of synthesis and "reconciliation" of both models, and not for rigid adherence to one or the other, regardless of appropriateness. For instance, an individual may be viewed as having a high degree of social, psychological, and somatic impairment or any quantitative combination of these sources of impairment.

2. RESTRICTION OF OBSERVATION: Related to one's psychiatric world view is the way this view defines and restricts what one observes. A frequent pitfall of milieu therapy workers is the failure to recognize and distinguish four interrelated areas of observing and interpreting phenomena: the social-systems (cultural) level, the interpersonal level, the ego level, and the intrapsychic (intrapersonal) level. In group situations and tasks these four areas of phenomena operate simultaneously. It is crucial for milieu workers to learn to recognize all four areas of observation and interpretation and to know when to intervene in each area. I know of no more complex task for therapists to master. As stated previously,

the most common error for clinicians is to miss the social systems level. Constant vigilance, awareness, and experience are requisite for mastery of these multisphere observations.

3. MODES OF DECISION-MAKING: In milieu therapy conflict occurs often around the method by which decisions are made. Generally patient participation is desirable and theoretically well grounded. But many factors influence the decision-making process, such as crises, level of trust, capabilities and willingness of patients and staff members to evidence responsibility, the category of event, superordinate institutional regulations, and the particular conceptual model. Decisions can be made by the staff with or without a patient advisory mechanism, mutually by patients and staff members, and by patients with or without a staff advisory mechanism. I consider the following guide lines essential: No decision potentially influencing the social system or policy should be made by the staff without communicating it in straight-forward fashion to the patients, and it preferably should be made only after consultation with patients; most decisions affecting policy can be made by patients and staff members together under the one-man, one-vote mechanism (recognizing that high-status people will tend to have, in effect, more than one vote); and in many instances patients can and should make decisions, particularly those concerning social behavior, without staff vote. It is also essential to recognize which mode is operating at any given time, that the degree of democratization depends on the situation, that democratization does not mean equalitarianism (a hierarchical order prevails in all groups), and that administrative decisions must be distinguished from policy decisions—the former require efficiency and delegated power, whereas the latter require consensus and dispersed power.

Roles

1. CONTRADICTORY BELIEFS ABOUT THE ROLES HELD BY PATIENTS AND STAFF MEMBERS: Staff members and patients possess attitudes and beliefs about themselves and one

another similar to most superordinate-subordinate relationships, but frequently act as though they did not or, even
worse, frequently act under the guise of a therapist-patient
relationship. In this regard, patients tend to see themselves
as sick, helpless, deprived, not responsible, and staff members as magical, powerful, responsible, and controlling. Staff
members tend to reinforce these beliefs by adhering to the
proper complementary ones despite idealized statements to
the contrary, i.e., they act toward patients as though the
patients were inferior, sick or lazy, unable to decide, and
needing control, while they profess a belief in human
potential, responsibility, equality, and the like. Transcending
the we-they attitude is terribly difficult for both patients and
staff members. This "syndrome" sometimes is manifested in
another way. The effort of staff members to enact humane
attitudes (warmth, hope, fairness, etc.) can come across in a
paternalistic and condescending manner. Still these con-
tradictions can be reduced by awareness, by making overt
the reality of authority and control, and by building in structures to limit staff dominance (e.g., meaningful patient
decision making).

2. PROFESSIONAL OMNIPOTENCE AND CHRONIC CASES:
Many mental health workers have a strong need to help
others and to maintain the view that in truth they are helping
others. These needs create a serious danger for the helping
person to despair of treating chronic patients. On the other
hand, these needs can produce the belief that patients are
getting better, being responsible, going to stop drinking, and
are trying, even when such things are not so. Clinicians want
to be good guys. Yet often it is not possible to be a good guy
and to "do good" well. With difficult cases being a good guy
means recognizing one's limits, staying on the side of reality
testing, and sometimes being confrontive with a truth that
hurts.

3. CONFLICT FROM SHIFT IN STAFF ROLES: Often milieu
therapy requires staff members in some degree to relinquish
important aspects of their traditional roles: direct delivery of

services and help, leadership, power and control, and personal anonymity. The shift toward becoming more advisory, facilitative, and consultative; more real and personal; and less dominant, powerful, and controlling conflicts with the more comfortable traditional role both because learned roles are not easy to relinquish and because the assumed role creates the anxiety associated with openness and exposure. Making the shift is basically an educational process. The shift is too frequently treated casually.

4. COVERT CONFLICT AMONG STAFF MEMBERS: Because milieu therapy produces role and concept changes, a certain amount of conflict is inevitable among individuals, clinical disciplines, and administrators. The effects of conflict among staff members are most harmful to patients when the conflict is hidden or covert. This effect can be minimized by making disagreements among staff members overt and known to the patients, and by suspecting covert conflict among staff members any time the amount of acting out and anxiety shown by patients increases.

Structure and Its Specificity

1. SPECIFYING PROGRAM GOALS AND MEANS: The psychotherapy training of mental health professionals emphasizes free association, unfolding of directions, open-endedness, and permissiveness. Mental health workers tend to be fuzzy or unclear in stating program or therapy goals, the specific means to achieve these goals, and time guides in which to attain the goals. We need to clarify as precisely as possible what the specific elements are that we think make a hospital or other milieu therapeutic, and then specify which elements are therapeutic for particular kinds of patients. Indeed, this failure to specify elements is one of the most serious pitfalls for mental health workers. For milieu therapists the ability to specify therapeutic components requires, as I indicated previously, a knowledge of social systems and organization structure, particularly the structure of bureaucratic organizations, of which mental hospitals are an example. It is

essential for milieu therapists to specify the therapeutic elements (or structures), to recognize the boundaries or limits on these elements, to recognize the changing interrelations among elements or structures and the changing hierarchy of importance of these components, and to assure congruency among elements and their relevance to life in the community at large. The lack of relevance or generalizability to life in the community at large is a frequent failure of milieu therapy. The staff must distinguish between good care and treatment. Creating a comfortable, secure, ideal treatment environment can inadvertently lead to the "sticky wicket" syndrome— the hospital environment becomes an end in itself, an occurrence that results in patients' functioning better in the hospital than either before or after hospitalization (the inverse "U"-curve effect). But the mental hospital is not the natural habitat of man. A permissive open-ended structure is not to be highly valued in most instances. The degree of prescribed structure, and of the coercion to conform to it, is always an issue in creating effective milieu therapy.

2. PATIENT TYPE AND THE MILIEU STRUCTURE: A common pitfall is the monolithic-milieu therapy program, a program organized to treat all patients uniformly. Yet the nature of the patient population, e.g., whether it is relatively homogeneous or heterogeneous, chronic or acute, rooted in or marginal to society, psychotic or nonpsychotic, highly or lowly motivated, is the crucial variable in determining the structure of the milieu. We must know and specify what structures are appropriate for what patients. Chronic steady-stay patients need a highly structured educational environment with a graded series of responsibilities and challenges, a concrete reward structure, clarity, protected paid employment, interdependent task groups, group membership, and environmental management experiences. Chronic "revolving-door" patients need a similar setting, except with somewhat less structure, a greater range of challenges and opportunities, anticipatory guidance, crisis orientation, maximal involvement in decision making and administration, and a

social-reward structure. Acute patients need a supportive low-demand situation initially (followed by a clearly open-structured dynamics-oriented environment), a social-reward structure, an interpersonal-relationships orientation, and an analysis of communications for dynamic meanings. In sum, the milieu therapist must provide alternate structures to meet differing patient requirements. A treatment "contract" is useful in specifying for all concerned the agreed goals, means, and time guides.

3. THE COMMUNITY MEETING: Alas, nowhere does ambiguity of purpose and means in milieu therapy more clearly evidence itself than in the so-called community or large group meeting. The function of the community meeting is to provide a vehicle for the demonstration and implementation of the elements considered essential to therapeutic milieus. Once again, the nature of the patient group should determine the structure of the community meeting. The community meeting with chronic and poorly motivated patients, those with primarily executive ego disorders, should be highly structured, task- and decision-oriented, and geared to social adjustment and to consequence of social behavior. With acute and highly motivated patients, those with primarily synthetic ego disorders, the community meeting should be loosely and openly structured, oriented toward interpersonal relationships, and geared to the dynamic meaning of psychological and social events. Awareness of these two basic types of community meetings can reduce ambiguity about the goals and structures of the community meeting and increase its effectiveness.

Process

1. THE PROCESS OF CHANGE: Although therapists have come to recognize the importance and perhaps dominance of process in psychotherapy, they frequently fail to recognize its crucial importance in milieu therapy. To conduct milieu therapy requires knowledge of social change and resistances to change. The stage of evolution or implementation of a

milieu program should significantly influence the structure, e.g., the amount of staff relative to patient decision making should be greater early in the development of a milieu program. (An exception to this recommendation occurs when a program starts from scratch; in this instance there is less previous culture requiring change.) Milieu therapists need to build in procedures for renewal, such as periodic brainstorming sessions, "plan-ins," and T-groups. Three strategies of organizational development—strategies of human relations, structure, and technology (e.g., computer application) —must be considered. Often the structural and technological strategies are neglected.

2. THE PHENOMENON OF OSCILLATION: The recognition and control of oscillation, i.e., the state of social organization and the fluctuations or phases of social organization from integration to disruption to reorganization,[70] are crucial in milieu therapy. When a milieu is in the integrated phase, it is relaxed, free, and cohesive. But the opposite obtains for the disintegrative phase. All milieus oscillate between these two poles. It is important to recognize these phases and to prevent deep disruptive troughs from occurring. Downward oscillation can be anticipated in association with an influx of new unacculturated patients, changes in key staff members, and crisis events. Oscillation alters the order of priorities and values. During downward swings the staff needs to be more active, directive, and controlling.

Individual Psychotherapy

An adequate discussion of the place of individual psychotherapy would require at least a volume in itself. Psychotherapy becomes a source of conflict in the conduct of milieu programs for several reasons. First, high-status professionals often overrate its importance. Second, artificial separation of administrative functions and psychotherapy functions is made. Third, therapists may try to accomplish long-range goals incompatible with reasonable hospital stay. And last, therapists may fail to distinguish with whom in particular psychotherapy is likely to be effective. If these pitfalls are recognized, psychotherapy in the milieu setting, even with chronic patients, can be effective.[64]

Assessment

In no way are mental health professionals more indictable than on the issue of effectiveness. The practitioners of milieu therapy are no exception. The problem for therapists is that in the absence of assessment all sorts of marvelous hopes arise and fall, direction and purpose become muddled, and tenacious but spurious views hold sway. Regularized assessment provides direction through the forest, provides a catalyst for change, and assures quality control. I believe that the woeful lack of multiple-criteria outcome assessment and cost-benefit analysis is inexcusable.

With this admonition, I think that it is time to move from past failings to speculations about what the future will bring.

THE FUTURE OF MILIEU THERAPY

First, we shall see the proliferation of many intentional social systems and intentional communities. These will involve a sophisticated synthesis of adaptation, role, organization, ego, education, and general systems theories and practices. I have noted that the potential of human organization for treating and stabilizing severely damaged people has barely begun to be recognized, let alone attained. The mental hospital as we have known it is not congruent with that potential. It has been a grave mistake to keep human beings in large structures designed for physical illness and incarceration. Intentional community architecture will encompass home design, group use, and social-recreational features.

Second, we shall see an increase in the specificity of particular therapeutic elements that are effective with particular patients. Programs will vary according to the type of functional disorder and offer comprehensive care and continuity of care. Global effectiveness ratings of treatments will be replaced by consideration of which particular treatment is effective with what type of population. The technological explosion will facilitate, perhaps even force, this specificity. Regularized outcome assessment, extensive computer utilization, with on-line access providing information immediately, cost-benefit analysis, and implementation research will become core treatment components.[83] Together with specificity facilitated by technology will come the era of comprehensive and diverse programs, programs and settings in which there will be a careful congruence between the program and patients' needs.

In particular, we shall see a diversity of community-based living situations providing some of the following features: alternatives to hospitalization, potentially permanent as well as transitional living, integration of mental patients with the general population, comprehensive care and follow-up (perhaps in the form of "super market" services[66]), and patient management and self-government encompassing a range of self- and patient care.

In a similar manner we shall see a variety of work situations (however work is defined) ranging from very protective to competitive employment. Work activity will include much needed human services, personal services, and reclamation services. Characteristics of employment programs will include integration with healthy workers, associations or agreements with private industry, and on-the-job preparation and skill training.

Third, we shall see proliferation of group experiences, such as sensitivity groups, family groups, motivation groups, task groups, social groups, personal development groups, and programmed groups. Staff members too will participate in group experiences, e.g., in training labs and "plan-ins," in order to keep relevant.

Lastly, we shall see more patient participation and management in the delivery of services of which patients are usually recipients. Complementing this development, traditional staff members will assume more consultative, advisory, and facilitative functions. In addition, new roles will emerge, such as mental health economist, program implementers, and social trainers.

The statements above are idealized and utopian. Nevertheless, there are definite pressures forcing changes in the directions indicated. Mental health professionals will be held accountable for the results of their programs. Social change is a force "blowing in the wind" and may even include the force of patient power. The new scholar, a combination of academic and action orientations, is becoming increasingly evident among mental health professionals. This new scholar-professional has a greater knowledge of processes of social change. Also, the impact of the community mental health centers will continue to diminish the role of the large mental hospital in the treatment of schizophrenia and other psychiatric disorders.

This foresighted vision also contains dangers. Many more partially disabled people residing in the community, some with genetic defects and others unable to perform parental roles, represent a potential, iatrogenically caused source for damaging children. Then there is the danger of institutionalization occurring in new settings—in small community facilities, as Epstein and Simon[32] have shown with community placement of state hospital geriatric patients. Lastly, emphasis on technological evaluation and effectiveness can lead to breaches of confidence, loss of humanness, and excessive reliance on hard data to the exclusion of such soft data as personal well-being and satisfaction.

Yet the vision of the future presented here is an optimistic one, based on the growing interest in man himself, his potential, and his capacities, as the remaining unexplored frontier.

SUMMARY

This chapter provides a perspective on milieu treatments and sees them as the current phase (with historical antecedents in "moral treatment") in the checkered history of the treatment of psychotic persons. Hopefully, this current phase will be extended by an increased recognition and understanding both of the therapeutic influences of social organizations and of the varying appropriateness of different social systems in the treatment of particular types of disordered populations.

The justification of this chapter's focus on human social organization is made in terms of its relevance to ego function and adaptation—man lives within, by, and through his social organization. The fabric of his life is patterned by his social environment. That being so, the varied and often conflictual characteristics of the mental hospital as a social system must be considered in any attempt to correct the ego dysfunction and socially disordered behavior of the schizophrenic. The subgroups of schizophrenic persons (i.e., the acute patients, the chronic "revolving-door" patients, and the chronic steady-stay patients) must be recognized so that the social organizations (e.g., the mental hospital) intended to treat these individuals may be optimally and appropriately designed. Each subgroup requires a somewhat different milieu.

A general treatment design or model entitled "intentional social-system therapy" is presented in this chapter and is based on a synthesis of various theories about the nature of man, ego psychology, roles, and social organization. The capability of and the desirability for patients to deliver the services they also receive is recognized in this model. The model also recognizes the need for specificity of therapeutic elements, anticipates varying beneficial results (depending on the type of patient and the nature of the setting) of different programs, and requires careful and continuing assessment of these results to assure a high level of treatment effectiveness. The generalizability of intentional social-system therapy may be seen in a variety of examples of milieu therapies treating chronic and/or acute patients in hospital-based, community-based, or comprehensive organizations. The chapter also includes a compilation of common problems in milieu therapy (related to models and concepts, roles, structure and

its specificity, process, individual psychotherapy, and assessment) and a presentation of some "helpful hints" for problem
solution.

The future of milieu therapy should see an increase in
the number and type of intentional social systems (and a
decrease in the use of large mental hospitals for the treatment
of disturbed individuals); an increase in the specificity of
treatment effectiveness (based in part on the increased use
of computer analysis); an increase in the variety of community-based living situations, work situations, and group
experiences available for patients; and a change in the roles
of patients and staff members to reflect the increased belief
in the capability of an individual (even one labeled schizophrenic) to serve while he is being served.

14

Dynamically Oriented
Individual Psychotherapy

INTRODUCTION

The chapter deals with long-term, individual, dynamically oriented psychotherapy with schizophrenic patients, many of whom were chronically ill. Such an approach is almost becoming an anachronism in this era of community psychiatry, prompt treatment, early discharge, heavy use of medication, etc. The approach has been accused of being "inefficient," and inefficient it is. As a matter of fact, from the point of view of doing the greatest good for the greatest number, it is about as inefficient a use of a psychiatrist's time as I can imagine!

As a learning experience it has no equal. I have learned more about the emotional lives of troubled people from the schizophrenic patients I have seen in long-term therapy (and more about my responses to them, a fact that is equally important) than from any other single training experience.

The jet plane gets one from San Francisco to New York in hours; the train takes days. If the plane flies over a cloud cover, one could go from coast to coast and never see the land. From the train it is impossible not to get to know the country at least slightly. If one drove, as did John Steinbeck in *Travels with Charley*,[24] one would get to know the terrain and the people very well, and, in certain ways, come to know oneself better, too.

The approach I am advocating in this chapter is a slow one. It may take years or a lifetime to get to one's destination with the patient. But the therapist's understanding of his patient and himself cannot help becoming enriched en route. It is a luxury no beginning psychotherapist can afford to miss.

In the early 1900s, Freud reluctantly came to the conclusion that the "narcissistic neuroses" (his term for the schizophrenic psychoses) were untreatable by psychological means.[9] His pessimism was in part based on his (incorrect) belief that schizophrenic patients were incapable of forming transferences to their therapists, and that therefore analysis of the transference, the keystone to his technique, was not possible. Classical psychoanalysis, using the couch and free association, indeed was not effective with such patients (it frequently made them worse), but the awareness of unconscious motivation and intrapsychic dynamics that derived from psychoanalytic investigation has been put to good use with different therapeutic techniques. I am subsuming this latterday collection of techniques that lean heavily on such awareness under the concept of "dynamically oriented psychotherapy."

Such therapy often takes place simultaneously with the kinds of structured, reality-testing techniques and use of medication, milieu, and hospitalization that were described in Chapters 12 and 13.

Dynamic psychotherapy with schizophrenic patients is difficult to do, and its results are even more frustrating to assess. There is evidence that certain therapists are able to work more effectively with chronically ill patients and bring about better long-term results than are others. Whitehorn and Betz[4, 5, 31, 32] showed that certain therapists, called the "A" group, had statistically significantly greater improvement in their schizophrenic patients (though not necessarily their neurotic patients) than the "B" group had, and these improvements were maintained five years later. The authors state,

. . . favorable outcome was found most
likely when the physician's Personal Diagnostic
Formulation shows some grasp of the personal
meaning of the patient's behavior; when he
aims at assisting the patient in modifications of
personal adjustment patterns and a more constructive use of assets rather than focusing on
psychopathology; when, in his day-by-day tac-
tics he participates with the patient in an active
personal way; and when a trusting, confidential
relationship develops between physician and
patient. These styles of transaction were again
found to be more characteristic of the A than
the B physicians.

In a large and well-controlled study, Rogers and his co-
workers[17] assessed a number of therapist and patient variables in work with chronically schizophrenic patients and
controls. They found that therapists who rated high on scales
of *accurate empathy* and *patient-perceived congruence* were
experienced more intensely by patients than were therapists
low on these scales. They report, ". . . the deeper the level of
the therapist's empathic understanding and genuineness with
his patient, the more the patient would reveal a deeper level
of self-experiencing and self-exploration at every point." They
further point out that these therapist traits, and the concomitant deeper experiencing of the patient, were positively
related to a number of criteria of improvement, including the
MMPI Sc scale, earlier discharge from the hospital, and
sustained improvement outside of the hospital.

When acknowledgedly skilled therapists attempt to describe what they do to effect such favorable outcome,
however, their statements are full of ambiguities and con-
tradictions. Rosenthal[18] makes the analogy of artists trying
to explicate their sources of inspiration and techniques of
execution, a notoriously difficult task. His analogy is apt,
because psychotherapy with schizophrenic patients demands
that the therapist have his intuition, his sensitivity, his appreciation of the unconscious, his knowledge of himself—in

short, his unique art—maximally available. This analogy does not mean he is entirely unable to describe his activities, just that to do so is extremely difficult.

In spite of these difficulties, there have been certain attitudes, principles, techniques, and goals that have been commented on by many therapists and that have some general applicability. Thus the views set forth below are a synthesis of my own experiences with patients and consultants and of my reading in the field. I would urge the reader who engages in such long-term dynamically oriented psychotherapy with schizophrenic patients to read the articles and books of Arieti,[2] Brody,[7] Burton,[8] Fromm-Reichman,[10] Hill,[12] Jackson,[13] Redlich,[7] Searles,[19, 20, 21] Sechehaye,[23] Sullivan,[25, 27, 28] and Will.[33] Even among dynamically oriented therapists, there is great diversity of opinion on technique; Boyer and Giovacchini[6] describe the use of a traditional psychoanalytic approach; Mendel and Green[15] apply psychoanalytic theory in an entirely different manner from that presented here.

An autobiographical account of intensive, dynamically oriented treatment is found in Hannah Green's *I Never Promised You a Rose Garden*.[11]

My exposition should serve to alert the reader to the issues and problems encountered in doing this kind of work; it should most definitely not be taken as any kind of complete statement. The beginning therapist should not only read in the field but have regular consultation, preferably using audio and/or video tapes, or direct observation, for his clinical work. The remainder of this chapter should be read in conjunction with the sections on treatment in the case histories (Chapter 3), especially the cases of Stephen J., Sylvia T., and Vivian L., and with the description of the patient's experiential world (Chapter 4) and his experiences with his family (Chapter 7).

ASSUMPTIONS

There are certain assumptions, philosophic positions, and therapeutic goals that must be made explicit. The first and most important of these assumptions is that the patient's experiential world is a meaningful one to him, and it is potentially meaningful to the therapist who has the patience and sensitivity to try to communicate with him. Authors state this position in different ways. Bellak[3] starts his book by quoting Terentius Plautus: *Homo sum; humani nil a me alienum puto.* ("I am human, I hold nothing human alien to me.") Sullivan[25] says, "Everybody is simply more human than otherwise."

Freud's pessimistic assumption about transference was unwarranted. If anything, many schizophrenic patients are transference-bound; they are unable to avoid forming strong and immediate transferences to anyone they have any contact with, as Searles[21] and Szasz[29] have indicated, and as the vignettes of Naomi N., Vivian L., and George M., in Chapter 4, demonstrate. As a second assumption, therefore, we may say that the apparent indifference and withdrawal of the patient often is in the service of containing and defending against these strong transference feelings. Vivian L. stated this dilemma most poignantly at the end of the therapy session in which we exchanged fairy tales. (That session is reported in greater detail in the section, "The Middle Stages of Treatment," in this chapter.) She said, "Too much friendship is like when a bear is cold and he sees the hunter's fire, and he comes over to get warmed and gets scorched."

A third assumption is that whatever the patient says may be taken as an indirect (unwittingly or occasionally deliberate) metaphorical statement about his perception of the state of the therapeutic relationship.

GOALS

The goals of the therapist should be modest, even if his hopes are great. There is a number of reasons why a therapist should not aspire to "cure" the patient and make him a normal-looking individual by the therapist's (usually) middle-class standards. Fromm-Reichmann[10] suggests that if such patients (referring to chronic patients) are able to find security and satisfaction in life without violating the law or hurting their neighbors, the psychotherapist has accomplished his major task.

In addition, if the therapist needs to cure his patient, he is implicitly prescribing a role that the patient must conform to if he is to please the therapist—the "well patient" role—which is a repetition of being forced into a role structure during childhood, albeit with less pseudomutuality in the relationship.[34]

Hill[12] speaks to this problem as follows:

> I would urgently advise any resident beginning his training to subject himself to a rule. The rule is that he will not cure or analyze anyone during the first several months of his training. The purpose of this rule is to remove the temptation *to do something* rather than *to be something* in therapy. The temptation is strong to invade a patient's extremely precarious balance with the intention of doing him good without the skill to avoid doing him harm. [Italics mine.—Ed.]

One of the dividends of not needing to cure a patient is that the therapist can come to know him better. He need not fend off or covertly discourage communications that sound sick, or that suggest futility and despair, in the service of maintaining his "cure." Such messages and feelings form a substantial part of the schizophrenic's experiential world. Furthermore, the therapists being open to all the patient has to communicate will convey to the patient that the therapist can tolerate and attempt to understand feelings that in the past others had treated as poisonous and unhuman.

With these cautions in mind, what are some of the goals the therapist can strive for? The first would be simply to understand the patient as best he can. Understanding any person fully is a difficult task, and understanding the schizophrenic is even harder. As the patient's previously repressed, distorted, and conflicting feelings and thoughts gradually emerge in the unfolding therapeutic relationship, the therapist should assist the patient in integrating the material thought to be "not-me" into "bad-me" and "good-me." In effect, he should help the equilibrium shown to shift to the left.

$$\text{Good-me} \rightleftharpoons \text{Bad-me} \rightleftharpoons \text{Not-me}*$$

Through this process the patient can gradually come to experience his feelings as belonging to him, rather than inflicted from without by voices, personages, and demons; and he can come to see that certain feelings, previously regarded as shameful and unhuman, are natural parts of the repertoire of human emotional responses.

PHYSICAL SETTING AND LIMITS

The traditional use of the psychoanalytic couch is strictly interdicted in doing psychotherapy with schizophrenic patients.† Such patients have enough difficulty in testing reality and assessing the nature of a relationship without having to endure the hardship of dealing with someone they cannot see. Instead, as Sullivan[27] recommends, two chairs, placed at 90-degree angles to each other, are desirable. In this position, patient and therapist can make or break eye contact comfortably without overtones of the "stare-down" contests of childhood.

Some patients cannot tolerate proximity with the therapist. If the therapist senses this atttiude, he would be well advised to separate the chairs by several feet. One therapist of my acquaintance is remarkably sensitive to how much closeness a patient can tolerate. He interviews while sitting in a chair with casters on it and scoots toward or away from the patient as he senses that the patient wants more or less closeness.

Some patients feel uncomfortable confined in an interview room. For such patients, a session conducted in the hallway or on the hospital grounds may be the way of initiating

* See Chapter 4 for further explication of these terms.
† For a different point of view, see Boyer and Giovacchini.[6]

a therapeutic contact. In other circumstances, the patient may try to evade any sort of therapeutic contact, and the therapist may have to force a meeting against the patient's will. I had one patient who had a remarkable capacity to conceal himself in laundry baskets, under furniture, or in presumably locked offices whenever it was time for his therapy session. On a consultant's suggestion, an aide and I hunted him down each time, and then locked him in an office with me for an hour, whether the patient liked it or not. Beneath his invective the patient gave a good deal of evidence that he enjoyed the hide-and-seek and the fact that he could get therapeutic attention at the same time that he was free to protest against it.

The length and frequency of sessions should be determined by more than a clock and a calendar. Initially, many patients grow restive after a few minutes; the therapist should allow the patient to leave if he gets extremely anxious. For patients in a catatonic stupor, one or several daily visits of from 10 to 15 minutes may help the establishment of rapport without taxing either the patient's or therapist's capacity to tolerate anxiety or silence. One patient was in a mute catatonic stupor for two months. Her therapist missed one of his daily visits, thinking they were not important to her. After she recovered, she commented on his absence by saying, "You were my bread and butter." Early in the work with Vivian, she frequently left the interview room after a few minutes but often returned voluntarily or with encouragement after her anxiety level had dropped. There are times when active encouragement is necessary, but there are times when it is not.

Many of these decisions about settings, scheduling, and encouragement are intuitive, and therefore it is impossible to set forth here rules for their application. Nevertheless, therapists should strive to meet any commitments that they have made and to explain unavoidable absences or changes simply and directly.

In recent years a few therapists have experimented with

multiple therapy, a situation where two or more therapists meet with a single patient.[35] Under these circumstances, the patient may dichotomize (or trichotomize) the therapist into The Good One, The Bad One, The Giving One, etc., projections of unconsciously perceived parts of himself. The gradual integration of these disparate personages may turn out to be one of the central tasks of therapy.

Physical violence in any of its forms should not be tolerated in a therapeutic relationship, as Fromm-Reichmann and Sullivan have pointed out.[10, 27] When violence threatens, restraint is needed. Often a simple show of force—the presence of several muscular aides—is enough to get the patient to back down. At other times a warm tub bath, cold wet packs, leather restraints, seclusion, and/or phenothiazines are helpful. The use of restraints should be judicious and humane, not punitive. Many patients have thanked personnel for containing them when they were losing control. That a patient is in restraints of one sort or another should be no contraindication to therapy. In fact, at such a time maintaining contact with other people is especially important to him; otherwise he will be most fearful that, in his omnipotent way, he has destroyed and depopulated the world that he needs. Many a therapy session has been conducted from the two sides of a seclusion-room door or with the patient in leather restraints. Vivian, during a particularly agitated phase of her treatment, had to be taken to seclusion on a few occasions when she started hitting and scratching. Gradually she learned to signal when she was getting unbearably tense and would voluntarily accept the suggestion that she walk alone to the seclusion room, sit in it while the door was left open, and return to the therapy session when she felt calmer.

THE STAGES OF THERAPY

Initial Stage

In the initial stage of therapy the patient should be offered the possibility of a relationship that will be profitable and interesting and not destructive or humiliating. Schizophrenic patients are fearful about the consequences of any relationship; if the patient indicates a willingness to spend time with the therapist, the offer should be accepted without comment. It is frequently very humiliating for patients to admit that they need help or want a relationship with someone, because such an admission puts them in a dependent and vulnerable position and leaves them open to rejection and disappointment.

Will[33] points out several facets of the dilemmas facing the schizophrenic starting therapy: patients are shy and afraid of close contacts; they are "remarkably susceptible to the behavior of others"; they have great difficulty explaining their ideas and feelings, especially the autistic sort, to others, and they are afraid that their feelings, especially those of anger, may destroy the therapist. The patient may also fear being engulfed, that closeness and relatedness will lead to mutual loss of identity and the destruction of both parties.

There is a story about a psychiatrist, walking along a river on a rainy day, carrying an umbrella. He spies a man slip down the bank, fall in the water, and go down for the first time. The psychiatrist hurries to the site and calmly watches the man surface and reach out, then go down for the second time. The man surfaces again, is about to go down for the third time, and gurgles out a watery "Help!" At this point the psychiatrist extends his umbrella and helps the man out. After he recovers, the man asks the psychiatrist why he didn't help him sooner. The psychiatrist said, "I just wanted to show you that you could learn to verbalize your need for help." Don't do that with your schizophrenic patients!

A vignette may help show how a patient can be intrigued with the possibility of a therapeutic relationship. I was admitting Mr. George K., a 34-year-old man being hospitalized for the first time. He made subtle and arcane references to a band of homosexual Communists and prostitutes that he had found out about and was collecting confidential information on. He smiled a superior smile and was quite loathe to give me any details because I might well be on the other side. Rather abruptly I asked him if he played poker. He looked surprised, said he did. I told him I would be afraid to play in a game with him. He asked why. I told him that though his demeanor might convey that he held nothing better than three-of-a-kind or a straight, and I would be feeling good holding a flush, when the cards were turned up, he would have a full house. He enjoyed this metaphor of the superior way he was handling our interview. He went then to the admitting ward but in a remarkably short time had managed to get himself transferred to my ward. He had been intrigued with the possibility of further contact.

Will[33] comments on some of the issues that arise at the beginning of treatment. He points out that because of past experiences the patient may see the therapist with suspicion, doubt, and contempt. The therapist in turn may doubt his readiness for his task, but, weathering such doubts, continues with his work. Therapy is largely concerned with understanding and correcting these verbal and nonverbal distortions of the relationship; the therapist must be sensitive to his own communications in the relationship.

Will further comments that loneliness is a frequent experience of the schizophrenic, and, though unpleasant for the therapist, must also be shared. Other experiences of the patient that therapists must be prepared to share are those of the anxiety of infancy, discouragement, fears of destruction and engulfment, and the wish to flee from the relationship.

Middle Stage

In the middle stages of therapy, usually starting after a few weeks and lasting from months to years, the emergence of the dissociated takes place. The patient reexperiences many previously repressed feelings in the context of the therapeutic relationship.

> *Example:* At one point with Vivian there
> was an emergence of previously repressed con-

cerns with nurturance, giving, and feeding. At the dinner table she had become a gourmand and the staff had to limit her from snatching food from the other patients' dinners. At the end of one of the therapy sessions, as she walked out of the door, she tweaked my shirt pocket, looking for a breast, and asked me what I had there. Ruefully I told her that all I had was cigarettes.

A month later, toward Halloween, we had a session in which she challenged me to exchange fairy tale stories with her. I told her I was willing, although I was not feeling too well that day, and invited her to start. [Informing her of my poor health ostensibly was to help her interpret any sour looks she might get as being due to a virus, not hostility. In fact, I was also looking for some mothering, something she picked up on and incorporated into her story.] She said, "You are Mrs. O'Leary's cow and you have a tick on your tit—giggle—I mean tail. I am Mrs. O'Leary and I am coming to milk you. I put the bucket underneath you and start milking you but you have tick fever [her perception that I had no milk for her that day, i.e., felt sick] and when I start, you jump around and kick over the pail and spill all the milk. I see that you have tick fever and go and get Farmer Brown. He and I ride back on horses through the snow and he gives you a shot of penicillin and cures you of tick fever and that's the end of my story.

I indeed felt mothered and thanked her for her nice story. Then I told mine:

There was a poor little girl who was out on the street and she was hungry and cold because she didn't have enough clothes or enough food. She walked by a candy store that was run by Maggie the Hag from Hagerstown. [Maggie the Hag was a character Vivian referred to frequently in her pre-Halloween fantasies]. The

> little girl went in and when Maggie asked her
> what she was doing in the store, the little girl
> said she wanted some candy. Maggie asked her
> how much money she had and the little girl
> said she had only a penny. Maggie said there
> were hardly any candies in the store that she
> could sell for a penny but she would go into
> the back and try and find some. While Maggie
> was in the back, the little girl stole all the candy
> she could jam into her pockets and ran out into
> the street and ate them. She knew what she
> was doing was wrong, but she had been so hun-
> gry that she couldn't stop herself, and finally
> she felt full and warm again, and that's the end
> of the story.

Vivian was quite intrigued with the story, which was
obviously an allegory that dealt with many of the themes
from earlier sessions, including her feeling that she didn't
need or didn't deserve therapy and maybe other people needed
it more (being too poor, emotionally, to afford it), her concern with eating and her inability to limit herself, etc.

It was later in that session that Vivian became solemn
and withdrawn, saying her change of mood had to do with
"friendship," going on to make the statement about the "bear"
and "the hunter's fire" mentioned previously.*

During the middle part of therapy, the patient will tend
to incorporate the therapist as an internal presence. The
therapist's face and voice will become very real to the patient,
and the patient may well rely on this introject to help him
meet anxiety-provoking situations. Examples of this phenomenon in two patients follow:

---

* Werner Mendel (personal communication) suggests another interpretation of the events of the end of this session: "It seems to me that the
patient's fairy tale clearly 'gives' to you while yours insists that she
must steal in order to have and judges her as wrong, although being
unable to stop herself. No wonder the patient was through with you after
you had spanked her hands in such a way." Mendel's point is a good one
and once again demonstrates the sensitivity of schizophrenic patients
to actual or implied rejection or reproof.

> A married artist of 27, a borderline character, complained of peculiar sudden "panic attacks" (they later proved to be displacements of anger from his job). He also became unbearably anxious whenever he had to leave the city limits for any reason. After eight sessions, his panic attacks had virtually gone, but leaving the city was still difficult. Shortly thereafter, he reported that he had gone on a day's outing and had overcome his fear at the Golden Gate Bridge approach by conjuring up the image of a "portable psychiatrist"—his therapist—carried in his car trunk, to be consulted if he had to.
>
> In Stephen T.'s treatment in his case history, the episode of his dinner invitation and how he distanced himself from his voices by using the internalized presence of the therapist is also a case in point.

Lewis Hill told his psychiatric residents that he sometimes used to give his patients a small empty bottle to carry around with them, "A little of Dr. Hill."

In the middle stages of treatment, the relationship is a very "real" one (in contrast to "therapeutic," to use Tarachow's distinction), for both therapist and patient.[30] Schizophrenic patients frequently manifest an uncanny ability to sense the therapist's sensitivities and needs and to put him to the test in a way neurotic patients rarely demonstrate.

There are at least two reasons for this ability of the patient to get to the therapist emotionally. First, patients frequently function more on the feeling than on the verbal level. Simple, straightforward communication was not an outstanding feature of the schizophrenic's childhood; certainly the schizophrenic patient uses words peculiarly. Without the currency of words, schizophrenic patients use nonverbal, feeling, empathic modes of communication, and these may well go beyond polite verbiage straight to gut-level experiences.

A second reason for the patient's ability to get to the therapist also derives from childhood experience, this time from the strange parental lack of respect for normal social privacy, social distance, and separation of the generations that most people know. The literature is replete with examples of parents intrusively entering into the private lives of their preschizophrenic children, refusing to let them develop a sense of separateness and self, betraying unmistakable signs of sexual interest in the children at the same time that they contradict their behavior with loud assertions to the contrary. Lewis Hill and Murray Bowen have pointed out in many places that the child must live for the mother, i.e., to keep her alive, or free from overwhelming anxiety, depression, or psychosis.* Thus, in the early years, the learning model for assessing social distance has been one of both unbearable and suffocating closeness and rigidly maintained distance rather than the great variety of flexible techniques to which most persons are exposed. And whether suffocating closeness or rigid distance was to occur was nearly impossible to predict.

If the quality of the relationship can have this much impact on the therapist, whose defenses are presumably in good working order, it obviously has an even greater impact on the patient. For these reasons, it is quite important that the therapist allow himself to be maximally sensitive to what is going on with his patient and help the patient handle his feelings in an adaptive manner. The situation is analogous to the love- (or hate-) stricken adolescent for whom the slightest gesture by the other person can have tremendous import, even when it is casually intended.

These remarks do not imply that the therapist retreat behind a façade of immobility just to protect himself from making a "wrong" response to the patient. On the contrary,

---

* This puts the child in the role of savior for the mother's (or, frequently, the whole family's) health and sanity. This role is analogous to Christ's role of sacrificing himself for all mankind and may illuminate the dynamics behind the assumption of the personality of Christ so often seen in male paranoid schizophrenic patients.

it is extremely important that the therapist be himself and not play therapeutic games with schizophrenic patients; intimate contact with an honest, genuine, and empathic person is a deficiency in the schizophrenic patient's life experience that the therapist can hope partially to correct, as Rogers' work suggests.[17]

A good therapeutic relationship can sustain a number of mistakes, ill-timed comments, and the like from the therapist. In fact, the therapist's willingness to admit to mistakes may be a refreshingly novel experience for the patient. In contrast, in an empty or precarious relationship, the therapist's well-phrased and well-timed statements may have little effect.

The therapist can enhance his awareness of the therapeutic process by a number of approaches. He should take note of feelings that appear spontaneously in himself, even if they don't seem to bear much relationship to the topics of the moment. They may, nevertheless, be echoes of feelings of the patient that are preparing to emerge into the open. Likewise, he should pay attention to the content of fantasies, daydreams, and night dreams that he has about the patient during or between sessions. If the therapist has a good colleague or consultant available, playing tapes of sessions can be an extraordinarily valuable learning experience. The consultant can see the forest often in a situation where patient and therapist are perforce preoccupied with the trees.

As noted before, for chronic patients, this middle stage of therapy may run months or years. It comprises the hard, patient work of therapy. As the feelings and thoughts, long repressed, emerge, they are usually seen as coming from outside the patient. They are attributed to the therapist, to the hospital, to outside forces, to the parents, to nearly anyone but the patient. However, as the work continues, the patient comes to see many of these complexes as being his own property: it is *his* own wish to be mothered that he has projected on the therapist; it is *his* own fear of (and wish for) homosexual closeness that he has projected onto his persecutors;

it is *his* own fear of rejection and humiliation that has caused him to make a schizophrenic retreat from human relationships. Some of "Not-me" has become "Bad-me"; some of "Bad-me" has become "Good-me."

If treatment has been successful and things that had to be handled in a psychotic fashion previously can now be handled in a more realistic way, patient and psychiatrist must prepare for termination and separation.

Final Stages

Even as proud and healthy parents find it difficult to emancipate their children, so therapists and patients may find termination difficult. Both should be able to acknowledge the pride and pleasure at a favorable outcome of therapeutic work. What may not be so easy to identify are the various sources of the sense of loss that occurs.

Searles[22] identifies some of these sources when he points out that there are at least four important contributants. First, the therapist has come to love and hold his patient in high regard, as a parent does a growing child, and does not want to give him up to the world. Second, some of the therapist's own repressed and unresolved oedipal feelings for the patient —countertransference feelings in the classical sense—will urge him to cling to the relationship. A third source, ". . . is to be found in the appeal which the gratifyingly improving patient makes to the narcissistic residue in the analyst's personality, the Pygmalion in him." The fourth source is the reality that a meaningful, productive, and intimate relationship between two people is nearing an end. Searles also points out that the importance of sources two and three, representing relatively infantile wishes on the part of the therapist, ideally should be a good deal less than the importance of sources one and four.

Another source of loss is that of the loss of the charming child. There is no doubt that many schizophrenic patients have a charm and a wit, a capacity for satire and mimicry (deliberate or otherwise), reminiscent of Harpo Marx, which is part of their illness. They can say and do things that are not permissible to the therapist. Growing up inevitably involves some sobering up. As the patient grows, the therapist may come to miss his delightful child.

Searles[22] has given an example of feelings about termination most poignantly:

> I think, for example, of a woman who was, at the beginning of our work some years ago, extremely unintegrated in her personality functioning. She behaved, from one session to the next, and often from one moment to the next, like a whole galaxy of utterly different persons. She has become, over the years, partly by dint of much hard work on the part of both of us, much better integrated. . . . But we have lost much too. . . . The beer hall bouncer I used to know is no more. The captured American pilot, held prisoner by the Germans but striding proudly several paces ahead of the despised prison camp guard, is no more. The frightening lioness has gone from her den. The incarnation of paranoid hatred, spewing hostility at the whole world, has mellowed into someone unrecognizably different. The endearing little girl can no longer hide the adult woman who is now part of her. . . . It is as though a whole gallery of portraits, some of them beautiful and some of them horrible, but all of them free from diluting imperfections, have been sacrificed in the formation of a single, far more complex and many-sided portrait, the relatively well-integrated person who now exists.

TECHNIQUES AND PRACTICAL PRINCIPLES

Anxiety

Sullivan and others have pointed out that the experience of more than modest amounts of anxiety is a disturbing and fragmenting experience that precludes useful learning about the factors leading up to the anxiety. Sullivan[26] has said,

> The first of all learning is, I think, beyond doubt in immediate connection with *anxiety*. I have already tried to suggest, and will again and again suggest, that severe anxiety probably contributes no information. The effect of severe anxiety reminds one in some ways of a blow on the head, in that it simply wipes out what is immediately proximal to its occurrence. If you have a severe blow on the head, you are quite apt later to have an incurable, absolute amnesia covering the few moments before your head was struck. Anxiety has a similar effect. . . .

In another context, Korchin and Levine[14] have demonstrated that there is an optimum amount of anxiety that will spur rats to solve learning problems. If they are subjected to greater than that optimum amount of stress, learning decays. The authors further found that the more complex the learning task, the lower the level of anxiety that would begin to impede performance. If the same principle holds for human beings, as there is every empirical reason to think it should, it follows that more than a little anxiety for a schizophrenic patient engaged in one of the most complex of all learning tasks—learning about his and others' feelings, thoughts, and conflicts—will have a deleterious effect on the patient's learning.

Anxiety must be recognized before it can be treated. Its most common indicators are autonomic reactions and their behavioral counterparts. Anxiety is signaled by tachycardia, "butterflies in the stomach," sweating of the palms and brows, frequent urination, restlessness and agitation, blocking and speech disturbances, etc. In its more extreme form, one sees a picture of great agitation, restlessness, panic, and sudden discharges of affect in flight or assault. When the patient seems mildly or moderately anxious, the therapist can simply point out to the patient that he is looking uneasy and anxious and ask him if this is the way he is feeling. If the patient says he is, indeed, anxious, both can deal directly with it in the ways mentioned below.

For certain schizophrenic patients, a singular kind of odorous sweating, peculiarly acrid and unpleasant, and totally unrelated to personal hygiene, may be the signal of anxiety.[16]

For most, if not all, schizophrenic patients, an increase in the amount of psychotic or primary process thinking and behaving signals a rise in anxiety levels. In the case of Sylvia T., an increase in delusional religious preoccupation served as a clue to increased anxiety. Stephen T.'s voices and fears that he was harming the therapist or others similarly indicated rising anxiety.

Another clue is the sudden awareness by the psychiatrist that he himself is becoming anxious. In subtle ways, schizophrenic anxiety is contagious at a nonverbal level; if the therapist finds himself becoming anxious, he should seek immediately to attend to the possibility that the patient is getting anxious about something, very likely something in the relationship.

If signs of anxiety have been detected, its meaning must be assessed. In Chapter 4 the central dilemma of the schizophrenic in maintaining distance and closeness while appearing to do neither was explored. Most frequently, the patient becomes afraid that something—often of his own thinking or doing—will adversely affect his relationship with the psychiatrist or with other important people, that something portends abandonment, rejection, or destruction by or of people he needs. Again, I must point out that to most of us, therapists included, mild or modest amounts of anxiety signify only mild or modest life stresses. The implication of anxiety for the schizophrenic takes on a much more immediate and all-encompassing meaning about his very being.

It then follows that, whenever possible, anxiety should be reduced to modest levels, in order to avoid its disintegrating and fragmenting effects on useful, therapeutic learning. If the anxiety appears suddenly in a therapy session, the therapist should seek to identify the threatening issues and reassure the patient whenever it is appropriate. This suggestion may be put into the form of a general rule: whenever the therapist notes signs that the patient is feeling emotions that threaten to disrupt, separate, or divide the therapeutic relationship, he should comment on them openly to the patient as frequently as necessary and seek to identify and dispel the unrealistic component and confirm the realistic component. These disruptive, or disjunctive, forces are often thought of as "negative transference," but I think that the term is not accurate. There are situations where negative, i.e., hostile and angry, feelings can serve to strengthen a bond while they are being examined; and there are times when positive feelings, i.e., love and affection, may grow so strong that they cannot be handled by one or both parties and may thus lead to the dissolution of the relationship. The relationship of George and Martha in *Who's Afraid of Virginia Woolf?*[1] was sustained by mutual hate and probably would have collapsed in a more tender atmosphere; many schizophrenic patients, especially women, have "fallen in love" with their therapists and have had to break off treatment because they could not master their feelings. The therapist should tend to leave conjunctive feelings alone, accept them gratefully, but try not to force the patient into the potentially humiliating position of discussing them.

In the sections on treatment in the case histories, there are at least two examples of identifying and dealing with disjunctive anxiety: Sylvia T.'s sudden repetition of the Lord's Prayer and Stephen T.'s fear of my making homosexual overtures to him; in both cases open comment caused an immediate reduction in anxiety.

For agitated and anxious patients, phenothiazines, as described in Chapter 12, are extremely useful. There was an era in dynamically oriented psychiatry when having to give a patient a pill was somehow thought to detract from the magic of the therapist's art. Now it is generally recognized that any measure, including drugs, hospital milieu, group therapy, and individual therapy, and the several other modalities extant should be employed whenever and wherever they might be useful in treatment.

Delusions, Hallucination, and the Countertransference

Inevitably, the patient will need to view the therapist in ways that are frequently quite different from the therapist's own self-perceptions. In some cases the distortions will be obvious and unthreatening to the therapist; in others they will be a definite threat to his *amour propre,* and his own anxieties will not only make it difficult for him to discern what is going on but make him defensive.

Patients see therapists in forms that may seem distorted to the therapist (even though the kernel of truth may be apparent to the therapist or his consultant), but it is important to the patient that he maintain these perceptions, at least during a given phase of treatment. In my opinion, the therapist should allow the patient to keep his perceptions, and should acknowledge that he recognizes that this is indeed the way the patient sees him, even if the therapist points out that he does not see himself the same way. Arguing with the patient in an attempt to demonstrate to him his poor psychological eyesight will probably serve to make him hold onto his perceptions all the more, just as maintaining tension on a sheep-shank knot causes it to maintain its form, whereas relaxing it causes previously unutilized loops of slack to fall out. The moral that persuasion is better than force applies as much to psychotherapy as it does to the rest of the world of human affairs.

> *Example:* The work with Vivian was becoming increasingly frustrating. She treated our sessions with a hauteur and condescension worthy of Queen Victoria. She came to sessions only sporadically and then found little to dis-

cuss. In turn, I was prodding her in various ways to "produce more material." In going over a tape with my consultant, he said that the situation suggested to him the picture of Vivian as a complacent cow and the therapist as a fly intent on irritating her and being flicked off with a casual swipe of the tail. In listening further to the tape, it became apparent to the consultant, and, reluctantly, with his guidance, to me, that Vivian was sending out subtle messages that she thought I was insensitive, stupid, and physically unattractive. In turn, I was unwittingly arguing with her to try to convince her of the falsity of her perceptions. In the next therapy session, I could allow myself to hear these commentaries for the first time, and commented a little sarcastically, "Well, Vivian, isn't it just your luck that of all the people on the face of the earth you could have gotten for a therapist, you got a dumb, stupid, ugly one like me."

She replied, "You're right, Mr. Rosenbaum, and I never thought you would ever know it." She then detailed several instances in which I *had been* dumb and insensitive. The pace of treatment picked up at that point.

Other reasons to acknowledge the patient's perception are set forth by Searles,[19] where he points out that patients may respond to unconscious processes of the therapist as if they were the patient's own processes, and the therapist, for his own reasons, cannot see these. He says,

In such instances . . . the patient's response is such a grossly exaggerated caricature of the therapist's actual behavior as to add to the therapist's unreadiness to recognize this connection. . . . But it is very important for the therapist to be able to recognize the nucleus of *reality*-perception which lies in the patient's response, for it is by encouraging the growth of

such fragments of reality-relatedness that he
can be of greatest value to these deeply ill patients.

It follows from this, then, that the therapist must be
willing to accept the possibility that he contains within himself, out of awareness, unresolved conflicts of the sort that
the patient demonstrates overtly. It is a fiction to believe that
any therapist, no matter how thoroughgoing his own psychoanalysis may have been, is ever completely freed of conflicts
about homosexuality, aggression, submission, fear of the
father and hatred of the brother, or love of the father and the
brother, or wishes for sexual conquest. Intensive work with
schizophrenic patients may well reach these recesses of feelings of the therapist, and he would be well-advised to allow
for this possibility.

Hill[12] points out that when patients make accusatory or
seductive statements to their therapists they may be issuing
a veiled invitation for the therapist to respond in kind, hoping
that he will refuse the invitation, but still not be too scared
by his own response to maintain a relationship with the patient.

One particular recurrent perception that patients may
have of therapists is that the therapist is going crazy, that
the patient's schizophrenia is somehow contagious, as shown
in the vignette of George T. in Chapter 4. Such perceptions
frequently come when the patient is seeking to incorporate
the therapist and make him a benign superego introject.
Hill[12] points out that the patient, as he improves, may magically assume that the evil in himself, his illness, is being left
with the therapist. It may be quite reassuring for the therapist
to inform the patient that he is not going crazy and that
he can maintain a relationship with the patient without being
adversely affected.

Silences

Silences often occur with schizophrenic patients of all
types, not just with mute catatonics. These silences can be

quite taxing, and the ways in which they may be dealt with depend both on the therapist's temperament and the quality and meaning of the silence. By this latter, I mean that the therapist's intuition may give him certain clues about what type of silence it is; it may be sad, angry, bored, excited, loving, depressed, contemplative, inarticulate, or combinations of these and others. I will suggest ways in which various therapists have handled silences, pointing out that this list is intended only as a beginning.

Don Jackson has used soliloquizing as a way of making contact with the silent patient. If the therapist finds his thoughts during a silence suggesting to him that it is a sad silence, he may think of a sad experience in his own life and say, "As I've been sitting here thinking, I remember the time when I was much younger and my pet dog got killed [assuming the incident did, in fact, take place] and I felt very sad about it. I wonder if what you are feeling today is something like that." Such a soliloquy leaves the patient free to respond, confirm, deny, or remain silent to the therapist's recitation. If the therapist has perceived the nature of the silence correctly, he has offered the patient evidence of his willingness to be an empathetic and sensitive human being, even if the patient is unable at that point to respond positively.

Frieda Fromm-Reichmann was said to have taken her knitting with her often when she visited a mute catatonic patient. By having something to occupy her hands, she did not need to burden the patient with a need to interact with her, while, at the same time, she was paradoxically more available to and in relationship with the patient than if she had cast the full brunt of her attentions his way.

In the early phases of the work with one patient, he was painfully shy, hid his face behind his hands, occasionally peeking out of the corner of his eyes at me, and responding to my questions with nothing more than a grunt. I had commented at some length on his shyness and fear of committing himself, but without noticeable result. One day I said, "Carl, I've been wondering about something. I wonder, if I stepped on your foot, would you have the guts to say 'ouch'?" He smiled broadly, and haltingly agreed that he just might. This marked the beginning of the end of his mutism.

Interpretations, Confrontations, and the Like

For the beginning therapist, his own rescue fantasties and need to prove himself a capable, sensitive, warm, giving, imaginative, helpful therapist (which is the ego ideal of most therapists, young and old) may lead him to make brash and premature interpretations that prove his psychological sophistication at the expense of the patient's self-esteem. Having seen more than a little of this in my own work, I would like to share a few observations that grew out of such experiences.

First, the therapist should side with the patient's superego or ego ideal whenever he can do so without perjuring himself. It is tempting for the neophyte therapist to envision the patient's parents, and the superego derived from them, as the villains in the piece and to suggest to the patient in a number of ways that he should abandon these corrupting influences, that he should start enjoying experiencing the hitherto repressed and forbidden id impulses. What the therapist ignores in such fantasies are a few basic facts of the schizophrenic way of life.

For example, the therapist is a stranger asking the patient to take his offer of help on faith; and the patient's experiences with strangers have generally not been particularly edifying in the past. Also, the parents (and their internal introjects) are the two people on the face of the earth whom the patient knows best. Half a loaf is better than none, and until the therapist has repeatedly proved to the patient that there is some substance to his offer of being a good listener, he will be regarded as no loaf at all. The quickness with which warring factions within a family, or other social group, will unite when outsiders threaten the integrity of the social unit, is legendary. The members of the families of schizophrenic patients appear to have formed unusually close and symbiotic relationships to one another, pseudo-mutual or otherwise, and the phenomenon of unity under attack by the outsider can develop with remarkable speed against the therapist who prematurely tries to show up the parents in a bad light.

Instead, the therapist can honestly acknowledge the patient's dependency on his family, on their mutual need for one another, on the factors that prevent a more satisfying kind of closeness, in a way that will not contradict the patient's perceptions and not threaten his few sustained object relations. If, later, anger about the thwarting of such feelings emerges in therapy, they can be much more constructively dealt with.

Second, the therapist should not be afraid to voice his intuitions of the patient's dynamics, but he should do it in a manner consistent with the patient's self-respect. That is, if the patient wishes to disagree with the therapist's ideas, the situation should be one in which he can do so without either person's having to lose face.

If the therapist is unsure of the correctness or timing of an interpretation, he can use a number of qualifiers that will allow the patient to disagree, for example, "It looks to me as if . . . ," "I get the feeling that . . . ," "My intuition tells me that . . . ," and ". . . how does that fit?" ". . . does that seem to make sense?" etc. The suggestion to Stephen that he had fears about our having an overt homosexual relationship is a case in point.

Therapists should suffer no loss of face if they are unable to follow a patient's train of thought. In fact, if the therapist sits and nods omnisciently when he is actually confused, he is doing the patient a disservice. Therapists in this situation would be well advised to say to the patient, "I don't think I'm following you. Does what you are saying mean such-and-such?"

There will be times when events in the life of the therapist will affect his behavior in therapy. Personal tragedies will depress him; personal illness will cause him pain. With the schizophrenic patient's propensity for omnipotent thinking, especially where alienation and pain are concerned, the patient may interpret signs of distress in the therapist as being his (the patient's) fault. At such times, the therapist may save the patient considerable anxiety by telling him in a simple way that his distress has nothing to do with the patient. If the therapist's distress is profound, it is in the best interests of all concerned to cancel a few sessions until the therapist has recovered somewhat; again, the patient should be given a simple and direct explanation of the reasons.

Borderline patients, or overtly schizophrenic patients who have a substantial amount of observing ego, may be quite appreciative of an explanation of the phenomenon of the double-bind. Being caught in a double-bind is, after all, a mystifying experience.[16] Such experiences may lead a patient to the conclusion, "I must be crazy." Explanation of the double-bind may make the mystifying environment a great deal more comprehensible.

> *Example:* In working with a markedly schizoid (but nonpsychotic) physicist, it became apparent that he had grown up in an incredibly chaotic environment. In one session I explained the double-bind to him. He absorbed the explanation with great interest and documented it with many incidents from his childhood.
>
> He visited his parents some months later and then reported, "I spent a week—I mean a day, but I guess it felt like a week—with my parents when I was back on this trip. It was one double-bind after another, and I cut short my trip before I lost my sanity."

The recovering patient may need to make special use of the therapeutic relationship so that it will live in his own mind and help him maintain his improvement. In an example of Hill's, a recovered patient sought out a friend of the therapist once or twice a year, and inquired after the therapist.

The patient would then proceed to do a 20-minute caricature of the therapist, treating the mutual friend as if he were the patient, thus reversing roles. The patient would then excuse himself and go his way. These occurrences went on for several years; Hill[12] interprets them as follows:

> He [the patient] kept him [the therapist], through the casual mutual friend, potentially available because it was always possible that the psychosis might again invade him and that he might need the therapist. You might say that he might need the therapist to fight the devil with fire.

Hill discusses the need to frame interpretations in the direction of the patient's self-esteem and healthier functioning as follows:

> A primary requirement is that all [the therapist's] behavior should be in the interest of supporting the real ego of the patient. This means supporting such activities on the part of the patient as are realistic and valid and supporting the patient's self-esteem, his confidence in himself, and his ability to cope with his anxiety without resorting to regressive defenses.

In this vein, there are many times when the therapist ought to make his feelings known to the patient, again, not masochistically, but in a simple, straightforward statement.

> *Example:* In the middle phase of the work with Vivian, she had taken to posturing and conducting herself in a rather sexy manner. One day she came into a session, and stood by the door in a sexy pose. I asked her to sit down. She said, "But you like this, don't you?"
> I replied, "You know I do, but it's too distracting and we can't get any talking done if you keep it up." She sat down willingly and we started talking.

On another occasion, I was due to take a month's vacation in Europe. A week before I was to leave, she consumed an unknown amount of an oxalic acid mixture used to clean metals in the occupational therapy shop. Emergency measures were called for, including phone calls to the local poison-control center, examination by the internist, administration of antidotes, and setting up regular observations of kidney function. It took three hours before we were sure she was not in danger.

At our regular therapy session that afternoon, as I was preparing to inquire in a kindly manner about any possible relationship between the impending vacation and the swallowing of the oxalic acid, I realized that I was furious with her for a number of reasons. So I said, "Damn it, Vivian, before we get started, there are a few things I want to get off my chest. Taking the acid this morning was a damn fool stunt. You took a serious chance on harming yourself; you got a lot of people upset; and you shot a morning when I had a lot of things I had to do."

She responded in one of the most open and nonschizophrenic statements I had ever heard from her: "Well, Mr. Rosenbaum, if you think you can go off to Europe and leave your patients behind without anyone to take care of them, well, Mister, you're just not much of a doctor!"

If Searle's patient was, at various times, a beer hall bouncer, a captured pilot, and a frightening lioness in her den, the therapist will be seen (and will often see himself) as a deserter of a sick patient, a lover, a torturer, a rescuer, a god, a gnat, a demon. When therapist and patient together can see themselves as all of these and as none of these, the work has been worth while.

References

CHAPTER 1

1. *Diagnostic and statistical manual—mental disorders.* Prepared by the Committee on Nomenclature and Statistics of the American Psychiatric Association, Washington, D.C., 1952.

2. *Diagnostic and statistical manual—mental disorders.* Prepared by the Committee on Nomenclature and Statistics of the American Psychiatric Association, Washington, D.C., 1968.

3. Bellak, Leopold (ed.). *Schizophrenia: a review of the syndrome.* London: Logos Press, 1958, p. 117.

4. Bleuler, Eugene. *Dementia praecox, or the group of schizophrenias,* J. Zinkin (trans.). New York: International Universities Press, Inc., 1950.

5. *Ibid.,* p. 9.

6. *Ibid.,* p. 36.

7. *Ibid.,* p. 56.

8. *Ibid.,* p. 378.

9. *Ibid.,* p. 90.

10. *Ibid.,* p. 92.

11. Kraepelin, Emil. *Dementia praecox,* R. M. Barclay (trans.). Edinburgh: E. S. Livingstone, Ltd., 1919.

12. Prince, Morton. Miss Beauchamp—the theory of psychogenesis of multiple personality. *Journal of Abnormal Psychology,* 1920, *15,* 67–135.

13. Redlich, Frederick C., and Freedman, Daniel X. *The theory and practice of psychiatry.* New York: Basic Books, Inc., 1966.

14. Thigpen, Collette. *The three faces of Eve.* New York: McGraw-Hill, Inc., 1957.

15. Yalom, Irvin D. Lysergic acid diethylamide. *Maryland State Medical Journal,* 1959, *8,* 14–17.

CHAPTER 2

1. Arieti, Silvano (ed.). *American handbook of psychiatry.* New York: Basic Books, Inc., 1959, pp. 1203–1221.
2. Bellak, Leopold (ed.). *Schizophrenia: a review of the syndrome.* London: Logos Press, Ltd., 1958, p. 157.
3. Bleuler, Eugen. *Dementia praecox, or the group of schizophrenias,* J. Zinkin (trans.). New York: International Universities Press, Inc., 1950, p. 213.
4. Bower, W. M. H., and Altschule, Mark D. Use of progesterone in the treatment of postpartum psychosis. *New England Journal of Medicine,* 1956, *254,* 157–160.
5. Brill, Norman W., and Glass, John F. Hebephrenic schizophrenic reactions. *Archives of General Psychiatry,* 1965, *12,* 545–551.
6. Cameron, Norman. Paranoid condition and paranoia. In Silvano Arieti (ed.), *American handbook of psychiatry.* New York: Basic Books, Inc., 1959, pp. 508–539.
7. Daniels, Robert S., and Lessow, Herbert. Severe postpartum reactions: an interpersonal view. *Psychosomatics,* 1964, *5,* 21–26.
8. Fondeur, M.; Fixsen, C.; Triebel, W.; and White, M. A. Postpartum mental illness. *Archives of Neurology and Psychiatry,* 1957, *77,* 503–511.
9. Garmezy, Norman, and Rodnick, Elliot. Premorbid adjustment and performance in schizophrenia: implications for interpreting heterogeneity in schizophrenia. *Journal of Nervous and Mental Disease,* 1959, *129,* 450–466.
10. Gjessing, L. R. Studies of periodic catatonia. *Journal of Psychiatric Research,* 1966, *2,* 123–134.
11. Hamilton, James A. *Postpartum psychiatric problems.* St. Louis: C. V. Mosby Company, 1962.
12. Hecker, E. Die Hebephrenie. *Virchows Archiv für pathologische Anatomie,* 1871, *52,* 394.
13. Hoch, Paul A., and Polatin, Phillip. Pseudoneurotic forms of schizophrenia. *Psychiatric Quarterly,* 1949, *23,* 248–276.
14. Jolian-West, Louis. The dissociative reactions revisited. Address at Stanford University, May 1967.

15. Kahlbaum, Karl L. *Die Katatonie oder das Spannungsiresein.* Berlin: Hirschwald, 1874.

16. Knight, Robert P. Borderline states. In Robert Knight and Cyrus Friedman (eds.), *Psychoanalytic psychiatry and psychology.* New York: International Universities Press, Inc., 1954, pp. 97–109.

17. Langfeldt, Gabriel. The diagnosis of schizophrenia. *American Journal of Psychiatry*, 1951, *108*, 123–125.

18. Melges, Frederick T. Postpartum psychiatric syndromes. *Psychosomatic Medicine*, 1968, *30*, 95–108.

19. Seager, C. P. A controlled study of postpartum illness. *Journal of Mental Sciences*, 1960, *106*, 214–230.

20. Towne, Robert D., and Afterman, Joseph. Psychosis in males related to parenthood. *Bulletin Menninger Clinic*, 1955, *19*, 19–26.

21. Weiner, Herbert. Diagnosis and symptomatology. In Leopold Bellak (ed.), *Schizophrenia: a review of the syndrome.* London: Logos Press, Ltd., 1958, pp. 107–173.

22. *Ibid.*, pp. 146–147.

CHAPTER 4

1. Arieti, Silvano. *Interpretation of schizophrenia.* New York: Robert Brunner, 1955.

2. Bleuler, Eugen. *Dementia praecox or the group of schizophrenias.* New York: International Universities Press, Inc., 1950.

3. Bowlby, John. Mother-child separation. In Kenneth Soddy (ed.), *Mental health and infant development.* New York: Basic Books, Inc., 1956.

4. Carroll, Lewis. *Alice's adventures in wonderland.* New York: Crowell-Collier and Macmillan, Inc., 1929.

5. Freud, Sigmund. *A general introduction to psychoanalysis*, J. Riviere (trans.), New York: Garden City Books, 1943.

6. ———. Dreams. In J. Riviere (trans.), *A general introduction to psychoanalysis*, Part III. New York: Garden City Books, 1943.

7. ———. The case of Schreber. In James Strachey (trans.), *Standard edition of the complete psychological works of Sigmund Freud.* Vol. XII. London: Hogarth Press, Ltd., 1958.

8. Fromm-Reichmann, Frieda: *Principles of intensive psy-*

chotherapy. Chicago: University of Chicago Press, 1950, pp. 153, 167.

9. Goldstein, Kurt. Methodological approach to the study of schizophrenic thought disorder. In J. Kasanin (ed.), *Language and thought in schizophrenia: collected papers.* Berkeley: University of California Press, 1944, pp. 17–40.

10. Green, Hannah. *I never promised you a rose garden.* New York: Holt, Rinehart and Winston, Inc., 1964.

11. Harlow, Harry, and Harlow, Margaret. Social deprivation in monkeys. *Scientific American,* 1962, 207, 136–146.

12. Hill, Lewis B. *Psychotherapeutic intervention in schizophrenia.* Chicago: University of Chicago Press, 1955.

13. Kasanin, Jacob. *Language and thought in schizophrenia: collected papers.* Berkeley: University of California Press, 1944.

14. Rapaport, David. *Organization and pathology of thought.* New York: Columbia University Press, 1951, p. 588.

15. Reik, Theodore. *Listening with the third ear.* New York: Pyramid Books, 1948.

16. Rosenbaum, C. Peter. Patient-family similarities in schizophrenia. *Archives of General Psychiatry,* 1961, 5, 120–126.

17. Searles, Harold F. Integration and differentiation in schizophrenia: an overall view. *British Journal of Medical Psychology,* 1959, 32, 261–281.

18. Spitz, Rene A. Anaclitic depression. In Ruth S. Eissler (ed.). *Psychoanalytic study of the child.* New York: International Universities Press, Inc., 1946.

19. Sullivan, Harry S. *The interpersonal theory of psychiatry.* New York: W. W. Norton & Company, Inc., 1953.

20. Szasz, Thomas S. A contribution to the psychology of schizophrenia. *Archives of Neurology and Psychiatry,* 1957, 77, 420–436.

21. Von Domarus, E. The specific laws of logic in schizophrenia. In J. Kasanin (ed.), *Language and thought in schizophrenia: collected papers.* Berkeley: University of California Press, 1944, pp. 104–114.

CHAPTER 5

1. Alanen, Yrjo. The family in the pathogenesis of schizophrenia and neurotic disorders. *Acta Psychiatrica Scandinavica,*

Monograph, Vol. 42, Supp. 189. Copenhagen: Ejnar Munksgaard, 1966.

2. Arieti, Silvano. *Interpretation of schizophrenia.* New York: Robert Brunner, 1955. For sale by Basic Books, Inc.

3. Bleuler, Eugen. *Dementia praecox, or the group of schizophrenias,* J. Zinkin (trans.). New York: International Universities Press, Inc., 1951.

4. Eliot, T. S.: The waste land. In *The complete poems and plays.* New York: Harcourt, Brace & Co., 1930, pp. 40–41.

5. Hilgard, Josephine, and Newman, Martha. Parental loss by death in childhood as an etiological factor among schizophrenic and alcoholic patients compared with a non-patient community sample. *Journal of Nervous and Mental Disease,* 1963, *137,* 14–28.

6. Kringlen, Einar. *Schizophrenia in male monozygotic twins.* Oslo, Norway: Universitetsforlaget, 1964.

7. Laing, Ronald. *The divided self.* London: Tavistock Publications, 1960.

8. Nameche, Gene; Waring, Mary; and Ricks, David. Early indicators of outcome in schizophrenia. *Journal of Nervous and Mental Disease,* 1964, *139,* 232–240.

9. Pollack, Max; Levenstein, Sidney; and Klein, Donald F. A three-year posthospital follow-up of adolescent and adult schizophrenics. *American Journal of Orthopsychiatry,* 1968, *38,* 94–109.

10. Pollack, Max; Woerner, Margaret G.; Goodman, Warren; and Greenberg, Irwin M. Childhood development patterns of hospitalized adult schizophrenic and nonschizophrenic patients and their siblings. *American Journal of Orthopsychiatry,* 1966, *36,* 510–517.

11. Pollin, William; Stabenau, James R.; Mosher, Loren; and Tupin, Joe. Life history differences in identical twins discordant for schizophrenia. *American Journal of Orthopsychiatry,* 1966, *36,* 492–509.

12. Pollin, William; Stabenau, James R.; and Tupin, Joe. Family studies with identical twins discordant for schizophrenia. *Psychiatry,* 1965, *28,* 60–78.

13. Prout, Curtis T., and White, Mary Alice. The schizophrenic's sibling. *Journal of Nervous and Mental Disease,* 1957, *123,* 162–170.

14. Sullivan, Harry Stack. *Clinical studies in psychiatry.* New York: W. W. Norton & Company, Inc., 1956, pp. 337–339.

15. Vaillant, George E. An historical review of the remitting schizophrenias. *Journal of Nervous and Mental Disease,* 1964, *138,* 48–56.

16. Weiner, Herbert. Diagnosis and symptomatology. In Leopold Bellak (ed.). *Schizophrenia: a review of the syndrome.* London: Logos Press, Ltd., 1958, pp. 119–121.

17. Wing, J. F. Five-year outcome in early schizophrenia. *Proceedings of the Royal Society of Medicine,* 1966, *59,* 17–19.

CHAPTER 6

1. Anastasi, A. *Psychological testing.* New York: Crowell–Collier and Macmillan, Inc., 1954.

2. Anderson, H. H., and Anderson, Gladys L. *An introduction to projective techniques.* New York: Prentice-Hall, Inc., 1951.

3. Aronsen, M. L. A study of the Freudian theory of paranoia by means of the Rorschach test. *Journal of Projective Techniques and Personality Assessment,* 1952, *16,* 397–411.

4. Ash, P. The reliability of psychiatric diagnoses. *Journal of Abnormal and Social Psychology,* 1949, *44,* 272–276.

5. Balkan, Eva R. A delineation of schizophrenic language and thought in a test of imagination. *Journal of Psychology,* 1943, *16,* 239–271.

6. Beck, S. J. Personality structure in schizophrenia: a Rorschach investigation in eighty-one patients and sixty-four controls. *Journal of Nervous and Mental Disease, Monograph No. 63,* 1938.

7. Becker, W. C. A genetic approach to the interpretation and evaluation of the process-reactive distinction. *Journal of Abnormal and Social Psychology,* 1956, *53,* 229–236.

8. Bellak, L. The Thematic Apperception Test in clinical use. In L. E. Abt and L. Bellak (eds.), *Projective psychology.* New York: Grove Press, Inc., 1959.

9. Bender, Lauretta. A visual motor Gestalt Test and its clinical use. *American Orthopsychiatric Association, Research Monograph,* No. 3, 1938.

10. Benjamin, J. D. A method for distinguishing and evaluating formal thinking disorders in schizophrenia. In J. S. Kasanin

(ed.), *Language and thought in schizophrenia.* Berkeley: University of California Press, 1951.

11. Billingslea, F. Y. The Bender Gestalt: a review and perspective, *Psychological Bulletin,* 1963, *60,* 233–251.

12. Binet, Alfred, and Simon, T. *A method of measuring the intelligence of young children,* Part II, Clara H. Town (trans.). Chicago: Chicago Medical Book Co., 1915.

13. Bochner, Ruth, and Halpern, Florence. *The clinical application of the Rorschach Test.* New York: Grune & Stratton, Inc., 1945.

14. Chapman, A. J., and Reese, D. G. Homosexual signs in Rorschachs of early schizophrenics. *Journal of Clinical Psychology,* 1953, *9,* 30–32.

15. Davison, A. H. A comparison of the fantasy productions on the TAT of sixty hospitalized psychoneurotic and psychotic patients. *Journal of Projective Techniques and Personality Assessment,* 1953, *17,* 20–33.

16. DuBrin, A. J. The Rorschach "Eyes" hypothesis and paranoid schizophrenia. *Journal of Clinical Psychology,* 1962, *18,* 468–471.

17. Eron, L. D. Frequencies of themes and identifications in the stories of schizophrenic patients and non-hospitalized college students. *Journal of Consulting Psychology,* 1948, *12,* 387–395.

18. Fine, H. J., and Zimet, C. N. Process-reactive schizophrenia and genetic levels of perceptions. *Journal of Abnormal and Social Psychology,* 1959, *59,* 83–86.

19. Frank, L. K. Projective methods for the study of personality. *Journal of Psychology,* 1939, *8,* 389–413.

20. Greenblatt, N., and Solomon, H. D. (eds.), *Frontal lobes and schizophrenia;* Second lobotomy project of Boston Psychopathic Hospital. New York: Springer Publishing Co., 1953.

21. Hathaway, S. R. Scales 5 (Masculinity-Femininity), 6 (Paranoia), and 8 (Schizophrenia). In G. S. Welsh and Dahlstrom, W. G. (eds.), *Basic readings on the MMPI.* Minneapolis: University of Minnesota Press, 1956.

22. Holt, R. R., and Havel, Joan. A method for assessing primary and secondary process in the Rorschach. In Maria A. Rickers-Ovsienkina (ed.), *Rorschach psychology.* New York: John Wiley & Sons, Inc., 1960.

23. Hutt, M. L., and Briskin, G. J. *The clinical use of the*

revised Bender-Gestalt Test. New York: Grune & Stratton, Inc., 1960.

24. Kataguchi, Y. Rorschach Schizophrenic Score. *Journal of Projective Techniques and Personality Assessment*, 1959, *23*, 214–223.

25. Klopfer, B. *Developments in the Rorschach technique*: Vols. I and II. New York: Harcourt, Brace and Co., 1956.

26. Lang, P. J., and Buss, A. H. Psychological deficit in schizophrenia: II. Interference and activation. *Journal of Abnormal Psychology*, 1965, *70*, 77–106.

27. Levy, S. Figure drawings as a projective technique. In L. E. Abt and L. Bellak (eds.), *Projective psychology*. New York: Grove Press, Inc., 1959.

28. Little K. B., and Schneidman, E. S. The validity of MMPI interpretations. *Journal of Consulting Psychology*, 1954, *18*, 425–428.

29. Machover, Karen. *Personality projection in the drawing of the human figure*. Springfield, Ill.: Charles C Thomas, Publishers, 1949.

30. Maher, B. A. *Principles of psychopathology*. New York: McGraw-Hill, Inc., 1966.

31. Marks, P. A., and Seeman, W. *The actuarial description of abnormal personality*. Baltimore: Williams & Wilkins Company, 1963.

32. Masling, J. The influence of situational and interpersonal variables in projective testing. *Psychological Bulletin*, 1960, *57*, 65–85.

33. Mayman, M. Rorschach Form Level Manual. Menninger Clinic, 1959 (ditto).

34. ———; Schafer, R.; and Rapaport, D. Interpretation of the Wechsler-Bellevue Intelligence Scale in personality appraisal. In II. H. Anderson and Gladys L. Anderson, *An introduction to projective techniques*. New York: Prentice-Hall, Inc., 1951.

35. Murray, H. A. *Explorations in personality*. New York: Oxford University Press, 1938.

36. ———. *Manual for the Thematic Apperception Test*. Cambridge, Mass.: Harvard University Press, 1943.

37. Murstein, B. I. *Theory and research in projective techniques*. New York: John Wiley & Sons, Inc., 1963.

38. Orme, J. E. The Rorschach sex response in a psychiatric population: 1,010 Rorschach records surveyed. *Journal of Clinical Psychology*, 1962, *18*, 303.

39. Piotrowski, Z. A. The Rorschach inkblot method. In B. B. Wolman (ed.), *Handbook of clinical psychology*. New York: McGraw-Hill, Inc., 1965.

40. ———. The Rorschach method as a prognostic aid in the insulin shock treatment of schizophrenics. *Psychiatric Quarterly*, 1941, *15*, 807–822.

41. ———, and Lewis, N. D. C. An experimental criterion for the prognostication of the status of schizophrenics after a three-year interval based on Rorschach data. In P. Hoch and J. Zubin, *Relation of psychological tests to psychiatry*. New York: Grune & Stratton, Inc., 1952.

42. Rabin, A. I. Diagnostic use of intelligence tests. In B. B. Wolman (ed.), *Handbook of clinical psychology*. New York: McGraw-Hill, Inc., 1965.

43. ———, and King, G. F. Psychological studies. In L. Bellak, *Schizophrenia: a review of the syndrome*. London: Logos Press, Ltd., 1958.

44. Rapaport, D. *Diagnostic psychological testing*, Vol. I. Chicago: The Year Book Publishers, Inc., 1945.

45. ———. *Diagnostic psychological testing*, Vol. 2. Chicago: The Year Book Publishers, Inc., 1946.

46. Rickers-Ovsienkina, M. The Rorschach Test as applied to normal and schizophrenic subjects. *British Journal of Medicine and Psychology*, 1938, *17*, 227–257.

47. Ritter, Anne M., and Eron, L. D. The use of the TAT to differentiate normal from abnormal groups. *Journal of Abnormal and Social Psychology*, 1952, *47*, 147–158.

48. Rorschach, H. *Psychodiagnostics*. Bern: Huber, 1942.

49. Sargent, Helen D. Projective methods, their origins, theory and application in personality research. *Psychological Bulletin*, 1945, *42*, 257–293.

50. ———, and Mayman, M. Clinical psychology. In S. Arieti (ed.), *American handbook of psychiatry*, Vol. II, New York: Basic Books, Inc., 1959.

51. Schafer, R. *The clinical application of psychological tests*. New York: International Universities Press, Inc., 1948.

52. Schmidt, H. O., and Fonda, C. P. Reliability of psychiatric

diagnoses: a new look. *Journal of Abnormal and Social Psychology*, 1956, 52, 262–267.

53. Singer, Margaret T., and Wynne, L. C. Differentiating characteristics of parents of childhood schizophrenics, childhood neurotics, and young adult schizophrenics. *American Journal of Psychiatry*, 1963, *120*, 234–243.

54. ————. Thought disorder and family relations of schizophrenics: III. Methodology using projective techniques. *Archives of General Psychology*, 1965, *12*, 187–212.

55. ————. Principles for scoring communication defects and deviancies in parents of schizophrenics: Rorschach and TAT scoring manuals. *Psychiatry*, 1966, *29*, 260–288.

56. Swenson, C. H. Empirical evaluations of human figure drawings. In E. I. Megargee (ed.), *Research in clinical assessment*. New York: Harper & Row, Publishers, 1966.

57. Tolor, A., and Schulberg, H. C. *An evaluation of the Bender–Gestalt Test*. Springfield, Ill.: Charles C Thomas Publisher, 1963.

58. Vernon, P. E. *Personality assessment: a critical survey*. London: Methuen & Co., Ltd., 1964.

59. Watkins, J. G., and Stauffscher, J. C. An index of pathological thinking in the Rorschach. *Journal of Projective Techniques and Personality Assessment*, 1952, *16*, 276–286.

60. Wechsler, D. *The measurement of adult intelligence*. Baltimore: The Williams & Wilkins Company, 1944.

61. ————. *The measurement and appraisal of adult intelligence* (4th ed.), Baltimore: The Williams & Wilkins Company, 1958.

62. Welsh, G. S., and Dahlstrom, W. G. (eds.). *Basic readings on the MMPI in psychology and medicine*. Minneapolis: University of Minnesota Press, 1956.

63. Wheeler, W. M. An analysis of Rorschach indices of male homosexuality. *Rorschach Research Exchange*, 1949, *13*, 94–126.

64. Wynne, L. C., and Singer, Margaret T. Thought disorder and family relations of schizophrenics, I and II. *Archives of General Psychiatry*, 1963, *9*, 191–206.

65. Zubin, J.; Eron, L. D.; and Schumer, Florence. *An experimental approach to projective techniques*. New York: John Wiley & Sons, Inc., 1965.

66. Zukowsky, Eugene. Measuring primary and secondary

process thinking in schizophrenics and normals by means of the Rorschach. Unpublished Doctoral Dissertation, Michigan State University, 1961.

CHAPTER 7

1. Ackerman, Nathan W.: The *psychodynamics of family life; diagnosis and treatment of family relationships* New York: Basic Books, Inc., 1958.

2. Alanen, Yrjo, et al: The family in the pathogenesis of schizophrenia and neurotic disorders. *Acta Psychiatrica Scandinavica*, Monograph Vol. 42, Supp. 189. Copenhagen: Einar Munksgaard, 1966.

3. Ibid., pp. 218–221.

4. Ibid., pp. 300–301.

5. Ibid., p. 528.

6. Ibid., p. 436.

7. Bateson, Gregory; Jackson, Don J.; Haley, Jay; and Weakland, John. Towards a theory of schizophrenia, *Behavioral Science, 1,* 251–264, 1956.

8. Bleuler, Eugen. *Dementia praecox, or the group of schizophrenias,* J. Zinkin (trans), New York: International Universities Press, Inc., 1950.

9. Boszormenyi-Nagy, Ivan (ed). *Family psychotherapy* New York: Harper & Row, Publishers, 1965.

10. Breton, Andre. What is surrealism? In H. E. Read (ed.), *Surrealism* New York: Faber & Faber, Ltd., 1936, p. 65.

11. Brodey, Warren M. Some family operations and schizophrenia. *Archives of General Psychiatry, 1,* 379–402, 1959.

12. Garmezy, Norman, and Rodnick, Eliot. Premorbid adjustment and performance in schizophrenia: implications for interpreting heterogeneity in schizophrenia, *Journal of Nervous and Mental Disease, 129,* 450–466, 1959.

13. J. Haley (ed.). *Family process.* Published jointly by the Mental Research Institute and the Family Institute, 1700 Bainbridge Street, Philadelphia, Pennsylvania, 19146.

14. Haley, J. The family of the schizophrenic: a model system. *Journal of Nervous and Mental Disease, 129,* 357–374, 1959.

15. Jackson, Don J.: Personal communication, 1964.

16. Lidz, Theodore; Fleck, Stephen; and Cornelison, Alice R.

Schizophrenia and the family. New York: International Universities Press, Inc., 1965.

17. Lu, Yi-Chuang. Contradictory parental expectations in schizophrenia. *Archives of General Psychiatry, 6,* 219–234, 1962.

18. ———. Mother-child role relations in schizophrenia. *Psychiatry, 24,* 133–142, 1961.

19. Mishler, Elliot G. and Waxler, N. E. Family interaction processes and schizophrenia: a review of current theories. *International Journal of Psychiatry, 2,* 375–413, 1966.

20. Phillips, L. Case history data and prognosis in schizophrenia. *Journal of Nervous and Mental Disease, 117,* 515–525, 1953.

21. Rosenbaum, C. Peter. Patient-family similarities in schizophrenia. *Archives of General Psychiatry, 5,* 120–126, 1961.

22. Rosenthal, Alan J.; Behrens, Manfred I.; and Chodoff, Paul. Communication in lower class families of schizophrenics: 1. Methodological problems. *Archives of General Psychiatry, 18,* 464–470, 1968.

23. Ryckoff, Irving; Day, Juliana; and Wynne, Lyman C. Maintenance of stereotyped roles in the families of schizophrenics. *Archives of General Psychiatry, 1,* 93–98, 1959.

24. Singer, Margaret T. Family transactions and schizophrenia: 1. Recent research findings. In John Romano (ed.), *The origins of schizophrenia,* Excerpta Medica Foundation, pp. 147–164, 1967.

25. ——— and Wynne, Lyman C. Principles for scoring communication defects and deviances in parents of schizophrenics: Rorschach and TAT scoring manuals. *Psychiatry, 29,* 260–288, 1966.

26. ———. Differentiating characteristics of parents of childhood schizophrenics, childhood neurotics, and young adult schizophrenics. *American Journal of Psychiatry, 120,* 234–243, 1963.

27. Watzlawick, Paul. A review of the double bind theory, *Family Process, 2,* 132–153, 1963.

28. Wynne, Lyman C. Family transactions and schizophrenia: 2. Conceptual considerations for a research strategy. In John Romano (ed.), *The origins of schizophrenia,* Excerpta Medica Foundation, pp. 165–178, 1967.

29. ——— and Singer, Margaret T. Thought disorder and family relations of schizophrenics. *Archives of General Psychiatry 9,* 199–206, 1963.

30. Wynne, Lyman C. *et al.* Pseudomutuality in the family relations of schizophrenics. *Psychiatry 22*, 205–220, 1958.

CHAPTER 8

1. Astrup, Christian and Ørnulv Ødegaard. Internal migration and disease in Norway, *Psychiatric Quarterly Supplement, 34*, 116–30. 1960.

2. Bateson, Gregory; Jackson, Don; Haley, Jay; and Weakland, John. Toward a theory of schizophrenia, *Behavioral Science, 1*, 251–64. 1956.

3. Buck, Carol; Wanklin, J. M.; and Hobbs, G. E. An analysis of regional differences in mental illness, *Journal of Nervous and Mental Disease, 122*, 73–9. 1955.

4. Clark, Robert E. The relationship of schizophrenia to occupational income and occupational prestige, *American Sociological Review, 13*, 325–30. 1948.

5. Clark, Robert E. Psychoses, income, and occupation, *American Journal of Sociology, 54*, 433–40. 1949.

6. Clausen, John A. *Sociology and the Field of Mental Health.* New York: Russell Sage Foundation, 1956.

7. Clausen, John A. The ecology of mental illness, Symposium on Social and Preventive Psychiatry. Washington, D.C.: Walter Reed Army Medical Center, 97–108. 1957.

8. Clausen, John A. The sociology of mental illness. In Robert K. Merton *et al.* (eds.), *Sociology Today, Problems and Prospects.* New York: Basic Books, 1959.

9. Clausen, John A. and Melvin L. Kohn. The ecological approach in social psychiatry, *American Journal of Sociology, 60*, 140–51, 1954.

10. Clausen, John A. and Melvin L. Kohn. Relation of schizophrenia to the social structure of a small city. In Benjamin Pasamanick (ed.), *Epidemiology of Mental Disorder.* Washington, D.C.: American Association for the Advancement of Science, 1959.

11. Clausen, John A. Values, norms and the health called "mental": purposes and feasibility of assessment, Paper presented to the Symposium on Definition and Measurement of Mental Health, Washington, D.C., 16 May 1966, mimeographed.

12. Clausen, John A. and Melvin L. Kohn. Social relations and schizophrenia: a research report and a perspective. In Don

D. Jackson (ed.), *The Etiology of Schizophrenia*. New York: Basic Books, 1960.

13. Dee, William L. J. An ecological study of mental disorders in metropolitan St. Louis, unpublished M.A. thesis, Washington University, 1939.

14. Demerath, N. J. Schizophrenia among primitives. In Arnold M. Rose (ed.), *Mental Health and Mental Disorder*. New York: W. W. Norton, 1955.

15. Dohrenwend, Barbara Snell and Bruce P. Dohrenwend. Class and race as status-related sources of stress. In Sol Levine and Norman A. Scotch (eds.), *The Study of Stress*. Chicago: Aldine, in press.

16. Dohrenwend, Bruce P. and Barbara Snell Dohrenwend. The problem of validity in field studies of psychological disorder, *Journal of Abnormal Psychology*, 70, 52–69. 1965.

17. Dunham, H. Warren. *Community and Schizophrenia: An Epidemiological Analysis*. Detroit, Michigan: Wayne State University Press, 1965.

18. Dunham, H. Warren. Epidemiology of psychiatric disorders as a contribution to medical ecology, *Archives of General Psychiatry*, 14, 1–19. 1966.

19. Dunham, H. Warren. Current status of ecological research in mental disorder, *Social Forces*, 25, 321–6. 1947.

20. Dunham, H. Warren. Social psychiatry, *American Sociological Review*, 13, 183–97. 1948.

21. Dunham, H. Warren. Social class and schizophrenia, *American Journal of Orthopsychiatry*, 34, 634–42. 1964.

22. Dunham, H. Warren. Some persistent problems in the epidemiology of mental disorders, *American Journal of Psychiatry*, 109, 567–75. 1963.

23. Dunham, H. Warren; Phillips, Patricia; and Srinivasan, Barbara. A research note on diagnosed mental illness and social class, *American Sociological Review*, 31, 223–7. 1966.

24. Eaton, Joseph W. and Robert J. Weil. *Culture and Mental Disorders: A Comparative Study of the Hutterites and Other Populations*. Glencoe, Illinois: Free Press, 1955.

25. Essen-Möller, E. Individual traits and morbidity in a Swedish rural population, *Acta Psychiatrica et Neurologica Scandinavica*, 100, 1–160. 1956.

26. Essen-Möller, Erik. A current field study in the mental

disorders in Sweden. In Paul H. Hoch and Joseph Zubin (eds.), *Comparative Epidemiology of the Mental Disorders.* New York: Grune and Stratton, 1961.

27. Faris, Robert E. L. and H. Warren Dunham. *Mental Disorders in Urban Areas: An Ecological Study of Schizophrenia and Other Psychoses.* Chicago: University of Chicago Press, 1939.

28. Felix, R. H. and R. V. Bowers. Mental hygiene and socio-environmental factors, *The Milbank Memorial Fund Quarterly,* 26, 125–47. 1948.

29. Frumkin, Robert M. Occupation and major mental disorders. In Arnold Rose (ed.), *Mental Health and Mental Disorders.* New York: W. W. Norton, 1955.

30. Fuson, William M. Research note: occupations of functional psychotics, *American Journal of Sociology,* 48, 612–13. 1943.

31. Gardner, Elmer A. and Haroutin M. Babigian. A longitudinal comparison of psychiatric service to selected socio-economic areas of Monroe County, New York, *American Journal of Orthopsychiatry,* 36, 818–28. 1966.

32. Gerard, Donald L. and Lester G. Houston. Family setting and the social ecology of schizophrenia, *Psychiatric Quarterly,* 27, 90–101. 1953.

33. Goldberg, E. M. and S. L. Morrison, Schizophrenia and social class, *British Journal of Psychiatry,* 109, 785–802. 1963.

34. Goldhamer, Herbert and Andrew W. Marshall. *Psychosis and Civilization.* Glencoe, Illinois: Free Press, 1953.

35. Green, Howard W. *Persons Admitted to the Cleveland State Hospital, 1928–37,* Cleveland Health Council, 1939.

36. Hagnell, Olle. *A Prospective Study of the Incidence of Mental Disorder.* Stockholm, Sweden: Svenska Bokförlaget, 1966.

37. Hare, E. H. Mental illness and social conditions in Bristol, *Journal of Mental Science,* 102, 349–57. 1956.

38. Hare, E. H. Family setting and the urban distribution of schizophrenia, *Journal of Mental Science,* 102, 753–60. 1956.

39. Hollingshead, August B. Some issues in the epidemiology of schizophrenia, *American Sociological Review,* 26, 5–13. 1961.

40. Hollingshead, August B. and Frederick C. Redlich. *Social Class and Mental Illness.* New York: John Wiley, 1957.

41. Hollingshead, August B. and Frederick C. Redlich. Social

stratification and schizophrenia, *American Sociological Review,* 19, 302–6. 1954.

42. Hughes, Charles C.; Tremblay, Marc-Adelard; Rapoport, Robert N.; and Leighton, Alexander H. *People of Cove and Woodlot: Communities from the Viewpoint of Social Psychiatry.* New York: Basic Books, 1960.

43. Jaco, E. Gartley. Incidence of psychoses in Texas, *Texas State Journal of Medicine,* 53, 1–6. 1957.

44. Jaco, E. Gartley. *The Social Epidemiology of Mental Disorders.* New York: Russell Sage Foundation, 1960.

45. Jaco, E. Gartley. The social isolation hypothesis and schizophrenia, *American Sociological Review,* 19, 567–77. 1954.

46. Kaplan, Bert; Reed, Robert B.; and Richardson, Wyman. A comparison of the incidence of hospitalized and non-hospitalized cases of psychosis in two communities, *American Sociological Review,* 21, 472–9. 1956.

47. Kety, Seymour S. Recent biochemical theories of schizophrenia. In Don D. Jackson (ed.), *The Etiology of Schizophrenia.* New York: Basic Books, 1960.

48. Klee, Gerald D.; Spiro, Evelyn; Bahn, Anita K.; and Gorwitz, Kurt. An ecological analysis of diagnosed mental illness in Baltimore. In Russell R. Monroe *et al.* (eds.), *Psychiatric Epidemiology and Mental Health Planning,* Psychiatric Research Report No. 22, the American Psychiatric Association, April, 1967.

49. Kleiner, Robert J. and Seymour Parker. Goal-striving, social status, and mental disorder: a research review, *American Sociological Review,* 28, 189–203. 1963.

50. Kohn, Melvin L. and John A. Clausen. Social isolation and schizophrenia, *American Sociological Review,* 20, 265–73. 1955.

51. Kohn, Melvin L. and John A. Clausen. Parental authority behavior and schizophrenia, *American Journal of Orthopsychiatry,* 26, 297–313. 1956.

52. Kohn, Melvin L. Social class and parent-child relationships: an interpretation, *American Journal of Sociology,* 68, 471–80. 1963.

53. Kramer, Morton. A discussion of the concepts of incidence and prevalence as related to epidemiologic studies of mental disorders, *American Journal of Public Health,* 47, 826–40. 1957.

54. Kringlen, Einar. Discordance with respect to schizophre-

nia in monozygotic twins: some genetic aspects, *Journal of Nervous and Mental Disease*, 138, 26–31, 1964.

55. Kringlen, Einar. *Schizophrenia in Male Monozygotic Twins*. Oslo: Universitetsforlaget, 1964.

56. Kringlen, Einar. Schizophrenia in twins: an epidemiological-clinical study, *Psychiatry*, 29, 172–84, 1966.

57. Langner, Thomas S. and Stanley T. Michael. *Life Stress and Mental Health*. New York: The Free Press of Glencoe, 1963.

58. Lapouse, Rema; Monk, Mary A.; and Terris, Milton. The drift hypothesis and socioeconomic differentials in schizophrenia, *American Journal of Public Health*, 46, 978–86. 1956.

59. Leacock, Eleanor. Three social variables and the occurrence of mental disorder. In Alexander H. Leighton, John A. Clausen and Robert N. Wilson (eds.), *Explorations in Social Psychiatry*. New York: Basic Books, 1957.

60. Leighton, Alexander H. *My Name is Legion: Foundations for a Theory of Man in Relation to Culture*. New York: Basic Books, 1959.

61. Leighton, Alexander H.; Lambo, T. Adeoye; Hughes, Charles C.; Leighton, Dorothea C.; Murphy, Jane M.; and Macklin, David B. *Psychiatric Disorder among the Yoruba*. Ithaca: Cornell University Press, 1963.

62. Leighton, Alexander H. *et al.* Psychiatric disorder in West Africa, *American Journal of Psychiatry*, 120, 521–5. 1963.

63. Leighton, Dorothea C.; Harding, John S.; Macklin, David B.; MacMillan, Allister M.; and Leighton, Alexander H. *The Character of Danger: Psychiatric Symptoms in Selected Communities*. New York: Basic Books, 1963.

64. Leighton, Dorothea C.; Harding, J. S.; Macklin, D. B.; Hughes, C. C.; and Leighton, A. H. Psychiatric findings of the Stirling County study, *American Journal of Psychiatry*, 119, 1021–6. 1963.

65. Lemkau, Paul; Tietze, Christopher; and Cooper, Maria. Mental hygiene problems in an urban district: second paper, *Mental Hygiene*, 26, 1–20. 1942.

66. Lin, Tsung-Yi. A study of the incidence of mental disorder in Chinese and other cultures, *Psychiatry*, 16, 313–36. 1953.

67. Lin, Tsung-Yi. Mental disorders in Taiwan, fifteen years later: a preliminary report, Paper presented to the Conference on Mental Health in Asia and the Pacific, Honolulu, March 1966.

68. Locke, Ben Z.; Kramer, Morton; Timerlake, Charles E.; Pasamanick, Benjamin; and Smeltzer, Donald. Problems of interpretation of patterns of first admissions to Ohio State public mental hospitals for patients with schizophrenic reactions. In Benjamin Pasamanick and Peter H. Knapp (eds.), *Social Aspects of Psychiatry,* the American Psychiatric Association (Psychiatric Research Reports No. 10), 1958.

69. Lystad, Mary H. Social mobility among selected groups of schizophrenic patients, *American Sociological Review,* 22, 288–92. 1957.

70. Mishler, Elliot G. and Norman A. Scotch. Sociocultural factors in the epidemiology of schizophrenia: a review, *Psychiatry,* 26, 315–51. 1963.

71. Mishler, Elliot G. and Nancy E. Waxler. Family interaction processes and schizophrenia: a review of current theories, *Merrill-Palmer Quarterly of Behavioral Development,* 11, 269–315. 1965.

72. Morris, J. N. Health and social class, *Lancet,* 7 February 1959, 303–5.

73. Myers, Jerome K. and Betram H. Roberts. *Family and Class Dynamics in Mental Illness.* New York: John Wiley, 1959.

74. Nolan, William J. Occupation and *dementia praecox, (New York) State Hospitals Quarterly,* 3, 127–54. 1917.

75. Ødegaard, Ørnulv. Emigration and insanity: a study of mental disease among the Norwegianborn population of Minnesota, *Acta Psychiatrica et Neurologica Scandinavica,* 4, 182–4. 1932.

76. Ødegaard, Ørnulv. Emigration and mental health, *Mental Hygiene,* 20, 546–53. 1936.

77. Ødegaard, Ørnulv. The incidence of psychoses in various occupations, *International Journal of Social Psychiatry,* 2, 85–104. 1956.

78. Ødegaard, Ørnulv. Psychiatry epidemiology, *Proceedings of the Royal Society of Medicine,* 55, 831–7. 1962.

79. Ødegaard, Ørnulv. Occupational incidence of mental disease in single women, *Living Conditions and Health,* 1, 169–80. 1957.

80. Parker, Seymour and Robert J. Kleiner, *Mental Illness in the Urban Negro Community.* New York: Free Press, 1966.

81. Pearlin, Leonard I. and Melvin L. Kohn. Social class, oc-

cupation, and parental values: a cross-national study, *American Sociological Review*, 31, 466–79. 1966.

82. Queen, Stuart A. The ecological study of mental disorders, *American Sociological Review*, 5, 201–9. 1940.

83. Rinehart, James W. Communication, *American Sociological Review*, 31, 545–6. 1966.

84. Robinson, W. S. Ecological correlations and the behavior of individuals, *American Sociological Review*, 15, 351–7. 1950.

85. Rogler, Lloyd H. and August B. Hollingshead. *Trapped: Families and Schizophrenia*. New York: John Wiley, 1965.

86. Rosenthal, David. Problems of sampling and diagnosis in the major twin studies of schizophrenia, *Journal of Psychiatric Research*, 1, 116–34. 1962.

87. Ryckoff, Irving; Day, Juliana; and Wynne, Lyman C. Maintenance of stereotyped roles in the families of schizophrenics, *AMA Archives of Psychiatry*, 1, 93–8. 1958.

88. Sanua, Victor D. The etiology and epidemiology of mental illness and problems of methodology: with special emphasis on schizophrenia, *Mental Hygiene*, 47, 607–21. 1963.

89. Sanua, Victor D. Sociocultural factors in families of schizophrenics: a review of the literature, *Psychiatry*, 24, 246–65. 1961.

90. Schroeder, Clarence W. Mental disorders in cities, *American Journal of Sociology*, 48, 40–8. 1942.

91. Schwartz, David T. and Norbett L. Mintz. Ecology and psychosis among Italians in 27 Boston communities, *Social Problems*, 10, 371–4. 1963.

92. Schwartz, David T. and Norbett L. Mintz. Urban ecology and psychosis: community factors in the incidence of schizophrenia and manic-depression among Italians in Greater Boston, mimeographed, 1963.

93. Schwartz, Morris S. The economic and spatial mobility of paranoid schizophrenics and manic depressives, unpublished M.A. thesis, University of Chicago, 1946.

94. Srole, Leo; Langner, Thomas S.; Michael, Stanley T.; Opler, Marvin K.; and Rennie, Thomas A. C. *Mental Health in the Metropolis: the Midtown Manhattan*, volume 1. New York: McGraw-Hill, 1962.

95. Star, Shirley. The screening of psychoneurotics in the army. In S. A. Stouffer; L. Guttman; E. A. Suchman; P. F. Lazars-

feld; Shirley A. Star; and J. A. Clausen (eds.), *Measurement and Prediction*. Princeton, New Jersey: Princeton University Press, 1950.

96. Stein, Lilli. "Social class" gradient in schizophrenia, *British Journal of Preventive and Social Medicine*, 11, 181–95. 1957.

97. Stenbäck, Asser and K. A. Achté. Hospital first admissions and social class, *Acta Psychiatrica Scandinavica*, 42, 113–24. 1966.

98. Sundby, Per and Per Nyhus. Major and minor psychiatric disorders in males in Oslo: an epidemiological study, *Acta Psychiatrica Scandinavica*, 39, 519–47. 1963.

99. Svalastoga, Kaare. *Social Differentiation*. New York: David McKay, 1965.

100. Tienari, Pekka. Psychiatric illnesses in identical twins, *Acta Psychiatrica Scandinavica*, 39, Supplement 171. 1963.

101. Tietze, Christopher; Lemkau, Paul; and Cooper, Marcia. Personality disorder and spatial mobility, *American Journal of Sociology*, 48, 29–39. 1942.

102. Turner, R. J. and Morton O. Wagonfeld. Occupational mobility and schizophrenia, an assessment of the social causation and social selection hypotheses, *American Sociological Review*, 32, 104–13. 1967.

103. Wechsler, Henry and Thomas F. Pugh. Fit of individual and community characteristics and rates of psychiatric hospitalization, Paper presented to the Sixth World Congress of Sociology, Evian, September, 1966.

104. Williams, Robin M., Jr. *American Society: A Sociological Interpretation*. New York: Knopf, 1951.

105. Wynne, Lyman C.; Ryckoff, Irving M.; Day, Juliana; and Hirsch, Stanley I. Pseudo-mutuality in the family relations of schizophrenics, *Psychiatry*, 22, 205–20. 1958.

CHAPTER 9

1. Abood, L. G. Current work on ceruloplasmin in mental illness. In F. A. Gibbs (ed.). *Molecules and mental health*. Philadelphia: J. B. Lippincott Company, 1959, pp. 3–6.

2. Baldessarini, R. J., and Snyder, S. H. A critique of recent genetic-biochemical formulations. *Nature*, 1965, *206*, 1111–1112.

3. Bellak, L. (ed.). *Schizophrenia: a review of the syndrome.* London: Logos Press, Ltd., 1958.

4. *Ibid.,* p. 174.

5. Berlet, H. H.; Matsumoto, K.; Pscheidt, G. R.; Spaide, J.; Bull, C.; and Himwich, H. E. Biochemical correlates of behavior in schizophrenic patients. *Archives of General Psychiatry,* 1965, *13,* 521–531.

6. Bishop, M. P.; Hollister, L. E.; Gallant, D. M.; and Heath, R. G. Ultracentrifugal serum proteins in schizophrenia. *Archives of General Psychiatry,* 1966, *15,* 337–340.

7. Böök, J. A. A genetic and neuropsychiatric investigation of a North Swedish population, with special regard to schizophrenia and mental deficiency. *Acta Genetica et Statistica Medica,* 1953, *4,* 1–100.

8. Bourdillon, R. E.; Clark, C. A.; Ridges, A. P.; and Sheppard, P. M. "Pink spot" in the urine of schizophrenics. *Nature,* 1965, *208,* 453–455.

9. Brown, D. D.; Silva, O. L.; and McDonald, P. A comparison of the urinary metabolites of L-Histidine-C-14 in schizophrenic and normal subjects. *Journal of Psychiatric Research,* 1962, *1,* 101–105.

10. Buhler, D. R., and Ihler, G. S. Effect of plasma from normal and schizophrenic subjects on the oxidation of labeled glucose by chicken erythrocytes. *Journal of Laboratory and Clinical Medicine,* 1963, 62, 306–318.

11. Cardon, P. V.; Sokoloff, L.; Vates, T. S.; and Kety, S. S. The physiological and psychological effects of intravenously administered epinephrine and its metabolism in normal and schizophrenic men: 1. Effects on heart rate, blood pressure, blood glucose concentration and the electroencephalogram. *Journal of Psychiatric Research,* 1961, *1,* 37–49.

12. Eiduson, S.; Geller, E.; Yuwiler, A.; and Eiduson, B. T. *Biochemistry and behavior.* Princeton, N.J.: D. Van Nostrand Company, Inc., 1964, pp. 101–107.

13. Erlenmeyer-Kimling, L., and Paradowski, W. Selection and schizophrenia. *American Naturalist,* 1966, *100,* 651–665.

14. Essen-Möller, E. Psychiatrische Untersuchungen an einer Serie von Zwillingen, *Acta Psychiatrica et Neurologica* (Suppl.) 1941, *23,* 1–30.

15. Feinberg, Irwin, and Evarts, Edward. Some implications

of sleep research for psychiatry. In J. Zubin and Shagass, C. (eds.); *Neurobiological aspects of psychopathology.* New York: Grune & Stratton, Inc. 1969.

16. Feldstein, A.; Wong, K.; and Freeman, H. The metabolism of serotonin administered by the intramuscular and the intravenous routes in normal subjects and chronic schizophrenic patients. *Journal of Psychiatric Research,* 1962, 2, 41–50.

17. Fessel, W. J. Disturbed serum proteins in chronic psychosis: serological, medical and psychiatric correlations. *Archives of General Psychiatry,* 1961, 4, 154–159.

18. ———. Mental stress, blood proteins and the hypothalamus. *Archives of General Psychiatry,* 1962, 7, 427–435.

19. ———, and Hirata-Hibi, M. Abnormal leukocytes in schizophrenia. *Archives of General Psychiatry,* 1963, 9, 601–613.

20. ———; and Shapiro, I. M. Genetic and stress factors affecting the abnormal lymphocyte in schizophrenia. *Journal of Psychiatric Research,* 1965, 3, 275–283.

21. Fessel, W. J., and Solomon, G. F. Psychosis and systemic lupus erythematosis. *California Medicine,* 1960, 92, 266–270.

22. Fieve, R. R. The relationship of atypical lymphocytes, phenothiazines, and schizophrenia. *Archives of General Psychiatry,* 1966, 15, 529–534.

23. Friedhoff, A. J. The metabolism of dimethoxyphenethylamine and its possible relationship to schizophrenia. In John Romano (ed.), *The origins of schizophrenia: Proceedings of the International Conference on Schizophrenia.* New York: Excerpta Medica Foundation, 1967, pp. 27–34.

24. ———, and Van Winkle, E. Isolation and characterization of a compound from the urine of schizophrenics. *Nature,* 1962, 194, 897–898.

25. Frohman, C. E.; Latham, L. K.; Warner, K. A.; Brosius, C. O.; Beckett, P. G.; and Gottlieb, J. S. Motor activity in schizophrenia. *Archives of General Psychiatry,* 1963, 9, 83–88.

26. Gerard, R. W. The nosology of schizophrenia: a cooperative study. *Behavioral Science,* 1964, 9, 311–333.

27. Gjessing, L. R. Studies of periodic catatonia: I. Blood levels of protein-bound iodine and urinary excretion of vanillylmandelic acid in relation to clinical course. *Journal of Psychiatric Research,* 1964, 2, 123–134.

28. ———. Studies of periodic catatonia: II. The urinary

excretion of phenolic amines and acids with and without loads of different drugs, *Journal of Psychiatric Research*, 1964, *2*, 149–162.

29. Gottesman, I. I., and Shields, J. Schizophrenia in twins: 16 years' consecutive admissions to a psychiatric clinic. *British Journal of Psychiatry*, 1966, *112*, 809–818.

30. Gregory, I. Genetic factors in schizophrenia. *American Journal of Psychiatry*, 1960, *116*, 961–972.

31. Haddad, R. K., and Rabe, A. An anaphylactic test for abnormal antigens in schizophrenics' serum. In *International congress of psychiatry*. Toronto: University of Toronto Press, 1961, pp. 658–661.

32. Halevy, A.; Moos, R. H.; and Solomon, G. F. A relationship between blood serotonin concentrations and behavior in psychiatric patients. *Journal of Psychiatric Research*, 1965, *3*, 1–10.

33. Heath, R. G. A biochemical hypothesis on the etiology of schizophrenia. In Don Jackson (ed.), *The etiology of schizophrenia*. New York: Basic Books, Inc., 1960, pp. 146–156.

34. ———, and Krupp, I. M. Schizophrenia as an immunologic disorder: I. Demonstration of antibrain globulins by fluorescent antibody techniques. *Archives of General Psychiatry*, 1967, *16*, 1–9.

35. ———; Byers, L. W.; and Liljekvist, J. I. Schizophrenia as an immunologic disorder: II. Effects of serum protein fractions on brain function. *Archives of General Psychiatry*, 1967, *16*, 10–23.

36. ———; Schizophrenia as an immunologic disorder: III. Effects of antimonkey and antihuman brain antibody on brain function. *Archives of General Psychiatry*, 1967, *16*, 24–33.

37. Heston, L. L. Psychiatric disorders in foster home reared children of schizophrenic mothers. *British Journal of Psychiatry*, 1966, *112*, 819–825.

38. Hirata-Hibi, M., and Fessel, W. J.: The bone marrow in schizophrenia. *Archives of General Psychiatry*, 1964, *10*, 409–413.

39. Hoffer, A. Mode of action of ergot hallucinogens. In F. A. Gibbs (ed.), *Molecules and mental health*. Philadelphia: J. B. Lippincott Company, 1959, pp. 44–59.

40. ———; Osmond, H.; and Smythies, J. R. Schizophrenia:

a new approach: Part II. Result of a year's research. *Journal of Mental Sciences,* 1954, *100,* 29–45.

41. Huxley, J.; Mayr, E.; Osmond, H.; and Hoffer, A. Schizophrenia as a genetic morphism. *Nature,* 1964, *204,* 220–221.

42. Kallinann, F. J. *Heredity in health and mental disorders.* New York: W. W. Norton & Company, Inc., 1953.

43. ———. The genetic theory of schizophrenia: an analysis of 691 schizophrenic twin index families. *American Journal of Psychiatry,* 1964, *103,* 309–322.

44. Karlsson, J. L. *The biologic basis of schizophrenia.* Springfield, Ill.: Charles C Thomas, Publisher, 1966.

45. Kety, S. S. Recent biochemical theories of schizophrenia. In Don Jackson (ed.), *The etiology of schizophrenia.* New York: Basic Books, Inc., 1960, pp. 120–145.

46. ———. Current biochemical research in schizophrenia. In P. Hoch and J. Zubin (eds.), *Psychopathology of schizophrenia.* New York: Grune & Stratton, Inc., 1964, pp. 225–232.

47. ———. The relevance of biochemical studies to the etiology of schizophrenic illness. In John Romano (ed.), *The origins of schizophrenia: Proceedings of the First Rochester International Conference on Schizophrenia.* New York: Excerpta Medica Foundation, 1967, pp. 35–41.

48. Kinsey, A. C.; Pomeroy, W. B.; and Martin, C. E. *Sexual behavior in the human male.* Philadelphia: W. B. Saunders Company, 1948.

49. ———; and Gebhard, P. H. *Sexual behavior in the human female.* Philadelphia: W. B. Saunders Company, 1953.

50. Kringlen, Einar. *Schizophrenia in male monozygotic twins.* Oslo, Norway: Universitetsforlaget, 1964.

51. ———. Hereditary and social factors in schizophrenic twins: an epidemiological-clinical study. In John Romano (ed.), *The origins of schizophrenia: Proceedings of the First Rochester International Conference on Schizophrenia.* New York: Excerpta Medica Foundation, 1967, pp. 2–14.

52. Kurland, H. D.; Fessel, W. J.; and Cutler, R. P. Clinical aspects of a serologic study of the psychoses. *Archives of General Psychiatry,* 1964, *10,* 262–266.

53. LaBrosse, E. H.; Mann, J. D.; and Kety, S. S. The physiological and psychological effects of intravenously administered epinephrine and its metabolism in normal and schizophrenic

men: III. Metabolism of 7-H³-epinephrine as determined in studies on blood and urine. *Journal of Psychiatric Research*, 1961, *1*, 68–75.

54. Landis, C., and Page, J. D. Sex distribution and the severity of illness among samples of schizophrenic twins. Cited by David Rosenthal, The offspring of schizophrenic couples. *Journal of Psychiatric Research*, 1966, *4*, 169–188.

55. Luxenberger, H. Some factors associated with concordance and discordance with respect to schizophrenia in monozygotic twins. Cited by David Rosenthal, Problems of sampling and diagnosis in the major twin studies of schizophrenia. *Journal of Psychiatric Research*, 1961, *1*, 116–134.

56. Mangoni, R. B., and Coppen, A. J. The effect of plasma from schizophrenic patients on the chicken erythrocyte system. *British Journal of Psychiatry*, 1963, *109*, 231–234.

57. Meehl, P. Schizotaxia, schizotypy, schizophrenia. *American Psychologist*, 1962, *17*, 827–838.

58. Mueller, P. Plasma-free fatty acid concentrations (FFA) in chronic schizophrenia before and after insulin stimulations. *Journal of Psychiatric Research*, 1962, *1*, 106–115.

59. O'Reilly, P. O.; Ernest, M.; and Hughes, G. The incidence of Malvaria. *British Journal of Psychiatry*, 1965, *111*, 741–744.

60. ———, Hughes, R. T.; Russell, S.; and Ernest, M. The mauve factor: an evaluation. *Diseases of the Nervous System*, 1965, *26*, 562–568.

61. Park L. C.; Baldessarini, R. J.; and Kety, S. S. Methionine effects on chronic schizophrenics. *Archives of General Psychiatry*, 1965, *12*, 346–351.

62. Pollin, W., and Goldin, S. The physiological and psychological effects of intravenously administered epinephrine and its metabolism in normal and schizophrenic men: II. Psychiatric observations. *Journal of Psychiatric Research*, 1961, *1*, 50–67.

63. Pollin, W.; Stabenau, J. R.; and Tupin, J. Family studies with identical twins discordant for schizophrenia. *Psychiatry*, 1965, *28*, 60–78.

64. Psheidt, G. R.; Berlet, H. H.; Bull, C.; Spaide, J.; and Himwich, H. E. Excretion of catecholamines and exacerbation of symptoms in schizophrenic patients. *Journal of Psychiatric Research*, 1964, *2*, 163–168.

65. Romanoff, L. P.; Rodriguez, R. M.; Seelye, J. M.; and

Pincus, G. Determination of tetrahydrocortisol and tetrahydrocortisone in the urine of normal and schizophrenic men. *Journal of Clinical Endocrinology and Metabolism*, 1957, *17*, 777–785.

66. Rosanoff, A. J.; Handy, L. M.; Plesset, I. R.; and Brush, S. The etiology of so-called schizophrenic psychoses. *American Journal of Psychiatry*, 1934, *91*, 247–286.

67. Rosenthal, David. Some factors associated with concordance and discordance with respect to schizophrenia in monozygotic twins. *Journal of Nervous and Mental Disease*, 1959, *129*, 1–10.

68. ———. Confusion of identity and frequency of schizophrenia in twins. *Archives of General Psychiatry*, 1960, *3*, 297–304.

69. ———. Sex distribution and the severity of illness among samples of schizophrenic twins. *Journal of Psychiatric Research*, 1961, *1*, 26–36.

70. ———. Familial concordance by sex with respect to schizophrenia. *Psychological Bulletin*, 1962, *59*, 401–421.

71. ———. Problems of sampling and diagnosis in the major twin studies of schizophrenia. *Journal of Psychiatric Research*, 1962, *1*, 116–134.

72. ———. *The Genain quadruplets*. New York: Basic Books, Inc., 1963, p. 609.

73. ———. The offspring of schizophrenic couples. *Journal of Psychiatric Research*, 1966, *4*, 169–188.

74. Shields, J., and Slater, E. Heredity and psychological abnormality. In H. J. Eysenck (ed.), *Handbook of abnormal psychology*. New York: Basic Books, Inc., 1961, pp. 298–343.

75. Silverman, J. Perceptual control of stimulus intensity in paranoid and non-paranoid schizophrenia. *Journal of Nervous and Mental Disease*, 1964, *139*, 545–549.

76. Singer, M. T., and Wynne, L. C. Thought disorder and family relations in schizophrenia. *Archives of General Psychiatry*, 1965, *12*, 201–212.

77. Slater, E. The monogenic theory of schizophrenia. *Acta Genetica et Statistica Medica*, 1958, *8*, 50–56.

78. Smythies, J. R. *Schizophrenia: chemistry, metabolism and treatment*. Springfield, Ill. Charles C Thomas, Publisher, 1963.

79. Solomon, George F., and Moos, Rudolf H. Emotions, im-

munity and disease: a speculative theoretic approach. *Archives of Genetic Psychiatry,* 1964, *11,* 657–674.

80. ———; Fessel, W. J.; and Morgan, F. Globulin and behavior in schizophrenia. *International Journal of Neuropsychiatry,* 1966, *2,* 20–26.

81. Sourkes, T. L. Cerebral and other diseases with disturbances of amine metabolism. In H. E. Himwich, and W. E. Himwich (eds.), *Biogenic amines.* New York: Elsevier Publishing Company, 1964, p. 196.

82. Stevenson, J. A. F.; Derrick, J. B.; Hobbs, G. E.; and Metcalfe, E. V. Adrenocortical response and phosphate excretion in schizophrenia. *Archives of Neurology and Psychiatry,* 1957, *78,* 312–320.

83. Tienari, Pekka. Psychiatric illness in identical twins. *Acta Psychiatrica Scandinavica,* 39, Suppl. 171. Copenhagen: Munksgaard, 1963.

84. Turner, W. J., and Chipps, I. A heterophil hymolysin in human blood. *Archives of General Psychiatry,* 1966, *15,* 373–377.

85. Wynne, L. C., and Singer, M. T. Thought disorder and family relations of schizophrenics. *Archives of General Psychiatry,* 1963, *9,* 191–206.

86. Zarcone, Vincent; Gulevich, George; Pivik, Terry; and Dement, William. Partial REM phase deprivation and schizophrenia. *Archives of General Psychiatry,* 1968, *18,* 194–202.

CHAPTER 10

1. Bellak, Leopold (ed.). *Schizophrenia: a review of the syndrome.* London: Logos Press, Ltd., 1958.

2. Goldfarb, William. Factors in the development of schizophrenic children: an approach to subclassification. In John Romano (ed.), *The origins of schizophrenia.* New York: Excerpta Medica Foundation, 1967, pp. 70–91.

3. Hamburg, David, and Lunde, Donald. Relation of behavioral, genetic, and neuroendocrine factors to thyroid function. In J. Spuhler (ed.), *Genetic diversity and human behavior.* Chicago: Aldine Publishing Company, 1967.

4. Handlon, Joseph H. A meta-theoretical view of the assumptions regarding the etiology of schizophrenia. *Archives of General Psychiatry,* 1960, *2,* 43–60.

5. Heston, L. L. Psychiatric disorders in foster home reared children of schizophrenic mothers. *British Journal of Psychiatry,* 1966, *112,* 819–825.

6. Kallman, F. J. *Heredity in health and mental disorders.* New York: W. W. Norton & Company, Inc., 1953.

7. Kringlen, Einar. Hereditary and social factors in schizophrenic twins: an epidemiological clinical study. In John Romano (ed.), *The origins of schizophrenia.* New York: Excerpta Medica Foundation, 1967.

8. Muncie, W. The psychobiological approach. In Silvano Arieti (ed.). *American handbook of psychiatry.* New York: Basic Books, Inc., 1959.

9. Pollin, William; Stabenau, James R.; Mosher, Loren; and Tupin, Joe. Life history differences in identical twins discordant for schizophrenia. *American Journal of Orthopsychiatry,* 1966, *36,* 492–509.

10. Pollin, William; Stabenau, James R.; and Tupin, Joe. Family studies with identical twins discordant for schizophrenia. *Psychiatry,* 1965, *28,* 60–78.

11. Rosenbaum, C. Peter. Metabolic, physiologic, anatomic and genetic studies in the schizophrenias: a review and analysis. *Journal of Nervous and Mental Disease,* 1968, *146,* 103–126.

12. Rosenthal, David. *The Genain quadruplets.* New York: Basic Books, Inc., 1963.

13. Tienari, Pekka. Psychiatric illness in identical twins. *Acta Psychiatrica Scandinavica,* Vol. 39, Suppl. 171. Copenhagen: Munksgaard, 1963.

CHAPTER 11

1. Alanen, Yrjo. Some thoughts of schizophrenia and ego development in the light of family investigations. *Archives of General Psychiatry,* 1960, *3,* 650–656.

2. ———, *et al.* The family in the pathogenesis of schizophrenia and neurotic disorders. *Acta Psychiatrica Scandinavica,* Monograph, Vol. 42, Suppl. 189. Copenhagen: Munksgaard, 1966, pp. 403–435.

3. Bellak, Leopold (ed.). *Schizophrenia: a review of the syndrome.* London: Logos Press, Ltd., 1958.

4. Beres, D. Ego deviation and the concept of schizophrenia.

In A. Freud (ed.), *The Psychoanalytic study of the child*, Vol. 11. New York: International Universities Press, 1956.

5. Fairbairne, W. R. D. *An object relations theory of the personality*. New York: Basic Books, Inc., 1954.

6. Freud, Anna. *The ego and mechanisms of defense*. New York: International Universities Press, Inc., 1946.

7. Freud, Sigmund. *The standard edition of the complete psychological works of Sigmund Freud:* Vol. VI. *The psychopathology of everyday life*, James Strachey (trans.). London: The Hogarth Press, Ltd., and The Institute of Psychoanalysis, 1901.

8. ———. *The standard edition:* Vol. XXII. *New introductory lectures on psychoanalysis and other works*, p. 80.

9. Jung, Carl G. The psychology of dementia praecox (1907). In *Collected Works:* Vol. 3. *The psychogenesis of mental disease*. Bollingen Series XX. New York: Pantheon Books, Inc., 1960.

10. ———. The association method. Lecture II. Familiar Constellations (1909). In *Analytical psychology* (Constance E. Long, ed.). New York: Moffat, Yard & Co. 1916.

11. ———. Instinct and the unconscious (1919). In *Collected Works:* Vol. 8. *The structure and dynamics of the psyche*. Bollingen Series XX. New York: Pantheon Books, Inc., 1960.

12. ———. Analytical psychology and education. Lecture III (1926). In *Collected Works:* Vol. 17. *Development of personality*. Bollingen Series XX. New York: Pantheon Books, Inc., 1954.

13. ———. Mind and earth (1931). In *Collected Works:* Vol. 10. *Civilization in transition*. Bollingen Series XX. New York: Pantheon Books, Inc., 1964.

14. ———. *The secret of the golden flower*. London: Kegan Paul, Trench, Trubner & Co., 1931.

15. ———. A review of the complex theory (1934). In *Collected Works:* Vol. 8. *The structure and dynamics of the psyche*. Bollingen Series XX. New York: Pantheon Books, Inc., 1960.

16. ———. On the psychogenesis of schizophrenia (1939). In *Collected Works:* Vol. 3. *The psychogenesis of mental disease*. Bollingen Series XX. New York: Pantheon Books, Inc., 1960.

17. ———. *Collected Works:* Vol. 7 (1916). *Two essays on analytical psychology*. Bollingen Series XX, New York: Pantheon Books, Inc., 1953.

18. ———. Recent thoughts on schizophrenia (1956). In

Collected Works, Vol. 3. Bollingen Series XX. New York: Pantheon Books, Inc., 1960.

19. ———. Schizophrenia (1958). In *Collected Works:* Vol. 3.

20. Klein, M.; Heimann, P.; and Money-Kyrle, R. *New directions in psycho-analysis.* New York: Basic Books, Inc., 1955.

21. McAlpine, I., and Hunter, R. *Daniel Paul Schreber— Memories of my nervous illness.* London: William Dawson & Sons, Ltd., 1955.

22. Metman, Philip. The ego in schizophrenia, Part 1. *Journal of Analytical Psychology,* 1956, *1,* 161–176.

23. ———. The ego in schizophrenia, Part II. *Journal of Analytical Psychology,* 1957, *2,* 51–71.

24. ———. The trickster figure in schizophrenia. *Journal of Analytical Psychology,* 1958, *3,* 5–20.

25. Perry, John W. *The self in psychotic process.* Berkeley: University of California Press, 1953.

26. ———. A Jungian formulation of schizophrenia. *American Journal of Psychotherapy,* 1956, *10,* 54–65.

27. ———. Acute catatonic schizophrenia. *Journal of Analytical Psychology,* 1957, *2,* 137–152.

28. ———. Image, complex and transference in schizophrenia. In Arthur Burton (ed.), *Psychotherapy of the psychoses.* New York: Basic Books, Inc., 1961.

29. ———. Reconstitutive process in the psychopathology of the self. *Annals of the New York Academy of Science,* 1962, *96,* 853–876.

30. Searles, Harold F. Integration and differentiation in schizophrenia: an overall view. *British Journal of Medical Psychology,* 1959, *32,* 261–281.

31. Stoller, Robert J. Passing and the Continuum of Gender Identity. In Judd Marmor (ed.), *Sexual inversion.* New York: Basic Books, Inc., 1965, pp. 190–210.

32. Sullivan, Harry S. *The interpersonal theory of psychiatry,* Helen S. Perry and Mary L. Gawel (eds.). New York: W. W. Norton & Company, Inc., 1953.

33. *Ibid.,* pp. 263–296.

34. *Ibid.,* p. 167.

35. *Ibid.,* pp. 319–320.

36. *Ibid.,* pp. 326–328.

37. *Ibid.,* p. 337.

38. Sullivan, Harry S. *The psychiatric interview,* Helen S. Perry and Mary L. Gawel (eds.). New York: W. W. Norton & Company, Inc., 1954.

39. Sullivan, Harry S. *Clinical studies in psychiatry,* Helen S. Perry (ed.). New York: W. W. Norton & Company, Inc., 1956.

40. *Ibid.,* pp. 12–14.

41. *Ibid.,* p. 24.

42. *Ibid.,* p. 40.

43. *Ibid.,* pp. 46–48.

44. *Ibid.,* pp. 63–67.

45. *Ibid.,* pp. 312–328.

46. *Ibid.,* pp. 320–321.

47. *Ibid.,* p. 342.

48. Sullivan, Harry S. *Schizophrenia as a human process.* New York: W. W. Norton & Company, Inc., 1962.

49. Szasz, Thomas S. A contribution to the psychology of schizophrenia. *Archives of Neurology and Psychiatry,* 1957, 77, 420–436.

50. *Ibid.,* p. 423.

51. *Ibid.,* p. 425.

CHAPTER 12

1. Blacker, Kay H.; Weinstein, B. J.; and Ellman, E. L. Mother's milk and chlorpromazine. *American Journal of Psychiatry,* 1962, *119,* 178–180.

2. Caffey, E. M.; Hollister, L. E.; Kaim, S. C.; and Pokorny, A. D. Antipsychotic, antianxiety, and antidepressant Drugs 1. *Medical Bulletin 11.* Washington, D.C.: Veterans Administration, 1966.

3. Casey, J. F.; Bennet, I. F.; Lindley, C. J.; Hollister, Leo E.; Gordon, M. H.; and Springer, N. N. Drug therapy in schizophrenia: a controlled study of the relative effectiveness of chlorpromazine, promazine, phenobarbital and placebo. *Archives of General Psychiatry,* 1960, 2, 210–220.

4. Casey, J. F.; Laskey, J. J.; Klett, C. J.; and Hollister, L. E. Treatment of schizophrenic reactions with phenothiazine derivatives: a comparative study of chlorpromazine, triflupromazine, mepazine, prochlorperazine, perphenazine, and phenobarbital. *American Journal of Psychiatry,* 1960, *117,* 97–105.

5. Delay, Jean; Deniker, P.; Green, A.; and Mordret, M. Le

syndrome excitomoteur provoqué par les médicaments neuro-leptiques. In F. C. Redlich and D. X. Freedman (eds.), *The theory and practice of psychiatry.* New York: Basic Books, Inc., 1966, p. 342.

6. Feinberg, Irwin. The current status of the Funkenstein Test. *Archives of Neurology and Psychiatry*, 1958, *80*, 488–501.

7. Forrest, Fred M., and Forrest, Irene S. Urine testing for phenothiazine and related drugs: its significance for achieving and maintaining rehabilitation of chronic mental patients. *American Archives of Rehabilitation Therapy*, March, 1963, pp. 1–4.

8. Freeman, Walter. Psychosurgery. In Silvano Arieti (ed.), *American handbook of psychiatry.* New York: Basic Books, Inc., 1959, pp. 1521–1540.

9. Gonda, Thomas A. Prediction of short-term outcome of electroconvulsive therapy. *Journal of Nervous and Mental Disease*, 1958, *138*, 59–72.

10. Himwich, Harold E. Psychopharmacologic drugs. *Science*, 1958, *127*, 59–72.

11. Hollister, Leo E. Personal communication, November 1967.

12. ———; Klett, C. J.; Caffey, E.; and Kaim, S. C. Drug treatment of schizophrenic reactions: VA cooperative studies of chemotherapy in psychiatry. Palo Alto, Calif.: Veterans Administration Hospital, undated.

13. Horowitz, W. A. Insulin shock therapy. In Silvano Arieti (ed.), *American handbook of psychiatry.* New York: Basic Books, Inc., 1959, pp. 1485–1498.

14. Impastato, Daniel J.; Berg, S.; and Gabriel, A. R. Practical elimination of fractures in electroshock therapy by succinylcholine: a control study. *New York State Journal of Medicine*, 1957, *57*, 2513.

15. Johns Hopkins University, Department of Psychiatry. Routine for electro-convulsive treatment. (Mimeographed material, pp. 37–39, undated.)

16. Kalinowsky, Lothar B. Convulsive shock treatment. In Silvano Arieti (ed.), *American handbook of psychiatry.* New York: Basic Books, Inc., 1959, pp. 1499–1520.

17. ———. Electric convulsive therapy after ten years of pharmacotherapy. *American Journal of Psychiatry*, 1964, *121*, 944–949.

18. Karreman, B.; Isenberg, I.; and Szent-Györgyi, A. On the mechanism of action of chlorpromazine. *Science*, 1959, *130*, 1191–1192.

19. Lewis, W. H.; Richardson, D. J.; and Gahagan, L. H. Cardiovascular disturbances and their management in modified electrotherapy for psychiatric illness. *Journal of Medicine*, 1955, *252*, 1016–1020.

20. Maas, James W. Reliability of the methacholine (mecholyl) test. *Archives of Neurology and Psychiatry*, 1958, *79*, 585–589.

21. MacLeod, John, and Middleman, F. Wednesday afternoon clinic: a supportive care program. *Archives of General Psychiatry*, 1962, *6*, 56–65.

22. Markowe, Morris; Steinert, Jack; and Heyworth-Davis, Freda. Insulin and chlorpromazine in schizophrenia: a ten year comparative study. *British Journal of Psychiatry*, 1967, *113*, 11–1–1106.

23. Matthew, J. R., and Conston, E. Complications following ECT over a three-year period in a state institution. *American Journal of Psychiatry*, 1964, *121*, 1119–1120.

24. Mendel, Werner M., and Green, G. A. *The therapeutic management of psychological illness: the theory and practice of supportive care*. New York: Basic Books, Inc., 1967.

25. Noyes, Alfred B., and Kolb, Lawrence C. Shock and other physical therapies. In *Modern clinical psychiatry*. Philadelphia: W. B. Saunders Company, 1963, pp. 538–542.

26. Osmund, H., and Hoffer, A. Massive niacin treatment in schizophrenia. *Lancet*, 1962, *1*, 316–320.

27. Patterson, E. S. Effectiveness of insulin coma in the treatment of schizophrenia. *Archives of Neurology and Psychiatry*, 1958, *79*, 460–467.

28. Pletscher, A. Basic aspects of psychotropic drug action. *American Journal of Mental Deficiency*, 1962, *67*, 238–244.

29. Redlich, Frederick C., and Freedman, Daniel X. *The theory and practice of psychiatry*. New York: Basic Books, Inc., 1966.

CHAPTER 13

1. Ackerknecht, E. H. *A short history of psychiatry*. New York: Hafner Publishing Company, 1959.

2. Atthowe, J. M., Jr., and Krasner, L. Preliminary report on the application of contingent reinforcement procedures (token economy) on a "chronic" psychiatric ward. *Journal of Abnormal Psychology*, 1968, *73*, 37–43.

3. Ayllon, T., and Azrin, N. H. The measurement and reinforcement of behavior of psychotics. *Journal of Experimental Analysis of Behavior*, 1965, *8*, 357–383.

4. Becker, E. *The revolution in psychiatry*. New York: The Free Press of Glencoe, 1964.

5. Bierer, J. The Marlborough experiment. Chap. 11 in L. Bellak (ed.), *Handbook of community psychiatry and community mental health*. New York: Grune & Stratton, Inc., 1964, pp. 221–247.

6. Black, B. J. Psychiatric rehabilitation in the community. Chap. 12 in L. Bellak (ed.), *Handbook of community psychiatry and community mental health*. New York: Grune & Stratton, Inc., 1964, pp. 248–264.

7. Borman, L. D. A revitalization movement in the mental health professions. *American Journal of Orthopsychiatry*, 1966, *36*, 111–118.

8. Braceland, F. J. Rehabilitation. Chap. 40 in S. Arieti (ed.), *American handbook of psychiatry*, Vol. III. New York: Basic Books, Inc., 1966, pp. 643–656.

9. Brill, H. Historical background of the therapeutic community. In H. C. B. Denber (ed.), *Research conference on therapeutic community*. Springfield, Ill.: Charles C Thomas, Publisher, 1960, pp. 3–16.

10. Brown, G. W.; Carstairs, G. M.; and Topping, G. Posthospital adjustment of chronic mental patients. *Lancet*, 1958, *2*, 685–689.

11. Cameron, D. E. The day hospital: an experimental form of hospitalization for psychiatric patients. *Modern Hospital*, 1947, *69* (3), 60–62.

12. Carstairs, G. M. Research in social psychiatry. *University of Edinburgh Journal*, 1962, *19–20*, 285–291.

13. ———; Clark, D. H.; and O'Connor, N. Occupational treatment of chronic psychotics: observations in Holland, Belgium, and France. *Lancet*, 1955, *2*, 1025–1030.

14. Caudill, W. A. *The psychiatric hospital as a small society*. Cambridge, Mass.: Harvard University Press, 1958.

15. Chittick, R. A., *et al. The Vermont story: rehabilitation of chronic schizophrenic patients.* Washington, D.C.: Division of Research Grants & Demonstrations, Office of Vocational Rehabilitation, 1962.

16. Clark, D. H. Background and present-day status of industrial and occupational therapy programs in English hospitals. *American Archives of Rehabilitation Therapy,* 1963, *11,* 35–47.

17. ———. *Administrative therapy.* Philadelphia: J. B. Lippincott Company, 1964.

18. ———. The therapeutic community—concept, practice and future. *British Journal of Psychiatry,* 1965, *111,* 947–954.

19. ———; Hooper, D. F.; and Oram, E. G. Creating a therapeutic community in a psychiatric ward. *Human Relations,* 1962, *19,* 123–147.

20. Conley, R. W.; Conwell, M.; and Arrill, M. B. An approach to measuring the cost of mental illness. *American Journal of Psychiatry,* 1967, *124,* 755–762.

21. Cumming, John, and Cumming, Elaine. *Ego and milieu.* New York: Atherton Press, 1962.

22. Daniels, David N., and Kuldau, John M. Marginal man, the tether of tradition, and intentional social system therapy. *Community Mental Health Journal,* 1967, *3,* 13–20.

23. Daniels, David N., and Rubin, Ronald S. The community meeting: an analytical study and a theoretical statement. *Archives of General Psychiatry,* 1968, *18,* 60–75.

24. Daniels, David N.; Zelman, A. B.; and Campbell, J. H. Community-based task groups in recovery of mental patients. *Archives of General Psychiatry,* 1967, *16,* 215–228.

25. Denber, H. C. B. (ed.). *Research Conference on Therapeutic Community.* Springfield, Ill.: Charles C Thomas, Publisher, 1960.

26. Devore, I. (ed.). *Primate behavior: field studies of monkeys and apes.* New York: Holt, Rinehart and Winston, Inc., 1965.

27. Dobzhansky, T. G. *Mankind evolving.* New Haven: Yale University Press, 1962.

28. Dumont, M. P., and Aldrich, C. K. Family care after a thousand years—a crisis in the tradition of St. Dymphna. *American Journal of Psychiatry,* 1962, *119,* 116–121.

29. Dunham, H. W., and Weinberg, S. K. *The culture of the*

state mental hospital. Detroit: Wayne State University Press, 1960.

30. Early, D. F. The industrial therapy organization: a development of work in hospital. Chap. 28 in H. Freeman and J. Farndale (eds.), *Trends in the mental health services.* Oxford: Pergamon Press, Inc., 1963, pp. 282–289.

31. Edelson, M. *Ego psychology, group dynamics, and the therapeutic community.* New York: Grune & Stratton, Inc., 1964.

32. Epstein, L. J., and Simon, A. Alternatives to state hospitalization for the geriatric mentally ill. *American Journal of Psychiatry,* 1968, *124,* 955–961.

33. Fairweather, G. W., *et al.* Related effectiveness of psychotherapeutic programs: a multicriteria comparison of four programs for three different patient groups. *Psychology Monographs,* 1960 (Whole Number 492), 74 (5).

34. Fairweather, G. W. *Social psychology in treating mental illness.* New York: John Wiley & Sons, Inc., 1964.

35. ———. *Methods for experimental social innovation.* New York: John Wiley & Sons, Inc., 1967.

36. ———, *et al. Community life for the mentally ill: an alternative to institutional care.* Chicago: Aldine Publishing Co., 1969.

37. Farndale, J. *The day hospital movement in Great Britain.* New York: Pergamon Press, Inc., 1961.

38. Fisher, S. H.; Beard, J. H.; and Goertzel, V. Rehabilitation of the mental hospital patient: the Fountain House Programme. *International Journal of Social Psychiatry,* 1960, *5,* 295–298.

39. Fox, Peter D., and Kuldau, John M. Expanding the framework for mental health program evaluation. *Archives of General Psychiatry.* To be published.

40. Freeman, Howard E., and Simmons, O. G. *The mental patient comes home.* New York: John Wiley & Sons, Inc., 1963.

41. Freeman, Hugh L., and Farndale, James (eds.). *Trends in the mental health services: a symposium of original and reprinted papers.* Oxford: Pergamon Press, Inc., 1963.

42. Freeman, P. Treatment of chronic schizophrenia in a day center. *Archives of General Psychiatry,* 1962, *7,* 259–265.

43. Frost, E. (ed.). *Proceedings of the Workshop on Compensated Work as Therapy.* Philadelphia: Institute of the Pennsylvania Hospital, November, 1963.

44. Garrett, D. Synanon: the communiversity. *Humanist,* 1965, *25,* 183–189.

45. Glasscote, R. M., *et al. The community mental health center: an analysis of existing models.* Washington, D.C.: Joint Information Service of the American Psychiatric Association and the National Association for Mental Health, 1964.

46. Goffman, E. *Asylums.* Garden City, New York: Doubleday & Company, Inc., (Anchor Books), 1961.

47. Goldschmidt, W. R. *Man's way.* New York: Holt, Rinehart and Winston, Inc., 1959.

48. Goveia, L. H. The Quarters: a case for community action. *Community Mental Health Journal,* 1965, *1,* 385–386.

49. Grad, J., and Sainsbury, P. Evaluating a community care service. Chap. 30 in H. Freeman and J. Farndale (eds.), *Trends in the mental health services.* Oxford: Pergamon Press, Inc., 1963, pp. 303–317.

50. Greenblatt, M.; Levinson, D. J.; and Williams, R. H. (eds.). *The patient and the mental hospital.* New York: The Free Press of Glencoe, 1957.

51. Gurel, L. Release and community stay in chronic schizophrenia. *American Journal of Psychiatry,* 1966, *122,* 892–899.

52. Harlow, H. F., and Harlow, M. Social deprivation in monkeys. *Scientific American,* 1962, *207,* 136–146.

53. Hollister, Leo E. Overgeneralization about therapy. *International Journal of Psychiatry,* 1967, *4,* 132–134.

54. Hubbs, R. S. The sheltered workshop in psychiatric rehabilitation. *American Journal of Orthopsychiatry,* 1964, *34,* 76–79.

55. Joint Commission on Mental Illness and Health. *Action for mental health.* New York: Basic Books, Inc., 1961.

56. Joint Information Service. *Fifteen indices.* Washington, D.C.: Joint Information Service of the American Psychiatric Association and the National Association for Mental Health, 1968.

57. Jones, M. S. *The therapeutic community.* New York: Basic Books, Inc., 1953.

58. ———. Therapeutic community practice. *American Journal of Psychiatry,* 1966, *122,* 1275–1279.

59. Kandel, D. B., and Williams, R. H. *Psychiatric rehabilitation: some problems of research.* New York: Atherton Press, 1964.

60. Kraft, A. M. The therapeutic community. Chap. 32 in S. Arieti (ed.), *American handbook of psychiatry*, Vol. III. New York: Basic Books, Inc., 1966, pp. 542–551.

61. Kramer, B. *Day hospital*. New York: Grune & Stratton, 1962.

62. Lambo, T. A. A form of social psychiatry in Africa. *World Mental Health*, 1961, *13*, 190–203.

63. Landy, D., and Greenblatt, M. *Halfway House*. Washington, D.C.: U.S. Department of Health, Education, and Welfare, 1965.

64. Mendel, W. M., and Green, G. A. *The therapeutic management of psychological illness: the theory and practice of supportive care*. New York: Basic Books, Inc., 1967.

65. Meyer, R. E.; Schiff, L. F.; and Becker, A. The home treatment of psychotic patients: an analysis of 151 cases. *American Journal of Psychiatry*, 1967, *123*, 1430–1438.

66. Miller, Dorothy. Alternatives to mental patient rehospitalization. *Community Mental Health Journal*, 1966, 2, 124–128.

67. Molholm, H. B., and Barton, W. E. Family care: a community resource in the rehabilitation of mental patients. *American Journal of Psychiatry, 123*, 1430–1438.

68. Pasamanick, B.; Scarpitti, F. R.; and Dinitz, S. *Schizophrenics in the community: an experimental study in the prevention of hospitalization*. New York: Appleton-Century-Crofts, 1967.

69. Rabiner, E. L.; Gomez, E.; and Gralnick, A. The therapeutic community as an insight catalyst: expanding the transferential field. *American Journal of Psychotherapy*, 1964, *18*, 244–258.

70. Rapoport, R. N. *Community as doctor*. Springfield, Ill.: Charles C Thomas, Publisher, 1960.

71. Ross, M. Extramural treatment techniques: an international overview. Chap. 9 in L. Bellak (ed.), *Handbook of community psychiatry and community mental health*. New York: Grune & Stratton, Inc., 1964, pp. 189–205.

72. Roth, Julius A. The public hospital: refuge for damaged humans. *Trans-action*, 1966, *3*, 25–29.

73. Sanders, David H. *Social psychology in the treatment of mental illnesses: a model approach for treatment of addiction— the effect of group membership on community adjustment*. A paper read before the Institute on Rehabilitation of the Narcotic Addict, Forth Worth, Texas, 1966.

74. Sanders, R.; Smith, R. S.; and Weinman, B. S. *Chronic psychoses and recovery: an experiment in socio-environmental treatment.* San Francisco: Jossey-Bass, Inc., Pubs., 1967.

75. Schwartz, M. S., *et al. Social approaches to mental patient care.* New York: Columbia University Press, 1964.

76. Scott, J. P.: *Animal behavior.* Garden City, N.Y.: Doubleday & Company, Inc. (Anchor Books), 1963.

77. Simon, W., *et al.* Long-term follow-up study of schizophrenic patients. *Archives of General Psychiatry*, 1965, *12*, 510–515.

78. Sinnett, E. R.; Stimpert, W. E.; and Strait, E. A five-year follow-up study of psychiatric patients. *American Journal of Orthopsychiatry*, 1965, *35*, 573–580.

79. Spitz, R. A. Hospitalism: an inquiry into the genesis of psychiatric conditions in early childhood. *Psychoanalytic study of the child*, 1945, *1*, 53–74. (New York: International Universities Press.)

80. Stainbrook, E. The hospital as a therapeutic community. *Neuropsychiatry*, 1955, *3–4*, 69–87.

81. Stanton, A. H., and Schwartz, M. S. *The mental hospital.* New York: Basic Books, Inc., 1954.

82. Strauss, A. L., *et al. Psychiatric ideologies and institutions.* New York: The Free Press of Glencoe, 1964.

83. Stroebel, Charles F., *et al.* Designing psychiatric computer information systems: problems and strategy. *Comprehensive Psychiatry*, 1967, *8*, 491–508.

84. Ullmann, L. P., and Berkman, V. C. Efficacy of placement of neuropsychiatric patients in family care. *Archives of General Psychiatry*, 1959, *1*, 273–274.

85. Vitale, J. H. The therapeutic community: a review. In A. F. Wessen (ed.), *The psychiatric hospital as a social system.* Springfield, Ill.: Charles C Thomas, Publisher, 1964.

86. Wessen, A. F. (ed.). *The psychiatric hospital as a social system*, Springfield, Ill.: Charles C Thomas, Publisher, 1964.

87. Wilmer, H. A. *Social psychiatry in action.* Springfield, Ill.: Charles C Thomas, Publisher, 1958.

88. Wing, J. K. Social treatment, rehabilitation and management. In A. Coppen and A. Walk (eds.), *Recent developments in schizophrenia* (Special Publication No. 1). *British Journal of Psychiatry.* London: Royal Medico-Psychological Association, 1967, pp. 79–95.

89. Yablonsky, L. *The tunnel back: Synanon.* New York: Crowell-Collier and Macmillan, Inc., 1965.

90. Zwerling, I. The psychiatric day hospital. Chap. 34 in S. Arieti, (ed.), *American handbook of psychiatry,* Vol. III. New York: Basic Books, Inc., 1966, pp. 563–576.

CHAPTER 14

1. Albee, Edward. *Who's afraid of Virginia Woolf?* New York: Atheneum Publishers, 1962.

2. Arieti, Silvano. Psychotherapy of schizophrenia. *Archives of General Psychiatry,* 1962, 6, 112–122.

3. Bellak, Leopold. *Schizophrenia: a review of the syndrome.* New York: Harper & Row, Publishers, 1962.

4. Betz, Barbara. Differential success rates of psychotherapists with process and non-process schizophrenic patients. *American Journal of Psychiatry,* 1963, *119,* 1090–1091.

5. ———. Validation of the differential treatment success of "A" and "B" therapists with schizophrenic patients. *American Journal of Psychiatry,* 1963, *119,* 883–884.

6. Boyer, L. Bryce, and Giovacchini, Peter L. *Psychoanalytic treatment of the schizophrenic and character disorders.* New York: Science House, Inc., 1967.

7. Brody, Eugene, and Redlich, Frederick C. *Psychotherapy with schizophrenics.* New York: International Universities Press, Inc., 1952.

8. Burton, Arthur. *Psychotherapy of the psychoses.* New York: Basic Books, Inc., 1961.

9. Fenichel, Otto. *The psychoanalytic theory of neurosis.* New York: W. W. Norton & Company, Inc., 1945.

10. Fromm-Reichmann, Frieda. *Principles of intensive psychotherapy.* Chicago: University of Chicago Press, 1950.

11. Green, Hannah. *I never promised you a rose garden.* New York: Holt, Rinehart and Winston, Inc., 1964.

12. Hill, Lewis B. *Psychotherapeutic intervention in schizophrenia.* Chicago: University of Chicago Press, 1955.

13. Jackson, Don D. In C. Whitaker and T. P. Malone (eds.), *Psychotherapy of chronic schizophrenia.* Boston: Little, Brown, & Company, 1958.

14. Korchin, Sheldon, and Levine, Seymour. Anxiety and

verbal learning. *Journal of Abnormal and Social Psychology*, 1957, *54*, 234–240.

15. Mendel, Werner M., and Green, Gerald A. *The therapeutic management of psychological illness: the theory and practice of supportive care.* New York: Basic Books, Inc., 1967.

16. Posner, H. S., *et al.* Cause of the odor of a schizophrenic patient. *Archives of General Psychiatry*, 1962, *7*, 108–113.

17. Rogers, Carl R. (ed.). *The therapeutic relationship and its impact.* Madison: The University of Wisconsin Press, 1967.

18. Rosenthal, David. Book Reviews. *Psychiatry*, 1961, *24*, 377–380.

19. Searles, Harold F. The schizophrenic's vulnerability to the therapist's unconscious processes. *Journal of Nervous and Mental Disease*, 1958, *127*, 247–262.

20. ———. The effort to drive the other person crazy: an element in the aetiology and psychotherapy of schizophrenia. *British Journal of Medical Psychology*, 1959, *32*, 1–18.

21. ———. Integration and differentiation in schizophrenia: an overall view. *British Journal of Medical Psychology*, 1959, *32*, 261–281.

22. ———. Oedipal love in the countertransference. *International Journal of Psychoanalysis*, 1959, *40*, 1–11.

23. Sechahaye, Margorete A. *Symbolic realization.* New York: International Universities Press, Inc., 1951.

24. Steinbeck, John. *Travels with Charley.* New York: The Viking Press, Inc., 1962.

25. Sullivan, Harry S. *The interpersonal theory of psychiatry.* New York: W. W. Norton & Company, Inc., 1953. Copyright, 1953, by William Alanson White Psychiatric Foundation.

26. *Ibid.*, pp. 151–152.

27. Sullivan, Harry S. *The psychiatric interview.* New York: W. W. Norton & Company, Inc., 1954.

28. ———. *Clinical studies in psychiatry.* New York: W. W. Norton & Company, Inc., 1956.

29. Szasz, Thomas S. A contribution to the psychology of schizophrenia. *Archives of Neurology and Psychiatry*, 1957, *77*, 420–436.

30. Tarachow, Sidney. *An introduction to psychotherapy.* New York: International Universities Press, Inc., 1963.

31. Whitehorn, John C., and Betz, Barbara. A study of psycho-

therapeutic relationships between physicians and schizophrenic patients. *American Journal of Psychiatry*, 1954, *111*, 321–331.

32. ———. A comparison of psychotherapeutic relationships between physicians and schizophrenic patients when insulin is combined with psychotherapy and when psychotherapy alone is used. *American Journal of Psychiatry*, 1957, *113*, 901–910.

33. Will, Allen O. Psychotherapeutics and the schizophrenic reaction. *Journal of Nervous and Mental Disease*, 1958, *126*, 109–140.

34. Wynne, Lyman, *et al.* Pseudo-mutuality in the family relations of schizophrenics. *Psychiatry*, 1958, *21*, 205–220.

35. Yalom, Irvin D., and Handlon, Joseph H. The use of multiple therapists in the teaching of psychiatric residents. *Journal of Nervous and Mental Disease*, 1966, *141*, 684–692.

Index